NADIA COMĂNECI AND THE SECRET POLICE

NADIA COMĂNECI AND THE SECRET POLICE

A Cold War escape

STEJĂREL OLARU

**TRANSLATED FROM THE ROMANIAN
BY ALISTAIR IAN BLYTH**

BLOOMSBURY ACADEMIC
LONDON • NEW YORK • OXFORD • NEW DELHI • SYDNEY

BLOOMSBURY ACADEMIC
Bloomsbury Publishing Plc
50 Bedford Square, London, WC1B 3DP, UK
1385 Broadway, New York, NY 10018, USA
29 Earlsfort Terrace, Dublin 2, Ireland

BLOOMSBURY, BLOOMSBURY ACADEMIC and the Diana logo are trademarks
of Bloomsbury Publishing Plc

First published in Romania by Omnium Publishing

English edition published in arrangement with Ilustrata Agency

First published in Great Britain 2023

Copyright © Stejărel Olaru, 2023

Stejărel Olaru has asserted their right under the Copyright, Designs and Patents Act,
1988, to be identified as Author of this work.

Translated by Alistair Ian Blyth.

Cover image: Romania Nadia Comăneci, 1976 Summer Olympics
(© Photo by Neil Leifer /Sports Illustrated / Getty Images)
(Set Number: X20678)

Bloomsbury Publishing Plc does not have any control over, or responsibility for,
any third-party websites referred to or in this book. All internet addresses given in
this book were correct at the time of going to press. The author and publisher regret
any inconvenience caused if addresses have changed or sites have ceased to exist,
but can accept no responsibility for any such changes.

Every effort has been made to trace copyright holders and to obtain their permissions
for the use of copyright material. The publisher apologizes for any errors or omissions
and would be grateful if notified of any corrections that should be incorporated in
future reprints or editions of this book.

A catalogue record for this book is available from the British Library.

A catalog record for this book is available from the Library of Congress.

ISBN: HB: 978-1-3503-2129-8
       ePDF: 978-1-3503-2130-4
       eBook: 978-1-3503-2131-1

Typeset by RefineCatch Limited, Bungay, Suffolk
Printed and bound in India

To find out more about our authors and books visit www.bloomsbury.com
and sign up for our newsletters.

CONTENTS

ILLUSTRATIONS

ABBREVIATIONS

A.C.N.S.A.S. Arhivele Consiliului Naţional pentru Studierea Arhivelor Securităţii (Archive of the National Council for Study of the Securitate Archives), Bucharest, Romania

A.M.A.E. Arhivele Ministerului Afacerilor Externe (Archives of the Romanian Ministry of Foreign Affairs)

A.N.I.C. Arhivele Naţionale Istorice Centrale (Central National Historical Archives), Bucharest, Romania

C.C. Central Committee of the Romanian Communist Party

C.N.S.A.S. Consiliul Naţional pentru Studierea Arhivelor Securităţii (National Council for Study of the Securitate Archives), Bucharest, Romania

F.I.G. Fédération Internationale de Gymnastique

N.C.P.E.S. (Romanian) National Council for Physical Education and Sport

R.C.P. Romanian Communist Party

S.I.E. Serviciul de Informaţii Externe (Romanian Foreign Intelligence Service)

EXPLANATORY NOTE FROM THE AUTHOR

The majority of the claims included in this book come from the Archives of the Securitate, the Romanian Secret Police. The Romanian Secret Police was established in 1948 and it was disbanded at the end of 1989 with the fall of the Communist regime in Romania. In the 1990s, following a lengthy legislative process Romania took steps to make the Securitate Archive available to the public. Today, it is administered by a Romanian state institution called the Council for the Study of the Securitate Archives.

The Securitate Archive is available to any member of the public, including researchers, and victims of the communist regime who wish to find out how the Secret Police surveyed them, so as to shine a light on the crimes and oppressive nature of the Communist regime.

The Securitate Archive is made up of information about people deemed to be 'of interest' to the Communist state. It even extended to those associated with 'people of interest'. These people who were followed and watched, sometimes for many years, were sometimes considered to be 'enemies of the state' in the eyes of the Communist regime. However, these people were often not wrongdoers. Today, we might consider some of them as heroes, people who have suffered and whose dignity has been wrongfully violated. Nadia Comăneci, for example, falls into this category.

Targets of the State Police have raised concerns about the contents of the Securitate Archive. They say that some of the information gathered and collated there was biased, incomplete, one-sided or even untrue. Some of these concerns are well-founded. In truth, many Secret Police informers were recruited through blackmail and threats. They were forced to work as informers against their will. It is because of this that there are questions surrounding the reliability of witness testimony and statements contained in the Securitate Archive, where information may have even been submitted by individuals who had an axe to grind.

It is for this reason that, wherever possible, my research has taken me beyond the Archive materials, to interviews with eyewitnesses, publications, such as biographies and autobiographies, and other contemporaneous material, such as press articles, scientific papers, documentaries, artistic films and video archive from that time.

Béla and Marta Károlyi did not respond to repeat requests for comment in respect of the allegations contained in this book.

ACKNOWLEDGEMENTS

In researching this book, I studied documents from the Diplomatic Archives of the Romanian Ministry of Foreign Affairs, the Romanian Central National Historical Archives, the Historical Archives of the Hungarian Secret Services, the Archives of the State Department (U.S.A.), and the Archives of the National Council for Study of the Securitate Archives. I am grateful to friends and colleagues who supported me in this endeavour, making the task of research the easier: Aurora Liiceanu, Claudiu Secaşiu, Ciprian Niţulescu, Elis Pleşa, Mihai Burcea, Marina Constantinoiu, Andreea Pulpea, Ioana Adobricăi, Bandi István, Roland Olah, Graham Buxton Smither and Virgiliu Ţârău, as well as the management of the Romanian Central National Historical Archives and the staff of the National Council for Study of the Securitate Archives. I would also like to thank some of the eyewitnesses to the events described in this book, who had the kindness and patience to guide me: late champion Kurt Thomas, Anca Grigoraş, Gheorghe Gorgoi, Gheorghe Condovici, Carmen Dumitru, Mariana Cojanu, Luminiţa Milea and Emanuel Fântâneanu. My thanks also go to my agents Livia Stoia and Oana Vasile from Ilustrata Agency.

1
SALTO IN THE DARK

On the night of 27–28 November 1989, seven people hurriedly but warily made their way towards the frontier between Romania and Hungary. Underfoot, the frozen earth creaked loudly, or so it seemed to them as they scrambled across the deep furrows of a ploughed field. At intervals, they heard barking in the distance, which came from the surrounding villages, and they took fright, thinking they might have been the ones who had disturbed the dogs. By now it was after midnight and the temperature had dropped so low that the cold had become a real danger, although it wasn't the only one, nor even the most significant, since the seven had embarked on the most perilous adventure of their lives: they were about to make an illegal border crossing between two communist states.

They had set out in the dead of night hoping that the danger of them being spotted would thereby be lessened, but the darkness hindered their progress and put their sense of direction sorely to the test. During their six-hour journey, they went up and down hills, crossed gullies, always at risk of losing their footing, and when the terrain allowed, they also ran. When they stopped to take a rest, they spoke in whispers and didn't so much as light a match, fearful lest the Romanian border guards catch sight or sound of them. The man who had taken on the risky job of acting as their guide was Gheorghe Talpoş, Ghiţă for short, a shepherd well known in those parts. Wearing a sheepskin cape and a black lambskin cap, he strode on ahead not only to lead the way, but also to show his sense of responsibility for the other members of the group, who came behind him in twos.

The border between Romania and Hungary stretches for almost 280 miles, with the Cenad frontier crossing situated not far from its westernmost extremity, about 45 miles north-west of the major city of Timişoara and 45 miles west of Arad. Talpoş was a local who knew the area around Cenad like the back of his hand. As it happened, it was also the best area for the escape, since here the border runs in a straight rather than a jagged line, which eliminated the risk that the group might unwittingly cross back into Romania if they lost their way. Talpoş knew that they had to keep moving northward, trying not to veer north-east, where the frontier lay at a greater distance, along the Mureş River, or west, onto the Pordeanu and Beba Veche plains, where the borders of three countries intersected to form the famous Triplex Confinium.[1]

If a Romanian army patrol had caught him walking by himself near the border strip, Talpoş would have been able to provide any number of plausible reasons for his being there, and besides, he knew some of the border guards personally. But things would have been far more complicated in the present situation, when his companions weren't locals, but had identity papers that gave addresses in Bucharest and other counties. The risk Talpoş was taking was compounded by the fact that one of the fugitives he was guiding to the border was Nadia Comăneci, the gold-medal-winning Olympic, World and European gymnast, whom dictator Nicolae Ceauşescu touted throughout the world as a symbol of national pride. The world's most famous gymnast was now fleeing her own country, which had been a repressive totalitarian régime for more than four decades. The shepherd would have had no excuse; there was nothing he could have said to exculpate himself if he had been caught with Nadia.

According to Talpoş, only that night, just before they set off, did he discover that Nadia was among the group he was to lead across the frontier. He was both amazed and intimidated by the discovery. 'How the hell can Nadia cross the border at night like a criminal? Hasn't she been abroad all those times? If she'd wanted to, couldn't she have just not come back?' was his reaction on learning her decision. He then went down into his cellar to drink two mugs of wine, saying, 'I want to be drunk if they catch me. At least I'll be able to say I was drunk.'[2] But the two mugs of wine failed to get him drunk – maybe because he was a hardened drinker, maybe because the cold and the bitter wind that night cleared his head. Wary, frightened, every member of the group followed his instructions; they obeyed his orders when he told them where to set foot, where to stop and rest, and when he warned them of potential hazards.

It had been about two weeks earlier that Nadia Comăneci joined that group of cross-border fugitives, who had come together without any prior plan. They included ordinary people from every walk of life, none of them public figures. Some were locals, some were from Bucharest. All of them were pursuing the dream of making a life for themselves in a better world: Dumitru and Gabriela Talpoş, the guide's brother and his wife, were from Cenad; Aurel-Adrian Biaş was from Sînnicolau Mare, a town near Cenad; Monica-Maria Marcu was a young engineer born in Sînnicolau Mare, but who worked at a factory in Bihor County; and George Paraschiv was a painter, but worked as an electrician at a factory in Bucharest.

Years later, their memories of those long, oppressive hours would be similar, although they differed in some details. George Paraschiv was struck by the fact that there was 'a large, full moon'[3] that night and felt menaced by the light it cast. But Nadia was to remember the dense darkness, which she found particularly ominous: 'When we stepped out into the night, we each put our hands on the shoulders of the person in front of us because once we moved away from the house, it was impossible to see. If I hadn't been touching the person in front of me, I would have gotten separated from the group and been lost.'[4]

Not all the members of the group viewed Gheorghe Talpoş in the same way. Unlike the others, Nadia regarded him as indecisive and she didn't agree with his decisions, although she didn't say so or openly oppose him. In her autobiography, she admits to feeling a sense of unease, even mistrust, in the man who was leading them to the border, whose directions seemed vague to her at best: 'I wanted to see a compass, or a map, or something. But there was nothing to do in the dark except follow the guy and hope he knew where he was going.' She remembers crossing an indeterminate stretch of dirt, without coming to the border, and thinking, 'I'm going to get killed, and all because I'm following a man with no sense of direction.' However, since it would have been dangerous to say anything, thereby breaking the silence, she resigned herself to 'concentrat[ing] on keeping my teeth from chattering.'[5]

Paraschiv thought that Nadia had no sense of direction in the given situation. He'd told her that the grassy strip separating the two territories looked like a road that would have to be crossed, and that it wouldn't take long to reach it, around an hour, and Nadia had believed him, unaware of how a frontier was marked out and guarded.

But given the strain they were under, it is no wonder that Talpoş's instructions for them to bear now left, now right didn't always inspire confidence, especially when they found themselves confronted with unpleasant natural obstacles that weren't easily overcome, such as a slushy pond in which Nadia sank up to the knees, praying that it wouldn't get any deeper before she waded to the other side.

But the greatest, most pressing danger came when, around two hundred yards in front of them, they saw the silhouettes of Romanian border guards marching away a man and a woman whom they had just captured trying to cross the frontier illegally. Talpoş made a sign for them to throw themselves to the ground and take cover in a ditch. In perfect silence, they then all listened as the voices of the border guards and the din of their barking dogs receded into the distance. They were able to make out the foulmouthed curses of the sentinels on the nightshift and the weeping of the captured woman. 'If they hadn't been busy with those people, maybe they would have caught us',[6] Nadia said to herself, and a similar thought crossed Paraschiv's mind: 'if we'd got there any earlier, we would have been the ones in trouble.'[7]

It was almost dawn when they reached Hungary, relieved that the most difficult journey of their lives had ended well. They knew they had crossed the frontier only when they came upon a milestone marking the end of Romanian territory, since, contrary to what Nadia had imagined, there were no barbed wire fences along the dividing line. They pressed on and only after a few kilometres did they stop to hug and kiss each other, realising that they hadn't celebrated the moment when they crossed the border. They were now in good spirits and grateful to Talpoş, having left behind them their fear of being chased by the dogs or surrounded by soldiers alerted to their position by flares.

Not long after that they came face to face with two Hungarian border guards, who loomed up as if springing out of the ground. Without realising it, they had been walking towards a watchtower, from which the two soldiers kept a lookout over the area. The soldiers immediately came down from the watchtower to apprehend them. They then took them to Kiszombor, a town near the frontier, where they were put through their first interrogation.

In keeping with procedures, before any decision regarding them was made, the cross-border fugitives were each interrogated separately, ordered to declare their identities, to explain the reasons why they had broken the law by crossing the frontier illegally, to say why they had made use of a guide, and to give a detailed description of the route they had taken. As a rule, fugitives from Romania could provide plausible motives, since it was widely known that living conditions in the country were abysmal and that the régime trampled on fundamental human rights.

Over the years since then, of the seven fugitives caught by Hungarian border guards on the morning of 28 November, only Nadia Comăneci, George Paraschiv and Gheorghe Talpoş have provided any information, in interviews and books they have written, about the manner in which they were treated and interrogated by the authorities at the Kiszombor frontier post. As is typical in such cases, the details they supply differ according to the attitude of each individual, according to his or her ability to observe and recall, or on the contrary, according to his or her desire to conceal facts that might be embarrassing. For example, the group's guide remembers: 'At the frontier post, the Hungarians interrogated us all, asked us who we were and what we wanted; the translator was Romanian, she was a fugitive like us,' whereas Paraschiv says that the Hungarian officer who interrogated them spoke perfect Romanian. Nadia claims that they were each interrogated separately, but Paraschiv claims that Nadia was taken to another room while the rest of them were kept together.

All of them remember one crucial detail, however, a detail regarding Nadia's conduct, which likely altered their fate, given that some members of the group were to have been turned over to the Romanian authorities after being denied leave to remain in Hungary. On learning the decision of the Hungarian border guards, Nadia's reaction was both swift and surprising: she said that she would go back to Romania with them if that was the situation. 'I admired Nadia for that: she had backbone!'[8] recalls Talpoş, who at the time probably didn't fully realise what would have become of him had he fallen into the hands of the Securitate.[9]

The Romanian Penal Code at that time treated illegal border crossings as crimes against state security, and those found guilty of such an act were given prison sentences of between six months and three years. Having acted as a guide, Talpoş would have received a harsher sentence, although it is hard to believe that he would have survived to appear in court, as he would have been subjected to unimaginable torture during interrogation for having had the audacity to help Nadia Comăneci escape from Romania. Consequently, even if Nadia raised the stakes far higher than she would really have been prepared to gamble, her gesture was still generous and it averted the danger as if by miracle.

With the exception of this detail to her credit, Nadia has never made public her negotiations with the Hungarian authorities. Therefore, we have no exact knowledge of whom she talked to at such length at the frontier post. In *Letters to a Young Gymnast*, she provides only a few neutral and highly summary snatches of that discussion, thereby preserving the mystery decades later. She recounts that when the border police saw her identification papers and realised who she was, they offered her asylum in Hungary on the spot: 'I was a famous gymnast and thus a hot catch in their minds. I think back on it now and wonder why I was so valuable to them. My career was over, and though I am considered a very good coach, what else could I really bring to Hungary?'[10]

The other defectors were each interviewed separately, but only two were given the same offer of asylum as Nadia, with the rest being informed that they would be returned to Romania the next day. Nadia recalls the obvious distress of those from her group who would have to face the consequences of being sent back to Romania and the bold, spur-of-the-moment decision it prompted her to make:

> 'Look', I told the police, 'I will only stay if the whole group is allowed to remain in your country.' The words were out of my mouth before I even considered what might happen. Gymnastics had taught me to be a team player, and in this case, my team was made up of my fellow defectors. I just thought that the situation wasn't fair. We'd all taken the same risks and crossed the border, and we should all have been allowed to stay. 'We came together, we'll stay together', I declared. To my complete surprise, the police agreed.[11]

George Paraschiv goes into far greater detail than Nadia when describing the interrogation as he remembers it. He was struck by the Hungarian border guards' excitement when they discovered who Nadia was. The soldiers offered their prisoners cigarettes and stood looking at them in obvious curiosity, even though they didn't speak Romanian and were unable to understand what the group were saying among themselves. The unit commandant, who then arrived and demanded the fugitives' papers, spoke perfect Romanian, however. Paraschiv describes the officer's immaculate uniform, his round spectacles and cropped hair, all of which gave him an intimidating air, which seemed not to bode well for his prisoners; the officer had 'a Nazi look about him', as Paraschiv puts it. The officer took their papers and neatly lined them up on his desk before making a show of examining them one by one. By Paraschiv's account, the commandant lost his icy composure on discovering the identity of his famous prisoner:

He starts to read out the names, as if making a roll call: Talpoş Gheorghe stands up, takes off his comically huge sheepskin cap; Biaş, Talpoş Gabriela, Talpoş Dumitru, Monica . . . Comăneci Nadia . . .

He is about to continue, but stops. He looks at her through those ridiculous spectacles and, screwing up his eyes, attempts a quip:

'I think this identity card must be stolen. Or is it a forgery?'

He grins from one corner of his mouth, as if expecting her to confirm it. He's jubilant!

Nadia stands up with a smile and says:

'It's really me, the gymnast, the Romanian champion, the world champion.'

The captain's face becomes contorted, he turns red, he turns pale, he starts trembling. [. . .] He leaves the room in a hurry.

Orders can be heard from the corridor. I don't understand what they're saying. Three soldiers burst in, line up in front of the door, holding their rifles.[12]

More than forty minutes later, the group heard a helicopter landing outside and shortly afterward the officer ushered a delegation of two generals and eight civilians into the room where Nadia and the others were being held. One of the civilians was Pál Schmitt, the chairman of the Hungarian Gymnastic Federation.[13] Schmitt, who spoke a little Romanian, greeted Nadia warmly and the two of them left the room together, with Nadia showing obvious relief at seeing a familiar, friendly face. After the generals and the civilian delegation filed out, the rest of the group were interrogated by the base commandant, who hung a large-scale military map of the Romanian-Hungarian frontier on the wall and made Ghiţă, the guide, describe their route in minute detail using a wooden pointer. Finally, Nadia returned to the room where the officer had been giving the group what Paraschiv describes as something resembling a school geography test:

The door opens and Nadia enters, alone. She sits down next to me, jubilant, beaming. The officer continues after a brief pause. It's as if we're in court. He reads out some articles of the Hungarian constitution.

I begin to understand what he's getting at. I'm nervous. He begins curtly:

'Talpoş Gheorghe, Talpoş Dumitru, Talpoş Gabriela, Biaş, in accordance with article number such-and-such I must surrender you to the Romanian authorities.'

My face turns white. I look at Nadia, she looks at me. Monica looks at her, too. Nadia jumps up, like a coiled spring.

'If that's your decision, then we'll all go back, we've all suffered the same, we'll all bear the consequences together,' she says solemnly.

The officer looks at her in amazement and then leaves the room, calmly, this time. We await the verdict. There is silence. Some of us are crying, they realise what the alternative is. I look at Nadia, I know that she's raising the stakes, that she has an ace up her sleeve.

The door opens, the Hungarian officer comes in. He's carrying a sheaf of paper. He hands out forms to us, we fill them in. We then receive temporary identity cards, which he stamps on the spot. 'We're all still together,' I say to myself, 'we've been really lucky.'[14]

Even though they had been captured by the Hungarian authorities and had grave fears as to their fate, the political context was in their favour. By 1989, the number of illegal border crossings had increased dramatically, with around nineteen thousand people clandestinely entering Hungary from Romania,[15] embarking on a course of action that put not only their liberty but also their lives at risk. To combat this phenomenon, the two states had negotiated bilateral accords on policing their shared border, the last of which was signed in 1983 and ratified in 1986. It was Romania rather than Hungary that was interested in having an impenetrable border, since it was only Romanian citizens who were making illegal frontier crossings. This is why the border between the two states was actually guarded by the Romanian army, while Hungarian border guards kept the adjacent area under surveillance rather than the borderline itself.

Among other things, the accord on policing the frontier stipulated that the two states were 'to inform each other of attempted or illegal frontier crossings, of the capture of persons who have infringed frontier legislation,' and captured fugitives were to be sent back 'within the shortest time, but no later than forty-eight hours.'[16] The Hungarians never had any intention of abiding by the accord, even though infringement might lead to serious repercussions under international law. This is proven by a top-secret document, Circular 0001/1985, issued by the Hungarian Ministry of Internal Affairs in July 1985, which states, 'information regarding Romanian citizens apprehended on Hungarian territory for illegal crossing of the shared border will be passed on only at the express request of the Romanian authorities and at a slow pace.'[17]

The reasons why Hungary no longer had any intention of applying drastic measures to Romania's so-called 'frontierists' were to do with political goodwill. Both states were communist régimes, but relations between them had long ceased to be 'fraternal', and by the second half of the 1980s they had deteriorated to their lowest level. This was looked on with alarm both inside and outside the Communist bloc. And not least, the two countries' relations with the Soviet Union presented a stark contrast: Soviet–Hungarian relations were very cordial, while Soviet–Romanian relations were very poor.[18]

Unlike the Socialist Republic of Romania, the Hungarian People's Republic had quickly adopted reforms similar to those introduced by Mikhail Gorbachev in the Soviet Union, embarking on a political, economic and social process aimed at salvaging 'communism with a human face.' Hungary had also launched a propaganda offensive whose aim was to prove that Transylvania was culturally Hungarian, while at the same time taking measures to support the Hungarian community in Romania, which it argued was subject to restrictions of the right to its own ethnic identity.

Romania for its part levelled vehement criticisms against its neighbour on account of the reforms on which Hungary had embarked, which were deemed unacceptable for a communist régime. Romania also accused its neighbour of a grave infringement of the principle of non-interference in the internal affairs of another state when Hungary voiced concern about the situation of ethnic Hungarians in Transylvania, an issue that had already been raised by international human rights organisations. But Romania was ruled by Nicolae Ceauşescu, a dictator devoid of all credibility, who was bogged down in a megalomaniacal project to construct a 'multilaterally developed socialist society' and was internationally isolated. Hungarian politicians justifiably believed that any normalisation of relations between Hungary and Romania was impossible to achieve as long as Ceauşescu was in power.

Obviously, ethnic Hungarians of Romanian citizenship enjoyed preferential treatment from Hungary. In any event, they made up the largest number of those crossing the frontier, and once they arrived in Hungary, they could consider themselves safe: they received political asylum, temporary residence permits, and even the right to continue their journey to the West, if they obtained the necessary documents. Circular 0001/1985 had actually been designed to assist ethnic Hungarians from Romania, regardless of how they reached Hungary, whether illegally or legally. This is to be understood from the very title of the aforementioned top-secret document, which makes veiled reference to the procedures to be applied in the case of 'certain' Romanian citizens. Verbal instructions made clear that the citizens in question were Hungarians from Transylvania, but in time the procedures also came to be applied to ethnic Romanians.

It was not a general rule, however. Some ethnic Romanian 'frontierists' were still sent back in line with the accord between the two states. The exact number is not known, but we believe that by 1989 they accounted for only a small percentage of the total number of cross-border fugitives.[19] The reasons recorded in the official documents varied, some of them lacking in seriousness, such as the fact that the cross-border fugitive didn't speak Hungarian or didn't have relatives in Hungary and consequently had no means of support in the country, or that he or she had crossed the border out of a spirit of adventure; while other escapees who were sent back had a criminal record.[20] More often than not, no reason was provided, and if Romanians were suspected of being Securitate informers, the deportation procedure was expedited, without any further explanations being given.

Neither Nadia nor any of her companions could claim the advantage of Hungarian ethnicity; all of them were ethnic Romanians. True, at the time the

Hungarian authorities had been spreading a rumour to the effect that Nadia Comăneci was actually from Transylvania and had Hungarian ancestry. The régime was supposed to have forced her to change her name from the Hungarian Anna Kemenes to the Romanian Nadia Comăneci. However, the rumour, which aimed to reinforce the idea that ethnic Hungarians in Romania were being forced to give up their identity, had no basis in fact; it was unconvincing and had also been deployed long before, in 1976, when Nadia had made an international name for herself, to the envy of neighbouring Hungary.[21]

Without access to the reports filed by the Hungarian border police, it is difficult to determine why the decision was at first taken to grant leave to remain in Hungary to only some of the seven. We may, for example, suppose that Gheorghe Talpoş had to pay for the fact that he had acted as guide. Likewise, in the case of Aurel Biaş, the reason may have been that a few years previously he had been caught trying to cross the border between Romania and Yugoslavia illegally.

Although specific details of Nadia Comăneci's interrogation – or rather, the friendly discussion with her – were not forthcoming, during it Hungarian officials, politicians and intelligence officers alike must have offered her more than just the papers needed for her to settle in the country. This was borne out a few hours later, on 29 November, when Pál Schmitt, the chairman of the Hungarian Olympic Committee, declared to the press that Nadia Comăneci was welcome to settle in Hungary if she so desired, to which end his organisation would provide her with every possible assistance. Moreover, from the first news items published by Hungarian journalists a few hours later, reporting information obtained from the authorities, it became apparent that during the discussion in question, Nadia complained of the fact that in Romania she had felt marginalised and deprived of the freedom of movement she needed in order to continue her career internationally. This was why she had given up material wellbeing in Bucharest, opting for freedom instead.

It is worth mentioning that according to some accounts, part of the discussion with Nadia Comăneci was recorded on video. The border guards introduced the film crew as reporters, but we have reason to believe they were intelligence officers.[22] The Hungarian authorities have never made the footage public, however, and it is probably stored in a secret state archive.

The seven were held for no more than a few hours, at the end of which the border guards provided them with provisory documents and allowed them to go free without any restrictions. The border guards even drove them by car into the centre of Kiszombor, where there was a bus stop. From there they made their own way to the Ministry of the Interior immigration office in Szeged – following the border guards' directions – where they formally applied for Hungarian residence permits. They were registered, they answered the questions put to all asylum seekers, and they were given meal and accommodation tickets. They spent their first night on Hungarian soil at the Hotel Royal, where the authorities sent all refugees, crammed together in the same room. General Department III[23] had stationed secret agents in the corridor, the bar and the restaurant. There were also a few journalists who had insider information that Nadia was in Szeged and were trying to meet her. For the time being, however, the Hungarian authorities made no official announcement.

The news broke the next day, 29 November, in a bulletin broadcast at eight a.m. on Radio Kossuth, Hungary's national station. In the tense political match being played out between the two countries, Hungary had scored another point against Romania, a decisive one. It showed the whole world that not even leading Romanian figures could stand any more of Ceauşescu and were even prepared to risk their lives to discredit his régime:

Former world gymnastics star takes refuge in Hungary

Yesterday, Nadia Comăneci requested political asylum in Hungary. Early on Tuesday morning, at six a.m., she illegally crossed the border into Hungary at Kiszombor with another six persons. They declared that they had crossed the border guided by a Romanian man. The crossing was planned in advance. The former Olympic champion left behind a nicely furnished home, a car, and a good life in order to choose freedom. She complained that even though she had received very many offers from abroad, she was not given permission to leave in order to become a trainer. She was unable to travel anywhere abroad, and in recent years she was no longer allowed even to visit Hungary. The curious Hungarian border guards were unable to refrain from asking her about Pacepa's book[24] and whether it was true she had had a relationship with Ceauşescu's son. Nadia denied it.[25]

The information revealed by the Hungarian authorities circulated with a swiftness that caught everybody off guard. Since further details were not yet forthcoming, the same news item was republished elsewhere, but couched in different words. The Magyar Távirati Iroda (MTI) press agency began its coverage of the sensational event by saying 'the greatest and most famous gymnast of all time' had fled Romania and was now in Hungary. The Magyar Nemzet daily smugly announced, 'Even Comăneci is now a refugee', while Hungarian state television, in various bulletins broadcast on 29 November, embellished on the subject, disseminating the first untruths in its evening news, when its Szeged correspondent claimed, among other things, that it was not Nadia's first attempt to flee Romania, since she had previously attempted to remain in the United States, but had been brought back by the Securitate against her will.

The international press picked up the story of Nadia's escape from Romania, and MTI journalists were inundated with phone calls from fellow reporters all over the world, even though they themselves knew little more than, 'Nadia has chosen freedom'. Deutsche Welle, the BBC, *Le Monde*, Agence France-Presse (AFP), U.S. cable news channels ABC, CBS and NBC, the *New York Times* and *Washington Post* were among the numerous outlets via which the news reached every corner of the world. From Brazil to Canada, from North Africa to the Middle East, from Yugoslavia to Sweden, no television station or newspaper could ignore such a sensational story, not even the Soviet press. The TASS agency relayed the initial MTI news item, and over the days that followed, Soviet newspapers *Trud*, *Sotsialisticheskaya Industriya* and *Sovetskiy Sport* all published stories.

Without even granting an interview, Nadia had struck the first propaganda blow. Merely the fact of her fleeing Romania set the Ceauşescu régime reeling: the whole of the international press now described it in the blackest terms as a régime so repressive that even people regarded as privileged in Romania were no longer able to endure it.

On 1 December, for example, the left-wing *Libération* published a story saying that Nadia had been a prisoner in her own country and her escape had come as a heavy blow, even an insult to the communist régime, given that she had fled to Hungary, a neighbouring country with which Romania had long had tense relations. The *New York Times* and *Washington Post* published photographs of Nadia on their front pages, with headlines such as: 'Nadia chooses freedom' and 'Nadia makes another amazing leap: to the free world'. There were television and radio stations in Canada which let it be known that the country was prepared to grant her political asylum. Radio Warsaw commented on the 'unusual situation that exists in Romania', which had led Nadia to take such dangerous, desperate action. Articles on the subject published in Spanish newspapers, such as *ABC*, were similarly harsh in their condemnation of the Ceauşescu régime. The *Times* of London reported a statement on the part of William Waldegrave, the deputy foreign minister, who promised that pressure would be placed on the Romanian government at every opportunity in connection with its human rights abuses, while Labour MP Paul Flynn told the BBC that he had demanded the government launch a Europe-wide 'crusade', using radio and international pressure to encourage Romanians in their march to democracy.

The whole world was looking for Nadia Comăneci, but she was nowhere to be found. Similarly, her six companions had vanished, which made their dramatic escape from Romania take on a different and far more spectacular dimension. Hotel staff told United Press International (UPI) journalists that although she had left her documents at the hotel, Nadia had left at half-past six in the morning on 29 November, stowing her luggage in the boot of a car with a Vienna number plate. In Budapest, a Ministry of the Interior spokesman confirmed that Nadia had left the hotel in Szeged for an unknown destination, probably Austria. According to the authorities, she was required to report to the police on 2 December, as her visa was valid for only three days – during which time she was free to travel around the country – but nobody expected to see her in Hungary again. For their part, officials in Austria declared that if Nadia arrived at the border without a valid passport, she would not be allowed to enter the country.[26]

The press in Switzerland took up the rumours according to which Nadia had already arrived in Berne, where she had been given refuge in the U.S. embassy. The source of this inaccurate information seems to have been Teodora Ungureanu, another great Romanian gymnast, who was at the time living in Grenoble, France. According to the AFP, Ungureanu had declared to the French press that Comăneci was in Switzerland. She admitted to already having had a telephone conversation with her, during which Nadia told her that she intended to travel from Hungary to the United States.[27] 'She's my friend. We were together for ten years. It's thanks largely to her that we won the team silver medal at Montreal in 1976. I'm very worried about her. Ever since her sporting career ended, in effect she's never left Romania. If she decided to flee the country, she didn't do it for sentimental reasons, or because she's in love with an American. She had problems in Romania, that's why she left,' added Teodora Ungureanu, who avoided making any further political comment for fear of reprisals against members of her family living in Romania.

On 30 November, at around three p.m., Michael Torff, the press officer for the U.S. diplomatic mission in Berne, publicly denied the information, in response to the journalists who had been phoning the embassy incessantly.[28] Margaret Tutwiler, a State Department spokeswoman, made a point of declaring that as of that moment, Nadia Comăneci had had 'no contact with the government authorities of any of our embassies.' Journalists with the UPI even went so far as to phone King Michael, whom the Romanian communist régime had forced to abdicate at the end of 1947 and who lived in exile in Switzerland. Although he had no information concerning Nadia Comăneci, he hailed her act of courage, said he was concerned her life might be in danger, and expressed his hope that she was safe.[29] For France-Presse, Queen Ana declared that the Romanian Royal Family was 'happy to learn that Nadia Comăneci had been able to escape the Romanian Gulag.'

From Thursday, 30 November onwards, the 'fake news' surrounding Nadia's disappearance swelled to even greater proportions. The main topic was that she was supposedly being hunted by the Securitate and her life was in danger. The night before, on 29 November, Radio France Info, quoting sources from the Hungarian authorities, had already announced that the Romanian Securitate had 'mobilised all its forces in Hungary to recapture Nadia Comăneci.' Reporters from the *Tribune de Genève* believed Nadia 'might be assassinated by the Romanian Securitate', while *Le Figaro* returned to the subject of Nadia's supposed first attempt to escape, when she was thought to have been captured by the Securitate and tortured by Nicu Ceauşescu, the dictator's son, although the paper admitted that it was 'hard to distinguish the truth among so many rumours about Nadia that are going around.' Similar stories were printed in the *Washington Post*: on 1 December, the paper gave credence to the rumour that Nadia had been kidnapped by Romanian agents and taken back to Romania.

Amid the international media furore, the British tabloids seized on the story, with the *Evening Star* publishing sensational headlines such as 'Kidnap team on Nadia's trail' and 'Come home or die'.[30] But over the course of Friday, 1 December, when officials from the U.S. Justice Department announced that Nadia Comăneci had been granted refugee status and an entry visa and was now on her way to New York, the alarmist stories about the Securitate agents trying to capture her vanished from the headlines. True, Nadia hit the headlines again a few days later, when she gave her first interview to the British press, confessing to *The Mail on Sunday* that she was still afraid of what the Securitate might do to her: 'If they can, they will try to get me back to Romania. (. . .) They don't want Nadia Comăneci in the West.'

A few hours later, on 1 December (early in the morning of 2 December, Romanian time), a Pan Am flight with Nadia Comăneci on board landed at Kennedy Airport, New York. She was met by two agents from the Diplomatic Security Service, whose task was to protect her until she boarded her next flight. She went through customs and was then taken to the airport conference room. Here, for the first time since she embarked on her escape, came face to face with the press. Hundreds of reporters desperate to see her bombarded her with questions during her short press conference, which she herself now views as not having created the best impression:

> With Constantin at my side, I told reporters in my best English (which wasn't very good) that I knew life would be different in the United States, but that 'I was nine times in the States, I know the life here'. Looking back, that statement wasn't just grammatically incorrect, it was horribly green. When asked how the Romanian government might feel about my defection, I said: 'It's not my business'.
>
> Those statements were the beginning of my downfall in the eyes of many Americans. They thought I appeared cold and wooden.[31]

But as Nadia herself says, it was hardly surprising she made such an impression, given that she had been bustled off the plane after a ten-hour flight and straight into a room 'packed with journalists shouting questions and flashing cameras', not long before which she had been crawling across freezing muddy fields and barbed wire, in fear of being shot at any moment: 'Suffice it to say that I was shell-shocked.'[32]

There were many questions that remained unanswered, while some of the answers that she did give were thought unsatisfactory. But at the time, Nadia wasn't criticised. The reporters thought that as she had only just arrived in the free world, there would be time for other press conferences. Nor was her lack of practice in expressing herself in fluent English deemed to be a barrier to communication; it was even thought she spoke English quite well. Her exhaustion did not go unnoticed, although she tried to hide it beneath an unaffected smile, and nobody was tactless enough to make comments about the inexpensive clothing she had been wearing for so many days.

Nadia's statement to the press was brief in the extreme: 'I want only to say a few words. I am happy to be in America, which is something I've wanted for a long time. But up to now I didn't have anybody to help me. This is my friend, who helped me to come here' – at which she looked around at the man behind her – 'and I want to thank him.' She seemed to feel vulnerable, and the avalanche of questions she was confronted with only made it worse:

'How long have you been planning to escape from Romania, Nadia Comăneci?'
'For many years.'
'What was the reason for you leaving?'
'I wanted to live a free life.'
'Did you leave because of events in Eastern Europe, dissatisfied that nothing is happening in Romania?'
'Yes and no, not necessarily. It's what I wanted. It was a personal decision.'
'Where will you be going after New York?'
'I don't know yet.'

These were just a few of the questions she was asked. But as Nadia herself remarks in her book, the audience was disappointed towards the end of the press conference in particular, when she was asked to comment on what impact her escape would have on the Ceauşescu régime, and she said only, 'It's not my business', repeating the same words in Romanian and then in English once more: 'Nu mă priveşte. Not my business', as if she wished to emphasise her disinterest in making any political comment. The reporters were, justifiably, expecting Nadia to launch into a list of grievances against Romania's communist régime and Nicolae Ceauşescu, having provided her with a witness box in the courtroom of the whole world. In this respect, her answer was disappointing. Although at first sight it might have seemed diplomatic, in actual fact it betrayed a lack of knowledge and lack of sensitivity to what Romanians had to suffer in their own country.

Undoubtedly, extenuating circumstances can be found. They would include Nadia's state of shock at the time and her inability to speak English fluently enough to present an argument easily, and she herself later put forward such reasons. We might also add her justified fear that expressing harsh political criticism would have increased the danger in which members of her family already found themselves in Romania. In addition, she feared that some reporters might ask her about her relationship with Nicu Ceaușescu – at the time, a number of newspaper stories were talking about this aspect of her life – thereby affecting her credibility, and this might have caused her to be more reserved when it came to making any comment about the Ceaușescu family.

But the blank the reporters drew with Nadia was filled in by others, since the media, in order to obtain the categorical statements they were after, contacted various Romanians who had also fled the country and who had worked with her as a gymnast or moved in the same circles. They included Béla Károlyi, her former trainer, and Géza Pozsár, the choreographer of the Romanian Olympic squad, who had defected to the United States in 1981. Both gave interviews critical of the régime to the Voice of America, which were noticed in Bucharest. Pozsár told reporters that in his opinion, 'Nadia's departure from Romania exposes the régime and draws the world's attention to the cruelty and backwardness in Romania,' while Béla Károlyi told the same radio station that Nadia's escape created an unpleasant situation for Nicolae Ceaușescu: 'In the past, political figures have left, even Pacepa, but this was more political, whereas when a sportswoman leaves, someone who was an idol not only to the president's family, but to the whole country, I think it affects him very unpleasantly and at the same time it signals something which in fact has been signalled all over Europe, people's movement towards democracy, towards freedom.'[33]

2
THE GREAT DANCE

When she fled Romania, Nadia had just turned twenty-eight. She was at an age when many people are often still finding their way in life, working towards achievement in their chosen careers, pursuing their dreams, accumulating experience and knowledge, settling down; an age when life starts to take on a deeper, more serious note, demanding a more sustained commitment in keeping with the chosen path. But at the age of twenty-eight, Nadia had already long since attained the highest pinnacle of achievement.

Born on 12 November 1961 in Oneşti, a small provincial town in Romania, she was the first child of Ştefania and Gheorghe Comăneci. They baptised her Nadia Elena, but of the two forenames it was ordinary-sounding, Slavic Nadia that won out over the mythically charged Greek name, which in the public mind has no association with the surname Comăneci. 'What do you want to go calling her Nadia for, Gheorghe?' the notary public supposedly asked, to which the father replied, 'I went to the cinema with the wife, it must have been about six months ago, and all of a sudden Ştefania takes my hand and places it under her ribs. "The baby's moving," she says. And because the little girl in the film was called Nadia, I told the wife that that's the name we'll give her if it's a girl.'[1] Although rather an unusual name in Romania, a few years later it was to become popular all over the world thanks to the girl from Oneşti.

Five years later, the Comănecis' second child, Adrian, Nadia's only sibling, was born. The Comănecis were an ordinary family of modest means, a family typical of the time. Although still a very young woman, Nadia's mother was a housewife. Nadia remembers her as always smelling of the kitchen from cooking all the time, while her father, who left early each morning for work, always smelled of engine oil, as he was a mechanic, who mostly repaired forestry machinery. Even if she did not have a childhood of plenty, Nadia was happy: 'As a child, I learned by creating and figuring out how to make things work (I can figure ways around any problem). Most people go and buy what they need, and if it doesn't work, they buy again. We didn't have that option. But I wouldn't trade my early years for anything.'[2] The fact that the town was surrounded by rolling, forested hills, which she roamed with the other children, and that she spent a number of years at her grandparents' house in Hîrja, a village in a beautiful valley near Oneşti, meant that Nadia had a kind of freedom unknown to children who lived in the big cities. She was rambunctious, full of energy, climbing trees and spending more time playing football with the boys than she did with the girls. Later she was to discover the pleasure of cycling, exploring both the town and the surrounding countryside.

Once she embarked on an intensive schedule of physical training, Nadia was forced to give up many of these outdoor pursuits, far sooner than she would have liked, both because she no longer had the time and because she was no longer allowed to. 'Nadia Comăneci frequently goes on bicycle rides outside town, thereby laying herself open to danger. The Head of the Ministry of the Interior Inspectorate for Bacău County has yet again warned the family and Nadia Comăneci about this behaviour with a view to ensuring her protection,'[3] reported Securitate officers from Bucharest on 23 September 1976, concerned that the gymnast might have an accident – as had previously happened – or might be at risk of attack or a kidnapping attempt.

Nadia took her first steps in the gymnastics world while she was still in nursery school. Small steps, for the time being. Practice sessions were held in a space with limited facilities that was provided by the town's sports club, named 'Flacăra' (The Flame). Nadia's parents, who hoped their daughter would become a pharmacist,[4] thought that it would be a way for her to burn off excess energy, which meant they would have more peace and quiet at home when she came back exhausted after training. But the reverse was true. Nadia began to learn exercises on the mat, the vault, the parallel bars, and the beam, doing things she wouldn't be able to at home. She was fascinated by the sport, which she viewed as pleasant way of spending time with the other children. 'Gymnastics was simply a pastime,'[5] Nadia recalls, and Marcel Duncan, her first trainer, knew how to be patient with the little girls whom he selected and taught their first gymnastics exercises as a form of fun and games.

In Oneşti in the early 1960s, there were no facilities for competitive sport. Marcel Duncan sometimes used to train the girls in the school corridor,[6] demonstrating his passion for gymnastics in circumstances where there were almost no resources available to him. Oneşti was a new town, still under construction, very much in the communist spirit of the times. It would soon be renamed after Gheorghe Gheorghiu-Dej, the first leader of communist Romania.[7] It was Gheorghiu-Dej who had made the decision to invest massively in the small Moldavian town. Oneşti already boasted a new refinery and a petrochemical plant, with other factories sprouting at a great rate. It was said that anybody who came to Oneşti would find work, the same as in other industrial model cities of the Communist bloc, like Magnitogorsk in the U.S.S.R., Nowa Huta in Poland, and Eisenhüttenstadt in East Germany. Labourers and engineers arrived from all over the country. To provide them with accommodation, small peasant cottages were demolished and conglomerations of Soviet-style blocks of flats were erected. The town's population tripled in the space of just a few years, although the town retained its small surface area. According to the March 1966 census, Oneşti had 35,663 inhabitants, of which 79.1 per cent were born elsewhere. The average age of the population was twenty-eight.[8]

A town synonymous at the time with its chemicals industry and youthful population, Oneşti was a place economically on the up. But even if the 'construction of socialism' had its own romanticism, its own specific atmosphere – the radio constantly broadcast bulletins about the town's remarkable achievements, and in 1963 singer George Bunea had a hit with the song 'Oneşti, Oneşti' – life there continued to be uneventful, drab. The town had just one cinema – the one where Nadia's parents had watched one of the many Soviet films that constantly played – or rather a room in an old building, fitted out with a screen and rows of wooden benches. There was just one decent restaurant and, situated on the main street of the old town, a cake shop, from whose window you could still see the maize fields at the edge of town. At the bottom of the hill, at the end of a cul-de-sac, there stood a church and the cemetery. Everybody knew everybody else, and the locals' routines were disrupted only when high-ranking officials came to visit. It was an opportunity for the people of Oneşti to see the most powerful Communist leaders of the time. For example, in 1962, none other than Nikita Khrushchev visited Oneşti with Gheorghe Gheorghiu-Dej, inspecting the town's industrial zone. A few months later, Walter Ulbricht, the leader of the German Democratic Republic visited. In April 1966, Josif Broz Tito, the leader of Communist Yugoslavia, came to the town, and in September of the same year, Nicolae Ceauşescu, the new Secretary General of the Romanian Communist Party, made Oneşti's industrial plants one of his first ports of call.

But sport in general and gymnastics in particular, which was soon to become a national passion in Romania, was not yet a priority when it came to the town's development plans. But even so, gymnastics had taken root. The Communist régime could take no credit for this, however, since the authorities did not plant the seed, although they were later able to reap the harvest. One might be forgiven for wondering what made the Romanian authorities decide to build the country's most up-to-date gymnastics facility in a town so far from the capital, with a relatively small populace, without any sporting tradition, a town that the régime had already earmarked for development as an industrial colony. A number of dedicated coaches can take the credit for Oneşti's achievements in gymnastics. Some of them had moved to that small town in Moldavia after being wrongfully penalised by the political leadership in Bucharest, which had for a time put the brakes on their careers.

In the mid-1950s, Marcel Duncan, Nadia Comăneci's first trainer, had worked as the chief technician at the Red Flame club in Bucharest, as well as in the Central Commission of the Romanian Gymnastics Federation (R.G.F.).[9] But in August 1958 he was sacked from the commission and demoted from category one to category two trainer, with a reduction in salary, after being accused of 'fostering an unhealthy spirit', because he had encouraged gymnasts to act like stars and shown indiscipline and cosmopolitanism.[10] In 1964, he ended up in Oneşti, as head trainer of the local Flame club, staying for just a few years, until 1969. He scouted for talent in the nursery and secondary schools and trained girls aged just twelve for national competitions. It was Marcel Duncan who had the stubbornness to persuade the local authorities to back sports in the town.

Marcel Duncan was joined by husband and wife Maria and Gheorghe Simionescu, who dedicated their lives to women's gymnastics. Maria Simionescu[11] arrived in Oneşti shortly after Duncan, having been demoted to 'low-level work'.[12] In Bucharest, before her demotion, she had been among the trainers of the national teams that took part in the 1956 Melbourne, 1960 Rome, and 1964 Tokyo Olympics, albeit with modest results. The authorities did not reinstate her as a Federation trainer until 1967, which allowed her to return to Bucharest.

Mrs Mili, as those who knew her respectfully called her, went to work in Oneşti partly because she knew Duncan. Duncan is supposed to have encouraged her to join him in developing the Flame club,[13] and Simionescu did so, establishing a gymnastics section of the local sports association in the late 1960s. Training sessions were now held in the Refineries Construction Trust industrial district of the town, which locals called the 'Snakepit' because of the poor living conditions there. They worked in a small gym, more like a hut, which was 'so cramped you had to start your run up to the apparatus from the toilet,'[14] as Gheorghu Braşoveanu, the head of the Oneşti sports lycée in the 1970s, remembers. But the girls were overwhelmed by it all and immediately took a liking to this new playground. There was a large green mat, the likes of which the girls had never seen before, on which they could run around without hurting themselves, and a shiny yellow beam.

For Mrs Mili, gymnastics was more than a profession; it was her calling. Stern in mien, especially in comparison with the mild-looking Duncan, Mili Simionescu was loved by her little gymnasts, who sensed tenderness behind the strictness she evinced. She used to ride a motorcycle, another reason why she was regarded as down to earth. Those close to her knew that everything she did was out of passion. It was Mrs Mili who gave the girls their first ballet lessons, and in the summer, on the expanse of concrete pavement by Belci Lake, she taught them exercises as they went round and round on roller-skates. 'She'd bought a sewing machine, she measured us and sewed our first gymnastics leotards, which were black with yellow bows, what joy!' remembers Anca Grigoraş, who to this day has happy memories of Mrs Mili for having 'taught us to like gymnastics.'[15]

Consequently, Marcel Duncan's ambition and devotion were what counted, and he was backed up by other enthusiastic P.E. teachers from the town, such as Mihai Ipate and Gheorge Braşoveanu. But Maria Simionescu's perseverance proved to be providential, since she was able to use her influence in such a way that the local administration was persuaded to invest in the necessary resources. True, there were already good reasons, since she and Duncan had begun to obtain their first positive results, as happened in November 1966, when at the Timişoara Championship for children and juniors the gymnastics team they had trained won first place, with individual team members winning first, second and third places in the individual floor event and exercises on the apparatuses. One of those juniors, the only one who would go on to have a gymnastics career, was Anca Grigoraş.

Taking inspiration from the methods of Soviet gymnastics, which at the time dominated the sport internationally, Maria Simionescu understood that a handful of trainers and just a few girls who loved gymnastics were not enough to win medals. What was needed was a new vision, as well as a team of devoted trainers, each of them specialising in a separate apparatus and willing constantly to better their achievements; a large number of gifted gymnasts, selected at an early age and enrolled in an intensive training programme; doctors; psychologists; physiotherapists; choreographers; musicians. In other words, an entire human infrastructure. But this was impossible to create without the physical infrastructure of a modern sports hall and a school to provide the young gymnasts with all the educational comfort they needed, without their parents feeling they had abandoned them far from home. It was a two-track enterprise. Trainers would be lured with the promise that the project would be up and running within the shortest possible time, while the investors would be eager to complete it in the shortest possible time given the great expectations of all those with a stake in its success.

With the support of Valerian Ghineţ, the town's mayor, and Andrei Erdely, the director of the Oneşti Industrial Constructions Trust, work on the gymnastics facility was completed at the end of 1967 and it was inaugurated in 1968. A year later, in September 1969, the Physical Education Lycée[16] opened its doors. The school's first headmaster was Gheorghe Simionescu, Mrs Mili's husband. Mayor Ghineţ, who was also head of the local branch of the Romanian Communist Party, continued to be generous and allocated twenty-six one-room flats for gymnasts and five flats for the trainers who had settled in the town. The town council also provided the trainers with medical services – the gym had been built in the centre of town, next to the hospital – and meal tickets at the town's best restaurant, where they had a room set aside specially for them, as well as other perks significant for the time. In Oneşti, a small town which, at the beginning of the 1950s, had only one P.E. teacher, Romania's first experimental gymnastics school began its work in earnest. The rudimentary huts located in the town's industrial district where the young gymnasts had once practised were now a thing of the past.

In the meantime, changes had taken place in Bucharest which had a positive influence on the development of the new sports centre in Oneşti. In July 1967 a national sports conference was held. It was decided that the Union of Physical Education and Sport should be replaced by a newly founded National Council for Physical Education and Sport,[17] which was the nationwide body supervising development in the sector. At the same time, general meetings of all the federations were held and they adopted new statutes and, above all, new managers. Elena Poparad was elected chairwoman of the Romanian Gymnastics Federation, and Nicolae Vieru secretary general.

The political context was also changing at the time, including the aberrant propagandistic discourse that had surrounded sport. In the 1950s, at the beginning of the Cold War, the drive to develop sport for the masses was extolled, as well as the exceptional merits and superiority of athletes from the Communist bloc. The new sport, which followed Soviet training methods, was treated as infallible, based as it was on Marxist-Leninist doctrine, and it was polyvalent, simultaneously constructing socialism and fighting for peace and friendship between nations – sport and peace were inseparable notions, since only if there was world peace could sports competitions be held. On the other side of the sporting Iron Curtain were 'imperialist' athletes, trained to become 'cannon fodder' for the West's armies. In the eyes of the Communist bloc, Western athletes were either opportunists out for their own personal gain, or they were ruthlessly exploited by their countries' capitalist régimes.

In Romania, Communist propaganda was to use sport as a weapon in the decades that followed, particularly after notable sporting achievements started to be made in the 1960s. But the discourse also become more nuanced. Taking advantage of sporting achievements, the régime was able to promote itself both domestically and internationally, claiming that such successes were based on a new type of thinking developed by Romania's communist system. Soviet sport was now no longer a model to be copied, but part of the competition.[18]

As part of this wave of changes, the Oneşti centre acquired greater importance, but continued to be viewed with reserve from Bucharest, sooner as a one-off experiment. The experiment might be a success, but what if it failed? Who would take the responsibility? Moreover, there were already other clubs – some of them with a long tradition – which laid claim to gymnastics, such as Dinamo Bucharest. Dinamo was Romania's strongest club, since it was part of the Ministry of Internal Affairs, which meant its athletes had the privilege of being able to compete internationally. The heads of gymnastics in Bucharest therefore deemed a degree of caution appropriate, allowing the local authorities in Oneşti the satisfaction of providing the Flame club a large amount of support, as well as responsibility to match.

Once the sports hall was inaugurated, the Ministry of Education, the National Council of Physical Education and Sport, and the Romanian Gymnastics Federation all supported those trainers and teachers prepared to be part of the new project to develop female gymnastics, and the Oneşti team expanded from one year to the next.[19] At the proposal of Maria Simionescu, who was now the Romanian Gymnastics Federation's teacher-trainer, supervisor and representative in Oneşti, technicians from all over the country whom she had noticed over the years were co-opted, and they were joined by the gymnasts they had been training. The new team was also joined by Marcel Duncan, who brought the girls he had previously discovered over the years, including Nadia Comăneci. From Autumn 1969, all the gymnasts were enrolled in the new gymnastics lycée.

It was the beginning of the journey. Over the years, when the results obtained internationally by gymnasts from Oneşti confirmed the value of the training centre, many of those in the upper echelons of Romanian sport made sure that they were the ones who reaped the laurels, to the detriment of those who actually deserved it. The name Marcel Duncan, who had laid the foundations of female gymnastics in the town after bringing the Flame club to life, was deliberately ignored. Maria Simionescu, who complemented Duncan's passion and had been ambitious enough to take the initiative for building a club of such proportions, could not be overlooked, however, thanks to the major rôle she continued to play in gymnastics. But her influence and decision-making power within the Oneşti centre were considerably reduced.

The coaches who settled in Oneşti at the time included Béla and Marta Károlyi. Still young and at the start of their careers, they didn't have any impressive achievements behind them, but how many gymnastics trainers did back then? Both of them were born in 1942, Marta in August, Béla in September. They had been students together in Cluj, at the recently founded Pedagogical Institute, in the Physical Education and Sports section. After graduation, they continued their education, enrolling as part-time students at the Physical Culture Institute in Bucharest in 1964. They had experience of both Soviet-style education, which began to be copied on a large scale in 1948, and the relative normality that took hold in Romanian education from 1962–64.

As a teenager, Marta had dreamed of becoming a teacher of the humanities. Or at least so it would transpire from a report dating from 1976, filed by the Securitate in Odorheiu Secuiesc, her home town, in which she is described as a young woman with good behaviour: 'The woman in question finished elementary school and general culture lycée in the town of Odorheiu Secuiesc, where she was known as a quiet pupil, studious, and with unblemished behaviour. At the time she did not have any interest in any branch of sport, mostly she was interested in philology, biology and the natural sciences, the subjects she studied for university entrance examinations. Failing on her first attempt, she abandoned the subjects in question and sat the examination for the three-year course at the Physical Education and Sport Institute in Cluj, from which she later graduated. It was here she met her present husband, Károlyi Béla, who was a student in the same class.'[20]

For Béla, who hated maths and science, sport was not a refuge, but had been an all-consuming passion since his youth. For that reason, he had had a tense relationship with his father, whom he disappointed when he chose a career as a P.E. teacher rather than becoming a construction engineer. Béla practised athletics at first. Of sturdy physique, from the age of thirteen he chose a track and field event unattractive to most: hammer throwing. Over the years, he also boxed and played rugby, finally settling on a career in handball, as both a player and a trainer, especially given that he had specialised in handball and skiing as a student in Cluj.

In 1963, after graduation, Béla Károlyi and Marta Eröss were sent to teach in two small mining towns in the Jiu Valley, twelve kilometres from each other: Béla in Vulcan, Marta in Lupeni. They married one rainy day in November 1963, without a ceremony, in the mayor's office of a town between Vulcan and Lupeni: 'We had a brief ceremony—she said yes, I said yes, and we were declared husband and wife. We kissed each other and then walked back to our respective jobs to teach afternoon classes. We spent our honeymoon in a small apartment we had rented in Lupeni. We were unbelievably happy,'[21] recalled Károlyi years later.

The enthusiasm of youth must have given them the strength to overcome hardships, since life in the Jiu Valley was not easy. Béla played for Vulcan's Future handball team, where he stood out, and Marta worked as a P.E. teacher in Lupeni. But before long, in 1966, they managed to move to Petroşani, the largest town in the area, where they both found jobs at the sports school, where they worked until 1968, when they moved to Oneşti.

Nicolae Vieru, the secretary general of the Romanian Gymnastics Federation at the time,[22] says that the Károlyis moved from Petroşani to Oneşti in the autumn of 1970,[23] but we have reason to believe that he is mistaken. Vieru also suggests that the transfer was thanks to Francisc Lövi, deputy secretary general of the Romanian Gymnastics Federation, at the request of Károlyi, both of whom were ethnic Hungarians and on friendly terms: 'Marta was a gymnastics trainer at the Petroşani Sports School. At the children's championship, the team she had trained came third. Because they had had a baby daughter who died, they wanted to leave the tragedy behind in Petroşani. They requested the Federation find them positions in a different town. They benefitted from favourable circumstances. At the Federation, the deputy secretary general was Lövi Francisc. He had a certain affinity for Béla, so he put him forward for the Oneşti Centre. At first, Béla worked at the sports school, teaching handball, and Marta worked alongside Maria Simionescu at the Olympic gymnastics centre.'[24]

In March 1975, in line with Vieru's suspicion, the Securitate did indeed conclude that Francisc Lövi 'shows favouritism in his professional work towards trainers of Hungarian ethnicity in our country'.[25] But even if in his memoirs he admits that Lövi put the proposal to him during a telephone conversation in early

January 1968, Béla Károlyi did not speak of the personal suffering he and his wife had been through, or about any links based on shared ethnicity with Francisc Lövi. In fact, Károlyi claimed that he and his wife arrived in Oneşti not on their own initiative, but at the request of the authorities, after their work in the Jiu Valley had been noticed in Bucharest. On 9 February, he made his first visit to Oneşti, to find out more about the project, to see the new sports hall, and to meet the team of trainers, and on 28 February, he and Marta arrived there with their luggage. It was not long after the town hall held the ceremony to inaugurate the new gym.[26]

The Károlyis therefore started all over again in a town that offered far more promising opportunities. Of course, at the time they could not have imagined that within a few short years later they would be representing Romania at top international events, but even so, their living conditions were now better than they had been used to and getting better from one year to the next. Given they were taking part in an experimental sports project, all that remained was for them to dedicate themselves to their profession and try to stand out as brilliant trainers.

At first, they were sent to work at different schools, and Béla didn't even teach gymnastics: thanks to his past career, he was made trainer of the girls' handball team at a sports school, which soon reached the finals of the Towns Cup. Marta, who also lacked experience in gymnastics, not having taken part in any international competitions either as a gymnast or a technician, was appointed gymnastics trainer alongside the far more experienced Valeriu Munteanu, from whom she was to learn the secrets of the profession.

The two trainers, Valeriu Munteanu and Marta Károlyi, were assigned a number of girls, including some who had been part of Marcel Duncan's group, as Maria Simionescu remembered years later: 'After the opening of the physical education lycée in 1969, [Nadia Comăneci] became a pupil at the school, having been assigned to Group A, where she trained with Marta Károlyi and Munteanu Valeriu.'[27] They continued to work as a team until Munteanu gave up gymnastics and returned to Bucharest. Nicolae Vieru says, 'Béla had had his eye on Nadia's group from the very start and did everything he could to take it over,'[28] which shows how ambitious he was, although we believe that Károlyi also knew how to seize an opportunity when he saw it. Marcel Duncan had already left Oneşti. He planned to emigrate from Romania and had applied to do so. Waiting for his application to go through, in 1969 he was moved to Galaţi, where he opened a new gymnastics centre and set up training facilities. Valeriu Munteanu had also left Oneşti: some think it was because his wife had not been assigned a department at the school there,[29] others because it was hard for him to work with two teams, the juniors from Oneşti and the seniors from Bucharest.[30] But whatever the reason, probably at the beginning of the summer of 1971, after a discussion with the head of the sports lycée and with Maria Simionescu, Béla Károlyi gave up handball and took up the position vacated by his predecessors,

Marcel Duncan and Valeriu Munteanu, becoming, alongside Marta, the second gymnastics trainer of the group that included Nadia Comăneci.

Over the years, Béla Károlyi never mentioned the rôle the two other trainers played, as if they hadn't existed, and when Romanian or foreign journalists asked him and his wife about the beginnings of their career, they said that they hadn't continued the work of anybody else and that Nadia's story began with them. Whenever he was asked about how he started training Nadia, Béla Károlyi recalled an episode in the schoolyard in Oneşti. He was there as a gymnastics trainer scouting for girls with an aptitude for the sport. He is supposed to have seen Nadia only after visiting a number of other schools and testing the speed, flexibility and balance of hundreds of other girls. 'Then, one day, I saw two blonde little girls turning cartwheels in a schoolyard. I went over to them and watched more closely: they had something special. The bell rang and the girls vanished back inside the school like arrows,' Károlyi recounts. Doggedly searching for them classroom by classroom, he finally found them, and one of the girls was Nadia Comăneci: 'I told them to tell their mothers that Béla Károlyi said they could be admitted to Onesti's experimental gymnastics school if they wished. They were six years old at the time'[31]

We don't know when he concocted this story, but he started telling it in public from 1975, after obtaining his first major gymnastics success at the European Championships in Norway. It is true that his tendency to usurp others' merits came to light earlier than this, but it had previously been couched in a certain ambiguity, as was the case in the interview he gave to *Sportul*, Romania's biggest sports paper, in April 1973, probably the first interview of his career, when he hinted at what he would shortly say loudly and clearly: 'Our interest in putting together a group of gymnasts to start intensive training [. . .] took us to a number of nursery schools in the town. Nadia stood out from the very start for her extraordinary qualities: mobility, range, speed, which is what we were testing for. Afterward, in the gym, she continued to stand out.'[32]

On 10 May 1975, *Sportul* published another interview with Béla Károlyi, this time a lengthy one, given on the plane on which he was returning from the European Championships in Norway. Constantin Macovei, the journalist who interviewed him, had covered gymnastics for decades. In answer to the questions, 'How did you discover Nadia? What attracted your attention to her seven years ago?' the reply was to become Károlyi's leitmotiv: in a nursery school in Oneşti, in 1968.[33]

It was four, not seven, years that had elapsed since Béla Károlyi started training Nadia, however, and his distorted memories, expressed with such nonchalance, provoked serious discontent among those it airbrushed out of history. But for a number of reasons, those memories could not be contested at the time. On the one hand, under the Communist régime, the press was under strict control and disputes of that kind were not allowed unless orchestrated by

Party chiefs. Even if his colleagues from Oneşti had dared to gainsay him publicly, no journalist would have been brave enough to allow them to give vent to such opinions for fear of a political scandal. On the other hand, Károlyi was by now a famous trainer, and the Communist régime was prepared to forgive him such minor vanities.

In fact, through its propaganda tool, the authorities went much farther than that, since in books about Nadia Comăneci, the women's gymnastics team, and the trainers from the Flame club in Oneşti published in Romania in the late 1970s, Károlyi's version of events was published without any mention of either Duncan or Munteanu. There were some, such as D. Dimitriu,[34] who even stirred the pot by claiming that a number of trainers had worked at the Oneşti centre but had had to give up because of they couldn't take the hardships, unlike Károlyi, who had the boldness to build something lasting and solid: 'Some stayed a year, others, two, others still, three, and that was about all. The lure of the big cities was a magnet far stronger than gymnastics for them. Some adapted here, others didn't. With their minds set on leaving more than they were on their work, it was normal that they wouldn't achieve much.'[35] Others were able to strike a more reserved tone, such as sports journalist Ioan Chirilă, whose book *Nadia* was a great publishing success in 1977. Chirilă, who must have known the truth, merely noted, 'Béla Károlyi *claims* to have seen Nadia for the first time while playing hopscotch' (emphasis added).[36]

Even if they were not public, discussions of this seemingly unimportant subject did exist, born of the indignation of some of those from Oneşti who knew all too well the rôle that Duncan and Munteanu had played, as well as when exactly Béla Károlyi had become a gymnastics trainer. They claimed that Béla Károlyi showed dishonesty towards his former colleagues, and their opinions quickly reached the ears of the Securitate. As early as March 1976, the Securitate had noted 'shortcomings in the moral character' of Béla Károlyi, given that 'after Nadia Comăneci's success he made declarations to the press and television that do not tally with the reality (that he discovered her and started training her, and the terrorised gymnast states likewise)'.[37] For this reason, in September 1976, the Securitate in Oneşti conducted an inquiry, with the results being reported to both the Bacău County Securitate Inspectorate and to Bucharest, and thence to the upper echelons of the Communist Party. This unusual investigation, which aimed to highlight Béla Károlyi's personality and working methods when training gymnasts, was conducted by Lieutenant Colonel Vasile Miriţă, who got to the bottom of the matter in just a few days. The informers were asked to put down in writing what they knew 'in connection with the discovery of gymnast Nadia Comăneci and the first period of her training,' with Miriţă holding open, unofficial discussions with those in charge of the centre and the lycée in Oneşti. All denied Károlyi's version and were unforgiving in their descriptions of his character and conduct.

Informer 'Nelu', for example, who was close to Károlyi for a long time, wrote in one of his reports, 'after the success of his pupil Nadia Comăneci, he declared to the press and television things that bear no relation to the truth (that he is supposed to have discovered Nadia and started working with her, the terrorised girl claims same thing. The source witnessed a scene at the 23 August Sports Field when Károlyi coached Nadia word for word as to what she had to say in reply to journalists' questions).'[38] More than a year later, 'Nelu' returned to the subject in another intelligence report, declaring, 'the first character trait of the aforenamed which I observed was that he <u>cultivates lies and manages to convince people of untrue things with unusual force</u>. For example, he told the source in great detail about how he "discovered" the girls at nursery school and how he fought with the school's heads to bring them for selection. The girls had to say the same thing, being constrained to lie.'[39] Gymnast Georgeta Gabor, a member of the Olympic squad, admitted, 'trainer Béla Károlyi taught us that in every circumstance, both at home and abroad, to answer those who asked us that he was the only one who selected us for the squad and carried out our training, which isn't true.'[40] Gheorghe Braşoveanu, the lycée's head, told Miriţă, 'Nadia Comăneci was selected by teacher-trainer Duncan Marcel,'[41] while giving an extremely negative account of Károlyi's character. Informer 'Pătru Ion' also confirmed that Duncan had set up 'the first gymnastics centre' in Oneşti and 'Nadia Comăneci was selected by Duncan Marcel when she was in the nursery school of the industrial district,'[42] describing Károlyi in the same negative light. Informer 'Gheorghe Daniela' said that Marta Károlyi,

not having been involved in competition gymnastics, took over trainer Duncan Marcel's small group when the lycée was founded and with teacher Munteanu Valeriu from Bucharest worked with the girls until Munteanu left in 1972. The group started training in 1968 at the Gheorghe Gheorghiu-Dej Flame club with Duncan Marcel, with whom they trained until the end of 1969.The group included Nadia Comăneci and Georgeta Gabor, members of the 1976 Olympic team.

In 1972, after the departure of Munteanu Valeriu, Károlyi Béla was also assigned to the lycée, having previously been with the handball team of the town's sports school. This can be verified against the archive documents, school registers, payrolls. (. . .) Károlyi Béla's claims to the press and television that he selected and trained them are not true.[43]

Informers 'Tudoran Gheorghe' and 'Măgureanu' declared the same thing, the second of them mentioning that Béla Károlyi had succeeded 'through various manoeuvres to drive out the other trainers and take everything for himself, according to the theory of "divide and rule".'[44] Drawing teacher Vişan was even unjust, refusing to recognise Károlyi's subsequent achievements: 'Béla Károlyi had greater luck than he did merit, Nadia was selected by the Simionescus and assigned to Károlyi for training, but it could have been anybody else and the result would have been the same.'[45]

On 30 September 1976, after Miriţă and his colleagues finished their investigation, the head of the Securitate from Bacău and the heads of Department One of the Securitate in Bucharest received the report from Oneşti, from which, for the time being, we shall quote only the conclusions as to who discovered Nadia Comăneci and when, since the document stretches for eleven pages and includes 'a number of unusual aspects' relating to the lives and professional careers of the Károlyis:

We report the following:

In 1965, in Gheorghe Gheorghiu-Dej Municipality, under the supervision of teacher-trainer Duncan Marcel, a female gymnastics sports nucleus came into being, which operated within the Flame Sporting Association. Subsequently, at the beginning of 1966, gymnast Nadia Comăneci was selected by Duncan.

In the same period, husband and wife Maria and Gheorghe Simionescu,[46] specialist teachers, were assigned to the Gheorghe Gheorghiu-Dej Municipality, who together with teacher Duncan Marcel made their contribution to training and laying the foundations of competition gymnastics.

The first competition gymnastics group began its activity in 1968 at the Flame Sporting Association, female gymnastics section, run by trainer Duncan Marcel until 1969, of which, among others, Nadia Comăneci and Georgeta Gabor were part.

Husband and wife Marta and Béla Károlyi were assigned to the Gheorghe Gheorghe-Dej Municipality during the course of 1968, respectively to the General Culture Lycée No. 1 and the Sports School.

In 1969, when the Female Gymnastics Lycée was established, teacher Marta Károlyi was selected and assigned to this school, where she took over the small group that had been trained by Duncan Marcel, and together with teacher Munteanu Valerică from Bucharest they worked with the group until 1972.

In 1972, when teacher Munteanu Valerică was recalled to the Romanian Gymnastics Federation, Károlyi Béla was appointed to replace him, having theretofore worked in the handball department of the local sports school. This competition gymnastics group, whose members included Nadia Comăneci, Teodora Ungureanu, Gabor Georgeta and others, was taken over with a view to continuation of training by the Károlyis under the supervision of federal gymnastics trainer Maria Simionescu and her husband Gheorghe Simionescu, who at the time was director of the lycée. This group, which included the best gymnasts, took part in national and international competitions, including the 1976 Montreal Olympics, Canada.

Duncan Marcel operated within the Municipality until 1969, when he left with his whole family, initially going to Galaţi, and at present he is in Israel (legal emigrant).

Husband and wife Maria and Gheorghe Simionescu are at present in Bucharest, the first a federal trainer and international gymnastics referee, and the second a gymnastics teacher at a lycée in Bucharest.

Munteanu Valerică is also in Bucharest, teaching at a sports school.[47]

As for Nadia, she tried to stand up to the trainer. Whereas in 1975, when she was just thirteen, she was obliged to tell journalists, 'from the age of six I got my start in the sport, with trainers Marta and Béla Károlyi,'[48] in the interviews she gave in the 1980s she no longer confirmed Károlyi's story, even if she did not mention all the names of her first trainers. 'I should read Béla's book, because his memories are a little different than mine, but he's close,' Nadia later said, in 2017, adding, 'I don't know exactly how he ended up with us, but he did.'[49] In her own autobiography she did mention the fact that the trainer who discovered her was Marcel Duncan, and that she took her first gymnastics lessons at the Flame Municipal Sports Club in Oneşti, while she was still in nursery school.[50]

For their part, those who were directly involved in the work of the Oneşti gymnastics centre have made similar statements since 1989, in the sporting press and in various books on the history of Romanian gymnastics, all of them feeling the need to repair the injustice to Marcel Duncan. Let us also add that it was not only Károlyi's insistence on telling his own imaginary tale that lay behind the fact that the name Duncan never appears in any of the books about Nadia Comăneci published in Communist Romania, but rather the fact that Duncan was viewed dimly by the régime. After the few years he spent in Oneşti and an equally short period working in Galaţi, Duncan left Romania for good. He saw Nadia again at the 1976 Montréal Olympics, but only from the stands, according to Nicolae Vieru, who remembers the moving scene: 'You ought to know that Marcel Duncan was in the stands in Montréal in seventy-six, on all the days of Nadia' glory! He was in the crowd, because he didn't have access to the delegation. He wasn't among the officials. But every day he came to the back, where the girls filed out, he greeted us and kept his eyes fixed on Nadia in admiration, after her Olympic performances.'[51]

Károlyi recounted the schoolyard episode so many times – in interviews, in his autobiography, in books by other authors, and even managing to introduce it into the script of a feature film called Nadia made in 1984 – that he himself probably ended up believing it was true. In the last interview to the Romanian press that he gave on the subject, in November 2011, he made the same claim, albeit admitting that Nadia 'may have had a gymnastics lesson or two with Duncan before that, just play, elementary stuff. You know, through the mist of the years, I no longer remember every single detail.'[52] In reality, the merit of discovering

Nadia Comăneci must go to Marcel Duncan, a cordial and passionate man, which in no way diminishes the great skill Károlyi later showed, opening up her path to perfection.

It should be said that Béla Károlyi was a man able to twist any fact to suit him. When he set out to influence the way a person thought or acted, he did so with great skill. Possessive by nature, he did not care about anything or anybody else when he wanted to fulfil a plan or satisfy an ambition.

He was a keen stamp collector and hunter, hobbies that might be regarded as extravagant under communism, as reserved for the privileged few. Although he gave the appearance of being very canny with his money, with some regarding him as miserly, he spent lavishly on his hobbies and devoted a great deal of his precious time to his nine hunting dogs, which were very dear to him and which he kept in the farmyard of a peasant from Oneşti. These pastimes and material indulgences on the part of the Károlyis, to the extent that they could afford them under communism, became more and more viable as the years passed, as their fame increased and their relations with the régime were consolidated.

Undoubtedly, within the team of technicians from Oneşti, Károlyi was a figure who stood out. There was something different about him. He liked to read, to improve his methodology and knowledge. He worked very hard, without pause; he built meticulously. He was voluble, full of energy. 'Károlyi is a stickler for tidiness, which makes you hesitate even before moving the ashtray on the table,'[53] said journalist Ioan Chirilă, highlighting the exaggerated attention to detail shown by the trainer. Nadia remembers that Marta Károlyi 'believed in discipline, and she was terribly demanding,' while Béla's 'attitude was light and easy compared to Marta's.'[54]

For as long as they lived in Oneşti, Béla and Marta Károlyi didn't have very many friends, due to their domineering, overbearing personalities. Perhaps Béla inherited this from his father, a civil construction engineer, who he himself said was a very disciplined and harsh man. But his father was also 'known for his good manners,' as a Securitate agent reported, noting that the son did not seem to have inherited them. In 1977, the Securitate drew up a report on Károlyi's character, concluding that he was impulsive and liable to fly into rages. In his relations with others, he was capable of courtesy only when he had an ulterior motive, and otherwise he was 'distant in his relations with colleagues, he is not characterised by comradely solidarity, but rather egotism.'[55] Obviously, those who described him thus were informers. Given that they worked for the secret police, the communist dictatorship's instrument of repression, and also given that some of the agents must have had tense relations with Károlyi, we might question their reliability; we might wonder whether their accounts were highly subjective, even vindictive. However, we cannot help but remark that, oddly enough, in none of these descriptions is Károlyi praised for his human qualities, only for his capacity to work. And since every informer pinpoints the same weaknesses and shortcomings, we believe that ultimately there is little exaggeration in their reports.

Moreover, the Securitate did not base its conclusions only on informers' reports, but also drew on information obtained from direct surveillance, since at various times there were hidden microphones installed in the Károlyi home. The recordings would have made plain what kind of relationship existed between the spouses, and what kind of attitude they had towards their colleagues and the gymnasts they trained. The opinion of the informers, who had already reported that the Károlyis quarrelled frequently, was thereby confirmed, as was the fact that he cared about nobody and nothing except his daughter and hunting dogs.

Late in his life, Nicolae Vieru publicly stated that Károlyi was a man devoid of all generosity, a man consumed by petty interest. But such a statement is no more offensive than others in which Károlyi is described as intransigent, unwilling to accept the majority opinion, convinced that he was always right. He compromised only when confronted with those more powerful than he, such as the leadership of the local Party organisation – although he himself claimed that it was only thanks to his connections that they kept their jobs – or members of the government in Bucharest, while continuing to make efforts to bend a decision in his favour. He was regarded as dictatorial, since he assumed unlimited powers within the team and fought to have those powers recognised at the highest level, in Bucharest. But whatever faults he may have had, the Securitate and the régime overlooked them and declined to interfere in his work, as they would have done had it been a different trainer. His ambition and huge capacity for work saved him, and the remarkable results he achieved served as a shield, protecting him for a decade.

Even with regard to his beginnings as a trainer, there is conflicting information. It is not known exactly when Valeriu Munteanu left,[56] and witnesses from the time no longer remember when Béla Károlyi started training gymnasts in Oneşti. Might it have been in 1970? Or was it the summer of 1971? Speaking of these early years in his autobiography, Károlyi himself is vague, giving almost no account of his work in the period from 1968 to 1971, as if trying to avoid the subject. In *Sportul*, there are a few clues to support the opinion that Valeriu Munteanu rather than Béla Károlyi was the gymnastics trainer in Oneşti at least up until the end of 1970. For example, in the 1 April 1970 issue, when *Sportul* published a long article about the establishment of a new gymnastics centre in Oneşti, the reporter made a point of mentioning 'the names of all those generous trainers that work here since they deserve it in abundance: Federal trainer Maria Simionescu, George Simionescu, the head of the Gymnastics Lycée, husband and wife Marine and Mircea Bibire (from Bacău), Tatiana Isar (Lugoj), Maria Raicu (Timişoara), Florica Dobre (Craiova), Petre Miclăuş and Valeriu Munteanu (Bucharest), Gheorghe Gorgoi (Cluj), Norbert Kuhn (Timişoara). Alongside them, full-time teacher Marta Károlyi also works in the gym.'[57] On 25 November 1970, Nicolae Vieru wrote a short piece for *Sportul*, titled 'Juniors on the cusp of maturity.' After a few remarks about Romania's youngest gymnasts, Vieru states that a number of technicians already stand out, including 'Valeriu Munteanu, Marta Károlyi (Gymnastics Lycée, Gheorghe Gheorghiu-Dej Municipality)'.[58]

Mariana Cojanu, one of the first gymnasts trained by the Károlyis, remembers that in the summer of 1970, when Marta Károlyi went to the seaside with the girls, 'Béla was with the girls from the handball team and came to help Marta out when we did exercises on the beach.'[59] We believe that Marta and Béla Károlyi officially became a professional couple at the end of the 1970–71 school year. Of the statements relating to that period to be found in the Securitate archives we believe to be correct that given by Gheorghe Braşoveanu, the head of the Oneşti Gymnastics Lycée in the 1970s. As Braşoveanu recalls, 'from 1971 Nadia Comăneci's training was continued by husband and wife Marta and Béla Károlyi.'[60] Mircea Bibire, a trainer in that early team, makes a similar statement: 'in 1971, Béla Károlyi arrived at the lycée and together with his wife Marta took over Nadia's team,'[61] while in a fiche from Károlyi's Securitate file, probably drawn up in 1976, we find, 'on 15 September 1971 he moved to the Gymnastics-Physical Education Lycée.'[62] Not least, there is a brief reference to this point in his career that comes from Valeriu Munteanu himself, in a declaration that reached the Securitate in June 1982, in which he states, 'I was Nadia Comăneci's trainer in Oneşti for two years.'[63]

At the national level, the lycée's first major success came in June 1970, at the junior championships in Sibiu. The team from Oneşti won first place, although this was not thanks to Nadia, far from it: aged just nine, she fell from the beam three times in just ten seconds, which prompted laughter from the girls in the team from Oradea as they sat on the bench, while some of her teammates started to cry in despair. Furious, frustrated, humiliated, Nadia suffered for having disappointed everybody – her teammates, her trainers, and herself. She was never to forget the episode of the three falls, describing it in *Letters to a Young Gymnast*, where she says that at the end of her catastrophic exercise on the beam, Marta was foaming at the mouth with fury. She was given a score of 7.25,[64] but her failure on the beam wasn't such a catastrophe after all, since the Oneşti team would have lost first place to Oradea only if she had received a 6.00.

Not long after that, the team had further successes, which were reported in *Sportul*, Romania's only national sporting paper. In April 1972, at the national schools gymnastics championships in Bucharest, held at the Floreasca Arena, Flame Oneşti once more triumphed. This time, Béla and Marta Károlyi are both mentioned, but journalist Horia Alexandrescu gets their name wrong, reporting, 'the pupils of Mr and Mrs Kiraly [sic] categorically won the team title and the first six places in the floor exercise.'[65] A few months later, on 3 July, Francisc Lövi, the deputy general secretary of the Federation, published a piece in *Sportul* titled

'You can count on tomorrow's generation of our gymnasts'. The piece gave the names of the trainers who had 'made a substantial contribution to obtaining remarkable results,'[66] including Béla and Marta Károlyi, but also mentioned Marcel Duncan, who by then was training the Galaţi team.

But up until the summer of 1972, *Sportul* coverage of the Oneşti team was summary, comprising just a few lines reporting its results, without any further remarks on the development of the young gymnasts. In the communist jargon of the time, *Sportul* reported that in Oneşti 'gymnastics has forged a solid tradition, ensuring for itself a future of great worth',[67] but noted that it was still early days for the girls now trained by the Károlyis. They were too little to be noticed by the Bucharest newspapers, which reported on established trainers such as Anca Grigoraş, Felicia Dornea, Paula Ioan, Elisabeta Turcu, and Maria Constatinescu, and older gymnasts such as Alina Goreac and Elena Ceampelea, who had already made a name for themselves at international competitions.

Nadia Comăneci was mentioned in the 14 April 1972 issue of *Sportul* alongside her teammates, without being singled out, in a long article about sport in Bacău County. But on 15 June, in an article that compiled information 'from all over the country', she was given a column headed 'A small . . . great hope',[68] which featured a photograph of her. Some of the details presented are incorrect – her date of birth and her surname, which is spelled Comănici – and her achievements, described as 'rich' for her age, actually refer to the team's, since she had yet to have accomplishments of her own. The by-line for the piece was Gheorghe Grunzu, a figure remembered only by those who worked with him in Oneşti at the time, since he wasn't a journalist, but rather chairman of the Municipal Council for Physical Education and Sport, a position he held for almost three decades.

At the end of June, when those in charge of the future gymnastics were choosing the members of the men's and women's national teams to take part in the 1972 Olympics, to be held in Munich, the Károlyis took their juniors to Sofia for the Friendship Cup. It was the first international competition in which Nadia's generation from Flame Oneşti took part, according to what Károlyi says in his autobiography. The competition was important since it brought together gymnasts from all the Communist bloc countries, who were very strong in the field. It was seen as a 'tournament of Olympic hopefuls', since as a rule it was here that future World and Olympic champions were noticed. 'Nadia won the all-round gold, and the team won the silver team medal,'[69] says Károlyi, but his memory is slightly exaggerated. In the apparatus events, Nadia won two gold medals (uneven parallel bars and beam), while Irina Shchegolova and Raisa Bichukina won gold on the vault and floor exercise, and Romania came fourth in the team competition. Romanian gymnasts came second in the medal rankings: three gold medals, the third won by Nicolae Oprescu on the men's still rings event, while the Soviet Union won eight gold medals.

It was a remarkable success. The Oneşti Juniors, without any experience of international competitions, demonstrated that they could compete with gymnasts from the U.S.S.R., Czechoslovakia, Hungary and East Germany, while Nadia 'Comănici', as she was again misnamed in the Bucharest press, stood out as 'the performer of the finale on the apparatuses'.[70] She had not yet reached the age of eleven.

After this significant development in Bulgaria, journalists seemed to take a greater interest in what was happening in Oneşti in general and in Nadia's budding career in particular. When the national junior championships was held in Cluj in November 1972, the young Flame gymnasts, now promoted to second category, swept away the competition. They won the team events, and Nadia won first place in the individual overall events after coming first in the beam, floor, and vault events. Journalist Constantin Macovei wrote that she was 'undeniably our greatest female gymnastic talent',[71] and a photograph of Nadia captured during her floor exercise was printed on the first page of the newspaper.

This great gymnastic talent, as Macovei called her, was by no means an exception, however. The gymnasts from Oneşti, whether trained by Károlyi or other technicians, proved to be the best, winning title after title. In 1973, for example, they won first place in every national competition, from category four to the masters, an absolute record, which must have depressed trainers and gymnasts from rival clubs such as Dinamo Bucharest and Sport Club Bacău, especially since the differences in points were substantial.

Macovei's assessment was borne out from one month to the next as Nadia took part in fresh competitions. In April 1973, at the International Gymnastics Championships held in Romania, Nadia astounded the world with her almost flawless execution on the parallel bars and beam, performing a torrent of handsprings on the bar and 720-degree corkscrew leaps on the floor, not moves that had been seen very often in competitions in Romania. She won every event, surpassing not only the other members of her squad, the far more experienced Alina Goreac and Elena Ceampelea, but also gymnasts from the U.S.S.R., East Germany, Poland and Czechoslovakia. At the Friendship Cup held in East Germany in August, the Romanian team, made up only of gymnasts from Oneşti, won third place in the team events. Nadia Comăneci won two gold medals, for the vault and parallel bars, and a bronze medal for the floor event, while Teodora Ungureanu won a silver medal for the beam event. But it is worth mentioning that in the composite individual event Nadia beat Nellie Kim, the Soviet gymnast who over the next few years was to emerge as her main rival. At another leg of the Friendship Cup, held in Pyongyang in 1974, the Oneşti team added to their collection of medals, winning first place. Nadia injured herself during warm-ups, but Teodora Ungureanu and Mariana Cojanu put in spectacular performances on the parallel bars, beam and floor.

From 1975, Nadia Comăneci was to compete in seniors competitions, including major international events. The year would bring genuinely significant triumphs, which by now drew the attention of the whole sporting world. She was Romania's best gymnast and the moment had come for her to prove it worldwide. In April, she took part in the Champions Cup in London, winning the competition trophy after beating Ludmila Savina of the Soviet Union and Avril Lenox of the United Kingdom. Károlyi's gymnast presented to the public for the first time in an international competition a double-twist dismount from the parallel bars, thereby launching a series of original moves that were to be named after her. Peter G. Shilston, the correspondent for *Gymnast* magazine and a declared admirer of Soviet gymnasts, wrote a piece in which he predicted: 'Nadia's genius [will] come to full fruition in time for the 1980 Moscow Olympics. But will the Russians let her take them apart on their home ground?'[72]

A few weeks later, in Skien, southern Norway, the European Gymnastics Championships were held. At the previous event, held in London in 1973, Alina Goreac had won one silver and two bronze medals, and Anca Grigoraş had won bronze, a real achievement given that Romanian gymnasts had not mounted the podium since 1959, when Elena Leuşteanu and Sonia Iovan had won silver and bronze.

According to the rules, each country sent two gymnasts to compete and two to be held in reserve. Romania had originally decided to send two gymnasts and one reserve from the Dinamo Bucharest Club. The Oneşti Club was competing with other sporting associations from Romania, but often Dinamo had an unfair advantage, as it was the club with the strongest political backing in the country. 'Our most ferocious enemy was the Dinamo club, the club of Romania's secret police. (. . .) Dinamo had a gymnastics club that enjoyed incredible facilities and financial support. Until the emergence of my team, the Dinamo club had dominated Romanian gymnastics,' Károlyi wrote in his autobiography, indignant that the Oneşti gymnasts, although regarded as the best, did not receive the go-ahead from the Federation to take part in the European Championships.

After exerting pressure in Bucharest, Károlyi managed to obtain a place in the team of gymnasts that was to represent Romania in Skien, and he organised a competition among his own gymnasts to see who would fill it. The real battle was between Nadia Comăneci and Teodora Ungureanu, although Nadia 'was visibly superior to the other girls on the team,' as Károlyi remembers. The decision to select her was to be decisive in the career of the young gymnast.

The Romanian team that travelled to Norway was made up of trainers Béla Károlyi and Nicolae Covaci and gymnasts Nadia Comăneci and Alina Goreac, who were joined by pianist Carol Stabişevschi,[73] since the floor exercise required live piano accompaniment at the time. The two gymnasts not only represented different clubs, Flame Oneşti and Dinamo Bucharest, but were from different generations. Nadia was thirteen, Alina was twenty-three, having also become national champion at the same age as Nadia.

In Skien, Peter Shilston's prediction of a few weeks earlier was proved wrong. Nadia did not have the patience to wait for the 1980 Moscow Olympics to demonstrate her genius, and she dominated the European Gymnastics Championships, becoming the youngest champion in history in the individual all-round event and the first Romanian gymnast to win the title. She won four gold medals out of a possible five and one silver. Alina Goreac won bronze medals in the vault and beam events.

At the time, given the excellence of Soviet gymnasts, in Romania it was said that in a competition with the Russians you ought to be content even to win second place. Nadia astonished not only the public, but also the opposing teams, who discovered a gymnast who, perfectly and unhesitatingly, could execute exercises of extreme difficulty, as Soviet trainer Vladislav Rastorotsky admitted.[74] She beat the competition favourite, Ludmila Turishcheva, who was the Olympic and World champion and who, in the previous European competition, held in London in 1973, had won all five gold medals. Nadia's medals therefore held the weight of world titles. Turishcheva came fourth in the parallel bars event,[75] and Nadia was later to remember the Soviet gymnast's disappointment:

I will never forget Ludmila's poise in defeat when she walked over to me at the championships and kissed me on the cheek. I still have the photograph of that moment because she was my idol. We couldn't communicate—we didn't speak the same language—but in that instant I knew that she was a true champion and that I wanted to take some of her grace and make it my own. I believe you can take the attributes you admire in others and incorporate them into your own life. You can't copy someone else's gymnastics style and come out on top, but you can make yourself a better person by learning from another's actions.

In retrospect, I realize just how terribly disappointed Ludmila must have been because the European Championships only happen every two years and she had won in 1971 and 1973. If she won in 1975, she would have been given the Challenge Cup for winning three times in a row. Later I would be the first gymnast in the world to accomplish that feat—in 1975, 1977, and 1979—and to receive the Challenge Cup.[76]

The international press warmly congratulated Nadia, proclaiming her a new star of world gymnastics. She had managed to change public perceptions of the sport thanks to the perfection with which she performed her routines. Most enthusiastic of all was Norway's press, with reporters asking readers whether they knew the Romanian anthem by heart now that they had heard it so many times being played at the podium in Skien and adding that they would probably continue to hear it many times more, whenever Nadia competed in a major tournament. The Russians were also courteous, and Nadia won plaudits in the Moscow press. *Sovyetsky Sport* published a piece titled 'The Right to a Smile', which was reprinted in full in Romania. The following is an excerpt:

> We knew that Nadia Comăneci's exercise on the uneven parallel bars ushered in something new in gymnastics. We will not list the elements of her routine, since they will be named after their inventor.[77] One thing may be said, however: Nadia is amazing. Her only visible hesitation was when she touched the bar after her second vault. But the ovations were so loud that they can only be compared with the 'explosion in the Olympic arena in Munich when Olga Korbut displayed her famed parallel bars element.'[78]

The results at Skien turned the spotlight on not only Nadia Comăneci, but also on the Károlyis and the Oneşti Centre, which reporters now called women's gymnastics' 'school of great expectations'. A year later, after her success in Montréal, the press was to praise the centre even more highly, calling it a 'school of champions'. After discovering the young gymnast, the Norwegians wondered whether she was nothing but a wunderkind, but answered their own question when they said, 'behind Nadia there are a dozen gymnastic talents in Romania who have attended the same training programme.'[79] People began to travel to Oneşti, to see for themselves the extraordinary things that were happening in the town. Béla and Marta Károlyi were now praised by the press, the public, and, above all, the authorities. It was they who had borne the real burden, undertaking the difficult task of triumphing in the competitions dominated for so long by the Soviets, and the gymnasts' toil would not have achieved results if the trainers had not tried out a revolutionary new method, as D. Dimitriu himself stated: 'At Skien, it wasn't Nadia's skill that won the day, but rather the revolutionary, intelligent ideas of her trainers, it was the triumph of a systematic method.'[80]

Not long after receiving invitations from the Ministry of Education, the National Council of Physical Education and Sport, the Romanian Gymnastics Federation, the National Council of the Pioneers Organization, and the Bacău Communist Party Central Committee to attend various prize-giving ceremonies, in November that year, a few days before her fourteenth birthday, Nadia Comăneci was awarded the title of World Sportswoman of the Year 1975, after a poll conducted by United Press International. From the excitement, Károlyi was unable to sleep all night:

> When I got the phone call from the radio and they told me that Nadia was the best sportswoman in the world, I asked Dan Voicilă to double-check to make sure they didn't mean best gymnast. It was an important difference. After I received confirmation, I couldn't suppress my excitement. Nadia was less

excited, since she isn't obsessed with rankings and works without being calculated about it.[81]

In 1975, when he saw his pupil on the podium in Skien, Béla Károlyi knew that his next goal would be to scale an even higher podium, in Montréal. In gymnastics nothing happens by chance. Success in Skien depended on success in London, at the Champions Cup, just as a victory at Montréal would naturally follow on from triumph at Skien.

But before they could be sure that they would take part in the 1976 Montréal Summer Olympics, the Károlyis had to go through the usual bickering in order to obtain as many places on the Romanian team as they could, since Dinamo gymnasts were once more given preference. As a result, a final selection was held in Bucharest at the 23 August National Sports Centre, in the form of an unofficial competition between the country's most important clubs. As chance would have it, a Party delegation visited the gym when Károlyi's gymnasts were practising and the Dinamo gymnasts were taking a break at the lido, which prompted indignation and the decision to appoint Béla Károlyi the head coach of the Olympic team, with complete discretion as to whom he would select for Montréal.[82]

The man behind the decision was Ilie Verdeţ, the head of the delegation that inspected the 23 August Gymnasium. At the time Verdeţ was a member of the Secretariat of the Central Committee of the Romanian Communist Party and chairman of the Council of Socio-Economic Organisation. He was one of the régime's most important leaders thanks to his close relationship with Nicolae Ceauşescu, and from 1967 to 1974 he had been first deputy chairman of the Council of Ministers. Before long he would hold the same position once more, and in 1979 Ceauşescu appointed him prime minister. A former miner, Verdeţ was familiar with the Jiu Valley, where Károlyi had also worked, and in the 1950s he had risen to become boss of the Hunedoara Communist Party. Verdeţ was delighted to see a young physical education teacher who had once worked in the mining community and was now an important national coach.

In his memoirs, Károlyi described this episode, so embarrassing to the Dinamo gymnasts and so favourable to him, claiming that Verdeţ took a liking to him from the very first and continued to support him in the years to come. Géza Pozsar, the choreographer of the Oneşti team, also described the same episode, but with a rather different take on the relationship between Verdeţ and Károlyi. According to Pozsar, the encounter gave rise to a genuine friendship, one extremely advantageous to the trainer, since he was able skilfully to exploit it over the years: 'One day, Ilie Verdeţ, the secretary of the C.C. of the R.C.P. visited us at the 23 August centre. Béla was able to make a good impression on Verdeţ and strike up a long-term friendship with him, as well as the head of his cabinet,

Hanea. He fostered the relationship by means of bottles of whiskey and cartons of cigarettes that he brought back from abroad, after competitions.'[83]

As a result, Béla Károlyi was the trainer who picked the squad for the Montréal Olympics, in which gymnasts from Oneşti were the most numerous: Nadia Comăneci, Teodora Ungureanu, Georgeta Gabor, and, as the reserve, Luminiţa Milea. They were joined by Mariana Constantin (Petrolul Ploieşti), Gabriela Truşcă (Sport Club Bacău), and Anca Grigoraş (a pupil from Oneşti, but who had recently transferred to Dinamo Bucharest), while Marilena Neacşu, the first reserve, represented the Sibiu Sports School. Grigoraş, aged eighteen, was the only 'veteran' of the squad, having previously competed at the Munich Olympics.

The selection of Károlyi caused discontent among other coaches, and a representative of the Romanian Olympic Committee even went so far as to criticise him in a report that he later submitted to the Securitate, in which he claimed, 'through decisions more to do with personal rather than national interests, Béla Károlyi has influenced the R.G.F. not to include gymnast Goreac Alina in the team for Montréal, thereby diminishing the team's potential.'[84] Károlyi had indeed been categorically opposed to selecting Alina Goreac, citing her age, which was not far short of twenty-four. But apart from the issue of her age, what mattered more to Károlyi was the fact that Alina was no longer an obedient child, submissive to her trainer, unlike the other girls in the team.

But thanks to his friendly relationship with Ilie Verdeţ, the influential protector who gave him a free hand and guaranteed that he could count on him to back his decisions as long as they won Romania medals, Károlyi easily rode out the storm of such opposition. Although it was obviously subjective to a certain extent, particularly since he had been given an unexpected opportunity to settle old scores with Dinamo, the Olympic squad the Károlyi put together in the summer of 1976 was genuinely remarkable, and Romania had never seen the like before.

By now, Nadia Comăneci's achievements were likewise remarkable: she had won numerous national titles, a European Championship title, and the award for best sportswoman in the world. Moreover, in the summer of 1975, both Nadia and Teodora had been invited to take part in the pre-Olympics competition in Montréal. Before they left, Béla Károlyi had wondered whether it would be a good idea or not, but finally he accepted that the gymnasts had to get used to the special conditions of such a competition: a long and tiring journey, jet lag, acclimatisation. It would therefore allow him to observe how they adapted and performed. The results were more than satisfactory: Nadia Comăneci came out ahead of Nellie Kim yet again, winning gold in the individual all-round and parallel bars events, silver in the vault and floor events, and bronze in the beam event. Teodora Ungureanu won a silver medal in the beam and bronze in the individual all-round and floor events, while Nellie Kim won gold in the vault, beam and floor events.

Unlike gymnasts from other clubs in Romania, the Oneşti girls had a very busy, almost overwhelming competition schedule. For example, 1976 began with a long tour of Canada and the United States, after which the team returned to Europe to compete against the West German team at Rüsselheim (6–7 March), where Nadia was awarded quadruple scores of 10. In March, there was also a competition between Romania and Holland, held in Bucharest. Once again, Nadia Comăneci was unbeatable, obtaining a 10 five times. Then came the first America Cup, held in Madison Square Garden, New York (27–28 March), where Romania was represented by Nadia Comăneci in the women's and Dan Grecu in the men's events. In New York, Nadia won the floor competition, receiving a 10, while Dan Grecu won the silver medal, with American gymnast Bart Conner, who decades later would become Nadia's husband, winning gold.

Regardless of the competition they were taking part in, be it in Romania or internationally, all the gymnasts in the team were counting down the days until Montréal, since the Olympics are the supreme test, bringing together the world's best in every sport, and it is Olympic success that defines a career.

At Montréal, the Soviet Union was the favourite in every event, not just women's gymnastics. The world's first communist society, engaged in the dramatic social experiment known as the dictatorship of the proletariat, used sport as a means of displaying its pride and the superior strength of the New Man. Soviet sport and its training methods were unbeatable, as proven by the fact that the country had won more Olympic medals than any other, although the reality that lay behind this success was little known.

Romania had not won an Olympic medal until the fifth games in which the country took part, at Helsinki in 1952, thanks to Iosif Sîrbu,[85] who won gold in the shooting event. After 1956, victories multiplied, and by 1972, the country had won another seventeen gold medals in boxing, shooting, athletics, rowing, Greco-Roman wrestling, and fencing. Athlete Iolanda Balaş and canoeist Ivan Patzaichin were true miracles, dominating their sports for many years.

But Romanian women's gymnastics had yet to make a large international impact. Romania had previously won just three medals in gymnastics, all of them bronze, at the 1956 Melbourne Olympics and the 1960 Rome Olympics, each thanks to Elena Leuşteanu.[86] The Olympic podium at the time was dominated by the U.S.S.R., whose team never failed to win gold, while individual gymnasts only ever felt threatened by Věra Čáslavská, the graceful gymnast from Czechoslovakia, at the 1964 and 1968 games, and by the experienced Karin Janz from East Germany, in 1972.

Not enjoying such a reputation, the Romanian team did not feature in any Olympic medal predictions at the time. It was thought that the ranking established by previous Olympics and by the 1974 World Championships in Varna – at which Dan Grecu won Romania's first gold medal at such an event, becoming world champion on the parallel bars – would be maintained at Montréal: the U.S.S.R.,

East Germany, Hungary. True, Romania had risen through the rankings in recent years, but it had yet to mount the Olympic podium. As far as the all-round individual event was concerned, Nadia Comăneci, as newly crowned European champion, was among the favourites, but Europe lay far outside the purview of the Canadian and U.S. public, which was unfamiliar with Romanian gymnasts and for which the Soviet team, whose members included Olga Korbut, Ludmila Turishcheva and Nellie Kim, outshone every other country. 'Nobody in the West knew us in 1976. We went to the Olympic Games in Montreal as a little-known team from a small and relatively unknown country. The Soviets were the reigning gymnastic champions – Ludmila Turischeva, and her teammate, Olga Korbut (already twenty-one years old), were the big names,'[87] Béla Károlyi later recalled. And it was for this reason that in July 1976, when Romania's gymnasts stepped out into the historical Montreal Forum arena, they did not feel the weight of a glorious Olympic past. Instead, they had many expectations to meet.

The confrontation was to be as momentous as it was arduous, especially since it had commenced even before the games began. The Soviet gymnasts were not only formidable, but also very famous, which gave them a psychological advantage. In the Canadian press, at first, the battle was as good as won by the Soviets, with Turishcheva, Korbut and Kim appearing in numerous interviews and television reports. On television, they appeared not only as gymnasts, but as stars, shown relaxing over tea with friends back home or walking in the forest outside Moscow, in the case of a feature on Nellie Kim. *Montréal Matin* published just a few lines about the Romanian squad, and was the only newspaper to publish a photograph, showing Nadia Comăneci.[88]

Not that Károlyi made any great efforts to court the press. The team, made up of three trainers, eight gymnasts, a pianist, and a physician, arrived in Canada on 6 July, but Károlyi opted to keep the squad hidden until the next day, moving them from the Olympic Village to a Holiday Inn about twenty kilometres outside Montréal. This move was agreed upon even before they left Romania, the reasoning being that the gymnasts needed peace and quiet the better to prepare. This was only half true, in fact, since Károlyi didn't like the arrangements at the Olympic Village, where the girls were put in 'pyramid A', while the men were assigned to 'pyramid B', as the ziggurats housing the delegations were named, which meant he was unable personally to supervise their schedule of rest and their diet. 'Since there had been a deadly terrorist attack at Munich in 1972, security was draconian,' remembers gymnast Georgeta Gabor. 'The women were housed separately from the men in the Olympic Village, and only the women were allowed to make visits. For us that wasn't a bad thing, since that way we had more time to rest and relax. We had a shared flat next to the head of the delegation, the great Mrs Lia Manoliu. Thanks to this, we had more facilities available to us than the other athletes. Likewise, since we had restrictions on certain kinds of food, because of our weight, after each training session we had the nice surprise of finding various goodies in the fridge, as a form of tacit solidarity among us gymnasts, which we ate immediately, lest we get caught.'[89]

Three of the gymnasts sustained minor injuries. Nadia Comăneci and Mariana Constantin suffered twisted ankles, and Anca Grigoraş complained of back pains. Károlyi, although worried about his gymnasts' health, recorded in his notebook positive progress in training: '11-12 July. The last two days at the Holiday Inn. It's a big success that we've avoided the atmosphere of the village or, more properly, the Olympic skyscrapers. We're putting the finishing touches. Mariana still has pains, but she's working shoulder to shoulder with the others.'[90] He also sent telegrams to Oneşti, one of them to choreographer Géza Pozsar, which was intercepted by the Securitate. The telegram reveals that he was worried about Nadia's injury, even if he didn't refer to it explicitly, and that he could barely wait for the games: 'Good day from Montreal, to you at least, since for us the days are anything but good. Things not going great and time standing still, seems like an eternity till the Great Dance begins.'[91]

Their return to the Olympic Village went almost unnoticed. On parting with the girls at the lifts, Béla asked Marta to make an inventory of the fridges in the room and closely to supervise their schedule. The days that followed, they continued training at a brisk pace, this time in the Forum, and waited for the competition to begin, the pressure and excitement increasing all the while. They didn't attend the opening ceremony on 17 July, since Károlyi deemed the four- or five-hour event would tire his gymnasts needlessly.

The 'Great Dance' began the next day, a Sunday. When he entered the arena, Béla Károlyi took a place in the stands, while Marta joined the gymnasts. According to the rules, male coaches weren't allowed to stay with the girls next to the apparatuses. 'I've got the best possible spot. I'll be right behind the goal posts—the Forum is also a hockey rink—thanks to the kindness of a former colleague of our pianist, who managed to wangle me a special invitation,'[92] Károlyi wrote in his notebook, grateful that although he didn't have the right to intervene, at least he was just half a metre away from his team.

The same as at any Olympic Games, the arena was packed to the seams with a noisy crowd impatient to watch the events. To thunderous cheers, the gymnasts assembled in their places, feigning indifference to their competitors. Nadia looked absent, casting occasional glances at the stands. Perhaps Nicolae Vieru had told the girls what he would later write in his memoirs: 'At Tokyo, I learned a lesson about taking part in major competitions in future, namely that the gymnasts and their trainers should focus solely on themselves, without looking at what the other teams and gymnasts are doing. Both our gymnasts and trainer Costache Gheorghiu watched with open mouths as the Japanese and the Russian gymnasts gave spectacular performances, the likes of which we'd never seen before, and influenced by what they'd seen in the competition, they dropped like flies from the apparatuses.'[93]

The all-round team events came first, then the all-round individual events and finally the individual apparatuses. In the all-round team event, the gymnasts competed by rotation on each of the apparatuses. All six gymnasts in a country's team competed, but only the top five marks counted. Of the twelve countries competing, Romania was in Group Four, the toughest, alongside the U.S.S.R., East Germany and Hungary. By the luck of the draw, the Soviet gymnasts started on the parallel bars, the East Germans on the vault, the Hungarians on the floor, and the Romanians on the beam. Georgeta Gabor was Romania's opening gymnast for all the events except the floor exercise, fully aware of the psychological pressure of the moment.

Watching the events, the crowd quickly realised that the real contest was between the U.S.S.R. and Romania, and the two nations' gymnasts were also the favourites of the television cameras. After the first exercises and the awarding of the scores, the commentators were critical, claiming that the marking was more generous than at previous competitions, even when the gymnasts had made obvious mistakes. As the teams switched apparatuses, the tension grew, even if the Soviet gymnasts had managed to pull ahead, winning by hundredth after hundredth. None of the Soviet gymnasts scored less than 9.65, and Olga Korbut won a 9.90 on the parallel bars, the first record of the competition, thanks to the move she had introduced at Munich in 1972, while Ludmila Turishcheva seemed to be dominating the floor exercise with her 9.90.

Károlyi's gymnasts scored between 9.30 and 9.90 and he was feverishly making calculations in his mind as he sat watching from the crowd. But it was obvious that Romania's team had no way of closing the gap with the Soviets. Károlyi didn't even stand up to cheer his pupils, except when Nadia and Teodora finished their exercises on a convincing note.

At the end of the all-round team events, Romania's gymnasts performed their routines on the parallel bars. When Nadia's turn came, silence descended on the whole arena. The exercises on the other apparatuses were almost finished, which meant that the whole crowd naturally turned its attention to her. Waiting for the signal to begin, again and again Nadia plunged her hands in the magnesium dust that helps gymnasts get a better grip. The uneven parallel bars, an apparatus that was introduced to the competition at the Helsinki Olympics, replacing the steady rings, were painful for the gymnasts, breaking the skin of their palms due to endless practice of the same element. It is both the most technical and the most unnatural apparatus, lying as it does outside normal human patterns of movement.

Former U.S. gymnast Cathy Rigby, commentating on the competition for ABC Sports, told viewers that it might be 'the highlight of the compulsory event' as Nadia attacked the parallel bars with a serious, almost frowning face, unaware that the whole crowd were on the edge of their seats, focused on her alone. Even the camera flashbulbs died down and the perfect silence was broken only when the crowd gasped in unison at particularly tricky moments in the exercise.

Nadia leapt straight to a support position on the high bar and cast away from it to perform a straddled front somersault while re-grasping the same bar. Her routine was marked by moments of exquisite balance as she performed handstands and her well-known full twisting somersaults between bars. Finally, using the spring of the lower bar for lift, she span through the air before sticking a perfect landing. The whole routine had lasted a mere twenty seconds.

The audience erupted into cheers, realising they had just witnessed an exceptional performance. As the bell that announced the score on the board was late in ringing, the murmurs of the crowd rose in volume to an uproar. The crowd was impatient, and the spectators variously chanted, booed, or cheered when, at last, the board showed a score of 1.00, which caused a moment's confusion. Could she really have been awarded such a drastically low mark? Nadia's gaze searched the crowd for Károlyi, but he was nowhere to be seen. He had stood up and taken a few steps in the direction of one of the referees, who held up all ten fingers in satisfaction. Nadia had in fact been awarded a 10. There was a decimal point after the 1 because the electronic scoreboard was programmed in such a way that it couldn't show a score higher than 9.99.

In the entire history of the Olympic Games nobody before Nadia had been awarded a score that denoted perfection. No sooner did Nadia rejoice at the referees' decision than marching music blared from the loudspeakers. The words 'a perfect ten' were already on everybody's lips and would make their way around the world. A gymnast from a small, distant country that the vast majority of spectators in the Montréal Forum had never even heard of had changed the history of the competition.

The Romanian journalists in the press centre, easily recognisable by the large badges they had to wear on their chests, were besieged by their counterparts from all over the world, who asked question after question about Nadia Comăneci. Who was she? Where had she come from? Every television station in Canada showed footage of her exercises on an unending loop, and in the press, not only the sports newspapers but also the major dailies featured her photograph on their front pages. The headlines all said the same thing: Nadia was incredible, brilliant, perfect. Almost perfect, said the more critically minded, no, *too* perfect, said those exhilarated by her performance. She was poetry in motion, sublime. Henceforward, gymnastics could be spoken on only in terms of before and after Nadia Comăneci, said journalists who had witnessed the event. Unexpectedly, the frail and enigmatic Nadia Comăneci had revolutionised the sport and become a legend. Words, no matter how suggestive, didn't seem to be enough, as writer Radu Cosaşu said in the copy he rushed off for his column in a sports gazette: 'Nadia Comăneci leaves behind the earth, grammar, the comparative form of adjectives, and all the more so the mechanics and mechanism of what we call celestial bodies, as well as bodies of judges.'[94] The fourteen-year-old Nadia was no longer a little girl, but had suddenly been transformed into a being endowed with preternatural skills. She was now the 'goddess of Montréal'.

And goddess she was to remain over the course of the remaining four days, as she worked one miracle after another. On Monday, Tuesday, Wednesday and Thursday, the gymnasts from Romania and the U.S.S.R. did battle with each other in the arena as if there weren't any other competitors. Teodora Ungureanu managed to thrill the crowd with an impeccable floor exercise, to the tune of 'Sleigh Bells', giving the general impression that her score of 9.75 was unjust. But Nadia was unstoppable. From one apparatus to the next, she soared, she floated, she enraptured the crowd. On 22 July she won the two finals, scoring perfect tens on the beam, that merciless apparatus on which penalty points are inevitable, and on the uneven parallel bars, which she seemed to master flawlessly. Over the course of the competition, her performances received seven perfect tens, demonstrating that the first was no fluke. Her worth and her excellence had been confirmed beyond all doubt.

At the end of the Olympic Games, the Soviets did not leave Montréal with their tails between their legs, far from it. The team as a whole returned with no fewer than one hundred and twenty-five medals, of which forty-nine were gold, which in itself spoke of Soviet sporting supremacy. In women's gymnastics, the Soviet team won the all-round event, while Romania took the silver medal. Like Nadia, Nellie Kim also obtained two tens and won gold in the vault and floor events. Romania's gold medals in the women's gymnastics events were all won by Nadia, after she came first in the all-round individual, beam and parallel bars events. The team as a whole won two silver medals and Teodora Ungureanu also took silver in the parallel bars event. Nadia also won a bronze medal in the floor exercise and Teodora in the beam event.

More than two decades later, in 2001, Nellie Kim was to recall the Montréal Games and her clash with Nadia Comăneci in an interview with Jean-Christophe Klotz, the presenter of *Les Grands Duels du Sport* on the Franco-German Arte channel. Even after so many years the disappointment Kim had felt at the time obviously still rankled when she said that while Nadia was a great gymnast and almost perfect, she was by no means superior to anybody in the Soviet team. 'I can't say that she was better than we were. Her routines were as difficult as those of Turishcheva, Korbut and myself. On a few apparatuses she was better than Turishcheva and Korbut, but on others, not quite. But the press turned her into the "goddess of gymnastics",'[95] she said, suggesting that it was not so much Nadia's performance that had counted, but the influence of Western journalists, who deliberately exaggerated her prowess.

Kim's opinion is only partly justified. Given that the Cold War was still at its height, Western journalists must have felt a bias towards anybody able to rock the myth of Soviet sporting invincibility. This had been the case of Olympic, World and European champion Věra Čáslavská, who at the 1968 Mexico City Olympics was done an injustice by the judges: the Czechoslovak gymnast had been forced to share the top of the podium with Larisa Petrik of the U.S.S.R. and had bowed her head and turned it to the right when the Soviet national anthem was played. Čáslavská was protesting not at the unfairness of the scoring to which she had fallen victim during the competition, but at the fact that her country had fallen victim to an invasion by the Soviet army just weeks before.

And the Western journalists loved her for it. But four years later, they also fell in love with little Soviet gymnast Olga Korbut at the Munich Olympics, recognising even then the decisive rôle she was to play in gymnastics. They dubbed her 'the darling of Munich', so captivating was her performance, which gives us to believe that regardless of political circumstances or personal sympathies, the international press was still able to preserve its objectivity in the face of obvious talent.

By the time of the 1976 Montréal Olympics, Romania had indeed gained its own separate image internationally, as Czechoslovakia had in 1968. The country was part of the Communist bloc, but a number of past political gestures on the part of Nicolae Ceauşescu had created the impression that Romania distanced itself from and sometimes even defied Moscow, an impression that was also bolstered by Bucharest's closer and closer ties with Washington and other Western capitals. Which is why the sympathy towards Nadia Comăneci on the part of both press and public could be viewed as all the more genuine.

But political circumstances could have no influence on how Nadia's performance was judged, where technique and artistic elements that were all that counted, and journalists could not award points in place of the judges. It was the fullness of Nadia's performance that was her secret, and it distinguished her from the Soviets, as Cathy Rigby remarked in her commentary for ABC: 'Oh look at that amplitude!' Nadia controlled her body in a way that stood out, without any tremor to betray hesitation, and with the ambition to control her balance to the utmost degree. She was fast, but at the same time elegant and certain, which made some of her movements seem unreal. The elements in the routines that won her scores of ten were achieved with flawless poise, seamlessly combined, in a style that Nadia was to make uniquely her own.

The International Gymnastics Federation's scoring code for the uneven parallel bars now includes the Comăneci Salto and Comăneci Dismount, named after the moves Nadia pioneered at Montréal. In the first, 'the gymnast begins in a support position on the high bar. She casts away from the bar and performs a straddled front somersault and regrasps the same bar'[96] – an element deemed to be of an extremely high level of difficulty. In the second, the 'gymnast begins in a handstand on the high bar and then pikes her feet onto the bar and does a sole circle swing around the bar. She then releases the bar first with her feet and then with her hands as she performs a half-twist immediately into a back somersault dismount.'[97] Such moves are only a few of those that were to inspire future generations of gymnasts, leading them to tackle elements of increasing complexity and even risk. In Munich in 1972, Olga Korbut had done the same thing. Likewise, Japanese gymnast Mitsuo Tsukahara revolutionised gymnastics with the spectacular vault that now bears his name. To this day, each generation of gymnasts takes inspiration from the daring of their predecessors.

The impact around the world of Nadia Comăneci's achievements at Montréal was remarkable. The popularity of the sport suddenly increased, and Nadia became an inspiration not only for younger gymnasts and even those of her generation, but also for countless little girls who dreamed of becoming like her. Some of those little girls went on to become champions, such as Mary Lou Retton, who watched Nadia at Montréal on television and was electrified by her refinement and natural grace. Others, even if they did not make a sporting career for themselves, remembered the event vividly and in years to come told of how it inspired them and nurtured their dreams to achieve something extraordinary. One example is Michelle Obama, who was twelve years old in 1976: 'I still remember Nadia Comăneci with that perfect 10, she dismounted from the beam, and I knew I could do that too. But I was never able to. My legs are too long for that.'[98]

It was also thanks to Nadia – and her trainers – that the Romanian gymnastics school gained worldwide renown and appreciation. After the Montréal Olympics, the Oneşti gymnasts received countless invitations to take part in show tournaments, which earned the Communist state serious amounts of hard currency, and many gymnasts and trainers from abroad showed an interest in visiting the Oneşti centre. There was a general recognition of the merits of the recently founded school.

There were many memorable moments at the Montréal Olympics, which awoke enthusiasm all over the world. The sacrifice that Shun Fujimoto made for his team was one of them: the Japanese gymnast made the decision to carry on competing after he dislocated his kneecap during the floor exercise, which led to the Japanese team beating the Soviet Union to the gold medal. There were also the superhuman efforts of the United States men's swimming team, which succeeded in beating East Germany. The East Germans had dominated the sport for years, but the real reason for this achievement was only discovered after the women's team was embroiled in a major doping scandal. But even if such thrilling moments will never be forgotten, the Montréal Games have gone down in history as 'Nadia's Olympics'. This is not so much because of the number of medals she won, and people today usually can't remember the exact number, but because of the impact her performance had on the history of gymnastics and of sport in general. At the same time, Romania earned an unexpected place in the upper echelons of world sport, and the country was henceforth to be identified as a women's gymnastics superpower.

The Soviet Union could boast Yuri Gagarin, the first man in space, the United States had Neil Armstrong, the first man on the Moon, and now Romania had

Nadia, the little heroine of the entire nation, but also beloved throughout the world. Being so young at the time, she had no way of knowing how deep an impact it would have on her in the long term. She had no way of knowing how much she had captivated the world; how famous she had become overnight. 'There were no appearances on David Letterman or Oprah Winfrey. I didn't do a photo shoot for the cover of a magazine. Sports agents at IMG and CAA never beat down my door; they didn't even knock. I came, performed, made my country proud, and left the arena via a bus, not a limousine,'[99] Nadia was to recall, but there can be no doubt that all those things would have been possible, given that every major press agency in the world was in pursuit of her, if the heads of the Romanian delegation and the Károlyis had not isolated her throughout the Montréal Games, except for a single appearance at a press conference.

But Nadia was impatiently awaited back home, as the whole country wished to celebrate her success at Montréal. On the afternoon of 27 July 1976, when the gymnastics squad landed at Otopeni Airport, thousands of Romanians were there to greet her. In a country where crowds were allowed to gather only at political rallies organised by the régime, such a welcome was not in the nature of things. But the régime did not try to prevent the crowd from welcoming her, instead encouraging it. Nicolae Ceauşescu was delighted at the countless messages of congratulations he received after the victories of Nadia Comăneci and the Romanian team. At the time, he did not feel threatened by the popularity of a gymnast of just fourteen, especially since he himself was able to gather laurels both politically and personally.

'I stepped out the door and down the stairs, and the thousands of Romanians who had come to meet our plane overwhelmed me.'[100] recounts Nadia, remembering the excitement of those moments. Wearing her five gold medals around her neck, carrying a travel bag on each shoulder, and holding a bouquet of flowers, she descended the steps from the plane and shyly led her teammates through the crowd there to greet them. Here and there, people were holding placards handed out by the authorities so that they would be visible on the television news. The love and the enthusiasm of the crowd were not staged, but the régime required the scene to have a propaganda touch, so there were placards that read, 'Bravo, Nadia! Ever onwards!' adapting the slogan of the Pioneers, while others were more explicit still: 'We thank the Party with all our heart for the wonderful conditions it has created for the sporting movement in our country!'

Although it looked as if people were able to crowd around the Olympic team freely, the Securitate was on full alert and had carefully filtered everybody who entered the airport. Department One assigned Lieutenant Colonel Emil Preoteasa to carry out the mission of protecting the members of the gymnastics squad and to prevent any possible 'hostile actions that might be initiated and committed by certain ill-intentioned elements.'[101] At the airport, Nadia was also greeted by a number of officials, including Miron Olteanu, the secretary of the National Council for Physical Education and Sport, and representatives of the Ministry of Education. And at the insistence of the Romanian and foreign press, the gymnasts also took part in a press conference, at which the usual references to the care bestowed on them by Nicolae and Elena Ceauşescu were by no means lacking: 'The congratulations and paternal words that Nicolae Ceauşescu, the Secretary General of our Party, and Comrade Elena Ceauşescu addressed to us encouraged us and inspired us to compete the better in order to secure new successes.'[102] After a night at the 23 August Centre, they set off for Oneşti, and were greeted by fresh crowds of people in the towns through which they passed. Once they were home, there were further celebrations, culminating in a spectacular event held in the town's sports stadium.

The Communist society into which Nadia was born and in which she lived cultivated shows of admiration and enthusiasm for outstanding achievements only to a well-balanced degree and in a specific political context. The achievements of Nadia, her trainers, her choreographer, and the entire Olympic team belonged to them, but not in their entirety: It was deemed that it was the Communist state that had created the conditions and the means whereby they were able to stand out, and their merits therefore ultimately had to be shared with the country's leader, Nicolae Ceauşescu.

As proof that Nadia's success was a natural consequence of Ceauşescu's vision for the development of sport, an event to legitimise the Communist régime was organised. The event was in perfect alignment with existing events to show off the new direction in foreign policy, whereby Romania's leader seemed to put an increasing distance between himself and the Soviet Union. Over the next few years, propaganda efforts were to be directed at constructing an elaborate mechanism to exploit Romanian's feelings of national pride, a determining factor in asserting the nationalist character of the régime, but without neglecting to play up a positive image of the country internationally.[103]

Plans for the first stage were laid at the highest level of the Party on 18 August 1978, when, at a meeting of the Executive Political Committee, it was decided to reward the Olympic medal winners. Nadia Comăneci received the highest honour, when by presidential decree she was declared a Heroine of Socialist Labour and awarded the Hammer and Sickle Gold Medal. Nobody so young had ever received such official recognition before. It was said that Nicolae Ceauşescu was determined to show his magnanimity and generosity, but in actual fact he was trying to turn the nation's heroine into a heroine of the Communist régime:

Comrade Gheorghe Rădulescu:[104] If you are in agreement, I propose that an illustrated postcard[105] be sold abroad in a few million copies. To this end, let us assign the task to the relevant foreign commerce enterprise and in this way, we will earn a handsome sum.

Comrade Nicolae Ceauşescu: We proposed that we issue a postage stamp.

Comrade Ilie Verdeţ:[106] An illustrated postcard of Nadia was issued, but it wasn't a success and it was withdrawn.

Comrade Nicolae Ceauşescu: Then let's see, let's make a nice one and you'll present it to me.

Comrade Leonte Răutu:[107] We had a very nice success at this year's Olympic Games, and Nadia Comăneci was the main heroine. It doesn't seem appropriate to me to confer the title of Hero of Socialist Labour on child of fourteen. We can give her an important medal, but not the title of Hero.

Comrade János Fazekas:[108] I'm in agreement with giving her the title of Hero of Socialist Labour, but what I propose is that all four who won gold medals be given the title of Hero of Socialist Labour.

Comrade Elena Ceauşescu: There aren't four, but two.

Comrade Ilie Verdeţ: We have four gold medals, but Nadia won three.

Comrade János Fazekas: I read in the Hungarian and Bulgarian press that they gave the title of Hero of Socialist Labour to their gold medallists, but they also gave it to the trainers who were responsible for them getting those medals.

Comrade Ilie Verdeţ: We gave Dîba[109] the Order of Labour, First Class.

Comrade Nicolae Ceauşescu: Nadia made an excellent showing of herself, and Dîba isn't at her level.

Comrade Elena Ceauşescu: We need to emphasise that.

Comrade Gheorghe Rădulescu. It was an outstanding performance.

Comrade Nicolae Ceauşescu: It's not a question of age here, but of what she achieved.

Comrade Leonte Răutu: It's a question of the nature of the title.

Comrade Nicolae Ceauşescu: It's why we introduced the title of Hero of Socialist Labour, to give it to people who make an outstanding effort in their field.

Comrade Ilie Verdeţ: If we've given it to peasants, to activists, we can also bestow it in the field of sport. Nobody else has won six medals at the Olympics.

Comrade Iosif Banc:[110] It's an achievement.

Comrade Nicolae Ceauşescu: The gymnastics our girls did turned it into an art form.

Comrade Leonte Răutu: I was referring to the nature of the title.

Comrade Elena Ceauşescu: It's awarded for labour.

Comrade Ion Ioniţă:[111] I agree with the report, with those who won medals, with Dîba, but there's one thing I don't understand, on page seven of the table, the sportsmen who came fourth and fifth were given medals, and those in athletics, who also came fourth and fifth, were given orders.

Comrade Ilie Verdeţ: It refers to Floroiu, in athletics, who came fifth and was given the Order of Sporting Merit, Third Class, and to those who came fourth, they put in the best showing of their entire careers, from fifteenth place they went to fourth. They would have come third, but there was bias against them in the deciding match. Whereas the girls, in the handball, didn't go all the way. That's the reasoning.

Comrade Richard Winter:[112] Nadia Comăneci's results were a result of her training by the main trainer. It wouldn't be lacking in importance, given that he shaped these achievements, besides the fact that he's been proposed for the Order of Labour, First Class, for him to receive a monetary stimulus too. What I think is that they always have equal rights to fifty per cent of the achievement. Let's give them not a Skoda or a Trabant, but a Dacia 1300 each.

Comrade Jánoş Fazekas: It wouldn't go amiss for the trainers to be given the title Hero of Socialist Labour.

Comrade Petre Lupu:[113] I don't know how they thought it through, but Argentina Menis is being given the Medal of Sporting Merit, First Class.

Comrade Ilie Verdeş: The medal isn't awarded for sporting achievement. There were norms that were abided by here. She made a contribution to the sport internationally and she's being given a medal.

Comrade Nicolae Ceauşescu: Let's give Béla thirty thousand lei and his wife twenty thousand.

Comrade Elena Ceauşescu. Make it fifty thousand, so it's half what Nadia gets.

Comrade Nicolae Ceauşescu: Let's also give Béla's wife a Skoda. He'll get a Dacia 1300 and she'll get a Skoda. We'll also think about something for Maria Simionescu.

Comrade Ilie Verdeţ: She works for the gymnastics federation.

Comrade Elena Ceauşescu: She's in charge of all the sports schools and she too has her merits.

Comrade Nicolae Ceauşescu: Let's give her a Skoda as well, then. Agreed? And in four years, if we have people like them again, we'll give them all cars.

Comrade Elena Ceauşescu: Although they should also be criticised as regards discipline. The handball team could have done much more, but we'll let them off for now. Apart from Nadia, the rest demonstrated quite a bit of indiscipline.

Comrade M. Dragnea: Comrade secretary general, we are aware of the fact that better results could have been obtained. This has given us a lot to think about. We promise you that we will do everything so that the glory of our sport will reach the highest pinnacles.

Comrade Nicolae Ceauşescu: All right, agreed.[114]

It was Nicolae Ceauşescu himself who awarded the medals at a ceremony held at the Palace of Sports and Culture in Bucharest on 19 August, an event that received extensive press coverage: 'It was an unforgettable evening, an evening when Romanian sport was given the priceless encouragement of the secretary general of the Party, Comrade Nicolae Ceauşescu, whose speech enthused all those who had won or lost in the struggle in Montréal.'[115] The newspapers and radio and television bulletins described the event in detail, placing at the centre of attention Nicolae and Elena Ceauşescu, on the one hand, and Nadia Comăneci and Teodora Ungureanu, on the other.

The 'vibrant enthusiasm' with which the sportspeople's faces manifested their gratitude to the Communist Party and its secretary general was also on show over the days that followed, as 23 August, the national day of the Socialist Republic of Romania, approached. Nadia's name and image featured on Party propaganda posters as a 'symbol of the enthusiasm and optimism of our homeland's youth'. Nadia also took part in the official parade held in Oneşti, marching at the head of the column of pioneers in the vanguard.

With 23 August 1944 – the day when Romania was 'liberated' by the Red Army – as the starting date, statistics were presented showing once and for all, lest anybody still doubt it, that in the last thirty-two years Romanian sportspeople had won ninety-eight Olympic medals, compared with just two before the country's 'liberation' by the Red Army. And in the last ten years, since Nicolae Ceauşescu took the helm as the country's leader, the biggest leap in the history of Romanian sport had occurred, with fifteen medals and 100.5 points at the Mexico Olympics of 1968 and twenty-seven medals and 179.5 points at the Montréal Olympics of 1976.

The sporting movement had seen a surge, Party activists claimed, since the decision taken by the Central Committee in February–March 1973 to develop physical education and sport, a measure that was cited as irrefutable proof of the genius shown by the leader of the Communist Party. Ceauşescu also made use of the occasion to deliver some of his famous 'precious indications', or rather empty words – 'we will have to apply ourselves, to make patient analyses, to learn lessons and to move towards a better organisation of our activity in every sector' – after which he urged sportspeople to begin thorough training for the next Olympic Games, to be held in Moscow.

The upshot was that while Nadia represented perfection, it was Nicolae Ceauşescu who was the genius.

3
REFLECTED IN THE MIRROR OF POWER: FROM BÉLA, GÉZA AND NADIA TO 'KATONA', 'NELU' AND 'CORINA'

The honours bestowed on the sportspeople, trainers and other members of the Olympic team[1] were of differing degrees, depending on the title and class, but they were more than just symbols of the régime's gratitude. They also came with material privileges extremely advantageous for the time: cash prizes, the opportunity to obtain a bigger flat, tax exemptions. Nadia Comăneci was the only one to receive the title of Hero of Socialist Labour, which came with a gold medal and was loftier than any other national honour or medal. Her achievement had to be set above the rest, as Elena Ceaușescu herself had suggested at the meeting of the Executive Political Committee, when she contradicted those who deemed it 'not appropriate' to give the nation's highest honour to a child of fourteen.

Teodora Ungureanu and Béla Károlyi received the Order of Labour, First Class, and Marta Károlyi was awarded the lesser medal of Sporting Merit, First Class, as was Maria Simionescu, while Nicolae Vieru had to make do with a medal of Sporting Merit, Second Class. The cash prizes and cars were given only to those deemed to have achieved exceptional results, but their value was not made public. For this reason, there were rumours that exaggerated the sums. 'I heard that Nadia got a Dacia 1300 car and around 300,000 lei, plus 80,000 dollars,'[2] a teacher from Onești told a Securitate officer in September 1976, which shows how easily facts could be distorted in a closed society. Nadia and her family had received just 100,000 lei and a car, in fact.[3]

On the other hand, some of those who were honoured, who knew the amount of the sums and the value of the gifts provided by the state, showed dissatisfaction at having been relegated to a lower category, since they believed their achievements ought to have been rewarded more highly. The most indignant of all was Béla Károlyi. Even years later, he still harped on the perceived slight, while distorting the facts, in his characteristic style, as a way of concealing his resentment:

> I received the highest award that anyone involved with sports or the arts could receive[4] — the First Grade Order of Labour. Marta also received an Order of Labour, as did Nicolae Vieru, the director of the Gymnastics Federation, and Géza Pozsár, our choreographer. However, Nicolae's award was a lesser grade than Marta's (. . .) Marta and I were happy with our Orders, but I knew that trouble was brewing. I have always been a bit frightened of going too high. I have a fear of losing step with reality. I knew that the Gymnastic Federation was frustrated by our growing importance, and that Nicolae Vieru, a powerful man in Romanian sports, had been deeply angered by the level of his award compared to mine.[5]

This passage from his autobiography gives us to understand that the honour he received elicited envy among others, and on the part of Nicolae Vieru in particular. But at the time, the Securitate reported that it was in fact Károlyi who was envious – not of Nicolae Vieru, but of Nadia Comăneci. In September, the trainer told a number of people around him, 'the title awarded to her is too big'[6] and 'that honour has made her "too big for her boots".'[7] It was also reported of him, 'he can't get through to her any more now that she has the title Hero of Socialist Labour, because he has a lesser title he can't "smack her bottom" any more,'[8] with reference to the fact that it was now harder for him to mete out corporal punishment to her, while in November 1976 a more detailed Securitate report stated that he behaved towards Nadia in a mocking way, addressing her as 'the heroine': 'After the return from Montréal and the decoration of the team and the technicians, Károlyi seemed dissatisfied that Nadia had received a decoration higher than his, and he alludes to her using the word "heroine".'[9]

While the two coaches thought Nadia was now too big for her boots, a number of people who knew them commented that shortly after their return from Montréal, 'the Károlyi family hasn't been able to handle success and they've fallen out with everybody.'[10] The reports of the Securitate officers include a number of denigrating remarks gathered from their informers, since at the time everybody who worked at the Oneşti gymnastics centre or who knew Nadia Comăneci was, without exception, under secret police surveillance. The surveillance had increased in intensity compared without previous years. Nadia had to be kept under comprehensive but discreet surveillance now that she was one of the country's most famous figures.

Similarly, since Oneşti had given birth to a prestigious brand – a school for élite gymnasts – foreign delegations from both the West and other Communist countries started visiting the small Moldavian town almost on a conveyor belt. Trainers, sportspeople, representatives of foreign gymnastics federations – they all wished to find out the Romanians' working methods and to meet the girls. 'Every five minutes the door to the gym opened and another delegation from this or that country marched through. They were accompanied by big shots from our government and the Gymnastics Federation. I had to stop practice, line the kids up, and present them to every delegation. It drove me completely crazy. The visitors, reporters, media were nonstop.'[11] Sometimes, to the great satisfaction of Nicolae Ceauşescu, who had embarked on a major drive to gain legitimacy at

Figure 3.1 Queen Fabiola of Belgium visiting Oneşti, October 1976, to meet Nadia Comăneci at the Physical Education Lycée. (Central National Historical Archives, dossier Primiri/Album 51, leaf 88, Bucharest, Romania.)

Europe's royal courts, even crowned heads showed a desire to meet the 'goddess of Montréal', as happened in October 1976, when King Baudouin of Belgium and Queen Fabiola visited Romania and the general secretary of the Communist Party arranged for them to visit the Borzeşti Petrochemical Plant and the Oneşti Physical Education Lycée, where they met Nadia Comăneci and Teodora Ungureanu. Consequently, given the star status of the gymnasts and the importance that Oneşti had gained, it is no wonder that, employing its usual modus operandi, the Securitate redoubled its efforts when it came to Nadia.

At the beginning of the 1970s, when sporting achievement was barely getting underway in Oneşti, the secret police did not find it necessary to make any intelligence checks on the nucleus of teachers, trainers and gymnasts that was beginning to form. They had little reason to do so. The local authorities didn't even pay very much attention to the disagreements that arose, given that Béla Károlyi was often at odds with the other technicians. It was thought to be only natural, as Károlyi was known to be both ambitious and difficult to get along with. Moreover, in a small town like Oneşti, it would have quickly come to light if the atmosphere within the squad was 'unjust', as they used to say.

Many of those who became informers were also members of the Communist Party. For this reason, they weren't assigned 'network' files, as informers' files were termed. After 1968, there weren't any files at all on those Party members who collaborated with the secret police, since Nicolae Ceauşescu wanted the Party to control the Securitate, rather than the other way around. Whenever the Securitate was faced with an operational situation in which they needed the collaboration of a Party member, they had to request the permission of the local Party bosses. Once permission was granted, the person in question would assist the Securitate for a limited time period, but without undergoing the usual recruitment procedure and therefore without having a network file opened on him or her. Nevertheless, the names of informers and Communist Party collaborators were recorded in a separate database, which has yet to be located in the archives, and the Securitate officers were referred to in various ways: 'official person', 'official liaison', 'operational liaison', and sometimes 'official source' or simply 'source'.

It should be said from the outset that the most significant informers, recruited not only to carry out comprehensive surveillance in Oneşti, but also to gather information and engage in operations to influence and control Romanian gymnastics, were leading figures in the sport. Maria Simionescu, for example, 'the first lady of Romanian gymnastics', was also held in high esteem by the Securitate, proving to be a valuable collaborator under the code name 'Lia Muri'. Likewise, Nicolae Vieru, the general secretary of the Romanian Gymnastics Federation, in his sober and conscientious style, collaborated with the secret police right up to its final days, in December 1989, hiding behind the code name 'Vlad'.

In the Securitate documents identified to date there are no details about the period when they became collaborators, how they were recruited, or whether or not they were subjected to pressure or blackmail. But 'Vlad' and 'Lia Muri' left deep traces. In the voluminous 'Sport' dossier their earliest reports and briefing notes date from 1974–75. Incontrovertible proof of their collaboration can be found in their personnel files, in which the officers of Department One record at an unstated date that they are 'source / 161 NI',[12] which clearly demonstrates their status.

Nevertheless, thanks to Securitate officer Nicolae Ilie, who for many years was her liaison and sometimes annotated her reports, we know that in November 1974 Mili Simionescu was already a 'trustworthy person'[13] and had undergone a fresh recruitment process. At the time, Ilie noted, 'Simionescu Maria is a Party member. She was the informer to our organs and was let go in 1973, when she became a p.m. [Party member] (. . .) Permission from the Party organs will be requested to use the aforementioned Simionescu Maria as a source to inform the Securitate organs.'[14] In February 1975, Ilie made a further note, at the end of one of his agent's reports: 'permission has been sought from the Party organs to make use of her,'[15] and by March she was a 'candidate'.[16] After which, she became a 'source'.

As far as Nicolae Vieru is concerned, he seems to have broached his collaboration with the Securitate more cautiously, at least in the initial phase. It was only later, in the 1980s, that he agreed to a code name and 'source' status, as his first reports are signed in his own name and presented as professional documents. Undoubtedly, his recruitment to the network of informers was a major success, since Vieru, after his appointment as secretary general of the federation, became one of the most influential people in the sport, contributing to every major decision regulating gymnastics and lives of gymnasts and their trainers until the mid-2000s. Those who knew him sustain even today that his achievements were remarkable. The Securitate sometimes noted in their reports that he had 'ascendency', by which was meant he enjoyed authority and influence, that he was esteemed or feared by his colleagues, an assessment that was wholly accurate. If we look at Romanian gymnastics as one big family, then it might be said that Vieru was the paterfamilias, even if he was subordinate to a number of people with political backing who served in the management of the federation or on the National Council for Physical Education and Sport up until 1989. He was also influential internationally, not only because he was a member of the Executive Committee of the International Gymnastics Federation and deputy chairman of the organisation over the course of a number of mandates, but also, above all, because he managed to develop a significant circle of relations and because he had a good reputation with foreign partners, be they sportsmen, trainers, journalists, or businessmen representing global concerns.

In this respect, the Securitate was always able to aim high, knowing no limits. Béla Károlyi was also considered for recruitment, and this is what happened, just a few days after his victorious return from the European Championships in Skien, where Nadia astounded the world with her memorable performance. But Károlyi was also a Party member. This is why, on 9 May 1975, Lieutenant Colonel Vasile Miriţă of the Oneşti Securitate submitted a report at the end of which he proposed that the Party organs should be approached with the request to allow Károlyi to be 'employed in operational work'. On 14 May, in accordance with the working procedures, 'the approv[al] of comr[ade] first-sec[retary] Ghineţ V. was obtained',[17] and Károlyi was recruited, becoming agent 'Katona'. Or so the Securitate believed, since although Károlyi did not openly decline to work for the secret police – he himself later admitted that he wrote a number of summary reports when he returned from foreign tournaments – he was swiftly dropped after it was realised that 'during collaboration he has demonstrated disinterest, revealing to others his connection with the Securitate organs.'[18]

In Oneşti, Lieutenant Colonel Miriţă, whose name we find in documents up to 1977, seems to have been tasked by the Bacău County Securitate Inspectorate with supervising and directing the network of informers at the gymnastics centre. Károlyi told his close friends that the officer visited him at home when he returned from abroad to question him and to have him sign a report about the trip. Károlyi admitted to sometimes defying the officer, telling him he was 'not obliged to tell him what he did during the trip in question.'[19] Károlyi was not lying: a number of his reports, from 1975, are either sarcastic in tone or cold and formal, demonstrating his attitude of insubordination towards an authority in which he did not believe. The reports he wrote at the urging of the Securitate officer were signed 'Prof. Károlyi', to which Lieutenant Colonel Mirinţă added 'source "Katona"', as if to reinforce the fact that the trainer was neither an 'official person' nor a 'candidate' but his own agent, although he would also be careful to mention that the report 'was provided at the officer's insistence.'

Not all Károlyi's reports were desultory and superficial, however. Sometimes he tried to take advantage of the Securitate's presence in his life, accusing colleagues of dishonest or vexing behaviour. For example, on 22 May 1975, he complained about young trainer Nicolae Moscu, whom he suspected – rightly, as it happened – of spying on him during training in order to steal the moves he invented, and he took advantage of the fact that Moscu was intending to emigrate to Canada:

In conclusion I insist on an inspection of the activity of teacher Moscu, who contrary to the instructions that the Ministry of Education sent to the heads of the Lycée, to the effect that he be removed from this educational establishment of national interest, nonetheless continues to be present during the process of training the Olympic squad, classed as a process kept secret from foreign persons and incompetent elements and persons engaged in suspicious actions. Under the circumstances, the presence of this man who will soon leave the country permanently is not at all desirable and might even bring considerable disservices.[20]

While Béla Károlyi made no effort to foster a secret relationship with the Securitate, it might be said of choreographer Géza Pozsar, who worked closely with the trainer, that his work as an informer turned out to be a vocation. Born in Oradea in 1950, Pozsar graduated from the Cluj Choreography Lycée in 1970 and was at first sent to work at the Trade Unions Club in Oradea, before being transferred to the Timişoara Opera. In 1974 he was recruited to work in sport, thanks to Maria Simionescu:

> We had been helping a local gymnastics trainer, Emeric Ban, who had a few girls in the national junior team. Maria Simionescu, a federal trainer at the time, came to visit the gym and seeing me work with the girls, she invited me to Bucharest, to join the national squad which was training at the 23 August Centre. After the Varna World Championships in 1972,[21] the team was broken up. It was proposed that I go to Oneşti, to the gymnastics lycée. At the same time, I was admitted as a part-time student to the Law Faculty in Bucharest. I met Béla on various occasions before I arrived in Oneşti. I started working with him in 1974.[22]

Géza Pozsar met Károlyi before he received the job offer in Oneşti and they had taken a liking to each other. Károlyi was very careful about whom he surrounded himself with, and Pozsár didn't seem to be either demanding or susceptible. As he was self-effacing rather than confrontational, he suited Károlyi very well. What also counted was that they were both ethnic Hungarians, which meant they could converse with each other in their native language, as well as the conjunction of circumstances at the time: Marta had fallen out with their choreographer thitherto. Maria Simionescu also supported Pozsár, intuiting that he would abide by her wishes. The young gymnasts also took a liking to him, calling him by his first name, since he was friendly with them and quickly won a reputation for being charming. Later, in a report for Lieutenant Colonel Miriţă that he wrote in February 1976, Károlyi praised Pozsár: 'professionally Pozsár's work hasn't shown any flaws, and he continues to demonstrate a consistent interest in perfecting himself, leaving behind him work of real quality, working with passion and competence.'[23]

Pozsár was recruited an informer on 26 February 1975 and given the code name 'Nelu'. 'He has given evidence of passion, sincerity and correctitude' and 'he has supplied intelligence materials that are valuable and have been confirmed,'[24] as the Securitate described him. We believe this description was accurate, since 'Nelu' turned out to be remarkably efficient and unsparing in his reports on Károlyi, finding in himself the strength required to conceal his personal disliking and hostility towards him. First recruited by the Bacău Securitate in the second half of 1976, Pozsár subsequently reported directly to Department One in Bucharest, and officer Nicolae Ilie instructed him on how to send his reports from Oneşti through the post in the form of letters to an imaginary fellow trainer in Bucharest, at Post Office Box No. 720, Post Office No. 1. From February 1975, 'Nelu's' reports began to flow regularly. And they flowed uninterrupted for six years, until Pozsár went abroad and failed to come back.

In the 2000s, when his collaboration with the Securitate became public, Pozsár, who now lives in the United States, denied it: 'I didn't have any connection with the Securitate. (. . .) I don't know what those files really contain. I'd really like to return to the country, to see them for myself, because a lot of things have happened since then.'[25] The years passed and with them his explanations changed, and now he claims that he became an informer after capitulating to Securitate blackmail. In 1974, Pozsár had met a young Frenchwoman. He fell in love with her and wanted to marry her, which led the Communist authorities to suspect him of espionage and, after being interviewed a number of times, they urged him to opt for the future without anxieties that collaboration would bring, as opposed to a grim future of interrogation, arrest and even imprisonment, in the event that he refused. Pozsár likewise claims that in his reports he only made reference to Béla Károlyi's abusive behaviour in the gym, as his main task was to protect Nadia.[26]

There is a grain of truth in Pozsár's claims, since he did have a love affair that attracted the notice of the Securitate, which was capable of absurdly believing that his French fiancée had been sent to spy on the Oneşti gymnastics school.[27] But 'Nelu's' reports went further than describing the relationship between Béla Károlyi and Nadia Comăneci. Apparently on his own initiative, he was eager to write page after page about everybody he came into contact with, regardless of their social position. If somebody made the mistake of telling him that he or she listened to Radio Free Europe or had met a foreign citizen, if somebody provided him with some item of information that might be of interest to the authorities, or if somebody made negative comments about the Party and State, 'Nelu' immediately reported it to Colonel Vasile Bucura of the Oneşti Securitate during the meetings they had at the 'Marin' safe house. He even wrote reports about his lover in France, as well as about her rival and his future wife, Maria Gîndea, about whom he said, for example, 'on 17 October 1975 teacher Maria Gîndea made injurious remarks about the Securitate organs.'[28] Miss Gîndea, who in 1976 became Mrs Pozsár, could herself hardly be said to have been an innocent victim of the Communist dictatorship, however. 'She married because she had a flighty life and had to gain respectability,'[29] reported informer 'Ionescu Ion' in April 1976, and there are a number of situations in her file which would seem to support this. For Maria Pozsár had been routinely recruited as a Securitate informer as early as the summer of 1972, when she was working as a guide at the Carmen Hotel in the Venus seaside resort.[30] 'I will continue checking him via source "Meda",[31] reported the Securitate officer on 27 February 1975 at the beginning of the process to recruit Pozsár. 'Meda' was in fact the code name assigned to Maria Gîndea.

The list of informers from Oneşti doesn't stop there. In the late 1970s, the Securitate continued its onslaught and recruited left, right and centre, as if desperate not to let a single person involved in the sports club slip through their fingers. We shall reveal the names of some of them in the pages that follow. The web of agents that the Securitate painstakingly wove in Oneşti combined with a network established in Bucharest within the Romanian Federation of Gymnastics and the National Council for Physical Education and Sport. For this reason, by late 1976, the Securitate was no longer able to be caught on the wrong foot. Intelligence officers knew everything about relationships between those in charge of gymnastics as they evolved in real time, they could anticipate events and intervene promptly to further the interests of the régime.

The large number of informers in itself demonstrates that the Oneşti centre had become a significant intelligence objective. But what was the specific mission of the informers? After Nadia became European Champion and more especially after she won Olympic gold, the Securitate's stated aim was to protect her. With her worldwide fame came risks and situations that might place her in danger. Evidence of that fame was the fact that the Comăneci family's postman had to deliver to their flat thousands of letters every month from not only Romania but all over the world.

In October 1976, a young man from France who had developed an obsession with Nadia waited for her on a bench near her block of flats in Oneşti for hours before accosting her on the street, telling her that he had come a very long way just to see her.[32] As the years passed and Nadia grew up into a pretty young woman, more and more young men sent her proposals of marriage, and the Securitate would promptly investigate them. In the files, there are reports of men from Canada, Mexico and Japan who 'sent her photographs and asked her to marry them.' In March 1979, a mentally disturbed man went looking for her at the headquarters of the Romanian Gymnastics Federation, claiming that she was his wife and he was there to take her home. His name was given to the authorities and more than likely he was committed to a psychiatric hospital. Similarly, 'in January 1988 a U.S. citizen presented himself at the N.C.P.E.S. claiming he was there to take her home—it was not possible to identify him,' while somebody from the Soviet Union tried to invite her to take part in activities 'against imperialist propaganda.'[33]

Given the draconian surveillance of the populace carried out by the Militia [the name for the Romanian Police during the Communist period] and Securitate, Romania had a low crime rate. Anybody who dared to commit a crime was usually identified and arrested within a relatively short time, since the police state functioned like clockwork. In September 1977, Nadia became the target of a criminal plot. Two young men already being held under arrest at Constanţa Militia station for other crimes, planned together to kidnap Nadia after their release. During the subsequent investigation, one of them confessed that the other 'was to wait for her in front of the school gym with a big bunch of flowers, holding it with his left hand in front of his head, and holding in his right hand a gun or flick-knife.' He would then demand she get into 'a van where I would be waiting for them. After that we were going to go back to Constanţa, on the coast, after which we would demand a ransom in hard currency and a guarantee we could cross the frontier.'[34]

We don't know whether they really intended to go through with such a naïve plan, a plan with no hope of success, because they were reported to the Militia by another prisoner in their cell. However, the Securitate took seriously the possibility that Nadia might fall victim to a terrorist attack either in Romania or abroad. 'As early as the Montréal Olympic Games there appeared signals that she might be targeted for kidnapping by terrorist groups,' a paper drawn up by Department One concluded in 1978, further stating, 'such signals have in some cases been confirmed by the police organs of the countries in question.' It was necessary to guard and protect Nadia, but also to prevent 'leaks to the outside of information connected with women's gymnastics in the S.R. of Romania and in particular with Nadia Comăneci, both as a gymnast and a private person.'[35]

But missions aimed at protecting Nadia were not set underway until after she won her first major international titles. Her international success in fact suited the régime perfectly, since the task of protecting her provided a legal framework for secret police surveillance. By late 1976, Nadia Comăneci and her mother had become persons of interest to the Securitate, but for different reasons entirely.

The informers recruited at the beginning of 1975 did not file reports on the gymnasts, since they were just children. Their task for to describe the mood within the team as a means of helping to prevent conflicts among the employees of the gymnastics school, to signal intentions to 'flee', in other words, to defect by failing to return to Romania after international tournaments, to monitor the voicing of hostile political opinions, to identify persons who maintained undeclared relations with foreigners, and to keep an eye out for anything else that might be of interest to the authorities. For example, in one of his first reports, dating from May 1975, at the time when the Securitate had set underway the procedure to recruit Károlyi and were constructing a psychological profile of him, Géza Pozsár observed, 'Károlyi Béla likes money and is quite thrifty with it,' also pointing out that when he travelled abroad he sought to take financial advantage of foreign partners.[36] Other informers showed greater zeal, making it a habit to report any marital infidelity on the part of their colleagues, their usual victim being Marta Károlyi.

For example, the following is one of Nicolae Vieru's first reports, dating from February 1975. The tone is neutral and the report provides a brief description of some of the trainers at work in Oneşti. Vieru, who was at the time only an 'official person', does not stoop to calumny, particularly given that at the time there was no conflict between him and Béla Károlyi, as there would be later:

I.M.   Top Secret
Department One   Sole copy
Recipient: Lt. Maj. Ilie Nicolae
Date: 04.02.75
FN/162/IN

Report on the cadres who work
at the gymnastics lycée in Gheorghe Gheorghiu-Dej municipality

The women's gymnastics lycée in Oneşti represents the no. 1 unit for the girls' Olympic squad with a view to the O.G. of 1976.

The main trainers of the section are spouses Béla and Marta Károlyi, very hard-working and dedicated persons, who currently have the most talented elements (Comăneci Nadia, Ungureanu Teodora, Gabor Georgeta, etc.). They came to Oneşti in the period 1967–68 at their own request out of a desire to work in gymnastics. They have a child and a quiet family life. They have had some minor conflicts with some of the trainers out of their desire to work harder than them and to make a name from themselves and perhaps from a certain egotism.

The supervising trainer of the section since 1973–74 was appointed by the Ministry of Education with the agreement of the federation: Hidi Iosif, a lecturer in the gymnastics department of the I.P.E.S. He is a man with experience, serious, perseverant in his work. The instruction programme has been better organised since he was assigned to the lycée. But he is a friend of the Károlyi family. He is married, has a son at school, his family being in Bucharest.

Pozsár Géza is employed by the school to carry out the girls' artistic training. He is a knowledgeable man, dedicated and serious. He is unmarried, having been assigned to Oneşti from Oradea. He works with the Károlyi trainers' group in particular.

Spouses Florin and Florica Dobre arrived from Craiova when the unit was established at the beginning of the 1969-1970 school year. They are professionally well-trained, serious and very hard-working. They are perhaps over-sensitive and sometimes suspicious. They work with the second echelon in terms of sporting potential.

Trainers Ipate Mihai, a local, and Dragomir Elena, who came to Oneşti after graduating from the I.P.E.S., are a couple who have yet to stand out with any exceptional results, although they work quite conscientiously.

Since the 1973–74 school year graduate Moscu Nicolae (a Jew) has also worked at the school, a hard-working and dedicated lad, but without experience or sufficient authority. Since the 1974–75 year he has worked with teacher Duicu Liana, assigned here from Tîrgovişte at her own request. (. . .)

I believe the issue of the national make-up of the cadres from the gymnastics lycée in Oneşti ought to be examined by our federation and the Ministry of Education.

03.ii.1975   Secretary general of the Romanian Gymnastics Federation
                 Nicolae Vieru
                 (signature illegible)

N.I. the material was supplied at the initiative of V.N. following the discussions with him in question.

Measures: request will be made to Bacău C.I. for mode in which those named in the report were identified and how they work, particularly about Hidi Iosif.

Hidi Iosif, lecturer in the gymnastics department of the I.P.E.S. will be identified and examined with a view to his recruitment.

Lt. Maj. Ilie Nicolae.[37]

From the document signed by Vieru we may observe at least two objectives on the part of Securitate officer Nicolae Ilie: the intention to gather information about other gymnastics coaches with a view to their recruitment – for the time being his sights were set on trainer Iosif Hidi – and a particular interest in the 'national make-up of the cadres', a phrase at the end of the report that refers to the non-Romanians among the Oneşti staff.

In other words, before he wrote his report, Vieru must have been questioned by Ilie about the Jews, Hungarians and other ethnic groups represented among the trainers, about whether their percentage had become too high, and whether the decision makers within the Federation and the N.C.P.E.S. and Ministry of Education had lost sight of the fact. There was no law forbidding persons from Romania's ethnic minorities from holding positions of responsibility, but it wasn't encouraged. From 1952 onwards, Gheorghiu-Dej set about Romanianising the central apparatus of the Party, inspired by the anti-Semitic purges that had taken place in the Soviet Union, but it was Nicolae Ceauşescu who imposed an emphasis on nation and state in the political discourse. By 1975, the nationalist discourse was flourishing, promoted in various forms. The media and cultural outlets saturated the public with works that claimed that Romania was a cradle of civilisation, that the Romanian people had a heroic past stretching from Burebista to the emergence of the Communist Party, a discourse that went hand in hand with a reserved attitude towards minorities, which by now were referred to as 'foreign elements' and who were denied any significant part in the country's history.

Therefore, in 1975, the Securitate was trying to gain a clear picture of the Oneşti staff and to recruit as many of them as possible, and each new informer that joined the network was pressured to write reports on his or her colleagues and the working atmosphere. The following year, by which time the number of agents had increased, and the volume of information had likewise burgeoned in consequence, it was as if the objectives on which the secret police thought they should concentrate also came into clearer focus, and the most important of these proved to be Béla Károlyi.

Although in the meantime he had achieved significant successes and had himself been recruited as an informer, Béla Károlyi became a target of systematic surveillance, for a number of reasons. His collaboration with the Securitate left a lot to be desired and it became increasingly obvious that he was going to be dropped as an agent. The Securitate officers in Oneşti and Bucharest, respectively Vasile Miriţă and Nicolae Ilie, didn't like him, due to his arrogance and even defiance. Agent 'Nelu', who wrote a number of reports about Károlyi during this period, signalled that he was saving up money and intended ultimately not to return to the country from abroad. He informed the Securitate that Károlyi sometimes alluded to the fact that Hungarians were discriminated against in Romania and was in the habit of making tendentious remarks about national leaders. But above all else, he reported that Károlyi was abusive towards the gymnasts he trained.

Some of these suspicions were to be borne out, but others were exaggerated. It was not clear at the time that Károlyi wished to defect, and Géza Pozsár presented no evidence other than what Károlyi was supposed to have said, things that anybody might say in private. This is what happened on 25 December 1975, when Pozsár reported that when the team were in training at the Piatra Arsă sports complex in the Bucegi Mountains, while taking a sauna Béla Károlyi said, 'if he ever leaves the communist bloc he will build a sauna like that with all the necessary facilities.'[38] Other such clues, if they might be called that, and corroborated by the fact that Marta Károlyi had an aunt in the United States, led the Oneşti Securitate to demand that during foreign trips, Béla should not be accompanied by his wife,[39] as he would abandon the idea of defection if his family was still in Romania. This is what should have happened in Montréal in 1976, but Béla Károlyi managed to overcome the obstacle thanks to his political connections in Bucharest.

The Károlyis' Hungarian ethnicity proved to be no impediment to their careers, but it could have been. The Securitate documents contain plenty of references to their ethnicity. Both Béla and Marta, as well as the other coaches, were allowed to display their ethnic identity as long as they did not thereby show hostility towards Romania. Of those listed by Nicolae Vieru in the report in which he brought up the 'issue of the national make-up of the cadres' at the Oneşti gymnastics lycée, more than half were ethnic Hungarians or Jews: the Károlyis, Géza Pozsár, Hidi Iosif, Nicolae Moscu. But the fact that measures were not taken to stifle their careers shows that there was no intention to discriminate.

The distrust of the Securitate, an institution in which many ethnic Hungarians worked together, had been aroused. This cannot have been accidental, somebody must have been behind it, and investigations continued in order to discover whether there might be a cell of Hungarian nationalists in Oneşti. A month after the discussion with Vieru, on 3 March 1975 Department One directed Maria Simionescu to write a report on Francisc Lövi, the assistant general secretary of the R.G.F., who was suspected of favouring ethnic Hungarian coaches. On the professional level, agent 'Lia Muri' did not have anything much to criticise Lövi for, but she still highlighted his 'preferences' and the fact that a group of ethnic Hungarians had come together in Oneşti:

> He works very conscientiously, intelligently in matters of organisation and at the administrative level. (. . .) The source did not observe chauvinist attitudes towards our cadres, volunteer activists etc., but he has preferences and at various meetings of referees-trainers can be observed a bias towards certain friends, e.g. Molnar Alfred, Albert Ion and Nagy Ecaterina—Cluj, Bodiş Francisc—Oradea, Deutsch Tiberiu—Bucharest, Katona Tiberiu—B Mare, Schroter—Sighet etc.
>
> (. . .) Regarding the training of the Olympic gymnasts from the gymnastics lycée in Mun. Gh. Gheorghiu-Dej, a group has formed: Károlyi Béla, Károlyi Marta, Hidi Iosif and Pozsár Géza, who work with these gymnasts. At present it's got to the point where only Hungarian is spoken in the gym. To replace the current head Braşoveanu Gheorghe, Mănăilă Gh. has been put forward, a good teacher, who as he is married to a Hungarian and in close relations of friendship with this group there are doubts about him.[40]

The situation was also signalled by Aurel Stoian, alias 'Relu',[41] assistant head of the Mass Sport Section and the Economic Section of the N.C.P.E.S., who in a report dated 5 October 1976 stated: 'Another issue raised by the source was the fact that at the lycée there are too many teachers and trainers of Hungarian nationality, some hired at the proposal of Károlyi Béla.'[42]

For the secret police, the most convenient solution to the problem was to recruit some of the ethnic Hungarians. Such was the case with Béla Károlyi, but even more so with Pozsár, whom the Securitate officer described, ironically or not, as having been persuaded to collaborate 'through gradual seduction based on patriotic sentiments', rather than as a result of blackmail, as Pozsár himself claimed.

At the beginning of 1976, the relationship between Károlyi and the Securitate deteriorated further, and he was accused of a number of faults, including 'a nationalist-chauvinist position.'[43] It was obvious that evidence was being sought, but despite painstaking efforts in this direction, it was late in appearing. The authorities in Cluj were also notified and told to carry out checks on Károlyi's family, after his father was supposedly discovered to possess books of an irredentist content,[44] but nor could this information be confirmed: the head of the Cluj Securitate replied that Károlyi's father was 'known to be correct and has a good position towards the policy of our Party and state.'[45] As emerges from covert Securitate recordings, when the Károlyis spoke in their mother tongue at home, Marta was sometimes caught making remarks interpreted as 'tendentious comments on the rights and freedoms of citizens of Hungarian nationality in our country,' while Béla claimed that in addition to his preference for Hungarian coaches, he also 'prefers to promote gymnasts of Hungarian nationality.'[46]

During the Montréal Olympics, one of the Securitate officers in the Romanian delegation claimed that Károlyi 'pressured Romanian judge Liţă Emilia, demanding that she ask the other judges in the uneven parallel bars brigade to award higher marks to a Hungarian gymnast so that she could win the silver medal instead of Teodora Ungureanu. I mention that Károlyi Béla exerted this pressure because he is friendly with the trainer of the Hungarian team, the gymnast in question being his wife. The Romanian judge categorically refused to do so, replying that Teodora Ungureanu was clearly superior to the Hungarian gymnast.'[47]

The Securitate continued to make a great deal of the fact that the Károlyi's were more Hungarian than Romanian and might even be secretly involved in what it termed 'hostile actions'. In December 1977, by which time a surveillance file on 'Katona' had been opened, a study draw up by Department One stated that during his frequent trips abroad 'he might be contacted and lured into disloyal actions by reactionary elements hostile to our country. To this can be added the fact that being a citizen of Hungarian nationality the target might be in the sights of hostile elements inside the country, as well as among reactionary Hungarian emigrants.'[48]

Did Béla Károlyi harbour nationalist prejudices? Even if only privately, did he proclaim Hungarian superiority over Romanians? Károlyi was too pragmatic to be a 'nationalist-chauvinist', and we believe the Securitate's accusation to have been ungrounded. Károlyi was enough of an opportunist to favour gymnastic talent regardless of ethnic background, and his preference for working with Hungarian gymnasts and trainers was only natural; any ethnic Romanian in Hungary would have done the same.

However, when the Károlyis later had serious conflicts with the Romanian Gymnastics Federation and frequently claimed they were marginalised because of their Hungarian ethnicity, such a position was also at odds with the truth. Ethnic insults were flung from both sides. During telephone calls recorded by the Securitate, Romanians whose relationship with the Károlyis was tense used to claim that Béla ignored all contrary opinions because he was a *bozgor* [an ethnic slur for a Hungarian],[49] while in 1976 Béla was recorded stating his agreement with the opinion that 'it's still the Hungarians who have to do the Romanians' jobs for them.'[50]

Whereas suspicions that the Károlyis intended to defect and displayed 'nationalist-chauvinist' attitudes were exaggerated at the time, when it came to the accusations regarding their abusive behaviour – towards other coaches and above all towards the gymnasts – there was plenty of persuasive and well-founded evidence. The main informer to describe the couple's abusive behaviour was yet again 'Nelu', and he did so in the very first reports he filed from the beginning of 1975. He has continued to do so to this day. In 2020, in an interview given to the two makers of a documentary film in the United States, Géza Pozsár testified that as trainers Béla and Marta Károlyi were both physically and verbally violent towards their gymnasts: 'He yelled at them and humiliated them. "Fat cow!" "Sow!" He slapped the girls and they were very frightened. Marta used to grab them by the throat and dig her fingers in. And she slapped them a lot. The girls had welts from her rings on their cheeks.' Asked whether he reported the Károlyis' violent behaviour to the authorities, Pozsár replied: 'Yes. I reported them, but you have to understand that nobody took any measures to stop them. In Romania it was tolerated.'[51]

Today, it is no secret that the Károlyis used to beat their gymnasts. Béla Károlyi's hand was so heavy that the victim of his abuse, a defenceless child, would be knocked over, bowled across the floor for a few metres. Pozsár's reports bear out his claim to have reported this abuse to the authorities. However, he did not report it to the police or the prosecutor's office, as the American filmmaker imagined – he couldn't understand why Pozsár's complaints did not result in an investigation – but to the Securitate, under the code name 'Nelu'. In his reports, Pozsár described in great detail the beatings, the insults, the dietary restrictions to which the gymnasts were subjected. And he was not the only one. Almost everybody who worked at the club made similar complaints, either as informers communicating such incidents to their Securitate liaison officer or among themselves while unknowingly being recorded by Securitate agents.

Perhaps the answer closest to the truth that Géza Pozsár might have given during the interview would have been that in Romania, Béla Károlyi's behaviour was tolerated. For not only were the accusations against the trainer never made public, but the Securitate never launched any inquiry into them. There was no political will to do so. In other words, Károlyi benefitted from protection at the highest level for long as he was a successful trainer.

This is proven by an incident that took place in 1976, before the team left for Montréal, when his gymnasts, too young to stand up to him, nonetheless sought help in a way that they imagined would bring them protection. They sent a letter to Bucharest that confirms that they had been subjected to physical and mental abuse. However, since the letter was anonymous, we cannot know who exactly wrote it. It was sent not to the Romanian Gymnastics Federation or the N.C.P.E.S., but to the Central Committee of the Romanian Communist Party, where it was received on 16 June. The letter, signed 'the Oneşti gymnastics team', opens with 'Comrade President', which shows that it was intended to reach the desk of Nicolae Ceauşescu himself.

The letter, which we reproduce below in full, contains numerous grammatical errors and is a jumble of words strung together without any ability to construct a sentence, but the accusations are grave. Béla Károlyi is described as a 'man without a soul', who 'is capable of killing us' and frequently resorts to 'beating'. The word 'slaves' is strongly underscored, thereby conveying the trainer's contempt and mockery of his pupils.

146/17.vi.1976[52]

We write to you after we read your speech at the socialist education congress and we thank you for everything you do for us, children of this country, for happy conditions of labour and education.

We are forced to write to you to ask you to do something to give us back our childhood which day after day this man without a soul steals from us who is called Mr Béla Károlyi. Thinking of his own good we have become like slaves.

We know that children shouldn't be beaten but we as it said in books do lessons like in the old circuses with beatings and punishments. We want to work and we proved it but not with the whip. We ask that this gentleman because he doesn't let us say different not work with us any more.

Do something so that he doesn't find out that we said how he treats us because he is capable of killing us—that's how he threatened Nadia if she doesn't win.

When visitors come from the television or the country he's slimy and they talk only to him and if we dare to speak it's the worse for us.

We are determined to work hard and to bring glory to our homeland all over the world but we ask you to look after our childhood.

We kiss you with much love,
the Oneşti gymnastics team.[53]

Obviously, when such accusations are made anonymously, they lose much of their weight. But if the Communist régime had wished to begin an inquiry, this hardly mattered, since the Securitate would have been capable of immediately finding out who wrote the letter. Although it raised concern when it arrived in Bucharest, the letter was covered up. From the Central Committee it was redirected to the Securitate, and the archives reveal that Ilie Verdeţ, a member of the Secretariat of the Central Committee, approached Teodor Coman, the Minister of the Interior, 'with the request to proceed in accordance with the agreement made.' As to the nature of the agreement between the two, a handwritten note from a Securitate officer enlightens us: 'The comrade interior minister orders that no checks be made in connection with the anonymous letter.'[54]

Nevertheless, on 12 November 1976, after fresh approval from the local Party organisation was obtained, monitoring of Béla Károlyi took a new direction, as this was the day when the Securitate opened an investigative file on him. It was a new stage in the surveillance of him. Thitherto, checks on him had entailed surveillance over limited periods of time in order to clarify various suspicions. But thenceforth, the operation was to involve more complex measures, since in the eyes of the Securitate, their suspicions had proven to be grounded.

In the documents that led to the opening of the investigation, 'Katona' was accused, among other things, of making 'tendentious comments', of engaging in 'unofficial relations with foreign citizens',[55] and of intending to 'flee', i.e. defect. It was not because Ceauşescu awarded him an 'Order' higher than the ones received by Vieru and other sportspeople, as Károlyi claimed in his autobiography. However, he must have sensed he was under surveillance, since in a report in his file dated April 1977, we find, 'the target shows evidence of suspicion and caution, being obsessed with the fact that the security organs are watching him,' and at the same time it is recommended that surveillance measures be taken 'in conditions of maximum subterfuge.'[56]

An increasing number of people around him were recruited, since 'Nelu', although highly effective, still sometimes had moments of tension with Béla Károlyi. The Károlyis' relatives also came within the purview of the Securitate. Bugs were planted in their home during certain periods – although Lieutenant Colonel Vasile Miriţă had already resorted to such a measure at the beginning of 1976. Informers from within the Federation and the N.C.P.E.S. were sent to Oneşti to gather information on Károlyi and influence him, and during tournaments abroad, he was always accompanied by a Securitate officer.

Once he was under full surveillance, the secret police became ever more convinced that Béla Károlyi was conceited, arrogant, egotistical, petty, although his merits were never denied: in various reports we find, 'both the target and his wife are recognised as exceptionally valuable from the professional point of view, domestically and internationally.'[57] In time, although the suspicion of 'nationalist-chauvinism' was set aside, more and more evidence was gathered to show that Károlyi's conduct was disloyal to the state.

By the second half of 1976, Béla Károlyi's life was an open book to the Securitate. But simultaneously, the lives of Nadia and her parents were also being monitored. Investigations focused on the trainer's working methods, examining his abusive behaviour and the way in which this impacted on the new Olympic champion. As Nadia was a national treasure from whom the political leadership expected further outstanding successes, as well as the youngest holder of the title Hero of Socialist Labour, the Securitate was responsible for protecting her – not only from terrorists, but also from her own trainer, especially now that she herself had begun to protest in her own way. After carrying out preliminary investigations, the Securitate moved on to interception of calls from the Comănecis' telephone the better to understand the evolution of the relationship between Béla Károlyi, alias 'Katona', and Nadia, alias 'Corina'. In reality, this was the principal reason why Nadia and her family were monitored by the Securitate from 1976 onward.

The summary reports on the Olympic squad drawn up by the Ministry of the Interior usually ended up on the desks of political decision makers: Elena Ceauşescu, Nicu Ceauşescu, Emil Bobu, Ilie Verdeţ, et al. The summaries described the 'inappropriate' atmosphere in Oneşti and the increasingly fraught relationship between Béla and Nadia. Sensing he was threatened by the unseen hand of the Securitate, Béla Károlyi in his turn did everything he could to preserve his political protection: 'Every week, on Fridays, Károlyi Béla telephones the cabinet of comrade Ilie Verdeţ, where he reports on the problems of the gymnastics team,'[58] we find mentioned in a Department One report from March 1977.

Paradoxically, the man who was eventually to become the most highly rated gymnastics trainer in the world knew nothing about the secrets of the discipline when he made his début in the profession. For a short time, he taught children gymnastics in Petroşani, but he only really learned the profession when he started teaching his first pupils in Oneşti, proving himself to be a remarkable autodidact. After giving up handball and becoming his wife's partner – as a gymnastics trainer she too had little experience worthy of note – Béla Károlyi decided to wager on very young gymnasts, whose age was much younger than had been usual theretofore. They were the girls that the Flame club had already selected, aged nine, ten and eleven, since none of the gymnasts the Károlyis had previously trained had stood out in any competition, which was also the case with the other coaches. The one exception was gymnast Rodica Horgoş. Károlyi mentioned her only once, saying, 'Rodica followed us to Moldavia from the Jiu Valley,'[59] but Horgoş is not included in the 1969–70 Oneşti Lycée Annual,[60] although a local Securitate informer seems to have referred to her, albeit not by name, in 1976 when he said that Marta Károlyi had selected and brought to Oneşti 'a girl with an aptitude for gymnastics.' But according to the informer, 'the girl was withdrawn by her parents after about a year since they couldn't tolerate any longer the harshness that Béla Károlyi practised during training.'[61]

Among the first gymnasts the Károlyis trained were Nadia Comăneci, Mariana Cojanu, Liliana Brănişteanu, Georgeta Gabor, Gabriela Sabadîş, Viorica Dimitriu, Constanţa Dilimoţ, Ana Barcan, Ionela Burlacu and Luminiţa Milea. In time, the make-up of the group changes, with some gymnasts leaving or being dropped by their trainers, while others joined to replace them. Such was the case of Teodora Ungureanu, the gymnast Andrei Kerekes discovered and trained in Reşiţa. Coach George Condovici recalled, 'I was in supervision and guidance at Reşiţa, as they called it at the time, where I met Teodora Ungureanu's mother, who told me that she wanted her daughter to go to Oneşti,' and Condovici wrote a positive report, which was approved by the general secretary of the Federation.[62] As a result, in 1971 Teodora Ungureanu joined Flacăra Oneşti.

Most of the gymnasts of that generation were born between 1960 and 1962, with the eldest, Liliana Brănişteanu, having been born in March 1958. Anca Grigoraş, whom Marcel Duncan discovered in 1965, was born in November 1957, but Grigoraş was not one of the Károlyis' gymnasts, having trained with them for just a few months, before the Montréal Olympics.

For this reason, when Béla Károlyi went to tournaments, there were jokes at his expense, to the effect that he had arrived with the nursery school or mistaken the tournament for a pre-school contest. In any event, it was a somewhat comical sight: the tall, heavily built Károlyi was gargantuan in comparison with the gymnasts, who themselves were made to look tinier than they really were. Other, more experienced, trainers pointed out to him that he ought to select more developed gymnasts, that his pupils were mere children who could not hold up against older competitors, but Károlyi stuck to his own theory with characteristic passion, employing solely theoretical arguments, given that he had yet to achieve any notable success. 'Some continued to criticise me for working with children,' he said, tired of the comments constantly made about him on the subject, 'that I'm playing a kind of badminton in gymnastics. Nobody can relinquish the image of the chubby gymnast who makes the parallel bars quake and leaves craters in the floor mat. I'm convinced that in gymnastics the future belongs to the children. How could it be otherwise? The child understands more easily, catches on immediately. The child has more time available. The child has greater courage.'[63]

Not only were the girls young, but also their bodies were delicate, undeveloped. Alongside the gymnasts of eighteen, twenty, twenty-two, they looked very frail, which sometimes shocked the public. The trend was in any case towards younger and younger competitors, but the change had been happening at a natural rate. From 1952 to 1964, the age of gymnasts at the Olympics was on a downward slope, reaching the youngest ever at the Moscow Olympics of 1984.[64] But the emergence of Nadia and her teammates speeded up the existing trend, leading to heated debates on the subject within the International Gymnastics

Federation and measures to impose an age limit after Nadia won the title at the European Championships in Skien aged just thirteen.

Another innovative training method that Béla Károlyi laid claim to was an emphasis on strengthening physical performance. 'I had taken my knowledge of athletics and transferred everything I knew into gymnastics. I knew that the stronger my kids were, the better athletes they would be,'[65] recounts Károlyi, convinced of the benefits of intensive, even harsh, training. Károlyi's theory was that the winner would be the one who trained the most, without resting and even when suffering from injuries sustained during training. The method gave rise to criticism on the part of experts, but in public this was expressed only in the form of positive comment, such as that to be found in D. Dimitriu's book: 'Of course, it is no secret to anybody that the working methods adopted by the Károlyis were not viewed with sufficient confidence at first. Most of the trainers criticised them for the large volume of work demanded of the pupils they were working with, believing that by proceeding in this way they were exposing their pupils to the danger of injuries.'[66]

Whereas at the beginning of the 1970s, training sessions lasted for two hours in the morning and another three or four hours in the afternoon, as the years passed and the gymnasts went on to greater and greater achievements, the sessions became longer and more intense, lasting seven or eight hours a day, although Béla Károlyi forced them not to admit this, but to claim they trained for just three or four hours a day.[67] 'Nadia Comăneci worked a lot. Between the ages of seven and nine, she worked for two hours, including plenty of time for play. After the age of nine, the quota increased to almost three hours. From the age of twelve she demanded more than was asked of her. Since then, the supplements have often increased,'[68] Károlyi told journalist Ioan Chirilă.

At the same time as the intensity of the training sessions was increasing, in the mid-1970s Béla and Marta began to impose drastic controls on the gymnasts' diet, the aim being to keep them below a certain weight, which they regarded as optimal. In gymnastics body weight is important, especially during the performance of acrobatic elements. During certain exercises, body weight is amplified and can cause failures and accidents. For this reason, it is physicians who are responsible for establishing a gymnast's ideal weight and her diet, whereas trainers aim to keep her below that weight so that she can perform gymnastic exercises more easily.

Károlyi never listened to the physicians, and when he observed that they didn't submit to his demands, he took steps to have them replaced. The informers' reports that reached the desks of the Securitate officers contain countless references to the suffering experienced by the gymnasts due to starvation. This was confirmed after the fall of the Communist régime by those with a direct knowledge of what happened back then, for example, Dr Ioan Drăgan, who was chairman of the Sports Medicine Society and director of the

Sports Medical Institute for a long time, as well as being an agent of the Securitate's Department of Foreign Intelligence, recruited in the late 1950s.[69] In his book, *Witness to 8 Olympics*, Drăgan recalls that he met Nadia and Teodora in the summer of 1975, during the preliminary competition before Montréal, and remembers his unpleasant impression of how they were fed: 'For a few days I eat meals with the gymnasts and with Béla and Marta Károlyi and see what our gymnasts eat (. . .) I feel ashamed to eat like a normal person in front of them, but Béla Károlyi encourages me and then I make bold, although still feeling embarrassed at the "poverty" on the girls' plates.'[70]

The lack of empathy is obvious. Béla Károlyi had a hearty appetite and ate his fill in front of the gymnasts, which amplified their suffering, as confirmed by Nicolae Vieru: 'the girls would be sent away from the table still hungry, despite the very hearty meal he ordered for himself.'[71] Informer 'Nelu' said the same thing in one of his reports, albeit choosing his words differently: 'he is a sadist, because even at meals, in the presence of the starving girls, he stuffs his face without a care.'[72] At the time, Károlyi did not even try to conceal from people outside the team the draconian diet he imposed on his gymnasts. It was not until the beginning of 1976 that he seems to have begun to avoid discussion of the subject. In his book, journalist Ioan Chirilă describes an episode at the restaurant of the 23 August Sports Complex, Bucharest, in February 1976, when after an intensive training session, 'Nadia ate a little meat (. . .) two salad leaves' and half an orange for dessert. 'That's how they eat,' Károlyi told the astounded journalist.[73]

But during the 1976 Olympics the situation grew so bad that most of the members of Romania's team tried to help the gymnasts as best they could, taking care to avoid the intransigent eyes of their trainers. In his memoirs, Dr Drăgan says that at Montréal 'the gymnastics girls are closely supervised by the Károlyis. The only place they didn't enter was the medical office – the gymnasts' working day began and ended in the medical office, for physiotherapeutic treatment of various locomotory injuries – and the staff took that opportunity to give Nadia, Teodora Ungureanu and the other girls fruit and a little chocolate as they underwent their treatment, since the hunger was terrible!'[74] Gymnast Anca Grigoraş did not forget how 'General Dragnea[75] used to come every morning to the room where we did physiotherapy. "Girls, I've come to see how you are doing," he would say, walking past us, he would give us a pat and slip into our hand a little container or two of honey, he would look in your eyes till you stowed it safely and then move on to the next girl.'

Grigoraş remembers that the girls became expert in stealing food without being seen by their trainers, and they were also furtively given food by the fencing team and former champion Lia Manoliu, who was in Montréal as deputy chairman of the Romanian Olympic Committee, who 'every day filled the fridge in the room claiming the food was for her,' as well as by one of the Securitate officers in the

Romanian delegation, Captain Ioan Popescu: 'we loved him for taking great care of us at Montréal, he would have blazing rows with Béla for the way in which he treated the girls. We all had the same uniform, the same clothes and bags. Popescu would come to the training sessions, he would glower at Béla, at intervals he would go out, but each time he would take a different bag with him. And we would find a yoghurt and an apple in the bags.'[76]

Driven by an obsession with controlling the gymnasts' weight, but without following the experts' recommendations, Károlyi started forbidding the gymnasts from going home except one day a week, suspecting them of eating too much when they were unsupervised. Which is what happened, since the girls were obsessed with quelling their hunger and enjoying forbidden foods. What the gymnasts were allowed to eat depended on the trainers' discretion, sometimes even on their passing moods, and since the girls did not eat enough for the physical exertion they put in, they obtained food from other sources. When they did so, they did not make balanced choices. Nadia, for example, particularly liked cheese and chocolate; her mother admitted that she 'had a liking for sweets.'[77] As a result, the trainers' drastic measures to maintain a certain body weight ultimately compromised the aim. If Károlyi had followed the physicians' recommendations on nutrition – a suitable diet both in quantity and quality – then the gymnasts' physical condition would have been much better, and during competitions they would not have been 'exhausted, more worn out than their opponents', 'as pale as convalescents after a long and arduous illness,'[78] as a representative of the N.C.P.E.S. remarked in a report to the Securitate.

Gymnast Georgeta Gabor best expressed the consequences of the trainers' ruthlessness when she said, 'they didn't sympathise with our problems. We had to deprive ourselves of many things, and I ended up developing an obsession with food. Maybe not all my fellow gymnasts thought the same as I did, but I know that at the time we were all outraged and each of us tried to manage as best she could.'[79] Given a life that demanded intense physical effort, drastic dietary restrictions, and the threat of the scales, since Károlyi checked their weight a number of times a day, food did indeed become an obsession for the gymnasts, as Georgeta Gabor said, and bulimia was a natural consequence of this obsession. When they managed to eat outside Marta and Béla Károlyi's supervision, they did so compulsively, wolfing down high-calorie food, which they then had to eliminate in order not to put on weight. The fact that some of the gymnasts in the squad ended up suffering from bulimia is now well known,[80] but at the time it was also brought to the attention of representatives of the Romanian Gymnastics Federation and the Securitate.[81]

Béla Károlyi was well aware of what his gymnasts were going through, but documents from the archives and the testimony of the gymnasts and other trainers show that he made no effort to seek treatment for some of the girls' bulimia or to relieve their sufferings.

Perhaps agent 'Nelu' was right when, in September 1975, he said of Károlyi, 'in general human suffering leaves him cold.'[82] The torture experienced by the gymnasts due to hunger made as little impression on him as it did whenever they fell ill or suffered injuries. Károlyi believed, 'achievements come more easily against a backdrop of exhaustion,'[83] which is why he insisted on excessive exertion, and this invariably also led to injuries. The instances when Nadia and the other gymnasts either trained or competed in major competitions while ill or injured were numerous and have been described by other coaches and by physicians, all of them outraged at Károlyi's callous indifference. Informer 'Gheorghe Daniela' brought to the knowledge of Securitate officer Vasile Miriţă the fact that 'in 1975, before Nadia Comăneci took part in the European Championships, she was suffering from a serious pulmonary virus and the physician ordered her not to make any physical exertion until she recovered, as there would still be plenty of time to train. Despite this, Károlyi Béla forced her to come to training with a high fever and to work at maximum intensity, which aggravated the illness and endangered her health. Only thanks to the competent care of Dr Bora, but still not fully recovered, was Nadia Comăneci able to take part in the London tournament.'[84]

In February 1977, Maria Simionescu reported to Securitate officer Nicolae Ilie, 'before leaving for the O.G., in Bucharest, at the 23 August Gymnasium, Nadia Comăneci, performing a double vault, fell on all fours and hit her forehead, also twisting her left ankle. She competed in the Olympics like that. In the same period, because of a violent episode, Milea Luminiţa walked away from training and went to stay with her relatives in Bucharest.[85] She was brought back and she was promised that it wouldn't happen again. Before the National Champ. in December, however, as she was fatter than was foreseen, she was dropped from the team. Nadia Comăneci told the source that [Béla Károlyi] upbraided her, once again far too severely.'[86]

In September 1976, Dr Iosif Corşatea told the Securitate:

Trainer Béla Károlyi was very put out when the physician, following an examination, took the decision to remove a gymnast from training. Béla Károlyi never followed the physician's instructions. [. . .]

Luminiţa Milea suffered a sprain and was given injections in the tendon, for which reason she had to take three days' rest. Marta Károlyi refused to take this into account and made her do normal training. Noticing that Béla Károlyi is in the habit of hitting the gymnasts on the head when they make a mistake, I pointed this out to him and told him to stop doing it, since it is very damaging and might lead to the loss of intellectual capacity.[87]

To return to one of the reports filed by informer 'Gheorghe Daniela', who provided the Securitate with other relevant details about how the coach saw fit to work with team physicians, we discover that Béla Károlyi 'ignored medical instructions to discontinue any physical effort over various periods, forcing the gymnasts to work when they were ill or injured, disregarding the medical staff, whom he described in front of the pupils and teachers as being insane and ignorant of their profession.'[88] The result, as the informer added, 'due to the way he behaved towards the medical staff, he drove away from the medical office even the nurses the lycée gymnasts greatly needed.'[89]

From such eye-witness accounts we may conclude that the Károlyis believed that when it came to nutrition and medical treatment, only they were competent to decide, not the doctors. If the team doctor believed that a gymnast had to weigh a certain amount, then the coach would lower that amount by a few kilos and alter her diet accordingly, and if the doctor prescribed a period of rest following an injury, the coach would force her to carry on training, convinced that it would toughen her up.

It is not surprising that physicians never remained in the Oneşti gymnastics squad for very long. In a report that is undated, but which seems to have been written at the beginning of 1977, Securitate officer Nicolae Ilie says that in Oneşti 'nobody can have a different opinion, otherwise he is removed—e.g. the case of former managing trainer university lecturer Hidi Iosif from Bucharest, the other two doctors that came and went before the current doctor.'[90] The Oneşti Securitate had also previously reported to Department One in Bucharest that Béla Károlyi did not take any notice of the doctor's instructions and

he proceeded in such a manner that the doctor reproached him for acting against the gymnasts' interests.

Béla Károlyi's reaction was prompt, inasmuch as he managed to have Dr Dragomir Teofil removed and replaced by surgeon Dr Lazăr Gheorghe. The latter provides medical assistance to the girls only with the approval of Béla Károlyi. The municipal Party organ had to intervene so that Dr Lazăr Gheorghe could provide medical assistance to Nadia Comăneci when she had a bicycle accident.

Even previously, he made the other gymnasts work when the doctor ordered a rest. For example, [one gymnast] has a pulmonary virus and a temperature of more than thirty-eight degrees, but was forced to work. He imposed the same thing on Luminiţa Milea, forcing her to remove a plaster cast and work.[91]

At the beginning of 1970 there were no specialist sports doctors in Oneşti. The gymnastics centre initially called doctors from the Gheorghe Gheorghiu-Dej Unified Hospital, but their experience was limited, and Béla Károlyi selected them based on the ones he liked and who would act in his interests. At first, he worked with Dr Teofil Bora, but he had him removed when he proved not to be as malleable as the trainer would have wished. In April 1975 he was replaced by Dr Teofil Dragomir, who became the gymnastics squad's doctor by decision of the Federation. At the beginning of 1976, the Securitate observed that Károlyi liked the doctor and was 'in relations of very good friendship with him (they go hunting together, pay family visits etc.)'[92] But on 25 September 1976 Dragomir too was replaced by Dr Gheorghe Lazăr, again at Károlyi's insistence. Lazăr, who was a surgeon and also a former volleyball player,[93] won Károlyi's trust and became part of his circle of friends precisely because he did not go against the coach's word or administer medical treatment except on his instructions. Under these circumstances, Nicolae Ilie reported, the young gymnasts were cared for only by nurse Ioana Martin, who was 'kept in the squad by the Károlyis because she has no personality and doesn't cause them any problems.'[94]

Károlyi was only willing to work with doctors who proved docile, although perhaps this was not his only criterion. Obsessed with the fact that he was kept under surveillance, he probably suspected that some of them collaborated with the Securitate. And he was perfectly correct in thinking this, of course. For a long time, the Oneşti Securitate had observed that the medical staff at the town hospital had formed 'cliques', and that some doctors 'at various meetings, have conversations that are hostile in nature,'[95] for which reason informers were recruited among them. For example, Dr Iancu Fâciu, who specialised in occupational medicine, had been recruited as long ago as 1953, due to his past Iron Guard sympathies, and was given the code name 'Măgureanu'. Dr Teofil Dragomir, the gymnastics squad physician for more than a year, was also recruited as an informer on 1 November 1977, after 'unreservedly' accepting the proposal of Officer Miriţă, and signed an agreement to operate under the code name 'Ionescu'.[96] Teofil Bora was proposed for recruitment much later, in 1985, but from his file it is not apparent whether the Securitate carried through on this.[97] As he had a 'close link' to Károlyi, surgeon Lazăr Gheorghe was recruited along with Dr Cezar Gămulescu, the Bacău County chief coroner.[98] Lazăr and Gămulescu were both part of Károlyi's close circle and sometimes went hunting or fishing with him.

As a result, it was easy for the Securitate to gather information from within the medical profession, and doctors provided many reports. At first, they wrote reports about each other, since they spent their free time together, fishing, visiting each other, playing bridge. For example, in one report, 'Ionescu' says that 'Măgureanu' is 'surly, very introverted, for which reason few people like him or seek out his company.'[99] Subsequently, they began to provide the Securitate with information about Béla Károlyi. Some of the earliest such reports were written by the surly Dr Fâciu, alias 'Măgureanu', who on 10 October 1974, for example, told the Securitate that ethnic Hungarians Béla and Marta Károlyi and Iosif Hidi were sabotaging their own ethnic Romanian gymnasts, preventing them from qualifying for the upcoming Montréal Olympics. 'To this end, highly subtly and skilfully, citing the need to intensify efforts, they cause the gymnasts, including Nadia Comăneci, to make efforts above and beyond the possible, to the point of physical exhaustion.'[100] He also mentions that the coaches do not follow the recommendations of the 23 August Medical Centre in Bucharest or those of the team doctor.

The report is obviously exaggerated. Fâciu still clung to the xenophobic Iron Guard mindset of his youth, as evidenced by his suspicion of other ethnic groups. It wouldn't be surprising if this report of October 1974 might in fact have sown the seeds of the Securitate's suspicion that the Károlyis were guilty of 'nationalist-chauvinism'. But the report did not distort the truth when it described the Károlyis remarkable resistance to any medical opinion.

Dr Teofil Dragomir, alias 'Ionescu', was more penetrating in his analyses. He came from a wealthy family, was highly sociable – although 'Nelu' claimed in a report about him that he was work-shy[101] – and circumspect in the information he supplied. For example, in September 1976, just after Károlyi dropped him from the team, Dragomir met Lieutenant Colonel Vasile Miriţă, to whom he explained that the first differences between himself and the coach had arisen in March,

when the squad was taken to the Slănic spa resort for recuperation. During this time, Béla Károlyi constantly countermanded the dietary regimen imposed by the physician and Federal manager Hidi Iosif and did not allow the girls to eat and instructed the gymnasts not to make any statements without his knowledge.

In March this year Béla Károlyi gave the gymnasts the categorical instruction that should they require medical assistance they should first inform him and obtain his permission to go to the doctor.

Also in March this year, one gymnast complained to the squad doctor claiming, among other things: 'I'm not staying [. . .], I don't have any new elements in gymnastics, he doesn't even look at me, I'm leaving, I won't stay any longer.'

Béla Károlyi's position towards the gymnast was adopted with the aim of getting rid of her from the team and bringing in Milea Luminiţa.

A month before the Olympics, gymnast Gabor Georgeta fell ill [. . .]. Despite the doctor's recommendation that she rest, trainer Béla Károlyi forced her to go to training, stating in front of the doctor and comrade secretary Intze: 'I gave the order, nobody is allowed to meddle with my squad.'

From personal observations, Károlyi Béla constantly addresses the gymnasts using insulting epithets: 'cows, stupid girls, hens, fat maids, animals . . .'[102]

Dr Gheorghe Lazăr, who replaced Dragomir, was not brave enough to stand up to Károlyi. This suited the coach down to the ground,[103] but it was also well known in Bucharest, whence Carmen Dumitru,[104] the Olympic gymnastics squad doctor, a specialist in sports medicine, was sent to Oneşti for two or three days every month. She examined the gymnasts and wrote individual reports on each, which she sent to the management of the Romanian Gymnastics Federation. Some of the reports also reached Captain Ilie, who wrote on them that they had been provided by source 'Carmen':

Source: 'Carmen'   Top secret
Received by: Cpt. Ilie Nicolae   001643/2
Date: 17.03.1977

Report

Medical-sporting issues regarding gymnast Nadia Comăneci
as of 27 February 1977

In the gymnast's development are to be noted:
1. An unusual capacity for physical exertion, exceptional nervous co-ordination, creative participation.
2. Satisfactory state of health, with some injuries at times of excessive reduction of nourishment.
3. She performed a very large amount of effort to which she adapted well.
4. Her regimen of life has been unusually drastic, even excessive.
5. Her dietary regimen, although recommended by specialists, has not been followed at the instructions of trainer Károlyi and some deviations on the part of the gymnast.
6. Scientific direction of training sessions has been possible to achieve only partially, due to a lack of receptivity on the part of trainer Károlyi.
7. The collaboration of the physician-coach in the process of training Nadia Comăneci has been sporadic, intermittent, being unusually difficult, because of the aforementioned coach, who at the slightest disagreement on the part of a physician has him removed (proven by the series of physicians that have abruptly and noisily ended their collaboration).
8. After the 1976 Olympics the moments of tension between coach and gymnast grew worse and more frequent, culminating in the emergence of inferiority complexes in Nadia, arising from her deliberately placing herself in disadvantageous situations (The Cluj National Championships 15 Dec. 1976, in training in autumn 1976 and winter 1977, the creation of a competition with exaggerated rivalry towards Ungureanu Teodora, invectives against gymnasts and other witnesses) which resulted in the gymnast refusing to work, in her running away from the gym etc.

9. At present Nadia is undergoing a quite difficult physiological phase—puberty—with especial physiological and psychological implications.

10. At the psychological level—as a feature to be emphasised in particular—Nadia is discouraged, she is afraid of the coach, she cannot and will not co-operate with him. She has not given up. She wants to work.

With regard to the above, as well as the tendency for such discords to be amplified, I the undersigned, as a doctor of sports medicine—specialising in gymnastics—who have worked with the gymnastics squad for sixteen years, propose:

1. That a training schedule be established in accordance with Nadia's present capacities.

2. That the technical side of the training be handled by a team of trainers, separately, and that this task be their priority.

3. That the biological side of the training be handled by a team (sports physician, psychologist, biochemist, nurse, masseur) and that they be in close contact with the relevant laboratories and institutes.

4. That the training be carried out in Bucharest, at least until the situation is rectified, because:

a. here the physical medical conditions (laboratories and specialists) can be guaranteed;

b. the moral climate is more favourable and acceptable to the gymnast;

c. the Party leadership will be able to exercise continuous control, since otherwise coach Károlyi will not implement the instructions he receives.

17.iii.1977
(Signature illegible)

Tasks: the source has been instructed to establish the reaction of those who come into contact with the gymnast and in particular that of coach Béla Károlyi

Measures: the material will be exploited at DUI Katona and the 'Corina' case.
Cpt. Ilie Nicolae[105]

A great sportsperson needs a trainer to match. The relationship between them, rather like that between master and disciple, is complex, special, many-layered, ranging from their conduct towards each other to the sincere affection they display. The relationship has to work both ways. The trainer is a protector, an initiator, the one who passes on learning and inspires courage and perseverance, while the pupil has to be receptive, to assimilate learning and act on it, to have complete faith in the trainer's advice. And if both are responsible and dedicated to each other, then the relationship will be long-lasting and cannot help but lead to success.[106]

The younger the pupil, the more the relationship resembles that between parent and child. Besides rigour and discipline, a young child also needs moments of affection to satisfy the need for protection, and such affection must be offered at the right time and in appropriate doses. But the decision belongs to the trainer and, depending on his own intellectual and moral make-up, he or she will be able to strike a balance between the various ways of demanding an effort from the pupil. Ultimately, the trainer's goal, like that of any mentor, is to transform the sportsperson into a winner, and he or she is responsible for the pupils' fate in this sense. The mentor projects himself or herself onto the disciple; the disciple is a product of the mentor. The trainer sees in the champion sportsperson what he or she would have liked to be, but perhaps was not able to become.

Therefore, what pedagogic style should the trainer adopt? There can be no doubt that there exists a power relation between trainer and pupil. The former makes demands and gives orders, while the latter complies and obeys. To achieve genuine sporting success, training must go beyond ordinary limits, it must achieve the greatest intensity, and the pupil must be urged to strive harder and harder. The genuinely gifted sportspeople are those that do not need to be pressured to achieve, because in them there is already an urge for perfection. The truly remarkable trainers are those who understand that before being cast into competition with others, the sportsperson has to be trained to compete with herself in order to overcome her limits. Ultimately, if she does not succeed in surpassing herself, she will not be victorious in any of the competitions in which she takes part.

Those who knew Nadia Comăneci in the gym described her as quiet, often inscrutable, withdrawn within herself, highly rational. She concentrated feverishly, worked enthusiastically, and practised exercises until she considered she had mastered them perfectly. But she also had obvious intuition. She was often the one who discovered a unique new element as an unexpected solution to finalise an exercise. Nadia had a remarkable gift, and the Oneşti trainers said she was so talented that even if you explained an element badly to her, she would execute it well. Fate must have looked kindly on Béla Károlyi for him to meet such a gymnast, and there can be no doubt that he quickly knew how valuable she was and what rôle she would play in his intrepid plan. Károlyi was also to prove his genius, since he was a challenging trainer who knew he had to encourage her to surpass herself both mentally and physically.

A pupil who wants to become a champion must undoubtedly lead a painful life, and it is also the trainer who lays down the limits of her toil and suffering, sometimes employing punishment as a means of instruction. But corporal punishment and persecution will prevent the pupil from being open and honest towards her mentor. 'As a trainer, if you're soft, you won't achieve the best,' Mariana Cojanu, one of the first gymnasts trained by the Károlyis told us: 'Harshness is necessary, but when you end up beating a child, slapping her or banging her head against the door, it's too much.'[107] In other words, in training his pupil for arduous, major competitions, the trainer must wield authority, but not resort to violence. Authority is based on respect and trust, feelings which in their turn give rise to mutual loyalty, whereas the intent to dominate the sportsperson through violence gives rise to fear.

Unfortunately, in this respect, the Károlyis went too far. Of course, they were not the only Romanian coaches who had a 'heavy hand', who resorted to beatings as a means of correction. There were coaches who used corporal punishment as a means of achieving success in other sports, not only in gymnastics. Their justification was the theory that results could not be obtained if training was relaxed, and that punishment was more effective than reward. But in gymnastics, because the results achieved by the Olympic squad were so exceptional, there were trainers from other clubs who took inspiration from the 'Károlyi method', since the abuse practised by Marta and Béla Károlyi was no secret: 'Very many trainers around the country have been working assiduously for years, maybe with fewer training facilities than the national team, and they always start from the initial selection. In their desire to achieve good results quickly, they copy what they believe to be the "key" to this success—beatings',[108] said Maria Simionescu in January 1980 in a report that refers only to this subject. The times were different and society allowed the deeply rooted practice of corporally punishing children, as typified by the saying, 'beating is heaven sent'. Traditionally, children were raised to be submissive, obedient to their parents, as a means of nipping in the bud any tendency to rebel.

Unlike in other situations, it was as if the life led by the young gymnasts alongside coaches Béla and Marta Károlyi was too harsh, too brutal. The two trainers were intolerant to the point of violence; they showed their inflexibility in not taking into account the gymnasts but only their own ambitions. Perhaps it was also significant that Béla Károlyi's own relationship with his parents had been almost devoid of affection, which seems to have become the standard by which he judged everything else in his adult life. 'My father never came to see me compete. He was not interested in any type of athletics. My mother spent her afternoons preparing the family meal, and she would never have come to watch me or cheer my efforts. Because of that, I have tried very hard during most of my coaching career to give that kind of parental petting and attention to the kids. I have always wanted them to have what I needed and never got.'[109]

Károlyi is obviously exaggerating for effect, since it was precisely 'parental attention' that was lacking in his relationship with the gymnasts he trained in Oneşti. The Károlyis' method was based on absolute discipline and on intensive training. They set little store by any affective relationship, since it would have been utterly at odds with the drastic rules whereby they demanded submission. Repeated blows, verbal violence and insults, starvation, excessive and aberrant control of medical care, and the inhuman demand to train and compete even when injured caused deep wounds in the psyches of the gymnasts, who distanced themselves from him, regarding him as cruel, and certainly not as a protective father figure. Only when there was a need to manipulate them did he tell the young gymnasts he cared about them.

True, unlike Marta, whose aloofness towards the gymnasts evinced obvious hostility, Béla could sometimes be affectionate. Mariana Cojanu recalls, 'Marta did not show her feelings, but he did. Before competitions he had an inspiring attitude, when he wasn't behaving nastily. And when we went on training camps, to the mountains or the seaside, he would sometimes organise games. Marta would also take part, but reluctantly.'[110] Unlike his wife, Béla Károlyi seemed to be ruled by two opposing personalities, since the despotic coach could abruptly become amiable, sociable, a man ready to entertain the gymnasts with jokes and various games. Sometimes, after a few glasses of wine, he would play the guitar with great pleasure, which made him seem even more cordial and friendly. But such moments were quickly forgotten once the door to the gym closed behind them all and training recommenced.

Yes, Béla was not like Marta, but there was something that united them: the boundless ambition to make a name for themselves as the architects of great champions, which fuelled their pride to the point of rejecting any other opinion, their intransigent refusal to listen to the doctors, and their scorn for other specialists in general, as if all that was required to mould an exceptional gymnast was their hands alone. They had to have complete control, and other than them, nobody else mattered.

Most of the gymnasts that the Károlyis trained in the 1970s have preserved to this day oppressive memories from the time, and we shall cite further examples of their abusive behaviour below. But when it comes to Nadia Comăneci, we are able to invoke only the secret documents from the Securitate archives that record such abuse. Nadia has avoided talking about the subject, and when she has done so, she has opted to be conciliatory, sometimes even laudatory, when referring to Béla and Marta Károlyi: 'I do not know the details of his coaching relationship with other gymnasts, but I do know that he is a good person. He motivated me as well as the rest of our team by the sheer force of his personality, which could be incredibly fun and animated when we tried our best or disappointed and sombre when we failed him and ourselves,'[111] claims Nadia, who considers that Béla Károlyi was never harsh with her, but only very strict. But in the interviews he has given to the press in recent years, Géza Pozsár claims that all the gymnasts with whom Béla Károlyi worked with in Romania suffered abuse, with the exception of Nadia, who was the only one who 'escaped without a beating.'[112] But was this really the case?

4

'TU SEI MIGLIORA DI TUTTE'

On the evening of 9 September 1977, Ştefania Comăneci's telephone rang at 21:51 hours. At the other end of the line was famous pop singer Benone Sinulescu, calling from Bucharest:

B[enone Sinulescu]. = Hello, Mrs Comăneci?

C[orina's mother]. = Yes.

B. = My respects.

C. = Mr. Benone?

B. = Benone calling.

C. = Yes, Mr Benone, what's wrong?

B. = It's about Nadia, I'm afraid, something's happened . . . don't be frightened, she doesn't want to go to Mexico.

The secret police were bugging the telephone at 'Corina's' family home in Oneşti at the time, and the long conversation between her mother and Benone Sinulescu, whose transcript in the Securitate files covers ten pages, provides numerous details about an incident that quickly reached the ears of a number of people in Bucharest, thanks to Benone Sinulescu and his friends. The singer was to have another telephone conversation with Nadia's mother on the same subject a few days later, likewise recorded and transcribed by the Securitate.

At the beginning of September, a number of gymnasts, accompanied by their coaches and a delegation from the N.C.P.E.S., left for Mexico to take part in a demonstration, having been invited by José López Portillo, the country's president. Six performances were held in Mexico City, Tijuana, Guadalajara and Monterrey, before large and appreciative crowds. The team then travelled to

Caracas, Venezuela, at the invitation of President Andrés Pérez, where they gave a further three performances. As she was ill, Teodora Ungureanu did not make the trip with her team mates Nadia Comăneci, Marilena Neacşu, Cristina Itu, Emilia Eberle, Gabi Gheorghiu, Marilena Vădărău and Ofelia Iosub.

However, on 9 September, the day before the team's departure, Nadia had left the hotel of the 23 August National Sports Centre in Bucharest without telling anybody. She had wandered through the city without knowing where she was going, although she did have a plan: she wanted to go home, to get as far away from Béla Károlyi and the gym as she could. First of all, she went to the main railway station, to find out the time of the next train to Oneşti, and then she slowly walked in the direction of the city centre.

When it was discovered that Nadia had left the hotel and nobody knew where she was, the alarm was raised: the Militia, the Securitate, top officials of the Romanian Communist Party, and representatives of the Romanian Gymnastics Federation and the National Council of Physical Education and Sport desperately searched for her all over the city, and unable to find her, they began to fear that she might have been kidnapped. 'I ran away, first I went to the station, then somehow I ended up walking to Victory Avenue. I went to a food shop and bought some cheese, because I couldn't stand being hungry any longer,' Nadia was to confess a few months later to some journalists from Bucharest who visited her at home.[1] The image of the Olympic champion wandering lost down Victory Avenue biting a chunk of cheese made a strong impression. The image wasn't one of self-sacrifice, as this would have implied a willingness to go without, but rather one of suffering.

Nadia managed to find out Benone Sinulescu's telephone number and he took a taxi to collect her. She had first tried to telephone singer Irina Loghin, but hadn't got an answer. Sinulescu had visitors when she called. 'I had a full house already, I mean, like they say, I'm a really big singer,' he boasted to Ştefania Comăneci, a few hours later, after her daughter left. In his book, Nicolae Vieru describes the same episode as follows: 'In the months after the Olympics, Béla's relationship with his lycée colleagues and with Nadia began to deteriorate. Twenty-four hours before the departure to Mexico, Nadia vanished from the National Sports Centre in Bucharest. There followed an alert at the highest level, and police and Securitate forces were mobilised to find her, also with the involvement of Cornel Burtică of the C.C. of the R.C.P. From the Federation, Adrian Stoica took part, because I was away on holiday. Finally, at the suggestion of the chief of the Oneşti militia, Nadia was found at the family home of Benone Sinulescu. He'd given a concert in Oneşti two weeks before and visited Nadia's mother.'[2] To make sure in future that they would quickly find out about Nadia Comăneci's unauthorised visits, as well as to monitor any information about her that might be communicated to others, the Securitate bugged the telephones of Benone Sinulescu and Ion Cernea, the husband of Irina Loghin, who was a former member of the national Greco-Roman wrestling squad, and requested that Unit T transcribe 'all telephone calls connected to Nadia Comăneci'.[3]

According to the Securitate transcription of the phone conversation, Benone Sinulescu described to Ştefania Comăneci Nadia's mood, assuring her that he had provided her daughter with every moral support:

> the poor girl, in a way she was frightened, because she was sick of Károlyi (. . .) I barely managed to get it out of her that she wanted to leave on the ten-thirty train. And I'm like, let me explain it to her, Nadia, you're valuable (. . .), you're valuable to the country, you're a national treasure, how can you think you can't go there and represent your country. (. . .) She thought that if they went to Mexico tomorrow, she'd stay behind and in the meantime, she'd rest and be able to eat. (. . .) Károlyi spoke to her nastily, said you'll be eating nothing but fresh air, but just one mouthful, because two will make you fat. (. . .) She'd made her mind up to take the train, wanted to see her mama. I want to go to mama, she says, I want to go to mama. She wanted to take a train somewhere and then change trains, she wanted to leave, to vanish. (. . .) It's very strange that a major came here, he asked me whether Nadia was here and he wanted her to go with him. Nadia had hidden, she was frightened. Mister, I said, hang on a minute, she's here, I said it quietly so as not to frighten her, because her heart was hammering. She'd made a kind of plan, if they came for her, 'I'm resting, I want to eat', she's just a child, how can she not eat.[4]

The second conversation between Benone Sinulescu and Ştefania Comăneci took place on the evening of 11 September. The singer returned to the subject previously discussed – 'Mrs Comăneci, it's me, Benone, let me tell you some more about what conclusions I came to about Nadia that evening when she came to me' – laying out the reasons which, in his opinion, explained Nadia's feelings of despondency: her coach's strictness ('She didn't want to [go to Mexico] because Károlyi had insulted her, he insults them, he won't let them eat anything but air') and the intensity of the training ('She said she was sick of the eight hours it lasts or who knows how long and of him treating her so roughly'):

> Mr Benone = (. . .) The poor girl, her heart was thumping when so many of them came after her. First a policeman came and she was so scared—she says, I want to go home to Mama, I can't take any more, and I want to go home to Mama, I swear. (. . .) She said that that man, Károlyi, said you can leave and after that she left the training centre. (. . .) She'd made a plan—by the 25th [of September] when we have to go back, I'll eat as much as I like and I'll have the time off, because I haven't had any holiday, I was sorry for her. [. . .] They were expecting some bigwigs there, at the training centre, they

were people with clout, not just anybody. [. . .] As you can imagine, the whole building found out, but what was terrible for me was the fact that so many policemen came to my door and everybody must have been like, what's he said, what's he done.

Ob[jective's] M[other]. = Had she calmed down when she left?

Mr Benone = She'd calmed down, she had a good feed at my house.

Ob. M. = The next day she'd put on a couple of kilos.

Mr. Benone = Never mind, she'll lose them again.

Ob. M. = They feed her nothing but air.

Mr. Benone = I pitied her, I swear.

Ob. M. = The things that child has been through.[5]

During the meal, Nadia complained to Benone Sinulescu and his guests about how she couldn't stand Béla Károlyi any more and wanted to give up gymnastics. She said she wanted to be an ordinary child, to go on holiday, to sleep in sometimes, to eat, because being Nadia Comăneci 'was very hard'.

Obviously, she got none of her wishes. After they collected her from Benone Sinulescu's, the Militia officers took her to the hotel at the sports complex, where everybody breathed a sigh of relief, and the delegation left the next day on the international tour. Béla Károlyi held firm to the threat he had made before they left, when he said that it would be hard for her in Mexico: 'you'll have nothing but air to eat. But you'll see even air makes you fat.'[6] Nadia confessed to the journalists who visited her in December, '"in Mexico, our teacher kept us on a diet. I was the only one he forced not to eat for three days, and because of that I put on weight one day and lose it the next." "You really didn't eat anything?" "Nothing, for three days I didn't eat."'[7]

The relationship between Béla Károlyi and Nadia Comăneci had become so tense by 1977 that no matter how significant the concessions they made to each other, they could no longer work together harmoniously. Quite simply, they could no longer stand each other. Whenever Nadia heard somebody mention his name, her face would fall and she would abruptly become gloomy, while Károlyi continued to persecute her like a strict guardian, often undermining her spirits, telling her it was time for her to give up gymnastics as she was no longer capable of top-level performance internationally. The conflict was defused for a time when Nadia Comăneci and Teodora Ungureanu were transferred from Oneşti to Bucharest in December 1977. Károlyi's two best gymnasts were thus taken away from him.

Years later, Károlyi was only partially to admit he was to blame. In his memoir he claimed to have made a mistake in not allowing the gymnasts to have a private life. He said he was wrong to have made excessive demands on them during training, but in and of itself his conduct would not have led to him being separated from the top gymnasts of the Olympic squad if political decision makers in Bucharest had not intervened and if Nicolae Vieru in particular had not been driven by envy and personal pride.

> I was fierce. I set up stricter rules. No family trips to endorse and promote this and that, no interruptions or disturbances in the gym, no flying to weekend government functions. I cut out everything I could. When I heard of a family party organised for foreign reporters (who always brought gifts for the kids), I stopped the party. I cleaned house and sent the kids to sleep.
>
> I was a policeman, which I should not have had to be. And I wasn't the least bit successful. The only thing I did was create a situation that gave the Federation the opportunity to step in and be the sugar daddy. I was the mean ogre, and they were the nice people who wanted the kids to enjoy their status and privileges. I was so intent on re-establishing the norm that I didn't even see it coming. (. . .)
>
> After I had refused to allow certain delegations into the gym, the Federation had told Ceauşescu and he had gotten extremely angry. He had made an off-hand remark that he wanted the team near him, that he wanted to watch and control them. (. . .)
>
> Nicolae Vieru had finally gotten his revenge. I may have been awarded a higher honour than him in 1976, but now he had my team and there was nothing I could do to get them back. The Federation had managed finally to kick us for their own frustrations. There was nothing to do but say goodbye in our hearts to Nadia and the rest. They had never called us; their families had never contacted us. It was a bitter situation. Most of the kids had grown up in our home more than in their own. They were part of our family and now they were gone. They didn't even say goodbye.[8]

As far as Nadia is concerned, in her account of this tense episode she has spoken with typical reserve and discretion about her former trainer, describing him with undeserved respect. She recalls, 'I began to have disagreements and misunderstandings with Béla by mid-1977. Just little things at first. I was trying to stretch my wings and grow up, and like any teenager, I had the desire and need to be on my own.'[9] Likewise, she believes:

> In 1977, I didn't comprehend the extent of the danger around me; mostly, I was just trying to sort out what to do next. I felt as if my gymnastics career was coming to an end and that I should move to Bucharest and start taking college classes so I could figure out what I wanted to study. Like any teen, I felt confused and restless and ready for the next stage of my life. I'd worked so hard to be a great gymnast, but suddenly it didn't feel like enough. My lack of desire to achieve and compete was so unlike me. I had always been focused on gymnastics and success. And I still believed in the value of

sportsmanship, which included professionalism, respect for my teammates and coach, and holding myself to the highest standards. But I was exhausted from the competitions and media attention, and I just couldn't do what my coaches demanded or my gymnastics and my team required.

From what I understood at the time, the Gymnastics Federation decided that the best thing was to grant a 'trial separation' between my coaches and me for a loosely defined period of time. The official reason for my split with the Károlyis was so that they could once again work as talent scouts and create a new training centre in the village (sic) of Deva. I left for Bucharest, where I was told that I'd train and compete for a few more years but would have the opportunity to go to school. Meanwhile, Béla, who says he was never told that I was being moved, arrived one day for our regular training sessions to find me gone. He was devastated.[10]

The Securitate also drew its own conclusions, seemingly the least biased of all. In a report on Nadia Comăneci dated 21 August 1978, more than half a year after the crisis was defused, General Dumitru Tăbăcaru, at the time head of Department One, summarised the matter as follows: 'the conflictual situation was generated both by the trainers, given they did not adapt the training methods and manner of behaviour towards the triple Olympic champion to the conditions arising in her personal, family and sporting life, and by the gymnast, who no longer accepted the effort of training and the methods imposed by the trainers in question. To this situation also contributed other interested persons, particularly her mother.'[11]

Given the complexity of the surveillance carried out on Béla and Marta Károlyi, each phase in this evolving conflict was known to the Securitate in precise detail. We have no doubt that some of the agents' reports were subjective, which obliges us to make use of additional sources in order to discover the truth. But such sources are numerous and chronologically speaking, they include information from as early as the first half of the 1970s.

For example, informer 'Gheorghe Daniela', also a trainer, stresses, 'in the 1972–1974 period the couple Károlyi Béla and Károlyi Marta worked in tandem with the other teachers in the gym, which made it possible to know how they behaved both towards the gymnasts and towards their colleagues.' The informer is correct in this observation, since at the time training sessions entailed multiple groups practising at the same time, with pairs of trainers working with their gymnasts on one apparatus for a given stretch of time before moving on to the other apparatus, in rotation. At one point, probably in 1974, as 'Gheorghe Daniela' maintains, Béla Károlyi decided he didn't want to work alongside the other trainers any more and altered his schedule so that only his and Marta's pupils would be in the gym. More likely than not, they didn't want the other coaches to see the new moves they were experimenting with, since the trainers copied each other, as Béla Károlyi himself claimed when he made a complaint about Nicolae Moscu for doing just that.

Up until 1974, the other coaches were able to observe the Károlyis' behaviour towards their gymnasts, as the Securitate agent herself states in her report: 'Towards the gymnasts he showed a terrorising attitude and a brutality that completely contravene pedagogical principles, for which he received a series of complaints on the part of the parents, made both to the school and to the Ministry of Education. The girls were sometimes beaten till their noses bled or punished by being made to do physical exercises to the point of exhaustion.'[12] The informer continued to list other details already known to the reader – Károlyi made the gymnasts train 'in situations of illness or injury', he treated the doctors and lycée teachers with contempt, calling them 'insane and ignorant of the profession', he insulted the other trainers, uttering 'indecent expressions even in front of the pupils' – and her report is not merely highly detailed, but also hostile. It may be said that all her informer's reports were written with the persistent aim of casting aspersions upon the Károlyis.

Nadia's mother complained to Maria Simionescu about the fact that 'her daughter is made to work until she can't take any more and the palms of her hands are bleeding and if it goes on like this she will give her to another trainer,' but the gymnast denied it when Mili Simionescu asked her whether it was true.[13] Gheorghe Braşoveanu, the head of the lycée, revealed the explanation for Nadia's denials. He told Lieutenant Colonel Miriţă that even though they were suffering, the girls refused to admit that the Károlyis were victimising them because it would have meant them being dropped from the team: 'In the 1974–1975 period, the parents of a number of gymnasts [. . .] complained in writing to the Romanian Gymnastics Federation and verbally to the heads of the lycée that their daughters were being beaten and insulted by Béla Károlyi using the words, "cow, stupid, foolish, fat, mucky" and so that this state of affairs wouldn't become known, he threatened them with giving them lower marks for behaviour and dropping them from the squad.'[14]

Despite complaints on the part of the gymnasts' parents, there was no improvement in the atmosphere. For fear of the repercussions, the gymnasts dared only to complain to their parents and to send an anonymous letter to Nicolae Ceauşescu, which changed nothing. But the Securitate continued to conduct surveillance, gathering piece after piece of evidence. Informers were instructed to write reports not only about the Oneşti centre, but also about the manner in which trips abroad unfolded and about international tournaments. These reports were analysed by Department One Domestic Intelligence and summaries were passed up the hierarchy to the head of the Securitate and thence to members of the Central Committee.

One such document drew on a report written immediately after the Romanian squad returned from Montréal. At the 1976 Olympic Games, the secret police planted five undercover officers in Romania's official delegation: Colonel Vergiliu Ionescu, head of Unit 0650 (Independent Foreign Trade Service), Colonel Vasile Pralea, retired, Major Gheorghe Untaru of Department Four Military Counterintelligence, Major Nicolae Ilie of Department One Domestic Intelligence, and Captain Ioan Popescu, who had previously worked in the Passports Department and who in 1976 was hired by the National Council for Physical Education and Sport. These agents enjoyed the assistance and protection of Marin Dragnea, head of the N.C.P.E.S. and the Romanian Olympic Committee, and the support of informers within the delegation (referees, coaches, doctors), while also relying on the highly useful work done by some of the Romanian journalists attending the games, who had also been recruited by the Securitate. The only report to have been identified in the archives that refers to the leg of the tour in Canada was written by Captain Ioan Popescu on 6 August 1976. It reviews a number of 'aspects' he deemed noteworthy:

REPORT
on certain aspects within the gymnastics squad taking part in
the Montréal Olympic Games in the period 6-27 July 1976

The women's gymnastics squad made up of eight gymnasts, three trainers, a pianist and a medic arrived in Canada to take part in the Olympic Games on 6 July 1976.

According to the understanding between the Romanian Gymnastics Federation and the Canadian federation, training sessions and preparation were held jointly. The squad was quartered at a hotel outside Montréal along with the Canadian squad, enjoying optimal accommodation and training conditions. This joint stage of preparation unfolded in the period 6-11 July 1976. In the period 11-26 July 1976 the women's gymnastics squad was quartered in the Olympic village.

Over the period of the stay in Montréal, I have to report the following exceptional aspects regarding the gymnastics squad:

— the squad arrived in Canada from the home country with three injured gymnasts: Comăneci Nadia, Ungureanu Nadia and Constantin Mariana, team coach Károlyi Béla having concealed this; they were given the appropriate treatment for recuperation until the beginning of the competition, thereby managing to attend the competition in a state of good health;

— originally the N.C.P.E.S. leadership established that the team coaches should be Károlyi Béla and Albu Atanasia. Subsequently, interventions were made at the Passports Department by the leadership of the N.C.P.E.S., particularly comrade secretary Emil Ghibu, so that trainer Károlyi Marta, the wife of Károlyi Béla, could also make the trip, it being made plain that she would stay with the gymnasts, she would look after them, and that her attendance at the competition was necessary. The proposal was made at the insistence of Marta Károlyi's husband, since the regulations of the International Gymnastics Federation forbid male coaches to stand with the girls on the competition podium, and so that coach Albu Atanasia would therefore not be given the opportunity to appear on the podium as co-author of any successes. [. . .]

— an especial problem within the gymnastics squad is the inappropriate behaviour of Károlyi Béla towards the members of the squad consisting in swearwords, insults and even the administering of beatings, creating an atmosphere of terror within the squad. Thus, none of the members of the squad are allowed to talk to persons outside the squad, to answer questions put to them except in the presence of the coach, or to say they are injured, any exception being punished with a beating;

— prevailing upon the fact that the gymnasts have to have an appropriate weight for the competition, he imposes on them an incorrect diet (as confirmed by team medic, Dumitru Carmen) according to his own opinion, without taking account of the recommendations of those authorised. This has led to injuries and participation in the competition of a number of gymnasts [. . .] in a condition below their potential;

— he nonetheless tacitly accepts that all the team members should be given supplementary food secretly, both in the home country and abroad, but in the event that a gymnast is unsuccessful he is still prepared to admit that this method was the reason;

— taking advantage of the emergence in Romanian gymnastics of innate talents Comăneci Nadia, Ungureanu Teodora and the work of other trainers (Simionescu Maria, Albu Antanasia, Bibire Mariana etc.), he had made the current gymnastics squad his personal property, demonstrating by any means that he is the sole author of the current success, seeking to advertise himself more widely abroad;

— in interviews given to various foreign newspapers and magazines, he has sought to explain that the success of Romanian gymnastics is the result of his own labour and discovery of special training methods;

— he claims for himself every success of Romanian gymnastics and the discovery of Nadia Comăneci. In reality Nadia Comăneci was discovered and trained by Petre Duncan, who has legally emigrated to Israel, and for a period of time she worked with Maria Simionescu, the federal trainer at the N.C.P.E.S.;

— although he granted interviews to foreign newspapers and magazines very readily, thereby trying to advertise himself, the reporter for the 'Sport' broadcast Octavian Vintilă, present in Montréal, had to badger Károlyi Béla for three days before he could realise an interview with Nadia Comăneci and Teodora Ungureanu for listeners of the broadcast in the home country;

— likewise, during the interview he gave to Canadian television, he said nothing about the excellent conditions created in the home country to obtain these results;

— after achieving success, Nadia Comăneci received presents and a lot of letters from admirers in various countries. A part of the presents she received was appropriated by Károlyi Béla, but Nadia Comăneci's correspondence is of interest to him only if it contains various souvenirs;

— after the prize-giving ceremony, the members of the squad personally asked me that the sums due to them as prize money should be handed to each of them on the basis of a signature, since trainer Károlyi Béla is in the habit of sharing out to them the moneys owing to them as he sees fit and at a greatly reduced sum, which is what happened during the tournament effectuated by the gymnastics team in Canada, the U.S.A. and F.R.G. in March 1976;

— during his stay in Canada Károlyi Béla made contact with Stăncilaş Ionică, a former Romanian citizen domiciled in Oradea, a legal emigrant to the U.S.A. in 1971, currently a physical education teacher at a school in the city of Cleveland. He met with him a number of times in the evening, outside the Olympic village, without informing the heads of the delegation. According to coach Albu Atanasia he knew Săncilaş Ionică in the home country and also met with him in March 1976 during a tournament in the U.S.A. Stăncilaş Ionică communicated to Károlyi Béla that in September-October 1976 he is going to open a gymnastics school in Cleveland relying on funding received from the American government, requesting his support by means of his presence in the U.S.A. for 1-2 months; (. . .)

— on 24 July 1976, the secretary general of the Romanian Gymnastics Federation Vieru Nicolae, who was present at the Olympic Games as a judge in the men's gymnastics competition, asked the permission of the comrade chairman of the N.C.P.E.S., lieutenant general Marin Dragnea, for the men's and women's gymnastics squad to take an excursion outside Montréal to a training centre of the Canadian Gymnastics Federation, for rest and relaxation. Receiving the necessary approval, the squad, made up of 24 persons, travelled to this centre, around 120 km from Montréal. Arriving there, I observed that it was not a training centre of the Canadian federation, but a camp site, privately owned by a Canadian citizen by the name of Robinson, an ethnic Hungarian. This camp site consisted of wooden huts, where children aged from eight to sixteen were staying, they were of Jewish origin, emigrants to Canada from the R.S.R., P.P.R., C.S.R., U.S.S.R., H.P.U., sent there by their parents for their summer holidays. Ascertaining this fact, I immediately told comrade Vieru that we were leaving, since it was inadmissible that the Romanian team, an Olympic vice-champion, headed by Nadia Comăneci, should come to this camp site and stay in such conditions till the next day. He did not agree to our leaving, claiming 'the people here have spent 1,500 dollars to provide us with this accommodation.' Asking him what these expenses represented, since the food and accommodation were very poor, Vieru Nicolae was startled, saying that he regretted entrusting the so-called expenses to the hosts. That evening we stayed in two completely inappropriate huts, sleeping on bunkbeds, and some people slept on mattresses on the floor. The next day I once more told Vieru Nicolae that we had to leave, since that trip to such a place had no justification, but he refused. Furthermore, during the afternoon, with the help of Károlyi Béla and Bădulescu Mircea, they organised a demonstration of the gymnastics team in a hut converted into a gymnasium and with make-shift apparatuses. All the children at the campsite were present and some of their parents, who lived in the surrounding area. Checking up on this situation I discovered from Liţă Emilia that the visit to this campsite was at the proposal of Bădulescu Mircea, the gymnastics coach at the Dinamo sports club, in Montréal as a judge in the men's competition, who entered into relations with a Canadian citizen, secretary at the judge's table, and who with her husband was employed as a teacher at this camp site during the summer holiday.

I estimate that this visit constituted a means of advertising the campsite of citizen Robinson and that for this he received the sum of 1,500 dollars, which was divided between Vieru Nicolae, Bădulescu Mircea and Károlyi Béla. Likewise, during this visit, Károlyi Béla instructed the girls to be friendly towards the children at the campsite, to give autographs and let themselves be photographed with them, which was at odds with his previous behaviour in such situations.

After returning to the home country I was informed that Vieru Nicolae and Károlyi Béla deposited at the Romanian Foreign Commerce Bank sums in dollars that were approximately equal to the moneys they were paid for the trip, which would have meant they made no expenditure or purchases, a fact at odds with the large number of items they bought and brought back to the home country.

Specialist Officer III
Cpt. Popescu Ioan

6 August 1976[15]

As for the subpar conditions at 'Camp Robinson' reported by Captain Ioan Popescu, the gymnasts themselves did not particularly notice them. They were just glad to be in the country and share moments of recreation with other children. They even thought that their stay at the campsite was at the request of the Securitate, so that they would be better protected, as Georgeta Gabor has said in a recent interview: 'After the Olympic Games, we were yearning to have a few days off, we didn't have holidays . . . to give you an idea, after the games we were supposed to stay in Canada a little longer, but we were brought back to Romania immediately, because it was rumoured that there was a risk that Nadia would remain abroad, but I don't know whether the rumours were true. They even took us to a place controlled by the Securitate, which was like a campsite, a nice place with a forest, but they didn't even let us stay there long. One morning they made us pack our bags, they left visit a supermarket for precisely two hours, and then we went to the airport and then home.'[16]

After the team's glorious homecoming from Montréal, the Securitate intensified its surveillance measures, with Nadia becoming a top priority. The secret police drew up a family tree, identifying her parents' relatives in order to examine their backgrounds, the family telephone was bugged, and friends of the family were also thoroughly checked. In the archive documents can even be found a diabolical plan on the part of the Bacău Securitate, mooted in November 1977, to monitor the relationship between Nadia Comăneci and Teodora Ungureanu: the Onești Securitate was ordered to recruit informers not only among the lycée's teaching staff, but also among the gymnasts' classmates, who were minors, aged just sixteen: 'categorise and study the girls in the class in question, and select from among them those appropriate for inclusion in the network.'[17] While Béla and Marta Károlyi were under surveillance because they were deemed disloyal to Romania and abusive in their relationship with the gymnasts they trained, Nadia Comăneci and her parents were monitored to protect them from Károlyi's actions and to prevent any reactions on their part that might have damaged the image of the Communist régime.[18]

In the second half of 1976 Nadia Comăneci and Teodora Ungureanu began to make it more and more obvious that they wished to break off their relationship with their coaches. But Károlyi made no concessions to them as a means of defusing the situation. At the seaside, where he had obtained official permission to take the gymnasts on a short holiday, Károlyi tried to stamp out what 'Nelu' claims he viewed as a 'star-like attitude' and subjected the girls to the usual spartan schedule: 'Very little food and limited physical training. (. . .) Gabor refused to follow this regimen and was kicked out of the team. The source found on the pupil a notebook in which she complained about the highly strict working regimen and in which she described the insulting words that Béla Károlyi addressed to the gymnasts before the Olympics, as well as the unkept promise to give them two weeks off after Montréal.'[19]

Because she had been keeping a diary recording his abuses and encouraged the other girls to insubordination, Károlyi had Georgeta Gabor removed from the squad. He did so in a dishonourable manner, claiming not only that she 'instigated the girls not to work' – making Nadia and Teodora give written statements in support of this[20] – but also that 'she admired those who left the country' and 'provided no moral guarantees regarding her behaviour abroad,'[21] which was hard to imagine in a fifteen-year-old who had spent almost all her life in a gym. For this reason, Gabor was placed in the situation of having to discuss the matter with a Militia officer[22] but the Securitate knew the truth, as is apparent from a report filed by the Bacău County Inspectorate on 22 October 1976: 'from investigations it transpired that the real reason was the discovery by Béla Károlyi of notebooks in which Gabor wrote down her impressions of daily training sessions and the position of the two trainers.'[23]

Nadia kept a similar diary. According to those who have seen it, she recorded not only her moments of satisfaction as a gymnast, but also her moods of despondency, the bitterness she often felt during training sessions. Informer 'Dan', about whom all we know is that he was a trainer at Oneşti, stated in June 1977:

Nadia's mother read to me from Nadia's personal diary where she made daily notes about all her personal feelings and in particular she read to me everything that happened to the girls when we went to Spain. From what her mother read to me from Nadia's diary the behaviour of coach Károlyi becomes apparent, the insults such as: you're cows, stupid, badly brought up by your families, you're good for nothing. Furthermore, he beat them when a training session didn't meet its target, saying they were to blame for the failure of the training. From the entries in this diary it is also plain that he didn't give them their full meal allocation, on the grounds that they had to lose weight and it was a shame to waste food on such good-for-nothings.[24]

Experiencing training as a great burden, Nadia began to miss sessions and to ignore the dietary restrictions, in which she was encouraged by her mother. Ştefania Comăneci complained about Béla Károlyi to all the heads of the N.C.P.E.S. and the Federation, even sending a letter to Nicolae Ceauşescu himself. The head of state decided to grant her an audience, news of which struck both the local Party organisation and Károlyi with the force of an earthquake. All of them mobilised to steer the situation in their favour, since if Nadia's mother got a chance to complain directly to Ceauşescu, the consequence would have been devastating to them. Béla Károlyi's telephone conversations, intercepted by the Securitate, reveal the stress he was under on 18 September 1976:

Com.[rade] I[ntze Ioan]: I think that Nadia's mother wants to cause us difficulties. She sent a letter to comrade Ceauşescu and asked to have an audience, she says she has something to tell him connected with the girl. What she wants to tell him I don't know. I just got a phone call from comrade Năstase in which he told me to tell her to be there on Monday morning at eight.

Ob.[jective Béla Károlyi]: What are you saying, who knows what she's got into her head, I told you that woman's capable of something stupid.

Com. I: I said maybe you know something, or maybe you'll find out from the girl what it's all about.

Ob. I'll find out. I had a training session with them today and if possible, I'll talk to the girl myself, see what she says.

Com. I: Yes, talk to her and see, at least tell her not to let her say anything stupid there. Tell me her phone number because I know she changed it and I have to inform her.

Immediately after this 'Nela' [Ştefania Comăneci] the mother of the ob. was telephoned and com. I. informed her that on Monday morning she had to attend an audience with com. Ceauşescu.

Com. I: Mrs Comăneci, did you send a letter asking to be given an audience at the C.C. with comrade Ceauşescu?

Mother of ob.: Yes, it's true.

Com. I: I received a telephone call from comrade Năstase, the secretary at the chancellery of comrade Ceauşescu, and he says I should inform you that you have to be there on Monday morning at eight, to go to entrance C, to have your identity card on you, because anyway I think they inform comrade Năstase there at the duty office of entrance C.[25]

To the relief of the persons concerned, the audience did not take place. Béla Károlyi immediately went to see Ştefania Comăneci, promising her he would meet all her demands, as a means of persuading her not to go to Bucharest. The next day, Géza Pozsár and Károlyi talked on the phone, a call which was intercepted by the Securitate, and 'objective Katona' told agent 'Nelu' that he wanted to go hunting, but abandoned the plan because he had to handle a delicate situation, which 'when you hear it, it'll give you chills':

Ob. I go there and Intze says: comrade Comăneci, on Monday at eight she requested an audience with comrade . . . and the man's secretary goes and phones him to say he'll receive her on Monday at eight.

Dn.: Listen carefully, Béla! Let me fill you in: I told you about her that time, so you wouldn't be discovered! I told you some things, take care! You know what she wants to attack you with . . . to do with health!

Ob.: Because that time I didn't let her go to . . .

Dn.: No, no! In general, to do with eating, she doesn't want to sacrifice her child, that sort of thing . . .

Ob.: She's cunning.

Dn.: What can be done about it now?

Ob.: I went to see her to shut her up.

Dn. And what does she say?

Ob. She said what she wanted to say. (. . .)

Dn.: Be careful, Béla! If she starts talking nonsense there, be careful, Béla! Do you know what she told me? That she knows even when you beat her and she also knows when you took her to Bucharest, for training, when she was ill, before the Olympics, and that you want to look after your own interests . . . that's how she put it. How can you defend yourself? Why don't you phone the (federation), somebody to make her think twice about who she talks to.

Ob.: She's not going any more.

Dn.: Unbelievable, Béla. That's really something else . . .

Ob.: That's right.

Dn. You ought to (vulgarities) those girls and get younger kids instead. That way you don't have any trouble, any headaches.

Ob. I said the same thing to my missus, the same thing.

Dn.: With the little'uns it's a pleasure. What do you need this for? Wasn't this the last thing you needed?

Ob. It was the last thing I needed (swears).

Dn. Unbelievable, that mother of hers . . . a good thing she's not going.

Ob.: You're right there!

Dn. And what was the price of her silence?

Ob. Think about it with a cool head . . . any problem still has to be resolved hierarchically, from the top down.

Dn.: A good thing you're in the clear . . . goodbye.[26]

After this tactical victory, Károlyi went on the offensive, sick of seeing his authority so easily undermined. On 28 September 1976, he went to the Romanian Gymnastics Federation and complained about Nadia's behaviour. According to Károlyi, she had put on 'a lot of weight, for which reason she is no longer in the necessary shape to be able to perform gymnastics exercises. He also claimed that she does not stay at the hostel reserved for the gymnastics team, also due to the influence of her mother.'[27] The attempts at mediation and official steps to defuse the conflict were unsuccessful, even though initial discussions seemed encouraging. Arriving from Bucharest, on 1–2 October, the delegation headed by General Marin Dragnea, the chairman of the N.C.P.E.S., tried to reassure the parents. Aurel Stoian, alias 'Relu', who accompanied Dragnea to Oneşti, explained in a report, 'in the presence of the Party organs they talked to the parents of the Olympic gymnasts whence it transpired that the sticking points between a part of them and Károlyi Béla had been resolved, including those between him and Nadia Comăneci's parents.'[28] The Securitate utilised informers such as Maria Simionescu and Nicolae Vieru to organise unannounced inspections in Oneşti, the concern being that 'Béla Károlyi has an obvious interest in discrediting Nadia Comăneci and forcing her to withdraw from the sport. In this respect, we have information from which it is plain that he insults her in a vulgar way, constantly, stating that to him the Comăneci chapter is closed.'[29] Valerian Ghineţ and other local Party leaders were also implicated in various operations to influence Károlyi, which, by late October, are supposed to have led to 'a change in the behaviour of the man in question.'[30]

Even if there the relationship between Károlyi and Nadia was no longer close and training sessions had suffered as a result, Nadia still displayed her talent at events worldwide and frequently made the front pages of newspapers. Her first public appearance after the Montréal Games was in France, where, in Antibes on 22–23 October, and Chamalières on 24 October, she took part in two show competitions that thrilled French audiences. On 5–7 November 1976, Nadia Comăneci, Mariana Constantin, Anca Grigoraş and Marilena Neacşu dominated the Balkan Championships in Thessaloniki, where Nadia won all the gold medals in the finals on the apparatuses, and Romania took the team title. Nadia was awarded two tens (in the floor exercise and vault event). In Japan, where she took part in the Kuniki Cup (Nagoya, 13–14 November), Nadia was again awarded two tens (uneven parallel bars and floor exercise), a 9.95 (vault) and a 9.80 (beam). Teodora Ungureanu won silver, and Mariana Constantin bronze, in a tie with Elena Davydova. In November, a number of Károlyi's gymnasts also competed in another two demonstrations in Hamburg. The final major competition of the year was to take place in Cluj: the finals of the National Championship and the Romania Cup.

A number of criticisms of Nadia found their way into the communist-controlled Romanian press, it is true. For example, in an interview Károyli claimed that in Antibes, Nadia had made a timid start, 'making a mistake on the parallel bars, obviously uncomfortable because of the spotlights,'[31] while Constantin Macovei, the correspondent for *Sportul*, reported from Thessaloniki that she had not made full use of her potential and was 'still not on top form,'[32] having made two errors on the beam and the parallel bars. As if making an insinuation, in the 2 November and 6 November issues of *Sportul*, there were even extensive pieces about the factors on which success depends in sport, with an emphasis on intensive physical training. 'Labour, the determining factor of sporting success,' claimed the October article, quoting Nicolae Ceauşescu as saying, 'in our conception of how to shape the new man we place the emphasis on work, as a determining factor of the whole of social activity,' while Károlyi was presented as the best example, in a piece titled 'The exigency of the trainer'.[33]

After the tournaments in Japan and the German Federal Republic, the conflict – or the 'inappropriate atmosphere', as Securitate documents referred to the state of affairs within the Olympic team – grew to even greater proportions. Captain Nicolae Ilie of Department One described the sequence of events and the actions of all those involved in a report written at the end of the year. A few days later, on 30 December 1976, the report reached the desks of the Party's upper echelon, but in a redacted form, which omitted any details that might reveal the identities of the officers and informers involved in the surveillance operation:

Department One   Top secret
162/IN

Report

After the competitions in Japan and the G.F.R., arriving in Oneşti, Nadia Comăneci began to miss training sessions, she refused to stay in the hotel, which led to her being dropped from the Milan tournament, as she was out of shape. This situation was ascertained by the heads of the N.C.P.E.S., which decided that she not make the trip to Milan, lest she be compromised.

Not even after this did she return to the hotel, continuing to live at home, during which time she did not make a sustained effort in training sessions, which caused her to put on weight.

On 11 December, Nadia Comăneci and Teodora Ungureanu were invited by the mayor of Gheorghe Gheorghiu-Dej municipality to take part in the opening of a literary club, to which comrade Radulian was also invited.[34]

Without informing coach Béla Károlyi, Nadia Comăneci went to this event, which led to a negative reaction on his part. Knowing this, Nadia stopped attending training sessions, not wishing to see him, although he, along with the general secretary of the R. Gymnastics F., tried to talk to her about it. Finally, secretary general Vieru Nicolae, who travelled to Oneşti to collect Nadia with a view to her making a trip to London, went to her house and on Monday, 13 December, they arrived in Bucharest. On 14 December, Nadia, together with secretary general Vieru Nicolae made the trip to London.[35]

On 15 December, coach Bél Károlyi arrived in Bucharest to voice his dissatisfaction at not having made the trip to London, but to do so he went not to the heads of the N.C.P.E.S. but to the C.C. of the R.C.P. (apparently, he went to comrade Ilie Verdeţ, as he himself has stated), after which he travelled to Cluj-Napoca to accompany the Oneşti lycée team. Here he had some unprincipled discussions with the heads of the R.G.F.

From Cluj-Napoca, coach Béla Károlyi insistently demanded that after her arrival from London Nadia Comăneci come to the competition,[36] threatening that otherwise he would suspend her from the sport, repeatedly making clear that he had the approval of Party organs to do so.

Returning from London to Bucharest, Nadia Comăneci asked secretary general Vieru Nicolae to allow her not to take part in the National Gymnastics Championships in Clujj-Napoca, since she was not feeling well and, in any event, did not want to see coach Béla Károlyi.

Secretary general Vieru N., observing that Nadia was in a mental and physical state unsuited to her taking part in the competition, decided with the approval of the heads of the N.C.P.E.S. that she should return to Oneşti.

At the insistence of Béla Károlyi, and also on the intervention of the instructor of the C.C. of the R.C.P. – (Gheorghe) Vlădica – the N.C.P.E.S. leadership decided that Nadia Comăneci should make the trip to Cluj-Napoca.

Thus, on the morning of 17 December 1976, it was decided that Nadia should return to Bucharest to be collected by comrade Verdeţ and after that to travel to Cluj-Napoca. In Bucharest they waited until the last plane to Cluj-Napoca for her to be met, which wasn't possible, since comrade Verdeţ was busy.

On the plane and on her arrival in Cluj-Napoca, Nadia Comăneci did not want to see coach Béla Károlyi, saying that she was afraid of him.

Before they met there were a number of discussions with both Nadia and Béla in order for the latter to show a conciliatory attitude towards Nadia, which did not in fact happen, since when he met her he adopted a harsh attitude towards Nadia, scheduling a test for her the next morning.

At the test, Nadia partially passed on two apparatuses (floor and beam), without attaining her own standard.

Before the official competition, Béla Károlyi was called before the Federal Office, assembled to examine whether or not Nadia would take part in the competition as part of the team on two apparatuses, since she had the approval of the higher organs of the Party. Finally, the Federal Office agreed that Nadia should take part in the competition, and at the end of the competition she should give a small demonstration along with her team mates.

Béla Károlyi was aware of Nadia's sporting form, but insisted that she take part so that she would lose, wagering not on compromising her as a gymnast, but on forcing her to work and to accept the conditions he imposed.

Nadia Comăneci's poor form is due to the following factors:

—After the Olympics the gymnast no longer wanted to work in conditions of total submission to her coach. In the sense that she no longer accepted being insulted in front of her older or younger team mates (medal-winning cow). She no longer accepted having her parents insulted. She no longer accepted the dietary regimen imposed by the coach, such that she resorted either to procuring foodstuffs (whether recommended or unrecommended) by herself or running away home, sometimes not turning up for training—this because she did not have the courage to face up to the coach if she made mistakes.

— The gymnast put on weight due to an unsupervised diet. The weight gain and loss is visible from one day to the next.

— Coach Béla treats Nadia in the same way as he did two to three years ago, ignoring the fact that she is aware that she is famous, that she is no longer twelve-thirteen years old, that biological changes have also occurred and she has become an adolescent, that she should not be treated in the same way and with the same methods.

— The gymnast is influenced by the conduct and attitudes of her family, who know about the way in which Nadia is treated and how her family are spoken of by coaches Marta and Béla Károlyi. (. . .) In any event, Nadia's mother has not given up on the idea of being granted an audience with comrade Ilie Verdeţ to discuss the above-mentioned issues, including the fact that the Károlyis together received much more after the Olympics than Nadia did.

— Coach Béla insisted that Nadia be in Cluj-Napoca so that from there he could take her to training camp in Băile Felix and after that to another training camp in Baia Mare, this in order to wrest her away from the influence of her parents, as well as other persons, wagering on returning her to the sporting condition that made her name. After Baia Mare he intends to find another place for training, after a short stay in Oneşti.

— Some gymnastics specialists believe that Béla Károlyi has acted well in giving her that lesson to Nadia Comăneci in Cluj-Napoca, and as regards removing her from under the influence of her family, they believe that this is urgently required.

— Nadia Comăneci is an intelligent adolescent, but lacking in education in every respect. Vain and full of herself, ambitious and determined, easily influenced. Towards her coach she is docile, she doesn't defy him, she doesn't have the courage to confront him. (. . .)

Cpt. Ilie Nicolae[37]

Finally, Nadia returned to the squad, and Károlyi managed to alleviate the tense mood, which endangered the training programme. At the end of December, the Károlyis and the gymnasts spent the holidays together at the Lily Pad Hotel in Băile Felix. Trainer Gheorghe Mănăilă, choreographer Geza Pozsár, pianist Carol Stabişevschi, Dr Gheorghe Lazăr, nurse Ioana Martin, and others joined them. Covert recordings made by the Securitate and, in particular, the highly detailed report written by Pozsár on 6 January 1977 show that the atmosphere over the holidays was quite relaxed, with only light training sessions and recreational trips for the girls. The diet, however, with the exception of festive meals, was as strict as ever. Pozsár reported: 'Nadia seems to want to lose weight, but she suffers from the hunger, since she asks me for apples. She really has lost weight. I think that she will work better.' 'Nelu', alias Pozsár, says that Károlyi behaved 'nicely' towards the gymnasts and adds that the coach went hunting a number of times with the county first secretary: 'We were supervised most of the time by others, since Béla was away hunting most of the time. (. . .) The girls can't much stand one trainer in particular, because he keeps a watch on them and snitches on them. Even less so another staff member, since she eats like a threshing machine in front of them, but screams at them if they eat more than they should. She smokes during meals with them, which doesn't seem to me to be either healthy or to set a pedagogic example.'[38]

On 5 January 1977, the team moved to the Borşa spa resort, where over the course of ten days they had a more intensive training schedule. Obviously, Maramureş County Securitate was there, too, planting bugs in the hotel rooms. After reproducing in his report all the information obtained by means of surveillance techniques – various conversations, the training schedule, and so on – the head of the county Securitate concluded, 'the mood within the squad is generally good.'[39]

The mood was not at all good, however. In February 1977, Nadia once more began to defy the schedule imposed by Béla Károlyi, and the conflict reignited, this time with greater ferocity. The dreaded coach, whom no régime official had dared to confront, given his successes, was pitted against an opponent aged just fifteen, but who was more than his match, since it would have been all but impossible to kick the world's top sportsperson off the national and Olympic squad.

During this period, Nadia's fame grew as she received further international recognition. She was awarded the Gold Medal of the City of Athens, and French sports paper *L'Équipe* gave her the Per Ludos Fraternitas trophy. The BBC and major press agencies on both sides of the Iron Curtain – Internationale Sport-Korrespondenz, based in Stuttgart, the Associated Press, Agence France-Presse, United Press International, and TASS, the Soviet news agency – declared her sportsperson of the year 1976 after carrying out polls. In Bucharest, an exhibition of photographs was held at the Salle Dalles to celebrate the Montréal victories of the 'doe of the Trotuş River', where visitors could admire a wonderful plaster statue of a soaring Nadia as she dismounted from the uneven parallel bars, atop a metre-high plinth. The work was made by sculptor Céline Emilian and was later cast in bronze and reproduced in marble. Nadia continued to appear in the Romanian press even when she wasn't taking part in international tournaments. Sometimes propagandistic articles were published, featuring photographs of Nadia alongside Nicolae and Elena Ceauşescu.

Károlyi therefore had to manage a highly complex situation, which must have caused him great frustration. One informer, who had been at university with him and whom he met again in January 1977, recorded Károlyi's remarks to the effect that he felt himself to be the victim of a deep injustice: 'Béla Károlyi was of the opinion that too much was given to Nadia in the beginning and she doesn't yet know how to gauge these honours correctly since she is still a child. That Nadia now looks on him as if he were her servant and not the teacher who launched her and helped her to become what she is.'[40] He complained to all his acquaintances, including representatives of the N.C.P.E.S., the R.G.F., and the Party that he could no longer work in gymnastics – 'the Comăneci chapter is over' – because she didn't listen to him any more. She no longer weighed forty-one kilos, the weight he deemed appropriate, but forty-seven or forty-eight. She was no longer in ideal sporting condition, she no longer had potential, she no longer respected him. In fact, said Károlyi, Nadia was too easily manipulated by her parents – particularly her mother – as well as by other persons from Bucharest, a reference to Nicolae Vieru, but without directly naming him.

Ştefania Comăneci was indeed at the centre of the conflict. Károlyi accused her of being motivated by personal gain rather than parental concern. There can be no doubt that she did frequently complain that Nadia's successes were not adequately remunerated and that she pursued various material advantages, which, however, she regarded as rightful recompense for her daughter's efforts. The Securitate noted her intention to seek audiences with members of the Central Committee to make such demands, discovering in advance what she wished to obtain. She also thought it was unjust that she wasn't allowed to visit the West with Nadia during tournaments, although it wasn't the Securitate or the Party that put a stop to this, but rather Béla Károlyi, who was convinced that during competitions the gymnasts had to be isolated from their families in order for them to be able to focus. The conflict between Ştefania and Béla simmered constantly and each made grave accusations against the other. Ştefania believed that thanks to her talent Nadia had made Károlyi the world's most famous gymnastics coach, while Károlyi claimed that it was the opposite, that thanks to his talent Nadia had become the world's top sportsperson.

Both Ştefania Comăneci and Béla Károlyi sought justice from the Party. During a telephone conversation with Nicolae Vieru on 3 December 1976, Károlyi said, 'the only one that can do it is the Party organ (. . .) to take care of those damned parents of hers, although of the two I'm telling you her father doesn't cause us any trouble.'[41] Obviously, Károlyi relied on the support of Ilie Verdeţ, and he continued to receive it, but in Oneşti the Party wasn't on his side. Maybe this was because Bacău County Securitate had a lot of clout with the local Party organisation. What was more, the secret police had all the latest information about Károyli, given that they had authorised the surveillance measures.

For example, on 8 February 1977, an important Party meeting was held in Oneşti at the sports lycée, chaired by Gheorghe Roşu, the first secretary of the county organisation. Besides other local leaders, lycée teachers also took part, as well as N.C.P.E.S. representatives from both Bucharest and Bacău, in other words, everybody who would have been able to bring charges against Károlyi and order the taking of disciplinary measures against him. One of the people taking part, a Securitate informer with the code name 'Simion', wrote a report that reached Captain Nicolae Ilie, from which it transpires that Károlyi was accused of not working with the other trainers, of not taking part in Party meetings and sessions of the teaching board, of not allowing other gymnasts and trainers access to the gym, and of chaining and padlocking the gymnastics equipment so that nobody else could use it. These and the other accusations listed by 'Simion' go on for two whole pages, some of them directly relating to Nadia Comăneci.[42]

Károlyi defended himself by going on the attack. He attacked now the local Party organisation, claiming it didn't genuinely support him, now Nadia's mother, accusing her of 'inciting' people against him. Finally, both sides were content to draw their own conclusions: the county first secretary believed Károlyi had 'understood the shortcomings in his work', while Károlyi 'said he didn't understand anything of what had been discussed, maintaining his own positions.' But a decision that might have affected his career seemed to be taking shape, since Nicolae Ilie noted in his documents that Miron Olteanu, the general secretary of the N.C.P.E.S. had confessed: 'he intends to propose to the relevant organs that after the European Gymnastics Championships in May this year Károlyi Béla should be removed from the Olympic squad, this because in every discussion with him lately he has threatened that if he is not allowed to work the way he wants then he will leave the Olympic team.'

Even if the pressures on him didn't let up, Károlyi remained as intransigent as ever. A few days later, on 17 February, in Bucharest he met Maria Login, the then vice chairman of the R.G.F. When he informed her of his gymnasts' progress, he emphasised the ambition and determination of Teodora Ungureanu, said Marinela Neacşu came second in terms of sporting worth, after Teodora, and Gabi Gheorghiu third. He said Emilia Eberle came last, and didn't consider her to be a great talent, although she was already capable of competing in major international competitions. According to Károlyi, at the European Championships to be held in a few months, he would select, in order of talent, Ungureanu, Neacşu, and Gheorghiu. Login, who was part of the Securitate's network of informers and signed under the code name 'Elena', reported:

I asked him why he had omitted Nadia from the selection list for the European Championships. He answered that since Nadia had missed training and was facing serious problems with her weight, which had increased, he didn't see her as being capable of making up for lost time or achieving a high level of training.

[. . .] That because of Nadia, of her family's interference in the training schedule, of her mother's repeated urging her not to submit to the rigours of the training process, they had ended up in a state of conflict both with her parents [. . .] that he went to Nadia's home and talked to her mother and father, that he humiliated himself so badly it made him sick. But despite his efforts, things weren't resolved, and the mother's assurances lasted not even a day.

He added that in his opinion behind Nadia's mother there are other people who urge her to take this recalcitrant attitude. That these people are determined to destroy them, their work and their achievements.[43]

Károlyi felt he was surrounded by enemies – Nadia's mother, the head of the sports lycée, the mayor of Oneşti, the leadership of the R.G.F., the first secretary of Bacău County, the Securitate – and he confessed to Maria Login that he would like to leave the town, asking for her help to do so. He said that there was nothing to keep him in Oneşti, that his electricity and telephone had been cut off, that his daughter had been turned away from nursery school, that the Mercury shop[44] refused to take his orders, and that while he was away in Băile Felix and Borşa, the Securitate had searched his home. 'They turned everything upside down, even went through the underwear drawers, and in some of the rooms, they'd pulled up sections of the parquet and then glued it back down,'[45] 'Elena' reports him as saying and also mentions that in particular he blamed Valerian Ghineţ, the local mayor and head of the Oneşti Party organisation.

All these actions, said Károlyi, are not unknown to comrade Ghineţ, who approves and even encourages them. Concluding that his home had been searched, he went to comrade Ghineţ, offering him the keys to his flat so a thorough search could be made, after which he should be left alone. He mentioned that he asked comrade Ghineţ why he should be under surveillance. Better they monitor the countless foreigners who come to the town, who go to Nadia's house to applaud her and give her all kinds of presents. Frenchmen, Italians and Japanese had made such visits, but nobody did anything about it.[46]

Probably what he told agent 'Elena' he was also in the habit of telling Ilie Verdeţ when he had the chance, but adding further accusations, as he was convinced that all those embroiled in the conflict had a share of the blame, apart from Marta and himself. His obstinacy, combined with the authoritarian decisions he made regarding the Olympic squad, meant that 1977 was to be the most controversial year in the entire time he trained Nadia Comăneci and the other gymnasts. In the Securitate files there is not a single month in which reports, transcripts of intercepted telephone calls and various other documents illustrating the escalating conflict were not filed.

In the spring of 1977, during intensive training for the European Championships in Prague, tensions peaked, once more putting the leadership of the N.C.P.E.S. and Romanian Gymnastics Federation on the alert. In March, during training in Cluj, Teodora Ungureanu ran away, boarding a train to Oneşti. The authorities were alerted, the Securitate intercepted her at the station in Tîrgu Mureş, and she was escorted to Bucharest. 'The gymnast gave as the reason for leaving the fact that she could no longer stand working with coach Béla Károlyi,' who 'persecutes her baselessly,'[47] the Securitate officers stated in their report. The N.C.P.E.S. leadership took the decision to send the gymnast back to Cluj, and on 20 April they send a representative of the Federation to attend the gymnasts' daily training sessions. In April and May 1977, while on a preparatory tour of Spain, Securitate officer Ioan Popescu, embedded in the Romanian delegation, reported that Béla Károlyi 'showed inappropriate conduct towards Nadia Comăneci and Teodora Ungureanu consisting in swearwords, insults, even beating them, because their weight was unsuitable for the competition,'[48] while Ilie Istrate, a N.C.P.E.S. instructor and Securitate operational connection,[49] reported, 'the girls were found weeping in their rooms because of hunger.'[50]

In the latter half of 1977, the Károlyis repeatedly found themselves in the situation where Nadia refused to carry on training with them. They continued to insult her, and in this respect Béla had a rare gift, being able to concoct and wield insults in a way that severely wounded the children's dignity. As if Károlyi's customary 'medal-winning cow' insult wasn't enough, during the October 1977 U.S. tour started telling people, 'all Nadia Comăneci is good for now is the circus and cabaret.'[51] Nadia was emotionally scarred by such remarks, they injured her self-esteem, and she ended up believing she her career had reached the end of the line. Károlyi also claimed, 'she doesn't want to lose weight because she's convinced she'll never be what she was'[52] and that she intended to retire from sport after the world cup to be held in France in 1978.[53]

Nadia's training was in any event deficient, and by the second half of the year, her weight had risen to fifty-one kilos. Securitate covert recordings from November 1977 reveal that typically she didn't turn up for training, claiming that Vieru had forbidden her to do so until the R.G.F. and N.C.P.E.S. took a decision about her. When she did attend training sessions, she would avoid practising alongside her team mates because she was 'embarrassed to work out in front of the girls.'[54]

In September, during the Mexico tournament, Károlyi confessed to Géza Pozsár that his and Marta's situation had become so complicated that 'now would be the moment to remain', meaning not to return to Romania, and that were it not for their child, whom they had to leave behind whenever they made foreign trips, they would do so the first chance they got. Pozsár immediately informed the Securitate. In Greece, a few days later, Károlyi claimed that in Bucharest there was increasing talk of his being replaced as coach for the Olympic team, telling 'Nelu' that when he and Marta arrived back in Romania 'it will be over for us'.[55] For his part, Pozsár urged Károlyi to take steps to move from Oneşti to Deva, where he could start all over again.

The scenario Károlyi feared did indeed play out, but the outcome was not as gloomy as he expected. Although there were plenty of arguments to expel the Károlyis from the sport, they were allowed to continue as coaches and were transferred to General School No. 7 in Deva, where they trained juniors preparing to take part in international competitions, while Nadia and Teodora, who no longer wished to work with them, were moved to Bucharest. From internal documents of the Federal Bureau of the Romanian Gymnastics Federation, it can be seen that punitive measures and public condemnation of the Károlyis were purposely avoided, as was typical in a Communist régime, nor were the gymnasts punished for having defied their trainers. In other words, the Federation aimed for a 'tactful approach to the measures that might be taken.'[56]

While the authorities were indulgent when it came to Béla and Marta Károlyi, they decided to take special measures to make sure that Nadia Comăneci would return to exceptional form in the shortest possible time. The World Championships were to take place in less than a year, in October 1978, and Nicolae and Elena Ceauşescu, who had been monitoring the conflict as it unfolded via secret Securitate reports, still had great expectations of Romania's best gymnast. At the beginning of every major international competition in which Nadia was taking part, Elena Ceauşescu was in the habit of demanding that she win 'two or three gold medals',[57] which translated into an official Party directive for the Communist leaders in charge of Romanian sport. Ştefania Comăneci was confident that the N.C.P.E.S. and R.G.F. decision would be in her daughter's favour. 'They're not going to give her up, because they're getting an earful from elsewhere,' she said on 16 November 1977,[58] and Maria Login, the vice-chairwoman of the R.G.F. made it quite clear at the time that efforts had to be made to support the gymnast not because she was Nadia Comăneci, but because 'she is, nonetheless, a Hero of Socialist Labour and mustn't be defamed'[59]

Just a few weeks later, the N.C.P.E.S. and R.G.F. ruled that Nadia Comăneci and Teodora Ungureanu should be transferred to Bucharest, and they arrived at the beginning of December. The official documents state that the main objective was 'special preparation of Nadia Comăneci with a view to successful participation in the World Championships in France from 22 to 29 Oct. 1978'.[60] The documents in question made no mention of the Károlyis. In order to achieve this objective, the Romanian Gymnastics Federation assembled in Bucharest a special training and medical team.

Nadia and Teodora left behind their years in Oneşti and were never to return there to train as gymnasts. In his memoir, Béla Károlyi recounts that Nicolae Vieru and other R.G.F. officials arrived in Oneşti one Saturday afternoon to collect Nadia and Teodora, going to their homes and waiting while they packed their bags. He found out about their departure only on Sunday morning, when they did not show up for training. He was surprised, indignant, saddened, because he had not had a chance to say goodbye and would have wished more than anything to hug them one last time. Vieru, the man who had been awarded a lesser medal than Károlyi's, had finally got his revenge: Vieru now 'had my kids', as Károlyi put it. Károlyi was unable to make any kind of protest, since Nicolae Ceauşescu himself had approved the decision, and 'my supporter, Ilie Verdeţ, was out of the country.'[61]

A more unvarnished description of the Károlyis' reaction at the time can be found in the reports of dedicated secret police informer Géza Pozsár, the Olympic team's choreographer. According to Pozsár, the Károlyis did indeed blame Nicolae Vieru, but they also blamed Nicolae and Elena Ceauşescu, and in the weeks that followed they painted themselves as the victims of a wider conspiracy: 'Béla claims that it was not his own attitude or behaviour towards Nadia that caused the Federation to take such a measure, but the fact that, since both he and the source are of Hungarian origin, the state is trying to strike at us and remove us from élite gymnastics.' 'Nelu' also mentioned that Marta cited the same reasons, claiming that ethnic Hungarians were deprived of their rights in Romania and 'a spanner ought to be thrown in Nadia's works at the World Championships'. Károlyi also told Pozsár that there was nothing for them in Oneşti any more and that they 'ought to leave'.[62]

One of the most telling Securitate documents in this respect was drawn up on 3 December 1977, on the eve of Nadia and Teodora's departure from Oneşti. It is not an informer's report, but the transcript of a discussion between the two gymnasts and two Romanian journalists who had come to Oneşti to write a story. Since the interview took place in the Comăneci family flat, which was bugged by the Securitate, the whole conversation was recorded. Both Nadia and Teodora recounted to the reporters a number of tense moments in their relationship with Béla Károlyi, and the dialogue speaks volumes:

Ministry of the Interior   Top secret
Bacău County Inspectorate   copy no. 1
Municip. Gh. Gheorghiu Dej Securitate
No. 00676/3.12.1977

REPORT

At the objective's[63] two comrades from the . . . (sic) newspaper are visiting to interview her. Teodora Ungureanu is also in the room.

C. = objective, tell me about your misfortunes, because I've heard you had a lot of misfortunes with the comrade professor. Is it true that story about the bracelet? Tell me what happened with the bracelet.

Ob. = American television[64] came to film us and at training only Mr Pozsár was there, the teacher always leaves when they're going to film, he doesn't want to appear, but after that . . .

T. = does he take the money?

C. = does he take the money, Teodora?

T. = yes, he takes the money.

C. = has it ever happened to you?

T. = I heard that he received I don't know how much from the C.E.C. [State

Savings Bank] after filming

C. = have you ever received anything for filming?

Ob. = no.

C. = how so?

Ob. = there was filming and at the end Flip[65] gave me a gold bracelet and said that only four people have that bracelet.

C. = Flip said that?

Ob. = yes, and Flip gave me the bracelet, then the next day the teacher came and he says that you did something stupid again and I say, mister teacher, what did I do? And he says, why did you take it, don't you know you're not allowed to, he says that the militia found out and were up in arms, I asked the militia and they said they didn't know anything about it. Before that he said go home and bring me that bracelet and I left it there, but I can't remember who I gave it to, but Luminița [Milea] said she saw Mrs Károlyi wearing it on her wrist.[66]

C. = amazing. Objective, tell us what happened in Germany at that sauna.

Ob. = they told us to take a sauna, we sat in there till we felt ill, I couldn't take it that long.

C. = how long?

Ob. = over an hour.

C. = is it true that once he locked you in the sauna and some lads had to come to unlock the door?

Ob. = no, we complained, but he didn't lock us in the sauna, but we complained that we couldn't stay in there any more. We did about six sittings, he would take us out, he would put us in cold water and then back in the sauna.

C. = when did this conflict between you and Béla actually begin? I know that after the European Championships you said you were going to give it up.

Ob. = no, that was after the Olympics.

C. = so, the first time was after the Olympics.

Ob. = yes.

C. = and what did you say to him then, did you really say you were giving it up or what started it all?

Ob. = it started before the America cup, after that I didn't want to do it any more and he kept putting it in writing that he wouldn't do anything else to us.

C. = you mean he undertook it in writing? To whom? Where did he send it, to the federation?

Ob. = yes, to Mr Vieru, Mrs Simionescu and the comrade general [Marin Dragnea].

C. = he made more than one undertaking in writing?

Ob. = more than once, about three times.

C. = and what did he write?

Ob. = that he wouldn't insult us any more.

C. = how exactly did he insult you?

Ob. = he said nasty words about us.

C. = can you tell me one of the words he said, for example, was there a particular word he used to say about you? What did he call you?

Ob. = in all kinds of ways, I wrote it down in that notebook, he'd called me fat, she told her, you'd think you were a . . . (she refers to 'T'), go on, say what he called you.

T. = you'd think I was a widow with fifteen kids, a drunken goose.

Ob. = he used to say flying lumps of lard.

C. = did he call you stupid?

T. = imbeciles.

Ob. = sad imbecility.

C. = but tell me something, ob., did you get any gifts abroad, gifts you received?

Ob. = we didn't get gifts, but I don't know when we received gifts, I didn't really keep track of what gifts he received, but in any case he received them, but in any case he said that for 'T' too, but I didn't see what exactly.

C. = Teodora told me about the necklace, they were all engraved, they had monograms, but she has an ordinary necklace, very ugly. I doubt that's really the one.

Ob. = I don't know anything about that.

C. = but did anything like that ever happen to you, for him to take one of those gifts you received?

Ob. = no.

C. = I know that there was a story about a cheque in your name for about ten thousand dollars, something of the sort, and in the end, the cheque disappeared, or what happened?

Ob. = some journalists called us and one of them said that for my achievements and for everything I'd done for the country, he said they'd give me that cheque for ten thousand dollars and two hundred and twenty-eight dollars. Before that Mr Vieru told me, you'll be receiving a cheque and mind you don't accept it, because you're not a professional.

C. = and you turned it down?

Ob. = no, Mr Vieru said to give it to him.

C. = and did you give it to Vieru.[67]

Ob. = yes, and he said he'd give me two hundred and twenty-eight dollars and he didn't.

C. = he said he'd give you two hundred and twenty-eight dollars?

Ob. = yes, the remainder.

C. = so that you could buy yourself something. So, he didn't give you it. After a brief pause. Is there anything else you want to tell me?

Ob. = yes. When I was in Mexico, the teacher kept us on a diet. I was the only one he made to go without eating for three days and because of that I put on weight one day, lose it the next.

C. = and you really ate nothing?

Ob. = nothing, three days I didn't eat.

C. = and how could you compete without eating?

Ob. = it wasn't during the competition. We were travelling. And he weighed me in the morning, I weighed 45 kg. After that I had a meal, I ate breakfast, after that I went into town, I did some shopping, I went back, I went to have lunch and when I weighed myself again I was 45.3 kg. It was the food but he said I was snacking on the sly again.

T. = yes, and that time in Spain, when he hit you so hard you almost banged your head on the scales?[68]

C. = did he hit you hard?

Ob. = he did.

C. = and it was actually only 300 grams?

Ob. = yes, after that I went to training, he made me run until I couldn't take any more. I said I'm not running any more, because my right side hurts.

C. = your spleen.

Ob. = and he said that it's just all that water you glug down you.

C. = yes, tell me, ob., I know there was a discussion with comrade Vieru, that either you present yourself at the team or you abandon gymnastics. What happened?

Ob. = he said either I go to Bucharest . . . (the telephone rings — wrong number)

C. = and what did you do? I heard that you didn't want to go to Bucharest either?

Ob. = I didn't want to go. I had some problems in the family and I couldn't go and leave my mother on her own.

C. = but is it harder in Bucharest?

Ob. = I'm doing my best to reach the top again.

C. = but I'm positive you'll succeed, you're an ambitious little girl, you're a Hero of Socialist Labour, you have your feet on the ground, and you're not ten years old any more. I think you have the determination to come back. But tell me something! You said that it's out of the question your working with Béla Károlyi again. What made up your mind? What was the last straw, why you didn't want to work with him?

Ob. = it wasn't just one thing that was the last straw. There were too many things piling up. I hadn't wanted to any more for a long time, but he kept saying, come on, come on, that it was just a month till the competition in America and he told me, come on, for this competition, because even so, it's the last of your career.

C. = that's what he told you?

Ob. = yes, and when we were coming back from Spain, he said on the train . . .

T. = that we should retire, that we were retiring as winners now.

C. = but did you think of retiring?

Ob. = no, but that's what he said.

C. = and what did he say about the younger girls? That they're better than you?

Ob. = that they needed to work. Each of them wants to be good.

C. = but what's your opinion?

Ob. = she's a good gymnast. But if he came to me at a competition and I was in good form . . .

C. = but has the teacher come lately to have a private talk with you, for you to talk with him.

Ob. = yes, he's come lots of times. Once when he came to school to ask me if I still wanted to work with him, I asked comrade Braşoveanu to say that I wasn't in school and the teacher went to the comrade general.

C. = but tell me, aren't you going to make it up with him? Does he seem strict as a trainer or does he seem like a bad man?

Ob. = I can't take any more, and when I see him . . .

C. = what do you think of the solution of you working with three trainers?[69]

Ob. = it's a good solution, and I think it will produce results. I've worked with comrade Condovici before. When he was here he taught me a lot of moves.

C. = a shame you can't find the notebook, because you could have told me those things better.

Ob. = but I remember them.

C. = you'll have forgotten some of them, but tell me some of the bad things you remember. When you were abroad anywhere, did he make a fool of you? (pause) Let me ask you something else. Do you really like sweets so much that you've been munching sweets for the last quarter of an hour?

Ob. = we like them.

C. = don't you eat too many?

Ob.= we're eating them because when we're on trips they don't let us eat. Ah, now I remember. Before we went to Mexico, in Bucharest . . .

C. = ah, I know the story. You ran away to Benone Sinulescu's.

Ob. = I ran away because the teacher said, look here, when we go to Mexico, you'll have to eat fresh air. But mind, even air makes you fat. I ran away, first I went to the station, then somehow I ended up on Victory Avenue, on foot. I went to a food shop and bought some cheese, because I was starving.

C. = and you ate the cheese? An Olympic champion eating cheese on the street! And then what did you do?

Ob. = I went to Benone's and I told him.

C. = but you still left. I heard you cried that evening.

Ob. = yes, because whenever somebody called me 'great' I didn't say anything about the teacher.

C. = it was nice that you did that, but it would have been better to say. Tell me something, they say that your putting on weight is an issue. How many extra kilos have you put on?

Ob. = about four or five.

C. = and how long will it take you to lose it?

Ob. = I can do it, because I've done it before. At one point I went from 45 to 36, and I could barely stand up any more. I did a double vault, fell on my head and injured myself.

C. = but didn't he help you on the double vault?

Ob. = no, and that's why I don't do it now.

C. = what's your opinion of the World Championships in Paris? It's one title you haven't taken yet. You're Olympic champion, you're . . .

Ob. = yes, I want it. I want to win some medals at the world championships. That's what I said before the Olympics too. (somebody knocks on the door. It sounds like the postman bringing two letters from 'the American'. The conversation continues). I'll go and try to win at least one medal, a gold if possible.

C. = you're modest, you don't think about winning them all.

Ob. = maybe I do think about it, but I don't say it.

C. = tell me something, I see you receive a lot of letters. About how many letters do you received.

Ob. = one day I got 109.

C. = and this is the American who you say writes to you every single day?

Ob. = yes.

C. = what job does he do?

Ob. = he hasn't told me.

The whole interview was recorded by the reporters. They are to film the objective the next day in the gym. The reporters left.

Eds. HG and ZC.

Typist. MM
two copies
1 copy to Bacău CI — Securitate
1 copy to Department One Bucharest.[70]

Fraught as the relationship between Béla Károlyi and Nadia Comăneci was in 1977, it was also a year full of international events at which Nadia was expected to confirm her exceptional performance at the 1976 Olympics. The Romanian Gymnastics Federation received numerous requests from all over the world for the 'goddess of Montréal' to take part in tournaments and demonstrations. She visited at least ten countries – France, the United Kingdom, Spain, Czechoslovakia, Italy, the German Federal Republic, Mexico, Venezuela, Greece, the United States – and countless cities, and if her relationship with Béla Károlyi had not been one of aversion and if her form as a gymnast had not suffered because of it, she would probably have been able to accept many more invitations.

Of the foreign tournaments in which she took part, the most important was held in Czechoslovakia, where the European Championships were held on 13–14 May and at which Nadia had to defend the title she had won at Skien in 1975. The competition proved to be the most controversial of all those the Romanian gymnasts had competed in, due to the fact that the team was withdrawn from the competition and the delegation was summoned to return to Romania. The reason? Deep dissatisfaction at the judging.

Károlyi and his team arrived in Prague on 9 May, travelling not from Bucharest but Madrid, where since 26 April they had taken part in two competitions at the invitation of the Spanish Gymnastics Federation. The same as he had done in the past, Károlyi had acted according to his own vision of what was best for his gymnasts, scheduling a foreign trip in the period just before a major competition. He thought that in the run-up to such tournaments it was better to keep the gymnasts far away from their homes and families, as a means of preserving their focus. This was also why he refused to let the girls' parents come to training sessions or accompany them on trips. Nadia and Teodora's mothers had initially obtained permission to travel with the Romanian delegation to Prague, 'but on finding out, Béla intervened with the R.G.F.'[71] to revoke it, according to an informer.

Likewise, the competitions and public training sessions in Madrid, Barcelona and Vitoria ought to have allowed the gymnasts to achieve sporting condition and get them in the mood to compete. This is what happened, if we ignore the fact that in Spain, according to the Securitate agents in the delegation, Károlyi starved, slapped and verbally abused the gymnasts, and Nadia and Teodora decided that after the European Championships in Prague they would be through with him.

In Spain, the host federation treated the Romanian delegation with great ceremony, despite the fact that only a few months previously Félix Fernández, the head of the organisation, was claimed to have made derogatory remarks about Nadia Comăneci, allegedly calling her 'a monster manufactured in a laboratory',[72] and also despite the living quarters laid on for the delegation being rather modest. Fernández was on friendly terms with Nicolae Vieru, as both were members of the Bureau of the International Gymnastics Federation, and it was he who persuaded him to come to Spain to take part in a tournament and training prior to the European Championships, rather than Federal Germany, which was Károlyi's choice.

The Spanish public was enthusiastic, however, and the arenas where Nadia Comăneci, Teodora Ungureanu, Gabi Gheorghiu and Marilena Neacşu performed were packed to the seams, with people even sitting on the floor, since all the seats were taken. The Spanish press, which had recently ended a strike, seemed to shake off its lethargy with the arrival of Nadia, who was at the centre of reporters' attention. Romania's gymnastics demonstration was commented on from every angle, both sporting and political. For example, Félix Fernández was accused of organising the event as a means of smoothing out his image, badly rumpled after scandals within the Spanish federation. Others argued that it was scheduled at an unsuitable hour, in the middle of the day, so that it wouldn't clash with the socialist rally to be held by Felipe González. It also gave González a big helping hand, since many of the spectators there to see Nadia stayed on to take part in his electoral rally. Throughout the tournament, press coverage was uninterrupted, culminating in an event held on 8 May, when Nadia was handed a trophy as part of a ceremony at the offices of AS magazine in Madrid.

But on 9 May, when the team arrived in Prague, they all sensed that the admiration and excitement that enveloped them in Spain had now been replaced with open hostility. They landed at four-thirty in the afternoon and spent one and a half hours in the airport without being provided with any assistance by their hosts in passing through customs. Only when they stepped outside the airport was the Romanian delegation met by a representative of the Czechoslovak delegation, but there were no reporters, no photographers, no members of the competition's organising committee. True, the Czechoslovak ice hockey team had just won the world title in Vienna, and the streets of Prague still showed signs of the jubilant celebrations, but excitement about the gymnastics championships was growing and it was strange that not one reporter had turned up to cover the arrival of a team that included an Olympic champion. The official reason given by the hosts was that the national hockey team had arrived at the airport a little earlier. But at the time, Romania was out of favour in Prague because in Bucharest the day before Romanian tennis players Ilie Năstase, Ion Ţiriac and Dumitru Hădărău had beaten Jan Kodeš and Jiří Hřebec in Davis Cup matches and the Czechoslovaks had made loud complaints about unfair umpiring.

Seventy gymnasts from twenty-three countries were competing in Prague and the tournament was broadcast on television in more than thirty countries, even as far away as the United States and Japan. More than five hundred journalists from all over the world were also there to cover the competition, proving how big an interest there was in gymnastics. Back in Romania, the whole country, including Nicolae and Elena Ceauşescu, was watching the event on television or listening to it on radio, eager to see Nadia claim a fresh European victory. Besides the members of the official delegation and reporters from Radioteleviziunea Română and *Sportul* newspaper, a group of trainers from various clubs, headed by coach Gheorghe Gorgoi, also accompanied the Romanian contingent, having travelled from Bucharest to study the gymnasts from all the other countries. Officials of the N.C.P.E.S. and R.G.F., headed by Nicolae Vieru, had arrived by train a few days earlier to handle matters of accommodation and accreditation.

'Immediately after leaving Spain, Károlyi Béla had a complete change of attitude towards the members of the squad, speaking to them nicely and doing everything in order to achieve the best possible results,'[73] Securitate officer Popescu reported after his return to Bucharest, an observation that throws into relief Károlyi's style as a coach. In the days before a major competition, a radical change would come over him and he would relinquish all harshness, with the aim of boosting the gymnasts' morale and eliminating any factor that might discourage them. The last unpleasant incident involving the coach and his gymnasts took place on the morning of their departure to Prague, and was reported by 'Nelu' on his return to Romania: 'Béla noticed that some of the sandwiches placed on the table were missing and without having any certainty that it was her he accused Teodora of taking them, for which reason he hit her in the head with his fist.'[74]

The Romanian gymnasts in general and Nadia in particular did not enjoy favourable press coverage in Czechoslovakia. Nicolae Vieru recalled, 'the Prague press praised the Soviet gymnasts, but had quite a hostile attitude towards our gymnasts, and even after Nadia won for the second time in a row the title of absolute European champion, the newspapers printed on their front pages a photograph of Soviet gymnast Mukhina, who had taken second place.'[75] But Nadia did enjoy the full attention of the press from the rest of the world. During the days in the run-up to the competition, she was mobbed by reporters everywhere she went and filmed for every second as she trained, right up until she left the gym.

Lots were drawn to divide the gymnasts into two series. The first series were to compete from three o'clock in the afternoon on 13 May, the second series from six o'clock in the evening. Scheduled for the same day was the overall competition to establish the European champion and the rankings in the individual all-round contest, and on Saturday, 14 May, the events to find the best gymnast in each of the individual disciplines were to be held. At the most important European tournament in women's gymnastics, there were more competitors than ever aspiring to a place on the podium, with each country now able to send three gymnasts rather than two, a change to the rules that the F.I.G. had adopted in 1976. Romania was represented by Nadia Comăneci, Teodora Ungureanu, and Marilena Neacşu, who replaced Anca Grigoraş after she refused to take part in any competition at which Béla Károlyi was coach. Another change to the competition rules was that eight gymnasts now competed in the finals for each discipline, in order of the marks they had received in the all-round competition.

As a result of the draw, Nadia and Teodora were competing in different series. The Romanian delegation voiced its dissatisfaction at the fact that Teodora was included in the same series as Soviet gymnasts Nellie Kim, Maria Filatova and Elena Mukhina, while Nadia was placed in the second series.[76] On the first day of the competition, the Romanian delegation moved from dissatisfaction to determined opposition to the judges' decisions when they considered Teodora Ungureanu to have been blatantly marked down in the floor exercise and uneven parallel bars events. One of the N.C.P.E.S. representatives claimed that Teodora had been 'robbed of two or three tenths of a point.'[77] The Romanian delegation believed that for this reason Ungureanu had been deprived of bronze or even silver, but their contestation was rejected. That evening, the tension eased when Nadia won for the second consecutive time the title of European Champion. She also broke the European Championships record in the individual all-round competition, obtaining a total score of 39.30. The previous record had been 38.965 points, won by Czechoslovak gymnast Věra Čáslavská.

The incident that led to the withdrawal of the whole team occurred the next day, during the finals for the separate disciplines, in the very first event, which was the vault. Nadia Comăneci and Nellie Kim were vying for first place. Two years previously, in Skien, Nadia had won gold and the European title in the vault event, while Kim had come third, in a tie with Alina Goreac. But at the Montréal Olympics in 1976, Kim had won gold in the event, which made her the reigning champion, while Nadia was the challenger.

The two rivals performed different variations of the Tsukahara vault. Kim did a Tsukahara vault with a full twist and was awarded 9.75 points, while on her second attempt she did a combined Tsukahara vault, receiving 9.70 points, which was increased to 9.80 after the judges' decision was contested by the Soviets. When her turn came, Nadia did a double Tsukahara, for which she was awarded 9.75 points, increased to 9.80 after contestation, and a combined Tsukahara on her second try, receiving 9.70 points. Nellie Kim's vaults were more difficult than Nadia Comăneci's, but they were performed with obvious errors, including defective landings, which gave the spectators the impression that the champion could only be the Romanian gymnast, who had performed her vaults very well.

The judges' initial decision went in Nadia Comăneci's favour and she was announced the winner. But after contestations by the Soviet team, the judges settled on a tie between the two gymnasts, and this was displayed on the official scoreboard. But as Nadia remembers, 'Our final scores were added to our preliminary day's scores, and when the official board flashed, Nelli and I were tied for the gold on the vault. When we marched towards the podium to receive our medals, my name was called for the silver and Nelli's for the gold. Somehow, my score had been lowered. I don't know how, by whom, or why.'[78] The crowd was thrown into confusion. Nobody could understand what was going on or how such an important decision could have been altered in the interval before the medal-giving ceremony, which had been extended far beyond what the regulations allowed.

Vieru recounts, 'right then, Cristian Ţopescu and Atanasia Albu, who were providing commentary for Romanian Television, caught off guard by this turn of events, reacted emotionally, loudly protesting that Nadia had been robbed, wronged.'[79] At home in Romania, viewers were also astounded, but above all revolted. Their indignation was inflamed by the commentary of Atanasia Albu, who shared the microphone with Ţopescu in Romanian Television's studio in Prague. Whereas Ţopescu was a sports commentator, famous in Romania for his measured, objective voice, Atanasia Albu was a gymnastics trainer who had worked with Nadia in Oneşti since the beginning, although she was not a household name. As a professional in the field of gymnastics, her opinions therefore bore far greater weight than those of Ţopescu when she confirmed that the judges had acted unfairly.

Unfortunately, no recording of the broadcast has been preserved in the archives of Romanian Television. We do not know how far the two commentators actually went, for example, whether they openly stated that the Soviet Union had robbed Romania. However, it is said that Nicolae Ceauşescu, watching the competition on television, reacted with fury when the gold medal, which should have gone to Nadia Comăneci, was awarded to the Soviet Union as a result of contestations. Provoked by the outraged commentary he was hearing, Nicolae Ceauşescu decided from his seat in front of the television set to withdraw the Romanian team from the competition.

By the time Ceauşescu's decision reached the heads of the Romanian delegation in the Palace of Sport, Prague, Nadia Comăneci had completed her exercise on the uneven parallel bars and been awarded 10 points. Nicolae Vieru, in the midst of the action, since he sat on the appeal jury recalls:

during the uneven parallel bars final, somebody came up to the jury desk, asked which one was Vieru, and tapped me on the shoulder. When I turned my head, I saw a young man with the 'face of a Securitate man' who informed me he was there from the Romanian Embassy, having been sent by 'comrade Ambassador [Teodor] Haş', who was passing on to us an order from Bucharest, sent by Foreign Minister Macovescu, to abandon the competition in protest at the injustice to Nadia Comăneci. Likewise, he told me that at 20.30 hours a special aeroplane was waiting to take our delegation back to the home country.

Shocked and outraged by this interference, I protested and demanded explanations, but not receiving any, I sent the messenger bringing this order back to the Embassy, along with 'uncle Iliuţă' Istrate, who had accompanied the delegation to Spain as the representative of the Romanian Olympic Committee.

Shortly after the uneven parallel bars final ended and Nadia Comăneci was awarded gold, and as the final on the beam was underway, I was called to the telephone and from the embassy, 'uncle Iliuţă' informed me: 'Nicolae, the order was made by Ceauşescu, who was listening to the commentaries on television, during the vault, and he gave us the order to withdraw immediately, so gather together the delegation and leave the competition as quickly as possible!'[80]

Vieru immediately obeyed, and on his instructions the Romanian gymnasts and delegation collected their things and left the arena. Károlyi has similar memories of the episode, albeit coloured by his usual tendency to exaggerate, since he claimed that the Romanian ambassador himself entered the arena and went to the judge's desk, took the microphone and ordered the delegation to leave the building, saying, 'I am the Rumanian ambassador. I have a mandate from Nicolae Ceauşescu, the President of the Rumanian Republic. You are immediately to evacuate.'[81] There are no documents or eye-witness accounts to confirm that Teodor Haş, the Romanian ambassador to Prague, entered the arena.

It is true, however, that Béla Károlyi and Nicolae Vieru initially resisted the order from Bucharest, until they realised that it came from so high a level that nobody could disobey it. In his subsequent report, Ioan Popescu, the Securitate officer within the delegation, did not dare to mention that Ceauşescu's order had initially been questioned by Károlyi and Vieru, instead claiming that all the members of the delegation were in 'complete agreement with the measure taken.'[82] But Captain Nicolae Ilie, who was not in Prague, later questioned some of the eyewitnesses to report their reactions at the time:

On receiving the instruction to withdraw, the secretary general of the federation, Nicolae Vieru, head of the delegation, voiced the opinion that it was not good for us to withdraw, pointing out that the International Gymnastics Federation would take measures to sanction us.

Coach Károlyi Béla was not in agreement with the withdrawal, giving as his reason the fact that after the withdrawal the Romanian S.R. team would no longer be able to take part in international competitions.

When the withdrawal of the Romanian team was announced, the chairman of the F.I.G. — Titov Yuri, U.S.S.R. — walked over to our delegation demanding explanations, and after these were provided, he went to telephone the Soviet embassy in Prague, then our embassy, demanding explanations regarding the withdrawal. He was told that the embassy of the R.S.R. does not provide explanations to the chairman of the F.I.G., on behalf of which he spoke.[83]

All this agitation unfolded as Nadia performed her exercise on the beam. One by one, the Romanians left the arena, and Károlyi waited for Nadia to dismount from the apparatus. Nadia had just performed a perfect exercise, closing with a cartwheel and impeccable double twist. She then jogged over to the coaches and beneath the gaze of the judges and more than ten thousand spectators, she disappeared: 'As I left the arena, I glanced back and saw my beam score. It was another 10,'[84] recalls Nadia, regretful at having just lost another European title.

The gold medal was given to Elena Mukhina, who had come second and was one of the best gymnasts in the world. Back then, the medal-giving ceremonies took place after the close of the contest on each apparatus, and failure to mount the podium meant forfeiting the title. By leaving the tournament, Nadia found herself in the situation of giving up not only her gold medal for the beam, but also any other medals she might have won over the course of the competition. In the end, she left the Prague European Championships in Prague with just three medals, two gold, for the individual all-round contest and uneven parallel bars, and one silver, for the vault.

As he left the arena, Vieru poured fuel on the fire by declaring to the crowd of journalists pursuing the Romanian delegation, 'we aren't happy with the current rules and until they're changed, we won't be taking part in any more competitions organised by the F.I.G.'[85] To the Soviets, and to Yuri Titov in particular, the chairman of the International Gymnastics Federation, this statement sounded like a threat, and Vieru, once things had calmed down, found a means of retracting it.[86]

After a brief stop at the hotel to collect their luggage, the members of the Romanian delegation went to the embassy, where they were joined by Romanian diplomats who then accompanied them to the airport to board the special aeroplane taking them to Bucharest. At 23.15 hours, they landed at Otopeni Airport, where officials, reporters and more than ten thousand people from Bucharest gave them a hero's welcome. The national anthem was sung, the crowd chanted slogans such as 'Good for you, Nadia!' and 'Long live, dignity, honour and fairness in sport!', and interviews were taken, with all those questioned stating, 'Quite simply we were robbed!' Vieru recalls:

We were met by the Mayor of the Capital Ion Dincă, General Dănescu – Deputy Interior Minister – and General Dragnea – head of sport – and Party officials, national television, lots of reporters.

After Nadia and Béla gave short interviews, an official motorcade of Mercedes Benz cars took us to the 23 August sports centre. It was midnight by then and Ilie Verdeţ was waiting for us, the secretary of the C.C. of the R.C.P. responsible for sport. At the hotel restaurant there was a bounteous and beautifully laid out meal waiting for us, but Béla sent the girls to bed, refusing to allow them to eat. The adults from the delegation and the chief officials present stayed behind to discuss matters for more than an hour, with Béla being the one who spoke the most as always, with feeling and imagination, recounting the competition, how Nadia had been treated unfairly, and the 'wise decision of our beloved leader'.[87]

For days, the team's withdrawal was the main subject in the Romanian press, and not only in the sports papers. Not one newspaper article or radio or television broadcast was allowed to state that it was Nicolae Ceauşescu who made the decision to withdraw from the contest. According to the official version, the decision was taken by the N.C.P.E.S. and the R.G.F. 'Biased judging', 'discriminatory actions', 'attacks on the rules of sport', 'preconceived ideas', 'backstage manoeuvring', 'violations of fair play, of the spirit of ethics and fairness, of honour' were just some of the headlines. In the press could be found analyses, interviews, opinion pieces, photographic essays, stances on the part of experts and people of labour, translations of favourable foreign newspaper articles, anything to bolster the Romanian position according to which 'the abuses committed by leading figures in the F.I.G. (. . .) led to the leadership of the N.C.P.E.S. and gymnastics federation to take the decision to withdraw our gymnasts from the competition, a dignified, firm decision, in full agreement with the opinion of the sport-loving masses in our country, which, watching the championships on the small screen, justifiably manifested their complete bewilderment and indignation.'[88]

It was the beginning of what was to prove a propaganda spectacular. But unlike in other situations when the régime had acted to spread ideas and concepts among the masses, this time it did not have to win them over, there was no need to lay down the official line, since everybody was already convinced of the injustice that had been perpetrated. Moreover, given Romania's complicated relationship with Russia over the course of history – the Romanian people had never loved either the Tsarist Empire or the U.S.S.R. – such resentments easily augmented the sense of injustice and created the critical mass for an emotional chain reaction. Had the fire not been put out quickly, it could have led to social ructions politically dangerous to the régime. For this reason, the Securitate realised that the popular mood had to be closely monitored.

On 14–16 May, the county inspectorates of the Securitate sent telegrams to Department One in Bucharest, reporting the honest reactions, criticisms and indignation of ordinary Romanians. There was talk of the matter everywhere, on trams and buses, in shops and the workplace, at home, and informers were there to report opinions wherever they were expressed.

Whereas on the first day ordinary people's criticism had been aimed mainly at the judges and hosts of the competition, while saluting the courage of the Romanian delegation in protesting by withdrawing from the tournament – 'we're not afraid of anybody when it comes to our country's prestige' – before long it was observed that the accusations were overwhelmingly aimed at the Soviet Union: 'what happened in Prague was a Soviet fix, the Soviets have compromised themselves in front of all the people in the world'; 'the Soviets didn't strike at Nadia Comăneci, but at world gymnastics, at the decency of the human race'; 'what the Soviets did in Prague is nothing new, either in sport or any other field of endeavour'; 'the Russians have started making sport political again, instead of contributing to friendship and peace, which is what they boast, but they do the opposite'; 'what will the foreign radio stations say because this incident will lead to political complications, anyway the measure taken was welcome, it's thought that the order was given with the approval of the highest leadership of the party and state'.[89]

The virulence of the popular tone was also observed by diplomatic missions to Bucharest. The U.S. Embassy sent a telegram to the State Department and to other U.S. embassies in Moscow and Eastern Europe describing the inflexibility of Romanians' attitude towards Soviet behaviour in Prague:

Cynics might say that in this case the Romanians ought to have expected to get as good as they had gotten lately, for example, at the Kodeš versus Năstase Davis Cup match two weeks ago, when there were quite a lot of questionable umpire's decisions, but nobody will convince the Romanian public that it was not treated unfairly yet again in favour of its Russian neighbour. It was an event that did not make much of a contribution to the promotion of Soviet-Romanian friendship through sport.[90]

Consequently, it is no wonder that on 16 May the Securitate intervened to rein in Romanian journalists, who were guiding public opinion, carried away by an illusion of newfound press freedom: 'All journalists on sports issues have received instructions not to make any further comments regarding the withdrawal of the gymnastics team from the European Championships, but only to report on favourable passages from the foreign press.'[91] Analysing Romanian newspapers and magazines, we may conclude that the instructions were followed to the letter. From 18 May, articles ceased to be trenchant, instead providing plenty of space for positive comments on the withdrawal made by leading figures in international sport.

The embassy of the U.S.S.R. in Bucharest was closely monitored, but Soviet diplomats were cautious and kept quiet, making no public comment about events in Prague. What is more, on 21 July 1977, Oleg Zhdetsky, the TASS correspondent in Bucharest, was sent to Oneşti to hand Nadia the agency's prize for best sportsperson of the year 1976.

There were frequent criticisms of the judging in gymnastics. Perhaps they were too frequent, but the stakes were also high: errors on the part of the judges and what the Communist press in Romania called 'behind-the-scenes fixes' had been signalled at major international competitions, including the European Championships, the World Championships, and the Olympics, where the judging ought to have been conducted with the utmost transparency. But it is not easy to unravel what actually happened, and there are few public accounts on the part of those who either may have been complicit or who were witnesses. The Securitate archive contains a number of documents that make reference to the judging issue, but they present only the Romanian side, a view that is limited and separate, but still useful to anybody trying to bring the truth to light.

Notorious for their readiness to criticise, Romanians made complaints to the organisers of all the Olympic Games in which they took part during the Cold War. For example, a report drawn up by the Council of Ministers Committee for Physical Culture and Sport after the 1952 Helsinki Games states, 'there were not countless blatant thefts as there were in the past. Nevertheless, we suffered as a result of biased judging (. . .) particularly in the women's gymnastics, overall, where we were deprived of medals.'[92] In 1956, after the Melbourne Games, the heads of Romanian sport claimed in internal meetings that they had been confronted with 'totally biased judging',[93] without accusing anybody in particular. Later, when Romania became one of the major powers in the sport, vying for supremacy as the equal of the Soviet Union, the finger of blame began to be pointed at the Soviets and the Communist bloc countries most loyal to them: Hungary, the German Democratic Republic and Bulgaria.

The representatives of the Soviet Union manipulated the scoring using means that were as simple as they were effective. The night before the contest, the judges from the Communist countries held meetings in their hotel rooms, where they agreed upon the rankings for the next day. Each judge supported his own country's gymnast and negotiated to obtain the best possible score for her in one of the events, while agreeing to support the other countries' gymnasts in the other events. For example, if a Soviet gymnast was to receive the highest score in the floor exercise, the East German gymnast would win gold on the beam. The negotiations suited all those involved, particularly the delegates from the smaller Communist countries, who were happy to be treated as equals by the 'great friend from the East'.[94] All this was to the disadvantage of the other competitors and of course trampled every moral principle of a sporting competition. The negotiated outcome was only possible if no unpleasant incidents intervened during the contest, however. For example, if a gymnast made a mistake so blatant that it couldn't be overlooked, the hotel-room bargain would be impossible to keep. But there were also situations in which, to the spectators' amazement, the judges closed their eyes to obvious mistakes and even falls from the apparatus, merely to keep their pact.

Representatives of federations from the West tried to do the same thing, as a natural reaction to the obstacles they came up against during tournaments. But this came later, and in the 1970s, they didn't have the necessary clout to pull it off: 'Who the hell can we come to an understanding with? Two judges are from the United States, two from Canada, and you know where the other forty-eight are from',[95] said former gymnast Frank Bare at Montréal in 1976. The co-founder of the United States Gymnastics Federation and executive director of the organisation from 1963 to 1980, Bare was talking about men's gymnastics, but the situation was no different in women's gymnastics. Things were later to change, however. At the World Gymnastics Championships held in Moscow in 1981, 'three groups of countries formed, e.g.: U.S.A., Canada, England, New Zealand, Australia (English-speaking), which were joined by the Chinese P.R. (. . .) The Nordic countries formed another group, Sweden, Norway, Finland, Denmark, whose representatives met, also before the contest, at the Arbat restaurant,'[96] reported the Securitate informers within the Romanian delegation.

As a result, control over the judges meant control over the competition. Since during the Cold War, sporting competitions were another front in the clash between the two ideologically opposed camps, federation judges from the Communist bloc, who were more numerous and more influential, formed a coalition to achieve their goals: to help the gymnasts from their countries to win medals, while demonstrating that the Communist school of gymnastics was not only superior to that of the free world, but invincible.

There was no question that the gymnasts of the Soviet Union, East Germany, Hungary and Czechoslovakia were the better. No other gymnast at the time would have been able to defeat Larisa Latynina, for example, who dominated every apparatus at three consecutive Olympic Games, in 1956, 1960 and 1964, and whose record of eighteen Olympic medals was not beaten for another forty-eight years, by American swimmer Michael Phelps. Paradoxically, therefore, the judges' fixes were not especially aimed at Western gymnasts, but rather at establishing the pecking order among the gymnasts from the Communist bloc. An episode at the 1968 Mexico City Olympics is relevant in this respect: Věra Čáslavská was marked down in the floor exercise and on the beam in favour of Soviet rivals Larisa Petrik and Natalia Kuchinskaya.

As part of the Communist bloc, Romania was familiar with these unfair behind-the-scenes practices. Federation judges described them in a number of documents, albeit not in reports to the N.C.P.E.S. and R.G.F., but in secret reports to the Securitate, since with few exceptions, the judges were also informers up until 1989. The following is a report written in 1975 after the European Championships in Skien. The author was Maria Simionescu, alias 'Lia Muri':

On the occasion of the Women's European Championships in Skien, Norway, 3–5 March this year, the attention of all the specialists present, of the press, of the television stations of very many countries and of the Norwegian public was focused on the performances of our gymnast, Nadia Comăneci. Discussions began among the judges regarding the Romanian gymnast's chances of winning the championship even as early as the training sessions preliminary to the contest.

To counter a possible defeat for her gymnasts, the evening before the contest Larisa Latynina held a discussion in her hotel room with the judges from the socialist countries, to which our representative was not invited and I do not know for sure whether the representative of the H.P.U. was either.

Those present were: Latynina, who chaired the discussion (Lidia) Ivanova, U.S.S.R., Matlochová (Jaro)Slava, C.S.R., Dimov Tzvetana, B.P.R., Bartowick Nina, P.P.R., Hlavacek Sylvia, D.D.R.

In principle the aim of the discussion was to establish a shared point of view in the judging. Larisa Latynina claimed that 'Nadia Comăneci is a good gymnast, but she is too young to win and has plenty of time to wait.'

We found out from the P.P.R. delegation, through their coach and judge, and from the Italian delegation (Miranda Cicognani, judge, Agabio, coach), since a trainer from the H.P.R. works for them, Erzsébet Baranyai, who found out from the H.P.R. delegation.

Cicognani and Agabio communicated to the source that they found out and that they would speak to other countries: France, Spain etc. to counteract if need be a bias in the judging of the other judges who had made an advance agreement.

'Lia Muri'[97]

According to Maria Simionescu, Larisa Ltynina, who had become a trainer for the U.S.S.R. women's gymnastics team after retiring from competition, never liked Nadia Comăneci. In the summer of 1975, realising that Nadia threatened Soviet supremacy, Latynina 'influenced people against our gymnast' and at the pre-Olympic competition in Montréal she even wanted to make a written contestation of Nadia's score for the uneven parallel bars exercise,[98] 'Lia Muri' reported in October 1975. At the time there were clear signals from not only Romanian judges and coaches, but also reporters. For example, Constantin Macovei of *Sportul* 'found out from a Soviet editor, a friend of his, that the Soviet trainers from the women's squads are in a panic and they have taken exceptional measures to cope with the new situation.'[99] As a result, at the end of 1975, after Nadia's successes in Skien and the pre-Olympic trial in Montréal, it was obvious that the Soviets had no intention of inviting Romania's representatives to their secret hotel meetings.

The situation worsened after the Montréal Olympics, when Yuri Titov of the Soviet Union was elected head of the International Gymnastics Federation, and East German Ellen Berger was made head of the Federation's Women's Technical

Committee. Before Berger, the committee had been headed by Hungarian Valeria Nagy, who made no secret of her aversion to Romanians. As 'Nelu' said in a report in June 1975, her antipathy was supposedly rooted in what he called 'chauvinist sentiments'.[100] For this reason, Valeria Nagy was in the attention of the Securitate for 'negative attitudes towards our country' and 'irredentist comments', a conclusion that was by no means exaggerated, and Maria Simionescu was instructed 'to contact the woman in question when she has the chance in order to establish her position towards our country.'[101] But from the summer of 1976, when Swiss Arthur Gander was replaced as head of the F.I.G. by Yuri Titov, and Valeria Nagy was replaced by Ellen Berger as head of the Women's Technical Committee, behind-the-scenes machinations seem to have become the norm.

In a report of 30 September 1980, Maria Simionescu described Ellen Berger as 'aggressive' towards Romanians: 'This aggression manifests itself against us in particular, turning problems she might have with our representatives into problems with "Romanians" in general. For example, at Thonon les bains she reproaches Jaroslava Matlochová (C.S.R.) for having come to Băile Felix in our country for a cure: "How could you go to Romania, to the Romanians?" She got a very nice answer from her, telling her how well she had been received and what a special people we were. The majority of recent meetings have begun with reproaches against us openly in the Committee. At the Moscow O.G., in the finals for the beam, Titov Yuri, U.S.S.R., with a direct interest, capitulated, but not Ellen Berger. She was married and has a son who she told me works in the D.D.R. Security. For many years she's lived with Helmut Grosse, an air force officer, who did specialist training in the U.S.S.R. They are both invited to the U.S.S.R. every year, and at the major competitions in 1979 and 1980 Grosse was invited home for dinner (all the time) by Soviet generals alone or with Ellen Berger.' When Berger visited Romania, the Securitate monitored her through a surveillance operation and bugs planted in her hotel room.[102]

In his autobiography Béla Károlyi says Ellen Berger 'pulled the strings for her country', and 'there was still a strong traditional Soviet setup.'[103] Géza Pozsár, in an interview from 2020, also admitted 'the Soviets and all the Communist countries judged to their own advantage. We tried to find for ourselves allies among the Western judges. I spoke French, the official language of the F.I.G., I could talk to them about certain situations: "look at the Soviets, they're killing us, we're better than them, we have to make sure that the judges from the Communist countries don't let the situation get out of control" and so we started doing politics, but everybody else did.'[104]

In January 1977, the Securitate recorded Béla and Marta Károlyi discussing the judging at the Montréal Olympics: 'There were wide-ranging discussions about the gymnastics events at the Montréal Olympics, remarking upon the lack of objectivity on the part of some judges (mostly Soviet) in scoring the exercises presented by our gymnasts and the bias in favour of the Soviet gymnasts. (In this respect, Titov, the chairman of the International Gymnastics Federation, before the Olympics, openly requested the support of gymnasts Turishcheva, Olga Korbut and Nellie Kim).' During the same discussion, the Securitate noted that the Károlyis had 'an attitude of aversion towards Soviet gymnastics'.[105]

The opinions of Károlyi and Pozsár are today also supported by other eyewitnesses. Frank Bare claimed that during the Montréal Olympics, Valeria Nagy illegally attempted to change the membership of the judging panel for the floor exercise, forcing the selection of judges from East Germany and the Soviet Union in order to reduce Nadia Comăneci's chances.[106] She was backed up by Ellen Berger, but Arthur Gander, Frank Bare and others managed to thwart the Soviet plan.[107]

Maria Simionescu, the first vice-chairwoman of the Women's Technical Committee was Romania's spearhead in these behind-the-scenes battles. Unfortunately, very few reports by 'Lia Muri' tackle the subject and those that do are separated by wide intervals of time. For example, in December 1975, aware that the Soviets were looking for ways to manipulate the judging at Montréal, she informed the Securitate that after talks with the Italians, 'they assured us of their direct help with very high scores at the Montréal O.G. on the part of the Italian judges,'[108] and in May 1980, before the Moscow Olympics, she talked to the Swiss judges, 'ensuring yet another judge in future who will not disadvantage us in major competitions.'[109] The same year, she drew attention to the fact that 'the mood against us, maintained and even created by E. Berger, is getting worse'.[110]

A more detailed report written by Simionescu in March 1980, when F.I.G. representatives from the Communist bloc countries met in Sinaia, provides an even clearer picture of the aims they wished to achieve, as well as the nature of the relationship between the Soviets and the Romanians: 'During official and unofficial discussions, Yuri Titov drew attention to the fact that the Romanian delegation might by its position create anti-Soviet propaganda. Likewise, on an occasion prior to the Sinaia conference, Titov warned Maria Simionescu that if she did not abandon her fair, principled position within the Technical Commission of which she is a member and did not follow his instructions, he might inform on the Romanian representative's suspect relations with delegates from the capitalist countries.'

At the plenary meeting, Titov,[111] according to Simionescu, 'went so far as to assign tasks and the countries that each delegation present had to influence,' with the Romanians being instructed to forge closer ties to the Chinese in order to recruit them to their select club, and 'the Cuban representative criticised the position of some socialist countries, referring to Hungary, which did not help his country's team at the World Championships in the U.S.A., Dallas, and requested that in future the socialist countries act in solidarity as a bloc in order to protect the interests of all and to fight the capitalist countries.'[112]

Although it had undercover officers among the members of the delegation, the Securitate played no part in the Prague conflict. Nevertheless, it is worth noting that although trainer Atanasia Albu, who provided television commentary alongside Cristian Țopescu, was a longstanding and steadfast informer of Bucharest's secret police, the outrage she expressed over the microphone was not part of any Securitate operation.

After the scandal erupted, the Securitate, under the guidance of Department One, took measures to safeguard the image of Nicolae Ceauşescu and his government and to counteract any negative consequences that might have affected the gymnasts, coaches and Romanian Gymnastics Federation as a result of decisions taken by the International Gymnastics Federation, where the Soviet Union held the levers via chairman Yuri Titov.

Reactions in the international press, closely monitored in Bucharest, were satisfactory, inasmuch as the major Western newspapers recognised that the successive alteration of the scores in the vault event, which led to Nadia Comăneci being knocked off the top spot in favour of Nellie Kim, had been unusual, and the manner in which the F.I.G. had organised the competition inspired scepticism. But newspapers in the free world also published articles critical of Romania, which worried the Securitate. One such alarm signal came from the Zurich-based *Sport*, in an article titled 'Telegram from Bucharest', published on 16 May, which was highly critical of political interference in sport. Although the article did not name Ceauşescu, it did claim that the Romanian team had been withdrawn not on the initiative of the Romanian federation, but at the orders of the government in Bucharest, an act that would have been unthinkable in a democratic country and which 'proves the danger of sport's dependence on government in the Eastern bloc.'[113] In order to obviate such criticism in the press, the Securitate realised that it would be necessary to win international public opinion over to Romania's side.

After her return from Prague, Nadia was in the country for only two days, before leaving once more, on 17 May, this time to receive the Grand Prize of the International Association of the Sporting Press, whose members were holding their congress in the resort of Milano Marittima on Italy's Adriatic coast. The trip to Italy was free of the usual tensions, and Securitate officer Ioan Popescu reported that Béla Károlyi 'allowed Nadia Comăneci and Teodora Ungureanu to eat all they liked, accepting an abrupt gain in their weight.'[114] The congress was the event best suited to achieve Romania's objective, since Nadia was admired and applauded there by reporters from all over the world. There were one hundred and sixteen reporters from press agencies, television and radio stations, newspapers and magazine from forty-six countries on four continents, along with one hundred invited guests from Italian and international sport.

The Italian press was lavish in its praise of Nadia, and the headlines included, '*Nadia, in Italia, per dimenticar*' (Nadia in Italy to forget). To the satisfaction of the

Romanian delegation, the unanimous opinion was that Nadia was the best sportsperson in the world. Even if the Soviet Union was not explicitly accused in public statements, participants at the event argued that what had happened in Prague was not the best example of fairness in sport. Károlyi also won praise, and the chairman of the Italian Olympic Committee invited him to mount the podium, congratulating him on the successes he had achieved throughout his career.

In order to maintain this favourable mood, it was decided to organise a gymnastics demonstration in Bologna. But here the Securitate had to intervene, as revealed by the archives: 'In 1977, after the withdrawal of the Romanian women's gymnastics team from the European Championships in Prague, it was necessary to organise a gymnastics demonstration with Nadia Comăneci and the other Romanian gymnasts as a riposte to what took place in Prague. Making telephonic contact with Giorgio Pagani and Duilio Fenara in order to fulfil this difficult task, they realised the need to organise the demonstration and thus in 48 hours they succeeded, after many difficulties, and the demonstration took place in the Palace of Sports in Bologna. The demonstration enjoyed wide international coverage.'[115]

The Bologna event was organised with the help of Aurel Neagu, the editor-in-chief of *Sportul* and a Securitate agent whose code name was 'Constantin'. He asked for the help of Giorgio Pagani, a post office clerk and the boxing correspondent for *Studio* and *Guerin Sportivo* in Bologna, where he lived, and 'a member of the Italian Communist Party, a close friend of the secretary general of the party, and of [Renato] Zangheri, a member of the political bureau of the party and mayor of the city of Bologna.' Agent 'Constantin' had an 'outstanding' relationship with Pagani, who had always shown a 'great liking for our country, proving himself to be upstanding and ready to support Romanian sportsmen and sports teams in Italy or other countries.'[116]

After an exhausting ten-hour journey, the Romanian delegation reached Bologna for the demonstration, which was hastily put together on 18 May. It was a day of torrential rain and the event was scheduled at a late hour, clashing with the UEFA Cup Final in Spain, Juventus Torino versus Athletic Bilbao, which Italians were watching on television with great excitement. But even so, it was a great success. More than four thousand spectators crowded into the Palazzo dello Sport, where Károlyi presented Romania's gymnasts, starting with the youngest – Emilia Eberle, Cristina Itu, Gabi Gheorghiu, Marilena Neacşu – and culminating with Teodora Ungureanu and Nadia Comăneci, who received a standing ovation from the crowd, which chanted *'Tu sei migliora di tutte'* (You're the best). Béla and Marta Károlyi, Maria Simionescu, choreographer Géza Pozsár, and pianist Stabişevschi were also introduced to the audience, and at the end, hundreds of people crowded around the changing rooms and around the buses outside to applaud them and to give them a rousing Italian-style send-off.

Although part of the Communist bloc, Romania was by now a dissident nation. But how much could the country afford to rebel against the 'fraternal' communist nations and against the U.S.S.R. in particular? The sword that Ceaușescu had raised in Prague, succumbing to fury, was double-edged, and the hand that wielded it was stayed by serious political constraints. The Securitate made note of this on the very eve of Nadia's departure to Milano Marittima and Bologna: 'there is talk that this action might have repercussions on the situation of the withdrawal from the European Championships. Inasmuch as all the federations of the socialist countries will begin a campaign to the detriment of our country.'[117] This had to be avoided.

For this reason, in the months that followed the steps to be taken to limit the fallout from the Prague incident were carefully calculated. In the Securitate archives it has not been possible to locate the reports filed by 'Vlad', the code name for Nicolae Vieru, regarding the manner in which the crisis should be handled or how the Securitate and upper echelons of the Party guided him in the matter. But in his autobiography, he says that he travelled to Moscow to persuade Yuri Titov to understand the situation and 'not to take measures against our federation.' During the other meetings that took place in the summer of 1977, 'I prevailed upon the fact that our leaving the contest was unprecedented and in the technical regulations such a situation and its consequences were unforeseen,' which was the Romanians' most suitable negotiating stance: 'After discussions, debates, criticisms etc. it was established that the Romanian Gymnastics Federation should be given a warning and that a clause be introduced into the F.I.G. regulations that in future, in the event of leaving a competition, the results obtained by those in question should be annulled.'[118]

It was not very complicated to defuse the situation, since each party had an aim to achieve, and those aims converged. It was the Romanians' aim that the F.I.G. should not sanction either the gymnasts, the national federation, or Maria Simionescu of the F.I.G. Women's Technical Commission, who ought not to have joined the Romanian delegation when they abandoned the contest, since she was representing the F.I.G. and was required to remain, no matter what happened to her home country's team. Yuri Titov did not wish to see his reputation further sullied, since the international press frequently suggested that he was responsible or to blame for the illegalities that had occurred. 'I think you have read the foreign press, you must have noticed the issues raised by the press in Switzerland, France and elsewhere. It would be a good thing if we were to calm things down, not to give the press of the capitalist countries the opportunity to publish new attacks against the socialist countries, against me, as F.I.G. president,' he told the Romanians during a discussion that took place in Moscow.

The F.I.G. chairman made the mistake of admitting to Nicolae Vieru and Maria Login, the deputy chairwoman of the R.G.F., 'the issue has caused him constant stress and given him a big headache.' Likewise, they added in a report that reached Department One of the Securitate, 'he confessed to us that his point of view has been discussed at the highest level of the Party Leadership. He expressed the opinion that we communists should tackle the problems in this way and that among us the spirit of working together and friendship should continue to predominate.'[119]

Maria Login, alias 'Elena', provided many more details of the talks held in Moscow and at other meetings. For example, she says that the first meeting between Vieru and Titov took place in Vernon, rather than Moscow, 'where Y. Titov mooted the proposal that things ought to simmer down.' Later, between 13 and 15 July, they met in Moscow, at a gathering of representatives from the gymnastics federations of the Communist bloc countries. The mood was very friendly and during talks nobody made the slightest allusion to the Prague incident. It was not until 15 July, after the talks ended, that Titov requested a meeting with Vieru and Login, at which he complained about the pressure he was under, mentioning that the heads of the F.I.G. from the Communist countries were demanding a special meeting and that measures be taken. 'We also have to talk about whether the Romanian Gymnastics Federation maintains the stance expressed by some of its representatives in interviews given to the Romanian press, about not taking part in future at women's gymnastics competitions organised by the F.I.G. This boycott of the F.I.G. would not be in keeping with our desire to calm things down,' Titov said, while nonetheless stating that the R.G.F. should still be 'given a warning' for having withdrawn from the contest without providing a written statement of its reasons. However, he added that such a warning would be just a 'formality', while Vieru replied that the Romanian side was against it. 'Likewise, he wanted to know whether we would employ those arguments that attacked him and his interference in changing the scores. When he saw that we had brought this argument into discussion, he gave up the proposal to sanction the Romanian Gymnastics Federation and agreed to look for other means and wordings. But we don't know how sincere or steadfast he was in giving it up.'[120]

On 27 August, at Bienne in Switzerland, where the Executive Committee of the F.I.G. held a meeting, Titov gave assurances that he would not exert pressure to sanction the gymnasts, federation judge Maria Simionescu, or the R.G.F. The Romanians already had the support of the Spanish, Italian, British, U.S., French, Yugoslav and Bulgarian federations. Titov claimed that he did not wish to 'make a drama of things' but to find a 'constructive solution': 'he proposed that we regard what happened in Prague as regrettable, that we bring the matter to a close, and that the report regarding the matter be rewritten.'[121] A compromise had been reached, and the conflict petered out. But scandals to do with biased judging were to continue.

5

THE ROCKY ROAD TO SUPREMACY

In December 1977, after being transferred to Bucharest, Nadia Comăneci and Teodora Ungureanu enjoyed a few weeks of relaxation aimed at improving their mood. They were sent to Deva to watch the National Gymnastics Championships, and they spent the closing days of the year at the Piatra Arsă resort in Prahova. Intensive training was to recommence on 3 January 1978. In the meantime, Maria Simionescu prepared a detailed schedule, and the Romanian Gymnastics Federation put together a team of doctors and coaches that included managing trainer Iosif Hidi, trainers Gheorghe Condovici and Atanasia Albu, pianist Corneliu Grigore, physician Carmen Dumitru, nurse Sanda Vereşteanu, and psychologist Doina Gheorghiu. Choreographer Géza Pozsár was asked to go to Bucharest to help with the national squad and Nadia, but Béla Károlyi strongly opposed it, which led to the decision to recruit ballet dancer and choreographer Victor Vlase instead.

The trainers in charge of the gymnasts – Iosif Hidi, Gheorghe Condovici and Atanasia Albu – were among the most experienced at the time. Condovici[1] had achieved the better results, but Hidi was older. However, Hidi, although he taught in the gymnastics department of the Institute of Physical Education and Sport and had taken specialist courses in the U.S.S.R., was of the old school, which relied on the principles of excessive effort and endless mechanical repetition of the same elements. The younger trainers regarded him as obtuse, incapable of showing any openness towards progress and modern methods. But the gymnasts liked him because he treated them kindly, tenderly, like a father, an attitude that the others regarded as a flaw, a demonstration of his lack of authority.

Gheorghe Condovici was intelligent, bold, but also highly irascible, since he was prone to lose his temper very quickly. He accepted the past and tradition, but constantly sought new solutions. He was the coach of the men's junior squad and at the time he could boast to having 'Varna 1974' under his belt: along with Costache Gheorghiu and Mircea Bădulescu, he had trained gymnast Dan Grecu, who won Romania's first gold medal at a world championship. He was also put forward by the R.G.F. to train Nadia Comăneci instead of Károlyi because he was close to Nicolae Vieru, who had been his trainer in the 1960s, when he was a gymnast. In 1976, he had spent a few weeks in Oneşti, and Nadia and Teodora remembered him later. But in 1977, when he was asked whether he would agree to be transferred to Oneşti to work with the two gymnasts, he declined. 'He said that as long as Károlyi was in the gym, he wouldn't come here,'[2] said Nadia's mother during a conversation with her daughter, which was covertly recorded by the Securitate.

Atanasia Albu, who likewise had definite professional qualities, was the team's third trainer, specialising in the beam. But her pupils never took a liking to her. Her colleagues all called her Sica, but she was never friendly towards the gymnasts. She was never in the habit of encouraging them and she was unforgiving when they made a mistake. Her dream was to become a federation trainer, which she achieved in 1973, and to hold the positions that Maria Simionescu held within the International Gymnastics Federation after she retired. Other trainers regarded her as duplicitous and self-seeking. The archives provide evidence of her ambition to reach the top of the career ladder. In the late 1950s she sometimes took part in Party meetings held within the Romanian Gymnastics Federation, to which she was invited as a leading sportswoman. For example, she attended the plenary meeting of the R.G.F. on 26 August 1958, at which Marcel Duncan and other coaches and sportspeople were harshly punished for falling prey to unwholesome bourgeois ideological influences. Young gymnast Atanasia Albu gave a speech criticising the fact that some coaches hide 'things from the plenary related to the deficiencies of the comrades in the squad.'[3]

The trainers and medical personnel were responsible for getting Nadia Comăneci back into physical, mental and technical shape, so that she could continue as a gymnast at the highest level. Condovici took care of acrobatic elements and exercises on the uneven parallel bars and vault, Albu the beam and floor exercises, while Hidi supervised them both.

The Securitate adapted to the new situation, deploying a new 'network to influence, protect and defend gymnast Nadia Comăneci,'[4] as it is named in the archive documents, and simultaneously conducting surveillance and covert recording. As Géza Pozsár was no longer part of Nadia's entourage, his reports from the first part of 1978 make only intermittent references to her. As a result, the secret police sought other solutions, and the measures they took starting from December 1977 entailed total monitoring: recording equipment in the gymnasts' rooms at the 23 August National Sport Hotel, background checks on all the members of the team that had been assembled, talks 'with a view to softening them up, in order to discover and prevent any action that might injure Nadia Comăneci', alerting Section 5 of the Militia to provide additional security and protection measures in the area of the sports centre, and the instruction of the 'three intelligence sources within the team of trainers and medics.'[5] Although Department One's report gives us to understand that there were already three informers tasked with monitoring Nadia Comăneci, in reality the number seems to have been higher.

Even if the documents show that the trainers were kept under surveillance, it was also true that they had already collaborated with the secret police, albeit not all to the same extent. In February 1978, Iosif Hidi was an 'operational connection'. He presented Captain Nicolae Ilie reports that he signed with his real name, followed by his title, 'I.E.F.S. head'.[6] Gheorghe Condovici was recruited as an informer in 1966 and was given the code name 'Iosifescu Dragoş'[7] but in the archives it has not been possible to find any reports he may have written on Nadia, which suggests that for unknown reasons the Securitate did not use him as a source. But Atanasia Albu, alias 'Monica', was a secret police collaborator so devoted that the Securitate probably regarded her as more valuable even than Géza Pozsár.

Carmen Dumitru, who was esteemed by gymnasts and trainers alike for the skill with which she practiced as a physician, was an 'official source'. She was not recruited as an informer by the usual procedure, but when information was required of her, she provided it. A specialist in cardiology and sports medicine, Carmen Dumitru treated members of a number of Romanian national squads,[8] but the Securitate was interested in obtaining from her information about Nadia Comăneci's evolving state of health in particular. In the same period, the Securitate also drew upon another informed, codenamed 'Lili', who was probably a nurse at the sports complex's medical office, but whose identity remains unknown. From her reports it may be concluded that she was instructed to win Nadia's confidence, and for a few months, she succeeded. Pianist Corneliu Grigore, who signed his reports under the pseudonym 'Lazarovici Traian', was recruited as an informer while doing his military service. Those who knew him describe him as a very good pianist, in love with what he did, a serious-minded and generous man, but overly timorous and lacking in courage. As an informer he filed only sporadic reports on the members of the national squad. As the intelligence machinery still included Nicolae Vieru and Mrs Mili – who continued their careers as informers 'Vlad' and 'Lia Muri' – the Securitate remained a presence in both Nadia's professional and personal life.

The freedom Nadia hoped to enjoy in Bucharest was limited, as she was not allowed to go anywhere unaccompanied or without giving her reasons and planned route in advance. Her daily schedule and trips were known in advance by Securitate officers. When she did manage to slip outside the sports complex without permission, the authorities would enter red alert. An army of Militia and Securitate officers would set out in search of her, while top officials from the Party and N.C.P.E.S. went to the 23 August Centre anxiously to wait for the officers to bring her back or for her to return by herself. It was said that in such situations, even the borders were closed, to prevent her being taken out of the country against her will in the event that she had been kidnapped.[9] Nadia lived out her life in the sports complex, which, no matter how comfortable it might have been, was too small and suffocating a world for a curious, developing adolescent.

Figure 5.1 Photo taken by the Securitate on 4–5 October 1977, during a surveillance of Nadia Comăneci in Bucharest. (Archive of the National Council for Study of the Securitate Archives [A.C.N.S.A.S], Documents Archive, dossier 13346, vol. 26, leaf 436 bis.)

Figure 5.2 Photo taken by the Securitate on 4–5 October 1977, during a surveillance of Nadia Comăneci in Bucharest. (Archive of the National Council for Study of the Securitate Archives [A.C.N.S.A.S], Documents Archive, dossier 13346, vol. 26, leaf 436, back.)

Figure 5.3 Photo taken by the Securitate on 4–5 October 1977, during a surveillance of Nadia Comăneci in Bucharest. (Archive of the National Council for Study of the Securitate Archives [A.C.N.S.A.S], Documents Archive, dossier 13346, vol. 26, leaf 436, back.)

Figure 5.4 Photo taken by the Securitate on 4–5 October 1977, during a surveillance of Nadia Comăneci in Bucharest. (Archive of the National Council for Study of the Securitate Archives [A.C.N.S.A.S], Documents Archive, dossier 13346, vol. 26, leaf 436 bis.)

The three-storey hotel where she lived was just a few dozen metres from the sports hall. Nadia and Teodora shared a room on the second floor, at the end of the corridor, and were kept under close watch by the hotel staff, who had been instructed to apply strict rules of surveillance. They woke up at seven in the morning, ate breakfast in the canteen, and Condovici confirms that together they established a menu to which nothing could subsequently be added.[10] Training sessions began at eight with a half-hour warm up, but unlike in Oneşti, where Béla Károlyi didn't allow any other trainers or athletes to be present during training, the 23 August Gymnasium was not reserved for the women's team, but also used by the men's team, which wasn't a problem except when the lads engaged in raucous games of football during warm-ups.

The World Championships to be held in France in the autumn of 1978 were the prime objective of the women's squad. In anticipation of this sporting event, where positive results would also prove that transferring the gymnasts to Bucharest had been inspired, a mood of excitement and irritation took hold of the team. At the beginning of the year, when they left for France, the whole team displayed plenty of enthusiasm, as Carmen Dumitru noted on 22 February in a report about the three coaches, whom she described as 'trainers of the highest quality, comrades of honest labour.' She went on, 'they work in an atmosphere of collaboration, intense preoccupation with solving technical problems, rectifying existing physical deficiencies. They show pedagogical tact, a behaviour attentive and appropriate to the demands of this level.'[11]

But there were plenty of obstacles. During a meeting held at the R.G.F. in mid-February, it was concluded that Nadia wasn't co-operating with the coaches or making an effort. According to Hidi, either she lacked the desire to train any more, flirting with the idea of giving up the sport, or she declared herself incapable of losing weight, requesting medicines to suppress her appetite. By now she weighed fifty-two kilos and refused to step on the scales every day. Choreographer Vlase said she swung back and forth, sometimes working, sometimes not, as if she had lost her vocation. Albu proposed that a separate group be set up just for her, while Condovici informed the heads of the federation that maybe they ought to think about not taking part in the autumn world championships. Nadia had reached a critical moment and needed to find motivation straight away, believed Maria Simionescu, urging her trainers to work with her in an individual manner.[12]

Over the following weeks, incidents involving Nadia occurred, this time described by Mili Simionescu in a report she submitted to Department One in April, but which makes reference to events in February:

Monday (27 February 1978), during the break between two training sessions, between 14 and 16 hours (Nadia Comăneci) left the centre, taking the train to Ploieşti. That evening, when she was brought back, she was quite relaxed. From discussions with her mother it emerges that coach Condovici Gheorghe was very angry. Likewise, coach Albu Atanasia found Nadia frightened on the third floor, Sunday morning, after training, with the gymnast declaring to her that she didn't want to be beaten any more, because coach Condovici had threatened her that if she didn't lose weight he would beat her.

Nadia Comăneci remarked to her team mates however that she felt 'under guard' and wanted to prove that if she wanted to she could escape even in such circumstances, but she didn't really intend to leave.

Her coaches were talked to so that they would be demanding, stern, but without violence; so that they would organise pleasant, relaxing activities outside school and training hours.[13]

In February, Nadia, who showed no signs of being able to stick to a diet and had even put on a few kilos, 'was admonished for the increase in her weight that she had registered lately,' reported agent 'Lia Muri'. Condovici, who was quick to lose his temper, frequently upbraiding not only the gymnasts but his fellow coaches, was regarded as a strict trainer. In a letter of 12 April 1978, intercepted by the Securitate, Nadia complained that he 'behaves badly' and 'boasts (shows off) on our account. Do you know what Mr Condovici is like? Twice as bad as Károlyi was. I can't stand him any more. I've had enough.'[14]

At the time, a friendship had formed between Nadia Comăneci and gymnast Kurt Szilier,[15] a member of the men's national team. He and Aurelian Georgescu were observed spending too much time with Nadia and Teodora, sometimes meeting them in their hotel rooms after lights out. Schpizi, as his fellow team mates nicknamed him, had come to the attention of the Securitate in January, when they compiled a file on him. From the file we discover that he came from a family that had suffered during the early years of the Communist régime, when his father had been a political prisoner, one of the very many arrested at the time.[16]

By February 1978, the Securitate regarded the young Kurt Szilier as a 'close connection of the gymnast'[17] and decided to take measures to ensure a better 'knowledge and surveillance' of him. Not long thereafter, the authorities decided that the two gymnasts, Szilier and Georgescu, should be moved to the hotel of the Dinamo Club, to the dissatisfaction of Nadia and Teodora. 'They moved Schpizzi and Relu from the 23 August Hotel where we're staying, because the people from the federation decided to break off the friendship between us. So it would still be better in Oneşti,'[18] Nadia confessed to a girlfriend a few weeks later, once more gripped by restlessness.

Nadia was now sixteen years old. She was no longer the little girl who had appeared at Montréal with a ponytail and a bow on her hair, a girl of just 1.52 metres in height and forty kilos in weight, who obediently looked to her coaches. She now had short hair, cut in a fringe, and she had shot up six centimetres and put on ten kilos. She was growing up, undergoing the bodily and emotional changes of adolescence. Having risen to the top of her sport while still a child, it was time for her to embark on a personal life of her own, breaking free of authority. Her aspirations were those of any other normal teenager, who felt the need to fit in and to be with people of her own age. Famous throughout the world, Nadia now craved the simple things in life: to have a boyfriend and to go for a walk with him in the park, to go to the shops, to go to the discotheque or cinema, without having to seek permission or justify herself to anyone.

But there were no such prospects on the horizon, and Nadia was probably well aware that she led a life devoid of affectivity, a life controlled by adults, even if she had no way of knowing how minutely that control had been imposed by the Communist régime. At the training centre, surrounded by coaches, team mates, representatives of the federation and N.C.P.E.S., Securitate officers both known and unknown, she lived in complete solitude, since she was not allowed to develop any relationships outside the entourage imposed on her.

In April, Nadia made an effort and lost five kilos in just a few days. However, the atmosphere during training did not change for the better, but continued to be 'hard to bear' both for the coaches and the gymnasts, as Carmen Dumitru said, having in the meantime altered her opinion. The gymnasts began to feel afraid of the trainers, while the trainers were afraid of Nicolae Vieru and Maria Simionescu, who constantly checked up on their progress.

Atanasia Albu viewed Vieru as a disturbance, as somebody given to machination more than he was to helping the national squad, and who undermined Maria Simionescu's authority the better to arrogate to himself all decision-making, as informer 'Monica' noted in a report dated April 1981, in which she described at length how training unfolded in 1978:

On 1 December 1977, with great fanfare they are brought to Bucharest and training begins. The source is part of the team of trainers. Everything went well. Nadia and Teodora (. . .) begin to train consistently. On 24 April 1978, Nadia begins a short tour of Italy, where she competes very well. On this tour, contest and demonstrations, Nicu Vieru, as leader, is satisfied. Again, it seems to him that M. Simionescu is not competent enough and arrogates to herself every right: leadership, organisation, technical instructions etc. Nadia becomes 'the girl' who is 'a gold nugget, not yet valorised'. (The expression is hers.) After this tour there follows another, Sweden-France, where Nadia once more excels, and after a short stop in Bucharest, she leaves again, this time to China (with her mother). Nadia, technically very well prepared, wins the contest in China,[19] and N. Vieru starts to find all kinds of 'weaknesses' in the team of trainers, along with M. Simionescu.[20]

'Weaknesses', as the informer called them, continued to appear. Especially during the summer, when Nadia continued to go through difficult moments, experiencing the feeling that nobody understood her, that she was kept under excessive surveillance, that she was exhausted and abandoned and consequently no longer had the strength to be a gymnast. 'Lili' drew attention to the fact that from late July Nadia sought to wriggle out of training sessions, citing various excuses. She asked Vieru for days off so that she could focus on losing weight, which she didn't do, or else she would complain that nobody believed her when she complained of ill health, after a commission of the best orthopaedic physicians from the Emergency Hospital examined her without finding anything wrong and recommended that she continued to make a physical effort: 'According to the opinion of the source, N.C. is sick of gymnastics; she has no desire to train or interest in doing so; she tries to get out of training by deliberately putting on weight. She knows that she has to remain in gymnastics till the World Championships (particularly since her mother wants it) and hopes that when her mother comes here it will give her the desire to work. It is certain that N.C. is at a moral impasse to which the caprices of her age also add other factors.'[21]

Requested to support the team, Géza Pozsár arrived in Bucharest at the beginning of August. But because Béla Károlyi had not resigned himself to the idea that Nadia and Teodora were no longer his pupils, Pozsár did not receive his permission to continue working with the national squad, and the choreographer was therefore forced to abandon the thought. Nevertheless, he wrote a brief report on 5 August, after visiting the training centre, and his opinion was similar to that of the other informers:

The source reports on the training of the women's gymnastics squad in Bucharest.

Throughout training chaos reigns. There is nobody in charge. The trainers are at loggerheads. Hidi Iosif is not the right man to run training with authority and competence. He does not have the appropriate presence in front of the girls. Condovici is impulsive and is at odds with Atanasia Albu, who would like to work, but also to be in charge, whence the disagreements with Condovici. The girls have learned many new things, but for the time being they are far from being ready to compete.

Nadia Comăneci declared to the source on the evening of 4 August that she no longer wishes to stay at the training centre, because she can no longer bear the working schedule. The source sought to explain it to her positively, but it seems that Nadia no longer wishes to work.

Teodora Ungureanu works harder, but it seems that she has a negative influence on Nadia.

The working schedule, the volume of work is very poor, there is a lot of 'shirking'.

If urgent measures are not taken, the world championships will be compromised. It seems that Nadia no longer wishes to compete.[22]

In the same document, Nicolae Ilie states, 'the issues signalled in connection with the three coaches will also be checked via information supplied by source "Elena",' with reference to the reports submitted by Maria Login. Likewise, he notes that he instructed Pozsár to talk to Nadia more often with the purpose of encouraging her to work, and that he established the agent's next mission, which was to find out as much as possible about the 'dissensions' between the three coaches. A few days later, however, there were a number of events that led to an unfortunate incident: on 8 August 1978, Nadia was taken to Bucharest's Emergency Hospital after a suspected suicide attempt.

For obvious reasons, the press in Communist Romania was not allowed to print any mention of the suicide attempt, although three years later, there was a single exception, in circumstances that we shall lay out below. Nevertheless, the news reached the ears of Western journalists despite Romania's isolation from the free world. The Western press was to embroider the account to the point of fantasy, however. On the other hand, they had no means of discovering further details or checking the facts, since it was impossible to communicate with Nadia directly.

Disillusioned by the distortions published in the press over the course of time, in her book, *Letters to a Young Gymnast*, Nadia Comăneci decided 'to set the record straight after so many untrue stories have been told. Yes, I was very unhappy in 1978. But no, I did not attempt suicide by drinking a bottle of bleach because I saw my boyfriend with another girl as the movie *Nadia* showed. I have heard many accounts of that day and what supposedly happened; some journals in Germany even wrote that I drank two bottles of disinfectant because I was heartbroken at the breakup of an affair with a poet.'[23] Nadia says that the subject, which some tabloids rehash even today, 'is ridiculous and completely untrue.' She has spoken about the episode countless times, both before and after 1989, since foreign journalists have placed her in the situation of having to answer questions aimed at raking up her private life. But her answers have not always been the same.

With the permission of the Communist régime, the first public reaction came in 1981, in the form of a confession. In a book entitled *Nadia. My Own Story*, which was published in London in the autumn of that year, Nadia described the incident in plentiful detail, with the aim of persuading readers that none of it was true. The book was written in partnership with Graham Buxton Smither, a photo-reporter, but has never been published in Romanian translation.[24] The following are excerpts from the book that deal with the subject of the supposed suicide attempt:

The worst, and most cruel, example of the kind of wild speculation I have been the target of was the report of my 'attempted suicide' which appeared in some journals in West Germany, Italy, and Great Britain. According to the first of these reports, I had drunk two bottles of disinfectant because I was heartbroken at the breakup of an affair I was supposed to have had with some forty-two your old poet (sic). (. . .)

It seems to have been a case of someone hearing part of a story, greatly enlarging upon it and then later interpreting as tacit admission the fact that it was never denied.

The truth was that I had swallowed something that violently disagreed with me and that I had been involved in a bitter row with some officials who were with me in Bucharest. To clear up this matter for once and for all, let me first set the scene.

I was staying at the 23rd August Sports Hotel in Bucharest, where I had been promised that I would be allowed more freedom than I had been used to under Béla and Marta. The team doctor had also given me permission to take a short break from training. This would give me a chance to recover from the strain of the previous months.

The day in question was my wash day and I had some leotards, gymsocks, and underwear to deal with. I decided to pop down the corridor to borrow some bleach from one of the other girls, but when I opened our outer door I was confronted by one of the women team officials who immediately asked, 'Nadia, where are you going? Is there something that you want?' Now ordinarily, that is not the sort of question that should upset anyone, but I was finding that every time I wanted to leave my room, there was somebody 'casually' asking what I was up to. I suppose that they felt nervous about being responsible for me, but I felt angry because I was being denied the extra freedom I'd been promised. At least under Béla, I always knew where I stood even if I didn't like it or agree with it. Anyway, I went to get the bleach and came back with a cup full. Instead of doing my washing right away, I decided to write a letter home and, putting the cup down on the desk in the corner of the room by the window, I sat there and wrote, mentioning the crazy amount of protection which I had to put up with. The more I wrote about it, the more it made me angry. I finished the letter, discovered that I needed some stamps and went to borrow some from one of my teammates. When I opened the inner door to my room, there were three of the officials playing cards outside my room. 'Going somewhere?' came the inevitable inquiry. I hit the roof I could take no more.

'What the hell are you doing here? Why is it that I can't even visit the TV room without being cross-examined. I am supposed to be here to relax, to get some peace and quiet. How can anyone feel relaxed with you people ready to jump on me at every corner? You are driving me mad! I'd rather be back with Béla. Just leave me alone!'

I hardly registered the stunned and silent faces of the three guards. In an almost blind fury I stormed back in my room and slammed the door behind me. I threw myself into the chair by the desk and banged my letter down on the top. I was shaking with rage. I had some fruit juice in one of the cups there, and I picked it up and took a huge gulp. I wanted to calm myself. Before I realized what I had done, I felt a hideous burning sensation in my throat and stomach—I had reached for the wrong cup. I had swallowed the bleach, though not all of it, mercifully. In agony, I called out for help from the girls in the room next to mine. I had tried to make myself sick but could not. I think it was Dana (Turner) who rushed in and called immediately for a doctor. Luckily, in the 23rd August complex, we have a Sports Medicine Centre, so help was very quick in arriving. Within two days, I was back on my feet as if nothing had happened.[25]

Thus, according to Nadia, it was an unfortunate accident, which occurred in a moment when she felt despondent and annoyed at the excessive surveillance of her every move and the authorities' unkept promises.

While the reason given by Western journalists, according to whom Nadia's reckless act was prompted by disappointment in love, itself the result of too strict a lifestyle, there were also authors who took a different approach, drawing on their own experience of high-level sport. Sándor Dávid, who was a member of the Hungarian junior fencing team and later a sports commentator for Hungarian television, published a book entitled *The Freedom of the Leap* in 1981, which sold out immediately. Dávid describes the huge effort made by sportspeople who become champions, the sacrifices they make and their physical and psychological impact. In the tenth chapter, in which he talks about gymnastics, Dávid mentions that Nadia Comăneci attempted suicide because she had to lose ten kilos in weight.

In late October 1981, a number of Hungarian newspapers, including *Képes Sport* and *Népsport*, published positive reviews of the book, but Nadia herself reacted not long afterward, with the permission of the Romanian censors. Her right to reply was published in the 21 November 1981 issue of *Scînteia Tineretului* (The Spark of Youth), in which she wrote a weekly column with the title 'Nadia Comăneci talks to readers', with the help of journalist Horia Alexandrescu, even though he was not given a by-line. In her column that Saturday, Nadia Comăneci criticised Sándor Dávid, saying that he neither did any research nor knew what he was talking about when he made such a claim in his book. It was true, she said, that when a sportsperson controls her weight, she has to do battle with herself, but in her case, it was a question of five kilos, not ten 'and five kilos means two days of strict dieting, intensive training, saunas and running, and not at all any reason to panic.' She then repeated the account already published in *My Own Story*, to which Romanian readers had no access. But there are a number of minor differences, which may easily be understood, since the account omits any mention of the fact that she was under permanent surveillance by the authorities at the 23 August Complex: 'Taking a mug, I went out into the corridor to ask for some washing liquid from the cleaning woman, making a noise. Inevitably, a coach appeared, chiding me for not being in bed after lights out. I showed him I'd been getting some detergent to wash my kit and went back inside my room, annoyed.'[26] Where, she goes on, she confused the cup of detergent for a cup of fruit juice.

Three years later, the tale was retold in the film *Nadia*, which Nadia herself cites as one of the sources of disinformation on the subject. It is worth looking at this film more closely.

At the beginning of 1983, film producer Jim Thompson and screenwriter Jim McGinn visited Romania with the aim of obtaining the permission of the authorities for a film they were eager to make: a biopic about Nadia Comăneci, which, naturally, would be entitled *Nadia*. For the film to be as authentic as possible, McGinn wished to shoot it in Romania, using American actors cast by director Alan Cooke. The National Council of Physical Education and Sport rejected the project. The rights Thompson was prepared to pay – two thousand dollars – were derisory, but the main reason for the rejection was the script. After examination of the forty-page screenplay, it was concluded that the film 'presents aspects that affect the gymnast's prestige, overdo the contribution of the Károlyis in shaping and developing the gymnast and overall the film does a service to the Károlyi family, creating publicity for them.'[27] By then, Marta and Béla Károlyi, and also choreographer Géza Pozsár, were no longer in Romania, as all three had defected to the United States and were now officially deemed traitors. The script went over the top in casting a favourable light on the two coaches, as the representatives of the N.C.P.E.S. noted, which would have been unacceptable to the Romanians, no matter how big the fee had been.

When his proposal was rejected, Jim Thompson went ahead with his project anyway, shooting it in the Serbian Banat, with the permission of the Yugoslav authorities, in order to capture the atmosphere of an East-European country. The film was shown at Cannes in 1984. The Securitate believed that one of the authors of the screenplay was Graham Buxton Smither, who was placed on Romania's list of undesirables for the next five years.[28] Visiting Bucharest early in 1984, he was beaten up one evening in the Labour Boulevard area: while waiting for a taxi he had ordered, three people climbed out of a black car, called out his name, and punched him to the ground. Before they sped off in their car, they told him they knew where he lived and that he should get out of Romania and stay away from Nadia, which is what he did.

Buxton Smither was indeed a consultant for the film, and maybe even the person who came up with the original idea for it. In January 1982, Department One monitored him when he came to Romania with the intention of visiting Nadia. According to the Securitate, he proposed to Nadia 'that they should make a film together (. . .) also involving the Károlyi family, who have already been approached.' The Securitate report claims, 'Nadia Comăneci was enthusiastic about Graham Buxton Smither's proposal, but rejected the idea that the Karoli family should be involved.'[29] Decades later, Smither recalls one of the more hair-raising episodes of the whole project: after Nadia gave him a letter agreeing to the making of the film, he had to smuggle it out of Romania as he was fearful it might be discovered in the event that his luggage was searched at Otopeni Airport. The plan itself had been hatched in the basement of the U.S. Embassy, which was equipped with a special room swept daily for listening devices. It went without a hitch, after which it was Jim Thompson's responsibility to get the funds directly to Nadia.[30]

Without the permission of the N.C.P.E.S., Nadia could not have been part of the project, and the script retained its initial form. Géza Pozsár claims that in actual fact the film was based not so much on Buxton Smither's book as on information provided by Béla Károlyi, the real author of the script,[31] and we have no reason to doubt this. In the first place, Pozsár himself was directly involved in the film, since he played himself. Secondly, the film's credits give the Károlyis as consultants, which confirms their involvement. Thirdly, Marta and Béla are among the positive characters in the film. Indeed, they are portrayed in a highly seductive light. Joe Bennett, the actor who plays Béla Károlyi, scolds Nadia in a few scenes, but do so with fatherly love. Marta is portrayed as a likeable, tender, understanding, friendly young trainer, which certainly was never the case. In the film, it is the Károlyis who lay the foundations of gymnastics in Romania, but come up against numerous obstacles and corrupt, nasty characters such as Nicolae Vieru and Ştefania Comăneci, Nadia's mother.

We do not know how audiences reacted to the film more than thirty-five years ago, audiences that had no way of knowing how superficial and full of falsities it was. It has never been screened in Romania, but Vieru had the opportunity to watch it at the time, as he recounts in his autobiography:

> Before the congress (of the F.I.G.) in Los Angeles a film entitled 'Nadia' was being shown in Los Angeles. The film had also been shown on flights to America, having been made by the ABC company, which originally wanted to shoot it in Romania, but was turned down, since it was also about Béla Károlyi. The film was made in Yugoslavia with American actors, who played the characters Béla, Marta, Pozsár, Maria Simionescu, Vieru, and, of course, Nadia.
>
> I was in the film as a negative character, a communist politician who manipulated Nadia to create an image for myself of being a big boss, whom Béla sternly stood up to.[32]

In May 1984, when it was known that the first screening of the film was to be made at Cannes, Constantin Oancea, Romania's Deputy Foreign Minister, wrote a telegram to the French ambassador informing him that Nadia was prejudicial to Romania, since it proffered 'calumnies and distortions against gymnastics in our country and against Nadia Comăneci.' He also urged that solutions be sought to prevent the organisers of Cannes from accepting the film, a demand that obviously had no chances of success: 'The career of Nadia Comăneci and her family are presented in an insulting and degrading way (her father as an alcoholic, her mother as a social climber, Nadia as attempting to commit suicide, a constant dispute between coaches and the federation). At present the most effective means of countering this defamatory act are being examined. Given the short time remaining before the opening of the international festival, we ask you to undertake those measures that you deem necessary in order to thwart this hostile act and urgently to convey proposals and suggestions regarding the means to be pursued in order that the organisers of the festival not allow the presentation of this film.'[33]

At Cannes, the film was not a critical success. But it did present to audiences both in France and in the countries where it was subsequently distributed the scene of which Oancea complained in his telegram: the story of Nadia's suicide attempt, as it was known to Béla Károlyi and Géza Pozsár, the production's consultants. Nadia was supposed to have resorted to this desperate act out of depression and demoralisation. She was suffocated by the régime's surveillance, she had quarrelled with Teodora Ungureanu, and out of the window she had seen her boyfriend Kurt Szilier with another girl. But Nadia was portrayed not only as a victim, but also as a great champion, who picked herself up off the ground and continued to fight, since in the film the suicide scene is meant to emphasise her strength and tenacity in the difficult process of making her way back. Obviously, the Károlyis are also given the credit for knowing how to support and encourage her, while Nicolae Vieru is portrayed as the villain of the piece.

Resident in the United States since 1990, Nadia has not been able to avoid questions about the episode. But this time her answers have been different, as was the case in March 1990, in an article published in *Life* magazine,[34] in which she recognised that it was only an attempt, or in an interview with Bart Conner for *The Magic and Mystery of Nadia*, broadcast on ABC Sports:[35] 'There were rumours that you tried to commit suicide. Can you tell me about it?' asked Conner. 'Yes. When they moved me and changed my trainers, I didn't like it in Bucharest. I didn't have anyone to talk to and I just wanted to attract people's attention, for them to know that something was wrong, that what was happening wasn't good for me. I drank a little shampoo, not to commit suicide, but to attract attention.'[36] She was undoubtedly telling the truth because her so-called suicide attempt in the summer of 1978 was her only means to cause a shock and consequently to make the Communist régime agree to make changes and improve her life.

The Securitate arrived at the same conclusion through its agents, including Maria Simionescu, a witness to events at the time. Mrs Mili described to Captain Nicolae Ilie the chain of events, starting on Sunday 6 August, when Nadia ran away from the training centre to singer Benone Sinulescu's flat. On 7 August, Nadia 'gave the heads of the Romanian Gymnastics Federation a written note in which she expressly demanded not to have to work with trainer Condovici Gheorghe any more, and concluded with a kind of ultimatum that otherwise "the Nadia Comăneci chapter in gymnastics will come to a definite close"'. On 8 August, around 16.00 hours, she drank a glass of detergent dissolved in water, she was taken to the emergency room of the sports complex by trainer Iosif Hidi, then transported to Emergency Hospital, Simionescu continues. After intervention by the doctors and after treatment, it was deemed that it was not opportune to keep her in hospital, and the gymnast was taken by Maria Simionescu to her flat where she could keep a better watch over her.

On 9 August, there was a further incident, the final episode of this rebellion. In the evening, coach Condovici went to Maria Simionescu's home to demand explanations as to why the gymnast had left the hotel of the sports centre and during heated discussions, Nadia was struck by the coach. After Condovici left, Maria Simionescu called to her home first Nicolae Vieru, 'who decided to remove coach Condovici Gheorghe from the squad' and then Captain Ilie: 'Allow me to report that I immediately went to the place in question and talked to the gymnast and the source, reassuring them that nothing else would happen.'[37]

The Securitate were well informed and, in the reports that they promptly drew up for their political superiors, they gave a clear account of how the crisis arose.

But they also deemed it necessary to take further measures to keep Nadia under tighter control, as they were incapable of understanding that her depression and despair were in fact a result of constant surveillance:

> In this situation, at the end of 1977, gymnast Nadia Comăneci categorically refused to work with trainers Marta and Béla Károlyi, which led to the Romanian Gymnastics Federation establishing a new team of coaches to look after the training of promising gymnasts, with the main objective of taking part in the World Championships in France in October 1978.
>
> After a relatively good start, nor did this new format achieve the training tasks stipulated for this period for a number of reasons including:
>
> The rethinking of the coach-gymnast relationship was carried out defectively, skimping on discipline in the training and comportment of gymnasts Nadia Comăneci and Teodora Ungureanu.
>
> No measures were taken to prevent negative and mutual influence between the two gymnasts in connection with the volume of work and privations of high-level sport, in particular the actions of gymnast Teodora Ungureanu, who incited Nadia Comăneci with the obvious aim of holding her back from the standpoint of training while she herself made progress. The 'sporting' rivalry between the two is well known.
>
> The emergence and exacerbation of misunderstanding between the three coaches, situations which the two gymnasts used to their own ends. Let us here mention that such misunderstandings also exist among the heads of the federation (the secretary general and federation coach). These factors do not have a unified course of action in their relations with gymnast Nadia Comăneci.
>
> Neither the federation nor the team of coaches have found solutions for co-operation with the families of the two gymnasts to support them in achieving their training objectives, although it is well known that what they pursue most of all is their own and the gymnasts' personal interests.
>
> This state of affairs led gymnast Nadia Comăneci to lose faith in her capacity for willpower and effort, and as a result she underestimates her potential and prospects of winning the World Gymnastics Championships this year.
>
> It is believed that thanks to this she sometimes resorts to limited actions to give up high-level sport, knowing that she does not wish to withdraw from gymnastics after defeat at an international contest.
>
> Besides this, the gymnast's personal dissatisfactions should also be taken into account, which arise from the way in which she deems she has benefitted from the material advantages obtained as a result of participation in international contests.
>
> Taking into consideration the opinion of the experts and in the context of the aforementioned, as well as in order to be able to prevent in future

uncontrolled acts on the part of gymnast Nadia Comăneci, we propose that the following be put forward to be examined by the comrade Minister of Sport, Emil Drăgănescu:

1. The induction of a climate of order and discipline within the entire collective, including among the coaches. In this respect let it be known that coach Hidi Iosif allows himself easily to be influenced by the gymnasts, and from the professional standpoint he does not rise to the level of the exigencies that are demanded of this sports squad, which sometimes explains his lack of personality and firmness within the collective, he is incapable of leading such a squad.

2. The establishment of a daily schedule, which will require of the gymnasts a volume of work at least at the level of that which they performed in Oneşti before the Montréal Olympics.

3. The elimination of any immixture in the activity of the collective on the part of factors from the federation or N.C.P.E.S., with one person being designated in this respect to carry out liaisons between the federation, N.C.P.E.S. and this collective.

4. The designation of persons of the female sex within the collective to ensure the gymnast is accompanied and kept under surveillance both during the schedule and outside it, including during the night.

5. Insurance of more rigorous control of all the gymnast's contacts, including with her family and the other gymnasts in the squad, particularly with Teodora Ungureanu, regarding whom there are suspicions that indirectly or even directly she is inciting her to uncontrolled actions.

6. Non-conditioning of the granting of a flat in Bucharest on participation in the World Gymnastics Championships, but rather discussion in the most serious manner of the fact that she will be awarded a much larger prize than the one for the Montréal Olympics.

7. Inopportuneness of discussion with Nadia Comăneci of the possibility of her taking part in the Moscow Olympics.

8. Appropriate instruction of receptionists at the 23 August Hotel in Bucharest not to allow her in question to leave the hotel unaccompanied by a member of the collective of trainers or one of the persons designated to accompany her.

9 Opportuneness of other measures to be taken by the organs of the Ministry of the Interior with the aim of preventing any eventual uncontrolled acts on the part of gymnast Nadia Comăneci.[38]

Late August was an extremely tense time, with decisions taken under emotional disturbance. Would Nadia Comăneci wish to carry on as a gymnast? Would she be able to motivate herself? Maria Simionescu continued to keep a close watch on her. Nicolae Vieru managed to wrest a promise from her that after a few days of complete rest, during which she would try to lose weight, she would report back to training sessions. Captain Nicolae Ilie urged 'Lili' 'to conduct herself in such a way as to be on intimate terms with gymnast Nadia Comăneci in order to prevent uncontrolled acts on her part.'[39] Carmen Dumitru was assigned to sleep in Nadia's room with her after she left Simionescu's flat, much to Nadia's chagrin: at the end of August, she told her mother over the phone: 'I can't stand having Dr Dumitru sleep in my room with me any more. I'm not allowed to be on my own.'[40]

The training programme continued to be deficient, due to the fact that too many people were jockeying to be involved. Nicolae Vieru was in the gym constantly, 'with instructions and talking over the federation coach (she too present constantly), as well as the other trainers,' reported 'Lili'. There was also a throng of doctors, nurses and psychologists. 'Naturally, probably all of them want things to go well, but it's well known that the road to hell is paved with good intentions,'[41] added the informer.

All of them had good intentions, but they made it hard for Nadia to concentrate, since they deprived her of self-confidence, and such a large number of people was hardly likely to motivate her. On 24 August, Maria Simionescu told Ilie that Nadia had made progress, but 'she believes that everybody is standing around laughing at her and that the adults around her follow her all the time. She talked to her mother, then her father, who came to visit her in the last few days.'[42]

A few days later, agent 'Lia Muri' penned another report in which she briefly laid out just how damaged Nadia's mental state was and described the tumult of the training process:

On 22–25 August, Nadia Comăneci requested not to work and to eat only carrots and milk in order to get back to the optimum body weight for training, which request was accepted. After this brief period, not only did she not lose weight, but actually put on weight. Her father paid her a visit, she showed him around the city and he talked to her, encouraging her and asking her to train seriously. On the morning of 25.viii there was a discussion with Nadia within the squad's management collective, at which her father was present. In the end it was decided that she should go to the heads of the N.C.P.E.S. and declare that she can no longer do gymnastics, but although she even got dressed to go there, she changed her mind and then embarked on a strict weight-loss programme, by means of exercise, sauna and sweating beneath mats, repeated rounds.

In the sauna she was accompanied by coaches Albu Atanasia and Iorga Silvia. Nadia was crying and saying that she would go to the comrade minister (of sport, Emil Drăgănescu) with a knife for he to kill her so that she wouldn't have to do gymnastics any more. In the end she calmed down and three hours later she had lost 1.5 kg.

She slept in her room with Dr Carmen Dumitru and by morning she once again had the same weight as before this forced training. (. . .) The source believes that it is necessary that her mother should be with her![43]

Both Simionescu and Vieru asked Ştefania Comăneci to come to Bucharest so that she could spend a few days with her daughter. Nadia had previously said that she would like to have somebody from outside the environment in which she lived to come and stay with her, somebody close to her, who would provide her with the care and protection she needed. On 28 August, at seven in the morning, Mili Sionionescu telephoned Oneşti and had a brief conversation with Ştefania Comăneci.

The objective's mother was telephoned by citizen Simionescu, the following conversation takes place:

S.: what will we do about the ob[jective].? She said she can't take any more. She said so in front of everybody. Com. Vieru will issue a written decision today.

Mother: what should I do? Talk to her? Don't let her go to the com. minister till I get there.

S.: I don't know what to do. I'm desperate. I tried to get in touch with you. I told the ob. that we won't make any decision till we talk to you. A lot of important things have happened and we haven't had the chance to talk. She says she can't even walk any more. How is she supposed to work? On the parallel bars she says her palms hurt. She's only done two or three elements. She runs and cries because I don't believe her. I say, make a little effort, dear, even if it hurts, but she says she can't at all. I say, what are you torturing yourself like this for, running and crying, falling on your head?!? It's impossible. There's no point. Everybody has finished training, and I'm working extra in the gym on Sunday just to work with her separately, so she won't see what nice progress the others have made. It's a shame. (. . .) When you encourage her or scold her, I don't know how you do it, but she does the work.[44]

The European Championships in Strasbourg were just two months away, and Nadia was in a very poor state physically and in terms of morale. It was hard to believe that it was possible for her to take part in the competition any more. Vieru was already getting ready to inform the heads of the N.C.P.E.S., after which they would inform the people in charge of sport within the secretariat of the Central Committee of the Communist Party that Nadia would no longer be a member of the national team. Securitate General Dumitru Tăbăcaru, head of Department

One, had already done so on 21 August, when he reported to the head of the institution, 'Nadia Comăneci is no longer willing to submit to the effort and privation demanded by high-level sport.'[45]

Throughout this period, Béla Károlyi had not been idle in Oneşti, content merely to look wistfully at the countless trophies he and his wife had accumulated in their two-room flat. Béla was tireless and therefore capable of coming up with a viable back-up plan, which is what he did in the first months of 1978.

There was nothing romantic or attractive about the town of Oneşti, and Károlyi now viewed it as desolate and hostile. After Nadia Comăneci left, he felt more betrayed and persecuted than ever before. He frequently complained that the atmosphere had become suffocating, that he was discriminated against because of his ethnicity, and that the authorities 'are trying to punish us and remove us from the gymnastics élite.' At the same time, he was still thinking about various moves he might make 'to compromise and annihilate'[46] Nadia, as 'Nelu' reported in February 1978.

Consequently, as early as January, he intensified his efforts to move from Moldavia to one of the larger cities of Transylvania. At first, he tried in Cluj, where his proposal to create a new women's gymnastics centre was rejected by the local authorities for various bureaucratic and economic reasons. Then he tried in Deva, which he visited in early February. Here, luck was with him, since his plan was enthusiastically embraced, and he was even asked not to delay his transfer there.

The Securitate obtained information about the progress of these talks and the speed with which Károlyi's plan unfolded, both through intercepted telephone calls and from agents among the people he met. For example, Maria Login reported that Károlyi was making preparations 'to finalise with the local Party and sport organs the ways and means of his and his wife's transfer as coaches to the town.'[47] However, she was unable give the Securitate officer the date when the Károlyis intended to leave Oneşti or any details of how they were to work with the federation once they had moved to Deva. What was known, however, was that Béla Károlyi had struck up a friendship with Viorel Jianu, the first vice chairman of the Hunedoara County Council for Physical Education and Sport, who became his most important backer once he had settled in Deva.

As a man of action, extremely energetic when he had a goal to fulfil, Károlyi needed only a few weeks to complete the bureaucratic procedures, and by mid-April he and his family had moved to Deva. They arrived on 18 March, holding a team training session there, after which they did not return to Oneşti. 'When we arrived, the entire town turned out to greet us. There was a huge celebration and all the townspeople hugged and kissed us. It was such a sweet feeling. After all the frustrations, we were finally home,'[48] recalls Károlyi.

The local authorities, enthused at the opportunity to engage in a sports project of such a scope, made every possible resource available. Money was no object, since a budget was passed the very next day, after a lightning session of the Party's county planning committee. According to Károlyi: 'The mayor, Party officials, and the directors of local industrial plants all attended. Thirty minutes later we had the money, the construction workers, and the support of the entire town to create a new gymnastics school and centre. The next day the bulldozers rolled in and construction began.'[49] A few months later, a sports hall was officially opened in the centre of town, a space fifty metres long and twenty-one metres wide. The sports hall had a number of annexes, including a sauna, and was equipped with cutting-edge equipment for the time, including a hi-tech music studio. The Károlyis and Pozsárs were provided with every personal comfort, living in a duplex villa on Strada Alexandru Sahia, right next to the sports hall.

And so began the experimental gymnastics programme hosted by General School No. 7 in Deva,[50] an educational establishment inaugurated in September 1978, at the beginning of the school year. Whereas ten years earlier, when the Oneşti centre opened, the Károlyis had not made any contribution to its founding, the entire Deva project was entirely thanks to their own efforts.

After they moved to Deva, the R.G.F. decided to give the Károlyis the responsibility for training junior gymnasts, but the World Championships in France were also the principal objective of the competition season for them. In an interview for *Sportul* at the beginning of February, Károlyi complained – albeit in a muted way – that the Romanian Gymnastics Federation had not kept its word and transferred other gymnasts to Oneşti to replace Nadia and Teodora. 'Although initially we were promised that our request would be met, up to now nothing has been done,'[51] said Károlyi, who introduced to the newspaper's readers the gymnasts he had been training in Oneşti at the beginning of the year: Emilia Eberle, Cristina Itu, Marilena Neacşu, Gabi Gheorghiu, and Marilena Vlădărău, who were joined by two beginners in early January, Simona Noja and Viorica Gyüjtö. Most of these gymnasts followed Károlyi to Deva, hoping to be selected for the national team in the weeks before the Strasbourg competition.

Károyli was driven by a desire to show the whole country, but especially Nicolae Vieru and the Romanian Gymnastics Federation, that he could discover gymnasts as gifted as Nadia and pave their way to glory, and that Nadia wasn't one of a kind. In January 1978 he hoped to succeed in his plan thanks to Cristina Itu, whose achievements he singled out in interviews, since at the time she was Romanian gymnastics champion. But Itu suffered a severe injury and had to undergo a long process of rehabilitation. 'A bigger misfortune couldn't have come down on us,' Marta Károlyi told Géza Pozsár on 26 January, in a phone call intercepted by the Securitate, adding: 'The slap in the face that Nadia dealt Béla, and she left, it was a comfort to him that that girl was doing well and he could at least win a medal with her. The only gold medal is gone. It's a very difficult time. She was the only girl in the official competitions able to compete with Nadia, to beat her somehow.'[52]

After Cristina Itu's injury, Károlyi turned his attention to Emilia Gertrude Eberle, a quiet, modest girl, who had won gold in the vault and uneven parallel bars events at the Balkan Championships in 1977 and whom Károyli now considered to be his secret weapon. Born in Arad in 1964, Eberle had trained under Barbara Frenkel, Géza Weinhert, and Pavel Rosenfeld. She arrived in Oneşti in 1976, when she was twelve, and Károlyi beat her from the very first day, after her mother entrusted her to the famous trainer, in the hope that he would soon make her a great champion.[53] To Károlyi it didn't even matter that both of them were ethnic Hungarians; his abuse continued for years, with traumatising effects on the gymnast that lasted into adulthood.[54]

Ten years later, the Securitate suspected Eberle of lacking loyalty, recording in her personal file that she came from a 'nationalist' family that instilled in her 'nationalist ideas—such as "Hungary is her country".'[55] In 1989, informers signalled that the former gymnast, by now a trainer, intended to leave Romania illegally, which is what she did, escaping to Hungary just a few weeks before Nadia Comăneci.

The Department of State Security followed Károlyi from Moldavia to Transylvania as surely as his own shadow. His Oneşti file was sent to Hunedoara County Securitate Inspectorate, and the Deva secret police appended to it the new surveillance file that they opened on 18 April, just six days after he moved to the town, entitling it the 'Gymnast' dossier. To meet the legal requirements of the time, on 11 May 1978 the first secretary of the county Party organisation asked permission for Party member Béla Károlyi to be monitored, which permission was granted the next day.

Thenceforth the Securitate focused on setting up a new intelligence network. The agents in Oneşti were no longer useful, with the exception of Géza Pozsár, who had come to Deva with Károlyi. The first reports in the 'Gymnast' dossier were written by 'Nelu' in April–August 1978, and 'Nelu' continued to keep Captain Nicolae Ilie of Department One up to date via letters sent to the old post office box in Bucharest or in face to face conversations whenever he had occasion to visit the capital. We discover details of Károlyi's activities during his first months in Deva from one such report, written by Pozsár on 5 August 1978, in which he refers to himself in the third person:

The source reports that coach Béla Károlyi and his wife and choreographer Géza Pozsár moved to Deva on 12 April this year, where they received a villa with two separate flats. Coach Béla Károlyi immediately after his arrival set to work organising a school unit specialising in gymnastics that would take the nature of a high-level sports centre. With the support of the local party organs, the establishment of the new gymnastics centre v. quickly took shape, in record time, which is due in large part to the energy of B. Károlyi and the generosity of first vice chairman of the C.C.P.E.S. Viorel Jianu, a person with whom Károlyi is in very close relations, materialising in perfect collaboration, as well as in familiar respects.

Károlyi has fitted out his home to his own specification and the local organs, bowing to his repeated requests, have given him every assistance in this. He has built kennels for his dogs and poultry that are of the greatest 'comfort', hassling the employees of the 'Castle' stadium near which the villa is located to carry out building work and often even putting to work the people he brought with him to Deva to be employed as teachers. Not wishing to have any rivals at the professional level, he brought professionally inexperienced teachers, but who are devoted to him. This is how husband and wife Ghenade and teacher Victor 'Cibi' from Bucharest came to be here.

Obviously, above all else Károlyi places his interest in getting rich, and the people from Deva have promised him that they will enlarge his living quarters by means of an extension. This expense will be borne by C.C.P.E.S. forums.

At the same time the Károlyis were invited to the C.C. of the R.C.P., to see comrade Cazacu, where they were promised help to set up the new centre. B. Károlyi's sentiments and ideas regarding the situation of the Hungarians in Romania have not changed, he often says he was provided living conditions in order to 'shut his mouth.'

Towards the President of the country his feelings have still not changed, when he has the chance he makes sarcastic remarks about him.

His behaviour towards the girls has changed for the better. He no longer makes use of beating and insults. His wife has not changed in this respect, often resorting to beatings without justification. The Károlyis have not made contacts in the town, the only families they visit are Oprişa (relatives of Béla whom he needs for Andrea and contacts for purchases etc.), the Jianu family and the Miron family, the secretary C.C.P.E.S. Their relations with their families in Odorhei and Cluj have cooled, since the two spouses don't keep in touch with them.

(. . .) Towards choreographer Pozsár he behaves better, and he receives more benefits than before, but if the opportunity arises Béla thinks only of himself the same as before.[56]

On 13 August, Pozsár filed further information about the Károlyis' abusive behaviour towards the gymnasts, which seems to have diminished in the first few months after their move to Deva, reporting, 'the famous trainer has resumed his old methods.' According to the agent, Károlyi had reverted to his old violent ways and was beating the gymnasts 'as badly as can be, particularly Eberle, Vlădărau and Gyütö. When he no longer has technical arguments, he thinks this helps him. The pianist has been saying there's general discontent among the girls, and some of them are even thinking of giving up Deva.' Likewise, Pozsár drew attention to the fact that 'the great trainer takes great delight in Nadia's failures,'[57] with reference to Károlyi being perfecting informed about the difficult period she was going through in Bucharest.

Satisfied with how many privileges he was given in Deva and no longer under any pressure from the central authorities, Károlyi concentrated on the programme to train the juniors, and he soon obtained his first significant results. Two successes are worthy of mention, particularly since both flattered Károlyi's pride and brought him press plaudits: the European Juniors Championship and the Romanian National Championships.

The tournaments took place in September 1978. The European competition was held in the Palace of Sports, Milan, where Károlyi's girls – Emilia Eberle, Gabi Gheorghiu, Marilena Vlădărău, and Anca Kiss – won the first five places in the ranking, and on 13 September Eberle became the first European Juniors champion. Trudi, as everybody called her, won three gold medals and one silver. Marilena Vlădărău completed this run of victories with a further two silver medals in the finals on the apparatuses.

After their return from Milan, Károlyi gave a statement to the Romanian press in Otopeni Airport, saying 'at the present time, Emilia Eberle cannot be defeated in our championships.'[58] What he meant was that Eberle was on the point of becoming a second Nadia Comăneci, and a few days later he had the satisfaction of his prediction coming true. At the National Championships and the Daciada, held in Bucharest, which were covered by a number of foreign television stations, including NBC, Emilia Eberle and Kurt Szilier became the country's new champions in the women's and men's gymnastics events. Eberle won the all-round competition and three apparatuses (vault, uneven parallel bars and beam), and was deemed the best gymnast in the contest.

Nadia did not take part in the competition, the same as she had not taken part in the Balkan Gymnastics Championships held in Cluj between 8 and 11 September, at which Teodora Ungureanu and Anca Grigoraş shared first place. There were vague references in *Sportul* to her absence, which was supposed to be because she was 'following a special training programme,'[59] although her taking part in such contests ought to have been a normal part of such training.

Immediately after his success in the National Championship, Béla Károlyi took charge of Romania's women's gymnastics squad once more. He recounts the episode in his autobiography, claiming that Nicolae Vieru, his old enemy, was the first to beg him to accept the proposal, and after he rejected it, he was accosted by Ilie Verdeţ on his way out of the building where the competition was being held. He could not turn down Ilie Verdeţ, obviously. As a result, on 20 September 1978, the Károlyis and the gymnasts they had selected returned to Deva to begin an intensive training programme in preparation for the World Championships.

Also among them was Nadia Comăneci, who, according to Károlyi, visited him at the hotel, which astonished him. Károlyi recalls that she had put on so much weight that 'she was huge, completely deformed', and her morale was very low. 'Béla, I want to go back with you,'[60] Nadia is supposed to have begged him, with tears in her eyes, and Károlyi agreed, but only after explaining to her how great an effort she would have to make to get back in shape. Nadia described the episode differently, however. In her account, it was Károlyi who visited her, at the sports complex: 'When I opened the door of my room, Béla looked horrified. (. . .) I had gained quite bit of weight, and I was out of shape. He sat down, and we began to talk. He wasn't angry; he was nice and parental. I know that I cried, remembering the old days and my past glory.'[61] On the morning of 17 September, Nadia phoned her mother to tell her the news that she was going to Deva. When she found out, Ştefania Comăneci was outraged and warned her of the consequences, but Nadia told her that her former coach had been the one who came looking for her, wanting to work with her again, and 'insisted' that she go with him to Deva, while admitting that Atanasia Albu and Iosif Hidi still didn't know anything about her decision.'[62]

Can Nadia have been suffering from Stockholm Syndrome? She did want to go back to her old coach, but it is not possible to conclude that she did so based on any liking for the man, since she was decisively influenced by other people to do so, people with a great deal of clout. Atanasia Albu pointed to Nicolae Vieru as the main plotter. He was supposed to have 'instigated' Nadia to go back to her old coach, 'who understood his mistakes and with whom she could work perfectly,' said the secretary general of the R.G.F. Vieru, backed up by Emil Ghibu, the vice chairman of the N.C.P.E.S., talked about it in secret with Nadia a number of times, starting in August, after her suicide attempt: 'One day, coaches Hidi Iosif and Atanasia Albu were unseen witnesses to a discussion between Nadia and N. Vieru, who told her to get in shape before B K returned from the European Juniors Champ. in Milan, because after that he would arrange for her to work with him again. Nadia obeyed and got in shape until she put on 9 kg, but nothing could be done about it then. In this way, N. Vieru placed Nadia however it pleased him, constantly trying to avoid responsibility, but at the same time to keep his only ace up his sleeve, Nadia.'[63]

Géza Pozsár informed the Securitate that at the beginning of August, when he visited the gymnast in Bucharest, he 'persuaded her to go to Deva.'[64] For her part, in a phone call with her mother, Nadia confirmed the part played by Pozsár, as well as the manoeuvres of Vieru and Ghibu: 'Nadia's mother asked whether anybody knew about it, to which N.C. replied that com. Ghibu, who helped her in this matter, com. Pozsár who helped them to meet up.'[65]

Károlyi could not conceal his satisfaction, since, as he said, it had been proven that he was the one who made Nadia a champion, and his was the sole methodology that was successful in Romania at the time. Informer 'V. Rădescu' reported Károlyi's reaction to the Deva Securitate: 'He is anyway convinced that Nadia Comăneci was transferred to Bucharest for a time in order to established whether the results obtained at the last Olympics were due primarily to B.K.'s methods of instruction or whether it's simply Nadia's talent. And they were convinced of the truth, which is why Nadia came to Deva.'[66]

In his autobiography, Károlyi insisted on showing how doubtful he felt when the gymnast confessed to him that she wanted to train with him in Deva in order to compete in the World Championships, believing at the time that it was almost impossible to restore her to the shape required by such a contest. However, from recordings made by the Securitate in the Károlyis' home, which they had bugged not long after their arrival, it can be seen that Marta was delighted with the Olympic champion's unexpected request. 'If Nadia can be brought back into shape, then we really will be able to make a formidable team,'[67] Marta Károlyi told Géza Pozsár on 21 September, the day after Nadia arrived in Deva.

In the privacy of the Károlyis' home in Deva, the Securitate recorded the coaches' opinions about the new Romanian gymnastics squad and reported them to their political superiors. Marta, Béla and Géza often talked about Itu, who had put on weight and was not viewed as persistent enough, about Melita Rühn – 'the best gymnast nobody knows about will be a Saxon' – and about Teodora Ungureanu, whom they deemed not to be ready and at odds with Nadia, since there was now 'terrible bad blood' between the two former friends,[68] while in Bucharest, Department One had concluded that Teodora Ungureanu 'won't even think about doing gymnastics under the guidance of the two trainers'[69] and didn't want to go to Deva.

But the thing that Béla, Marta and Géza talked about the most were Nadia's chances of regaining her mental balance and bolstering her stamina. There were just three weeks to the World Championships. When she arrived in Deva, Nadia weight more than fifty-six kilos, and her training had been intermittent during the months she had spent in Bucharest. Would she have the strength to recover in so short a time? Without a doubt, it was a 'force majeure situation', as Károlyi described it in a brief phone call on the morning of 26 September with a person he addressed only as 'comrade minister':

I can inform you that according to my assessment she has lost about 3 kg. Her capacity for effort has increased, she's capable of moving, today she pulled off the first exercises she was made to do. It's an extraordinary success that after 3 days she's able to move. When she arrived she couldn't even lift her leg. Her capacity for effort is completely gone. I've been putting her through a kind of massage procedure. She gets an underwater massage, underwater douches, Scottish douches, a masseur whom we managed to hire for this period takes special care of giving her an overall massage after each training session, likewise we've put her on a diet, but which I don't control as strictly as before, so as not to create direct divergences, that is, so as not to create panic in her mind. I don't want to frighten her.[70]

A few days later, in keeping with the custom of holding a training camp and a friendly competition before a major international competition, Károlyi and his gymnasts went to West Germany. The national team was made up of Nadia Comăneci, Emilia Eberle, Marilena Neacşu, Gabi Gheorghiu, Marilena Vlădărău and Melitu Rühn, while Teodora Ungureanu and Anca Grigoraş, who refused to work with Béla Károlyi any more and were now trained in Bucharest by coach Gheorghe Gorgoi, joined them a few days later. In Germany, Nadia continued her special training programme, one of the most arduous she had thitherto undergone. All the exercises were performed while running a long and exhausting lap, rather like in military training. There was no moment's pause or relaxation from one apparatus to the next, but instead Nadia had to do a series of sit-ups or squat thrusts. As well as daily runs, she had to take countless saunas, all of which were aimed at helping her to lose weight rapidly and strengthen her muscles.

Before Strasbourg, Nadia had not had occasion to take part in any other world championships. The public were to discover a different gymnast, one who looked very different. Unlike at Skien, Montréal and Prague, where spectators had become familiar with the sight of a fragile little girl who was also a consummate gymnast, at Strasbourg, they were to see an athlete who was taller, physically more developed, on the cusp of adulthood.

Nadia captured the attention of both public and press not only because she was the reigning Olympic and World champion. At the time, information defamatory to her was circulating and had been picked up by the international press. It was said that she had had a nervous breakdown, that she had attempted suicide, that she had put on too much weight. Her conflict with Béla Károlyi was also known, and the coach was described by American sports journalists as a 'slave-driver'.[71] Even if none of this could be substantiated, it stimulated even further the interest in Nadia and the Romanian team.

The women's competition began on Tuesday, 24 October, the day after the men's events. Spectators eagerly took their seats in the Rhenus arena, breathlessly anticipating the contest about to begin, but due to a television workers' strike, it was not possible to broadcast the event live. There could be no doubt that the crowd loved Nadia. During the competition, they applauded her as they did no other gymnast, they whistled and booed when they thought the judges had marked her unfairly, as was the case in the vault event. And when she made a mistake, a collective 'ah' would be heard from the stands, followed by an oppressive silence, as if the eight thousand spectators were sharing Nadia's suffering.

The main battle in both the team and the individual events was between the U.S.S.R., East Germany and Romania, although the United States was also beginning to make inroads when it came to Communist bloc dominance. Gymnast Marcia Frederick, who had a poster of her idol Nadia Comăneci on her bedroom wall, proved to be the biggest surprise, becoming the first U.S. gymnast to win gold at a world championship. There were no tens on the scoreboard, and the highest mark on any apparatus was to be 9.95. Nadia was awarded a 9.90 for one of her beam exercises, but she was unable to impress the judges in the floor exercise, while her performance on the uneven parallel bars, usually her secret weapon, visibly lack amplitude, probably due to her weight, which easily makes itself felt on that apparatus. On the final evening of the competition, attempting to create a faster rhythm on the uneven parallel bars, Nadia failed to grasp the upper bar and fell while shifting balance from one bar to the other. Her final score was 9.25. For the first time in a major international competition, the Olympic champion had made a mistake, and it caused a sensation.

'On the vault exercises, in the optionals, Nadia was badly placed in the running order,[72] because Béla Károlyi believed in Eberle, although she was more poorly ranked in the set exercises. I persuaded Béla arguing that Nadia had better chances, he was receptive, although tardily, I managed to alter the order, so that Nadia won silver in the final,' wrote Vieru in his autobiography. He also outlined a number of incidents involving Yuri Titov, the F.I.G. chairman, which were reminiscent of the tournament in Czechoslovakia: 'The team came second, this after the floor exercise when we stopped our gymnasts from mounting the podium because the first two gymnasts had been give very low scores. After a lengthy discussion with chairman Titov and the head of the floor panel, we resumed our participation in the contest and things returned to normal. In the discussion in question, Titov said to me: "Again you want to do like you did in Prague?"'[73]

Things were the same as they had been in Prague, but the Romanians once more voiced their dissatisfaction with the judging, particularly in the compulsory events and the optional exercises. Although not as vehement as they had been in May 1977, the Bucharest press published a number of critical articles by Aurel Neagu, who was the *Sportul* correspondent for France, and also a Securitate agent. The judges proved to be petty, wrote Neagu, because they drastically and undeservedly marked down Romania's gymnasts, and he suggested that once again Ellen Berger and Yuri Titov were behind it.[74]

In his autobiography Nicolae Vieru makes little reference to the judging at the World Championships in France. But in a report dated November 1978, filed with the Securitate, he laid out step by step how the Romanian gymnasts had been marked, pointing out that Maria Simionescu, the head of one of the judging panels, had made efforts to gain them higher scores. He also mentioned Yuri Titov, who accused Simionescu of 'chauvinism',[75] but he also recalled the mistakes that Nadia made during her exercises:

In Strasbourg, as head of the judging panel for the set exercises on the beam, com. Simionescu processed the exercise on this apparatus in front of the judges based on the model for interpretation of the exercise in question by our team, despite the fact it was composed (drawn up) by the U.S.S.R. federation. The members of the beam panel (DDR., Norw., Holl., Yug.) caused us to be judged severely. As there were no discrepancies among the scores, the head of the panel was not entitled to intervene. The scores of the head judge are nonetheless mostly higher than those of the panel. To the team total for the set beam exercise our gymnasts achieve 48.15 points, 0.30 points behind the U.S.S.R. and the team's second highest score in the four competition events. The panel remarked of Nadia Comăneci's execution that on entering she touched the beam, which is correct. Therefore, there was no chance of increasing the scores.

In the free exercises event, with com. Simionescu as head judge in the floor exercise, she fought with all her might against the panel of judges (U.S.S.R., C.S.R., U.S.A., Austr.) which very seriously marked down our team, the panel was convened four times by the head judge, as there were large discrepancies between the scores, particularly from the U.S.S.R. and Cz.S.R. judges.

In discussions with the panel chairman Titov also intervened, who, losing his temper, told Maria Simionescu that she was making 'demonstrations against the Soviet Union.'

In the finals on the apparatuses, as head judge for the vault, Maria Simionescu, according to the new rules, was doubled in the judging by another member of the F.I.G. Technical Commission, Jaroslava Matlochová (C.S.R.). For Nadia Comăneci the whole panel gave her first vault 9.80, including the heads of the panel, and for the second vault two judges awarded 9.90, and two 9.80, the regulation average being 9.85. (. . .) When our delegation protested, with M. Simionescu arguing the score should be raised to 9.90, the panel disagreed and moreover announced that if we maintained the contestation it would be reduced by 0.50 points, since Nadia wrongly showed the no. of the vault executed. At the same time, the Soviets made a contestation to increase Kim's score.

The panel in the end rejected both contestations, despite the insistence of M. Simionescu and our delegation.

Comrade Simionescu, making use of her position, intervened to support contestations for Eberle on the uneven parallel bars and floor exercise, where in the end the scores were increased. Likewise, via connections and friendships forged by M. Simionescu over the years with various judges, we were assisted and marked fairly in other events, such as the free exercise on the beam, where Nadia, with great hesitation, was awarded 9.90 and likewise the rest of the team received high scores, as well as in the compulsory exercise on the parallel bars.[76]

For the Romanian team, the world championships in Strasbourg were a very difficult tournament, given that the Communist régime was exerting increasing pressure for them to win more and more medals. The gymnasts had grown up, and Nadia Comăneci was going through a complicated time. Although she had managed to lose nine kilos, her weight was not optimal, and her absence from training during the summer had taken its toll. Teodora Ungureanu found herself in a similar situation, and her training had suffered in the months before the competition. Anca Grigoraş no longer seemed to fit into the team, Marilena Neacşu was competing with a number of slight muscle lesions, and Gabi Gheorghiu and Marilena Vlădărău were not yet ready to be cast into a world-class contest.

Nevertheless, a number of important victories for women's gymnastics were won. The Romanian team came second, after the Soviet Union, a notable result, given that it was the first time in its history that it had gained the silver medal in the world titles. Secondly, Nadia Comăneci won gold on the beam, likewise a remarkable victory, since it was the first world title she had won on an apparatus, as well as being a first for Romanian women's gymnastics. Moreover, Nadia was awarded silver on the vault, while Emilia Eberle won three bronze medals, on the parallel bars, beam and floor exercise.

But on closer examination of the gymnasts' performances, the results were disappointing. In vain Neagu sent articles from Strasbourg declaring himself proud to be Romanian, in vain Mili Simionescu declared, on arriving back in Romania, 'our girls were up to the mark.'[77] Even if it was not publicly recognised, expectations had been far higher, particularly expectations of the Olympic champion. Some said that Nadia Comăneci had not been able to do better because of hostile judging, which deprived her of a gold medal for the vault, while others claimed that she won as many medals as she was capable of at the time. Proving her own impartiality, Nadia herself recognised that in Strasbourg she had felt humiliated and could hardly wait to leave the arena: 'I wasn't ready at the World Championships and struggled to finish my floor routine. Five weeks was not enough time to make up for a year without discipline. (. . .) The floor and bars were the worst because I simply couldn't carry any extra weight and be as good as I had been.'[78]

Having returned to Romania, Béla and Marta Károlyi did not make a show of being disappointed with the results, particularly given that they felt a brilliant future now awaited Emilia Eberle. The international press had now discovered the fourteen-year-old gymnast, and Károyli had great plans for her. During a telephone call with a journalist from The Flame, when asked to say something 'about Emilia, about her future', he made so bold a claim that the journalists could not disguise his bewilderment: '"Emilia made me glad when she obtained the results she obtained. But I'm even more glad that she didn't obtain more than that." "I beg your pardon?" "You heard me right. I glad that she didn't obtain more than was absolutely normal. If the tragedy of our first gymnast had happened to Emilia too, it would have been a disaster for the Moscow O.G."'[79]

Obviously, such a declaration on Károlyi's part could not be printed in the Romanian press.

As far as foreign reporters were concerned, the bewilderment had to do with Nadia Comăneci, who many claimed was 'finished'. Two medals – gold on the beam, silver on the vault – were not deemed to be victories but signs of irreversible decline. 'Is her career bottoming out?' asked some papers, such as *People*,[80] voicing their scepticism as to her taking part in future competitions, particularly the Moscow Olympics, to be held less than two years thence.

'Nadia is still Nadia', was the response of the Romanian press, which published articles lauding her. Some columnists criticised the performance of the Olympic champion, but did so in a very subdued way, couching the criticism in tender words of encouragement. They expected her to become European, World and Olympic champion once more, arguing that she was an example not only to her younger team mates, such as Eberle, whose time to excel had arrived, but also world gymnastics in general. But they added that if she was really to be ready for Moscow, then Nadia would have to 'set aside caprice.'[81]

'Look, Grigore,[82] dear, did you see yourself?' Béla Károlyi would ask Nadia, pointing out favourable articles in *Sportul* and *Scînteia Tineretului* on the morning of 1 November. Nadia was just getting ready to go home to Oneşti for a few weeks, before taking part in a tour of the United States at the end of November and returning to Deva on 1 January 1979 to begin training.

But the coaches were still sceptical about her. After Nadia left the Károlyis' on 1 November, Marta told Béla, 'she'll come back weighing 60 kg again. There won't be anything we can do about it. People will be depressed and discouraged that she's nothing now,' adding a remark that shows she had no great hopes of her: 'But in any case, we'll get on with our own business, we don't need to rely on her in any way. When we think about it in perspective, we make all our plans without her, and if she's very good, then I won't say she's not good.' the conversation came to a close when Béla told his wife, 'I'm not wasting any more time with her,' to which Marta assented: 'Yes, don't make your schedule around her, because she has caprices from one day to the next.'[83]

The tour of the United States due to take place from November to December 1978 was one of the reasons why Nadia Comăneci agreed to carry on training with the Károlyis in Deva. It was the idea of Twentieth Century Fox Television Sports, whose agent, Sheldon Saltman, contacted Nicolae Vieru in Strasbourg during the World Championships. The régime in Bucharest approved the plan without delay. Twentieth Century Fox was to pay the Romanian government a fee of two hundred thousand dollars, while Nadia was to receive the special gift of a motorcar. Shows were scheduled in six cities on the West Coast, kicking off in Los Angeles – where the Romanians were due to fly in on 21 November – and ending in Seattle. Peeved at all the attention being paid to Nadia, Marta Károlyi claimed that in order to receive the present she was eager to have, 'she's been told that all she has to do is turn up'.[84] Béla insisted that there was more than one gymnast in the team and everything seemed to be progressing well both in Romania, where they were making the final preparations, and in the United States, where Twentieth Century Fox had organised a major advertising campaign in the weeks before the tour.

It was to be one of the biggest sporting events of the year. The arenas had been booked and the tickets were on sale, with people braving a blizzard in Seattle and torrential rain in Portland to get their hands on them. Twentieth Century Fox proved to be generous to the Romanian delegation not only financially, but also in terms of the programme, which included plentiful opportunities for luxurious recreation: formal dinners, a cruise on a luxury yacht, a trip to Disneyland, a visit to the studios where Alan Alda filmed the highly popular *M*A*S*H* serial and a film set where they would meet Telly Savalas. In each of the cities where performances were to be held, there would also be special ceremonies to present the Romanians with the keys to the city, a rare privilege usually granted only to visiting heads of state.

The entire Fox Sports team worked tirelessly to make it happen, from Ron Beckman, the company president, and Sheldon Saltman, his deputy, to employees on the ground, all of them excitedly awaiting the Romanians' arrival. But on 21 November, the day when the Romanians were due to fly in, Frank Bare, the executive director of the United States Gymnastics Federation, received two telegrams from Bucharest within a few hours of each other. The first gave the names of the members of the delegation and the flight details; the second curtly announced that the tour had been cancelled.

Bare responded furiously, sending a harshly worded telegram to the Romanian Gymnastics Federation. The situation was unthinkable, given that the tour had cost 'so much it's indescribable.' The Romanian decision, said Bare, was 'intolerable and undignified', and the manner in which it had been taken was 'a mockery'. He immediately informed Twentieth Century Fox, causing an uproar at the film company's headquarters, where the indignation was total, especially given that the Romanians had provided no explanation. The telephones then started ringing at the Romanian embassy in Washington, with calls from congressmen, senators, film and television executives, and reporters, but the Romanian diplomats had no idea what had happened. Everybody was disgruntled: organisers, promotors, and above all the thousands of spectators who had already bought tickets. What had been set to be a resounding success and an excellent public relations opportunity for Romanian gymnastics had turned into a media nightmare.

To show how serious he was, Frank Bare declared to the press that he was cancelling the U.S. gymnastics team's tour of Romania, scheduled for the following year, and withdrawing Romania's invitation to take part in the international competition to be held in New York in March 1979. He also demanded that the F.I.G. suspend the Romanian team from the upcoming European gymnastics championship and said that he would take legal action against the Romanian Gymnastic Federation. Even Yuri Titov declared that the Romanians should be sanctioned to prevent such a thing happening again.

Nobody knows exactly why Romania pulled out, and any public discussion of the subject was forbidden at the time. The decision to withdraw from the tour must have been passed down from Cabinets One and Two of the Central Committee, as Nicolae and Elena Ceauşescu were the only ones capable of issuing such an order. In the secret documents, the Securitate makes no mention of the reason, which is yet further reason to believe that it was a decision on the part of the Ceauşescu family. Vieru mentions the episode in his autobiography, but without providing any explanation even after all these years: 'Twenty-four hours before departure, the tour was cancelled, which unleashed a very unpleasant conflict with the American federation, which had invested a lot in organising it. After I explained to him how things had unfolded in Romania, offering him my sincere apologies, the chairman of the American federation, who was a good friend of mine, said to me, "Nicolae, friendship is friendship, but I've lost 200,000 dollars".'[85]

A number of clues may nonetheless be detected in a report filed a year later, from which it is apparent that the spark that caused the explosion came from Ştefania Comăneci, who went to an audience at the Central Committee 'to address the higher leadership of the Party with the aim of obtaining a sum of money, a motorcar, and a flat in the capital.' Nadia's mother was still demanding full payment of the prize money promised to her daughter for her success at Montréal, as well as other material benefits, including the old cheque for ten thousand dollars, all of which the authorities deemed absurd, cynically replying: 'Don't teach children to be grasping.' 'Thanks to this undisciplined act, it was ordered that the U.S. invitation for the Romanian Gymnastics Federation to take part in a champions' tour with Nadia and the other gymnasts should not be taken up—and they were sent back to Deva from Bucharest on the day when they were meant to leave by plane,'[86] the report states.

If Ştefania Comăneci's demands really did annoy the Party chiefs and lead to such a decision on the part of Nicolae Ceauşescu, then it was all the more absurd, since it was preferred to cancel an event that could have brought financial benefits to the country and created a positive image, all to show who was in charge and set an example of intransigence. Furthermore, relations between the Romanian and U.S. gymnastics federation suffered as a result and it required intense diplomacy to restore them to their previous footing.

The authorities in Bucharest obviously could not have cared less about Twentieth Century Fox's financial loss. The company took steps to try and recoup the sum it had invested, requesting the assistance of Lloyd's Underwriters in the

U.S., the insurance firm with which it had taken out a contract. Recovery of a part of the investment was conditional upon the cancellation having resulted from illness or injury. Although it was not true, the Romanians declared that Nadia Comăneci was ill and Emilia Eberle had incurred an injury, delivering false medical documents to the U.S. embassy in Bucharest. The purpose was not to help Twentieth Century Fox, but to justify cancellation of the tour by means of a lie. On 15 December 1978, when D.J. Taylor, the agent of Lloyd's Underwriters, visited the Romanian Gymnastics Federation and requested to see Nadia Comăneci in order to wish her a speedy recovered, he was told that this was impossible and 'we cannot consent to anybody interfering in this matter.'[87] After which Taylor was invited to leave the premises.

Not having any involvement in the scandal, the Károlyis and the gymnasts returned to Deva, where they carried on training, far from the sound and fury in Bucharest. On 26 November, Marta said, 'she comes to Deva with her pretensions. We left Oneşti to get away from this circus,'[88] which allows us to conclude that Nadia Comăneci had agreed to continue training at the Deva sports centre, but under conditions different than in the past. For example, she no longer lived in a hotel with the other gymnasts, but in a flat of her own and was to be given deferential treatment by the coach.

In the months that followed, the relationship between coaches and gymnast improved considerably, with the Károlyis becoming more reasonable and conciliatory. Pozsár believes that in 1979 Károlyi treated Nadia like a young lady, and their connection became more like a partnership on an equal footing. The partnership still wasn't perfect, of course, especially given that Béla constantly complained that Nadia 'has devoured my life.' Marta, on the other hand, regarded Nadia as somebody who went to different extremes, and was dissatisfied with her wanting 'to live her life and to obtain good results, but I don't know whether she's capable of it.'[89]

Given that Nadia decided to stay in Deva, on 12 January 1979, Hunedoara County Securitate approved a plan of measures to set up a network of informers among the people around her, to plant bugs in her new flat in Deva by 10 March, and other actions to bring about more efficient surveillance.[90] Over the course of the year, Nadia made a number of attempts to get out of training, running away to various places in the town so that she couldn't be found, and the days when this happened – 28 August, 1, 6 and 17 October – were recorded in the Securitate's report on the sports centre. On 6 October 1979, referring to one such incident, Béla Károlyi told Viorel Jianu, the vice chairman of Hunedoara C.C.P.E.S., that he was at the end of his tether: 'I feel like my liver's about to burst. All I want is for this circus to end, it can't go on like this,' while also wondering why the Securitate didn't intervene ('Why doesn't that Iovan[91] follow her if that's his duty?'[92]

The Securitate established that in the first part of 1979, in public Béla Károlyi radically changed his behaviour towards Nadia, even if at home, when talking to

Marta, he still insulted her. A report dating from April that year says, 'he behaves nicely, no longer swears, flings insults,' and as a result 'in Nadia Comăneci's behaviour can be observed greater maturity and full control over herself in all she does, both in training and in relations with the coach and other gymnasts.'[93]

Károlyi's political clout had increased considerably since March 1979, when his protector, Ilie Verdeţ, was appointed prime minister. 'Béla Károlyi would phone the Central Committee and set us all trembling,'[94] Condovici recalled, and those who trembled included the Securitate officers, who now took care to conduct their surveillance operations as discreetly as possible and not to disturb the peace at the sports complex. Károlyi, aged just thirty-eight at the time, was influential, making use of his own authority and powerful connections in order to get what he wanted. He drove the only Mercedes in Deva and one of the few in the whole of Transylvania, he frequently held parties at the 'Roe Deer' chalet near Deva, laying on food and resources from the school, he went hunting with the highest official of the state, including not only Ilie Verdeţ but even Nicolae Ceauşescu himself, and his decisions were not to be opposed by anybody at the local level, with the exception of the Party leaders, who were promptly informed by the Securitate. In Deva, Károlyi acted like a king, and the gym was his kingdom.

The gymnasts, on the other hand, had the feeling that their lives were hemmed in, and they continued to fall victim to his uncontrolled temper and aggression. At Károlyi's orders, the gym was kept under permanent guard, and nobody apart from the members of the national gymnastics squad – the trainers, medical staff, pianist, choreographer – had access, not even the gymnasts' parents. He kept up the high-intensity training, including publicly, in interviews given to the press. On 4 November 1978 he explained to a journalist from *Flacăra*, 'what is imperative is that we shape a national team under the auspices of a single working concept, under the rule of an exceptionally intense, orderly style of working, guided by an idea of discipline, of complete, devotion, and then our key problem will be solved.'[95] In January 1979, Károlyi declared to *Sportul* that in Deva, he, Marta and the ten gymnasts he was training – Nadia Comăneci, Emilia Eberle, Marilena Vlădărău, Marilena Neacşu, Rodica Dunca, Melita Rühn, Dumitriţa Turner, Anca Kiss, Claudia Dragomir and Viorica Gyütö – were 'a real family,'[96] a typically exaggerated claim on his part.

As for Nadia, her plans for the future were constantly changing. Whereas in September 1978 she had told her mother that she would stay in Deva only until the World Championships, after which she would retire from sport and go to live in Bucharest,[97] in Strasbourg, she told a reporter that she would be withdrawing from competitive sport after the 1980 Moscow Olympics.[98] But before the Moscow Olympics there were still a number of important tournaments in 1979.

In films and novels can often be found the theme of the spectacular, often heroic, comeback of a sportsperson who finds glory before losing it all and then climbing back to the top. Most of the time, such characters are fictional, but there have been real-life stories of sportspeople who have stood out for their talent and perseverance and who have clawed their way back after the world had written them off.

Nadia Comăneci is one of them. In 1979 she made the most spectacular comeback in the history of gymnastics, achieving a new record: the first gymnast to win the European title three times in a row.[99] To dominate such a sport for six years running is a remarkable achievement, given European competition was fierce indeed, the judges were often biased or downright hostile, and age and exhaustion can diminish performance. That year, Nadia won gold medals at almost every tournament in which she took part: the Champions Cup, Romania's International Championships, the European Championships, the World Cup, and the Balkan Championships, failing only to win the title of overall world champion.

On 7 April, she made her first official appearance since Strasbourg at the Champions Cup in London. The *Sportul* correspondent reported that thousands of spectators had come to Wembley just to see the Olympic champion. But on the morning of 9 April, having just got back home, Béla Károlyi was covertly recorded by the Securitate as saying, while he unpacked his bags: 'When we went inside for the official training session, Nadia, the great Nadia, went almost unnoticed. I felt really bad about it. It made me downright furious. Not even during the contest was there much applause. Nadia was great. By the end, they were a little more enthusiastic.'[100] Nadia was indeed great, winning the trophy for the second time – after an interval of four years – defeating Elena Naimushina of the U.S.S.R. and Andrea Horacsek of Hungary, and only a hesitation on the beam meant that she didn't get a point ahead of the number two in the rankings. Then, a few days later, Romania's International Championships were held in Bucharest, with gymnasts from sixteen countries competing. Nadia won the individual all-round title and the whole world realised she was now in remarkable form.

From 11 to 13 May the European Championships were held in Copenhagen. With a figure reminiscent of when she competed in Montréal, Nadia was elegant, but also full of energy. She had lost a lot of weight, which visibly helped her to regain strength and balance. Her sweeping breadth, her control of her movements, combined with her growing maturity and mastery of new and highly difficult element, reminded spectators that Nadia was still the same international symbol of perfection. She won the European title in the all-round individual events for the third time, and on the second day, during the finals on the apparatuses, she won another two gold medals, on the vault and floor exercise. She won bronze on the beam because of a hesitation, and failed to win a medal in the uneven parallel bars event because she came too close to the upper bar during a leap and fell. But the figures speak for themselves, revealing her overall dominance of her opponents. She amassed 39.45 points, a new record – beating her own record, set in Prague, while Emilia Eberle, in second place, won a total of 38.85 points. With her third consecutive victory, Nadia laid definitive claim to the trophy of the International Gymnastics Federation.

The reporters at the press centre in Brøndbyhallen had forgotten that a few months previously they had been predicting the end of her career. 'A spectacular comeback,' reported France-Presse, while Associated Press declared, 'she put matters straight, taking back the supremacy she lost last year.'[101] The whole of the foreign press, even the Soviet agencies, employed the same admiring tone.

Béla Károlyi was also at the centre of attention, garnering praise from the world's press for his two gymnasts, Comăneci and Eberle, who had brought Romania such remarkable victories. Even Securitate captain Nicolae Ilie, undercover among the members of the delegation, posing as a sports instructor, was effusive in his assessment of Károlyi when he filed his report back in Bucharest, on 22 May 1979:

Throughout the period, within the gymnastics squad there was a mood favourable to the competition, determined by coach Béla Károlyi, who on this occasion demonstrated professional competence and seriousness in his work.

I should state that the coach has changed his attitude, comportment and the methods he uses in training the gymnasts and Nadia Comăneci in particular. It was observed that in the majority of cases he co-operates with Nadia Comăneci in achieving special training of the gymnast in question. Likewise, he treats her differently than the other gymnasts, being more conciliatory towards her, doing so in order to have her be closer to him.

On this occasion coach Béla Károlyi did everything possible to create greater publicity for gymnast Nadia Comăneci in both the press and on radio-television, doing so, as he himself stated, in order to counteract the publicity created for the Soviet gymnasts by the press and television in Denmark.

At these European championships, the same as at other international competitions, the Soviet delegation, headed by Yuri Titov, the chairman of the International Gymnastics Federation, attempted to employ every means possible so that the Soviet gymnasts would win, starting with a campaign against our gymnasts, and against gymnast Emilia Eberle in particular, and culminating in the attempt to influence and intimidate the judges in order to disadvantage our gymnasts.

The Károlyis behaved appropriately towards me as a Securitate officer within the delegation, and in some cases were even courteous, assisting me to carry out my mission in the best conditions.[102]

By the middle of 1979 everything seemed to be going wonderfully. Károlyi was no longer so strict with Nadia and he overlooked her caprices. The successes gained by the national women's squad were so impressive that even the Communist Party and the Securitate turned a blind eye to Károlyi's shortcomings. For her part, Nadia continued to be in excellent form. Having remembered her glorious past, she had now regained her identity, rediscovering the inner strength she had lost for a while.

Nadia continued to sweep all before her. At the Tokyo World Cup games in June, Károlyi's gymnasts lost the world cup, but won all four gold medals in the finals on the apparatuses, Nadia Comăneci coming first on the vault and floor exercise, Emilia Eberle on the uneven parallel bars and beam. The Romanian gymnasts received a standing ovation from the thirteen thousand spectators in the Yoyogi Arena, after witnessing Nadia set a new record: two scores of ten in the floor exercise. It was the first time in an official competition held by the International Gymnastics Federation that the victor had amassed twenty points in this event. At the Balkan Championships in October, held in Ljubljana, Nadia won four scores of ten, three gold medals, and the title of Balkan champion.

The year's last major competition, the World Championships, was held in Fort Worth, Texas, early in December. It was the only individual title that Nadia had yet to win. Given her astonishing run of success over the course of the year, it looked like nothing could stop her from taking the title, but the tournament was to be marked by drama and frustration, both for Nadia Comăneci and the Károlyis.

The tournament opened with the team competition between the world's best gymnasts, with Romania represented at the Fort Worth Convention Centre by Nadia Comăneci, Emilia Eberle, Rodica Dunca, Dumitriţa Turner, Marilena Vlădărău and Melita Rühn. As is well known, the official result in the team competition is based on the scores of the five first gymnasts, with the sixth, lowest score being discarded. After the set exercises, Nadia was in first place, but the next day, due to an open wound on her left hand – an abscess caused by a streptococcus aureus infection – she was no longer able to compete. She was taken to All Saints Hospital, where the pus was drained and she was administered a perfusion of antibiotics. 'I was at the judges' table,' recalls Nicolae Vieru, 'before the optional exercises, and I was called to the warmup room, where Béla told me that Nadia couldn't compete. I talked to Nadia, who showed me her inflamed hand and tried to put her weight on it, but she couldn't stand the pain.'[103]

Károlyi kept her in the competition, hoping that his other gymnasts would give satisfactory performances. He told her to go to the apparatuses when her turn came, touch the bar, present herself, and then return to the bench, to the bewilderment and regret of the crowd. She received a score of 0.00, but had to make the gesture in order to avoid disqualification. 'I just knew that keeping Nadia in the competition might help somewhere down the line,'[104] recalled Károlyi, and his decision turned out to be inspired.

Even though the world's best gymnast wasn't competing due to an injury, the Romanian team still did remarkably well in the uneven parallel bars event. But when it came to the beam, Emilia Eberle unexpectedly made two mistakes, causing Károlyi's hopes to crumble. She fell during her bar routine and lost her balance when performing her double handspring on the dismount, receiving a low score: 8.95. Melita Rühn obtained the Romanian team's best score, a 9.80, but it wasn't enough, especially since the Soviet team was dominating the floor exercise. Károlyi looked at the scores, made a calculation, and then turned to Nadia:

> Nadia did not say a word as I stared at her. She just looked into my eyes and then turned towards the beam.
>
> The green light went on and Nadia walked up to the beam. I will never forget that moment. I was facing away from the beam, waiting to hear the public's reaction. I couldn't look—I thought Nadia might turn around and never start her routine. Even if she did start, I was 90 percent sure that she would fall. Silence. Total silence in the arena. I turned around.
>
> There was Nadia, one hand and three fingers from the other hand on the beam, moving slowly, perfectly, into her handstand, quarter turn-out, step-out, and then the familiar rhythm of her beam routine. She threw her first back handspring, one-handed of course, then layout, layout—a powerful routine, beautiful. When she threw her dismount she stuck it! And at that moment all hell broke loose in the arena. It was so obvious, with her big bloodied bandage, that she was injured. and therefore so incredible that she had performed a near-perfect one-handed routine. The public went wild. The score came up, 9.95. We were back in first place.[105]

Thanks to Nadia, who performed the beam exercise one-handed, Romania won first place in the team competition. It was Romania's first title in the history of post-war gymnastics, during which the U.S.S.R. had won six of the eight world championships. According to Nicolae Vieru, at Fort Worth the Russians were even in danger of losing second place, but were able to cling on thanks to secret help from the Romanians, which is to say, Vieru himself and federation judge Maria Simionescu: 'Titov came to me and asked to talk to Maria Simionescu and tell her not to mark down Nellie Kim, since the D.D.R. would then overtake the U.S.S.R.'[106] In the finals on the apparatuses, Romanian gained another two world champion titles, with Dumitriţa Turner winning gold on the vault and Emilia Eberle in the floor exercise, while Melita Rühn won bronze in the individual all-round event and the floor exercise.

When Romania's women's gymnastics team mounted the highest step of the podium at Fort Worth, Béla Károlyi was invited to join his gymnasts, the same as the Soviet and East German coaches had done, standing on the second and third steps. The jubilant Károlyi raised his arms in the air and saluted the crowd alongside the gymnasts, as if he were the man of the moment and the victory was his alone. At one point, turning to face another side of the arena, he gave Nadia Comăneci a slight shove, but it was accidental, since there was little room on the podium. Nadia raised her head towards Károlyi, casting him a questioning look that evinced profound unease.

Victory was greeted with jubilation, particularly in Bucharest, where the press praised the Károlyis to the skies and lauded the medal-winning gymnasts. Nor was Nadia forgotten, and it was said that even when in great pain, since everybody had seen her hand injury on television, she had shown 'admirable devotion'. When their plane landed at Otopeni Airport, however, Nadia had not been the first to disembark, as was usually the case, but rather Emilia Eberle, Dumitriţa Turner and Melita Rühn. To the waiting press, Béla and Marta Károlyi made no mention of any sacrifice or devotion on the part of the Olympic champion, but emphasised that the Romanian team was now strong enough to win victories even without Nadia, saying that the other gymnasts had rallied perfectly. Although it was undeclared, everybody could sense Károlyi's hostility towards Nadia.

But what actually happened at Fort Worth? Why had Nadia's injury become so serious that it kept her off the medals podium? Years afterward, the people involved told the story in interviews and autobiographies, but their accounts differed. Nadia has never said much about it, merely explaining that she had scratched herself on a buckle and 'chalk, friction, sweat and dirt caused an infection,'[107] with the result that she was unable to use that hand.

Nor did Nicolae Vieru say much else about the incident, although Béla Károlyi placed him in an unpleasant situation in which he ought to have reacted. In his autobiography, Károlyi claims that Nadia suffered a minor scratch, which he himself bandaged the night before the competition. But Vieru is supposed to have taken the decision, without Károlyi's permission, to take her to hospital, and the doctors' radical intervention, which entailed giving her stitches and injections, meant that she was no longer able to compete. Károlyi even suggests that Vieru was thereby trying to undermine him.

Károlyi's account is, as ever, harsh, but we do not think it reflects the truth. It is not confirmed by any information in the Securitate files, to wit, the reports written by the officers who were embedded within the Romanian delegation. Moreover, Béla and Marta Károlyi also spread a different theory, within their own close circle, in the days after they returned from Fort Worth to Deva, where the Securitate resumed its secret surveillance of them in their own home. In conversations with various friends in mid-December, the Károlyis claimed that Nadia Comăneci had trained very well for the U.S. tournament, better than ever, in fact. They said that the Fort Worth competition was exceptionally well-organised and that the crowd was amazing. When asked to describe the dramatic moments during the tournament, Marta claimed that Nadia had 'deliberately infected herself so she wouldn't have to compete. There was a whole circus around her. "Poor girl" and all that.'[108] According to Marta, 'she herself nicked herself and wiped dirt on it to make it infected,'[109] knowing that she would be forced to take part in the competition against her will. Why? Because 'she had some material demands, as well as wanting her mother to come,' which the coach hadn't met. 'Have you ever heard anything like it?'[110] Marta Károlyi complained to her friends.

The accounts of Géza Pozsár, alias 'Nelu', and Major Dumitru Iovan of Deva Securitate, both of whom went to Fort Worth, provide a better understanding of such startlingly cruel claims. In the reports they filed after their return to Romania, they laid out the reasons that led to Nadia's rebellion, but they did not confirm Marta Károlyi's theory.

It all began with the coach's decision to organise a tour before the World Championships, as was his custom, except that this time he went completely over the top. The Romanian team left the country on 22 October and did not get back until 11 December, with the gymnasts having been separated from their families for more than a month and a half. Their parents later accused Károlyi of insisting on this gruelling trip for personal rather than professional reasons. During the tour, the restrictions were more drastic than at home, with the coaches keeping the gymnasts under constant supervision. 'The entire team looked gaunt and pale when we arrived in Texas,'[111] remembers Nadia.

The tour took in Norway, West Germany, Britain, Mexico and the United States, an itinerary that neither the gymnasts nor their parents knew about in advance. They found out only when they arrived in Norway: 'The first part of the tour went normally, meaning the Norwegian leg. After the competition in Norway, the girls were informed that they would not be returning to the homeland, but would go to the G.F.R. The Norwegian organisers were barely able to provide the team with accommodation, meals and a hotel, and the last night was spent in a night shelter in wretched conditions, since it wasn't possible to pay for the hotel,' says informer 'Nelu', from whose report we quote below:

The next leg was the G.F.R., where we stayed in Rüsselheim, in normal conditions. It was here that the scandal with Nadia began, as she didn't want to work, complaining of a back pain. Béla intercepted a letter from Nadia to her mother in which she said that she would do everything not to compete, saying that Béla was behaving nastily with her etc. The letter exists. After this letter, Béla managed to convince everybody that Nadia wanted to defect and remain abroad. She was guarded in her room in shifts. Gymnast Vlădărău was given the task of keeping her under surveillance and reporting everything she did. But Nadia didn't work.

Pozsár claims that in Germany Béla Károlyi continued to humiliate Nadia. He gave interviews to the press 'blowing his own trumpet and exposing Nadia's dark period in Bucharest.' In England, Károlyi confined Nadia to her room and had a serious row with Major Iovan when he found out that he had taken her food. In Mexico, 'he staged a practical joke, placing with his own hand bottles of Pepsi by the girls' doors' and then accusing them of breaking their diet. 'Béla beat Eberle to back him up in his lie,' recounts 'Nelu'. The informer also reveals just how much care the coach took of Nadia's injured left hand, which Károlyi claims to have tended in his autobiography:

After Mexico the team went to the U.S.A., to the World Championships. Béla wanted at all costs to force Nadia to compete, contrary to Vieru, who didn't want to compromise her, as Nadia was in precarious physical condition. Béla told the source that she must at least be seen to compete on the first day, and after that she could compromise herself in the optionals, all the better. Nurse Borş alerted Béla in a timely fashion that Nadia had an infection in her hand, but he didn't allow the nurse to give her antibiotics. Marta claims that Nadia did it to herself. There is no clear proof in this respect.[112]

'Nelu' must have told Captain Nicolae Ilie the same thing when he returned to Romania, since on 18 February 1980 Ilie informed his superiors, 'the appearance of the boil and its known evolution were due to underlying poor personal hygiene, malnutrition and the fact that the doctor and nurse intervened only when it had reached an advanced form, due to the interdiction on their doing so made by coach Béla Károlyi. We should state that doctor Oană Ioachim was instructed by the trainer to take care of our country's men's gymnastics team'[113]

Securitate Major Dumitru Iovan laid out similar information in his report, but provided greater detail, including references to the amorous liaisons of members of the delegation during the tournament. He described the restrictions placed on the gymnasts and their morale.[114]

None of this would have come as any surprise to anyone, but Iovan also made note of an important detail, namely that on the day of the departure to Fort Worth, Béla Károlyi had had 'heated discussions' with Nicolae Vieru regarding his refusal 'to work in future with Nadia Comăneci, claiming that he would bear whatever consequences came of it. Moreover, in interviews to the press in Bucharest and the declaration he made on arriving in Deva, he made it clear that he no longer accepted her, repeating the phrase that Romanian gymnastics had grown so much that it no longer depended on one individual.'[115] Without a doubt, after their return to Deva, the Securitate was expecting Béla and Nadia to stop working with each other.

A few weeks later, on 8 February 1980, Nadia Comăneci, alias 'Corina', remembered Károlyi's conduct in Fort Worth. She did so in a brief statement to Romanian reporters visiting Deva to gather material to promote her in the foreign press. The reporters told her they had been sent from Bucharest to talk to her, since 'at the present time both the Soviet and the Western press are speculating in all sorts of ways, the Italians reported that you had committed suicide, while others said that you've stopped coming to training. They publish all kinds of stupid things in the press.' But the reporters quickly realised how tense things were in Deva and explained to Nadia that if she wished, they would convey any complaints she might have to the Central Committee or even Nicolae Ceaușescu, if need be. 'What is the truth? Obviously, insofar as you want us to inform the highest levels,' asked the two reporters.

Mr: Did you have serious confrontations with 'Barbu'?[116]
'Corina': I had plenty, but the World Championships brought it to a head.
Mr: Meaning?
'Corina': I competed on the beam with a swollen hand and after I dismounted, he called me a 'cur', for taking that point. After that he came here to Deva and said he managed to win first place even without 'Corina', with five girls.
Mother: He's made her unpopular here.
'Corina': He said that I did that to my hand myself so as not to compete. He gave the order for me not to be given any medicine.
Mr: To the team doctor?
'Corina': Yes.
Dr: The doctor didn't treat you?
'Corina': No.
Mr: That's against the oath he swore.
Mrs: But why did he do that, sabotage like that?
'Corina': Because they saw that I couldn't go on and he wanted me to make an embarrassment of myself.[117]

It was true that after they came back from Fort Worth, Béla and Marta Károlyi claimed that Nadia Comăneci had made no contribution to the victory in the World Championships. In private conversations in their home they loudly and repeatedly claimed, 'she didn't get any medal' and 'the truth is that for the first time we won gold in the team contest. And that was without 'Corina', who's thought to be a world wonder', while Maria Pozsár, the choreographer's wife, told Marta, 'I was even overjoyed it was like that. She'd been the only one winning.'[118]

But who could gainsay the two coaches who at the beginning of 1980 could boast that in 1979 they had won almost everything and were therefore entitled to enjoy every privilege? They returned from London with the Champions Trophy. In Bucharest they dominated the International Championships, and in Copenhagen the Romanian team won the largest number of medals: three gold, three silver, and one bronze. They won another seven medals in Tokyo (four gold, two silver, one bronze), in Ljubljana they won every title, and at Fort Worth, they gained the world title and six medals (three gold and three bronze), putting Romania once more in first place in the unofficial ranking of the nations. In addition, Emilia Eberle was now established as a major international name, another wager that Károlyi had won.

By the end of 1979, no other coach in the world could boast such a brilliant record, given that he achieved it all by himself, in the school he had set up, in a small town in Transylvania, where the Károlyis trained a group of just ten gymnasts. *Sportul* called them 'admirable coaches Marta and Béla Károlyi' and the whole of the Romanian press published paeans to them. The Securitate noted that Károlyi was already 'expecting to be awarded the title of Hero of Socialist Labour', the Communist régime's highest accolade. The Securitate who reported this was even inclined to agree with Károlyi: 'This would provide a permanent guarantee that in future, in one or another situation, the risk of him taking an undesirable decision would be completely removed.'[119]

Károlyi believed he was more meritorious than his gymnasts. What other explanation could there be if 'the great Nadia' hadn't produced any results when she trained in Bucharest? He would fly into a rage if anybody suggested a different explanation, which was what happened in Copenhagen in the spring of 1979, where Nadia won her third European title. Alexandru Mogoş, the head of high-level sport within the N.C.P.E.S., whom some people, including the Securitate, regarded as 'conceited and arrogant, egotistical and professionally ill-prepared',[120] told the Karoylis, 'it's Nadia who makes you somebody' and 'I'm returning with a sack of medals again.' Mogoş's words 'provoked a strong reaction in them' and 'a serious disagreement',[121] said agent 'Lia Muri', who witnessed the discussion. Mrs Mili neglected to say just how serious the argument was, but there can be no doubt that her expression points to a violent argument, verbally at the very least.

Results were being obtained in Bucharest, hitting the front pages of the newspapers, but they couldn't compare with the achievements of the sports centre in Deva. Emilia Liţă and Gheorghe Gorgoi were training Teodora Ungureanu and Anca Grigoraş, who were rumoured to be reaching the end of their career. Ungureanu had been suffering from illness, and Károlyi said of her that she had long since lost her form, but in 1979 she took part in the World University Games in Mexico City and won gold in the individual all-round event, becoming triple world university champion and spectacularly defeating Maria Filatova and Elena Davydova by just a tenth of a point. In the finals on the pieces of equipment she won two gold medals, on the uneven parallel bars and beam, a silver medal, in the floor exercise, and a bronze medal, on the vault – four medals in one day – while Anca Grigoraş won silver on the beam and bronze on the parallel bars.

None of these gymnasts intended ever to work with Béla Károlyi again. Teodora Ungureanu even publicly declared her intention, in an interview with *Flacăra* magazine. Provoked into doing so by Géza Pozsár, Károlyi commented on the interview in his own inimitable style:

'Onea':[122] Did you read the <u>Flame</u> that came out while we were away? The piece about Ungureanu?

M(arta): I might have read something.

'Onea': First one gets going, then the other.

Ob(jective Béla Károlyi): It's the third piece about comrade Ungureanu in <u>Flame</u>. I've read two. For her to say in that newspaper, 'at last the time has come to tell you the truth.' That 'thanks to such-and-such trainers who saved me from the hell I was living through.' The swine. Any minute now there'll be an article about the other swine. I can almost sense it. Informing the public opinion.[123]

In January 1980, after the conflict between the Karoylis and Nadia Comăneci was reignited, Nadia stopped going to the gym, claiming the coach didn't want her there, while Béla either said he didn't want her in the team any more or complained that he waited for her to show up at training sessions, but she refused to take part. Nadia's mother, on the other hand, once more tried to obtain the financial rewards promised by the authorities, but which still hadn't materialised. She demanded the cheque for ten thousand dollars that Nicolae Vieru had taken from Nadia in the past, full payment of the prizes promised to her for her success at Montréal – it hadn't been paid on 'orders from above', according to the Securitate, which meant the Central Committee had blocked it – and a flat in Bucharest for her daughter, paid for by the state, as she had discovered that other Olympic medallists had received one.

Each party sought to make complaints at the highest level in Bucharest, where they knew justice was done. On 17 January, Károlyi had a brief discussion with Emil Drăgănescu, the minister of sport in the Verdeţ government, but he declined to get involved in the conflict: 'he showed me the door and left. He said he didn't want to hear anything about it. People were sick of it,' revealed Károlyi in a conversation with a representative of the N.C.P.E.S. Nadia made a similar attempt, and Károlyi waited in Deva to be called to the capital, as intransigent as ever, as proven on 19 January, when he told Alexandru Mogoş over the phone: 'Let me tell you what it will be like: — Comrade, why haven't you taken steps to persuade the poor innocent child and I don't know what else. I'm sick of it, I'm getting out of it until the situation is cleared up, and after the Olympics, if it's to be, it'll be, and I'll go back into gymnastics. Until then I'm telling you I can't go on. It's made me ill. I don't want to lose my mind here. I'm telling you the whole caboodle that was here has been ruined. There's the smoke of battle all over town because of that bitch. (. . .) I'm the one who wants to destroy the national monument.'[124]

A few weeks later, the war diminished in intensity and the smoke began to disperse. Béla and Nadia continued to harbour strong feelings of mutual hostility, but they started talking again and training resumed. Maria Simionescu increased the frequency of her visits to Deva, Emil Drăgănescu spoke with Károlyi over the phone in order to be constantly informed, and Nicolae Vieru phoned Nadia, promising her things would soon be sorted out. 'She is not at all ready and is going to lose,'[125] declared Vieru during a meeting of the federation, an opinion Atanasia Albu considered to be unfounded, given that Nadia had easily won first place in the all-round individual events at the Romanian International Championships in April 1980.

After the tournament, Nadia did not go back to Deva, remaining in Bucharest so that she could take part in a sustained programme of training. It was less than three months until the Moscow Olympics. Documents from this period are missing from the Securitate archives, as if it were deliberately intended that there should be no record of the discussions that led to Nadia withdrawing from the Deva training programme or any mention of the decision makers involved. All that remains is a report written a year later by General Aron Bordea, the head of Department One, in which we discover that even though Nadia also wanted it, the decision was taken by 'the higher leadership of the Party':

In this period Vieru Nicolae made insistent overtures to gymnast Nadia Comăneci that she should return to Bucharest, luring her with a series of promises of a material nature.

Against the backdrop of her refusal to accept the working regimen imposed, the gymnast manifested dissatisfaction, making direct contact with the heads of the National Council for Physical Education and Sport, where she made clear that she refused to train under the supervision of Károlyi Béla.

In February 1980 this situated was examined by the higher leadership of the Party, where gymnast Nadia Comăneci formally agreed to carry on training in Deva.

After the International Championships of the S.R. of Romania in April 1980, Nadia Comăneci refused to return to Deva and, on 15 May 1980, the higher leadership of the Party decided to bring her to Bucharest, where she would continue training under the supervision of federation secretary Vieru Nicolae and trainer Gorgoi Gheorghe, with Karoli Béla periodically to attend her training.[126]

6
THE NINETEEN-EIGHTIES

The rivalry between the Romanian and the Soviet schools of gymnastics began in earnest in the mid-1970s. It was to last for decades and proved to be one of the fiercest clashes in the history of sport. It was often lacking in fair play, with some results being decided before tournaments even began, but the gymnasts from the two countries knew nothing of these behind-the-scenes machinations and in every contest, they gave their very best to win on each apparatus.

Communist jargon held that the Soviet experiment was the prime factor in developing the creative spirit of the working class. In gymnastics this was by no means an empty slogan. The Soviets were genuine pioneers, bold innovators. In every major competition, the Soviet gymnasts stood out for their acrobatics and exceptional grace. In the decades immediately after the war, the Romanians watched Soviet women's gymnastics with admiration and tried to learn from it as much as they could during educational trips and exchanges organised as part of the two countries' bilateral relations. They took part in competitions held in the U.S.S.R. and maintained links with trainers there, not only because they said it was a pride to learn the secrets of the sport from 'the big brother to the East', but because the Soviets genuinely were the best.

In 1973, the Romanian Gymnastics Federation took a decision that showed collaboration between the two countries had become closer than ever, hiring Soviet trainer Aleksandr Bogdazarov as manager of the women's national squad. Bogdazarov was given the task of training the team for the 1974 World Championships in Varna and supervised four groups of Romanian trainers: Ioan Pătru, Gheorghe Condovici, Gheorghe Gorgoi, Atanasia Albu, Norbert Kuhn, and Elena Leuşteanu, alongside whom worked choreographer Géza Pozsár and pianist Carol Stabişevshi. Bogdazarov's results were not spectacular, but by 1976, the Romanian team had risen two places in the ranking, compared with the 1972 Munich Olympics.

From 1975, the comradely spirit between Romania and the U.S.S.R. began to deteriorate. It was in 1975 that Nadia Comăneci first made an international name for herself, winning the Champions Trophy in London. The Soviets saw that their supremacy was in danger. Mircea Bibire,[1] a gymnastics trainer in Oneşti and a longstanding informer, confessed to a Securitate officer in late April, after returning from a trip to the U.S.S.R., that the young gymnast from Romania had caught the Russians' attention: 'On return from the U.S.S.R., prof. Bibire Mircea recounted to me the enormous interest that the Soviet specialists have in gymnast Nadia Comăneci from Gh. Gh. Dej. He even found it suspect that they were obsessed with knowing as much about her as possible and he confessed his fear that they might undertake "unsporting" measures against her in question, who threatens their supremacy in women's gymnastics. He signalled to me that the sanitary assistant who takes care of the gymnast's food is of Russian ethnicity and he is afraid that they might act via her to ruin the gymnast's form.'[2]

Although she was praised in the Soviet press, with *Sovietsky Sport* calling her 'the most brilliant' gymnast of the new generation after her success in Skien, the Securitate was picking up more and more signals that the Soviets were seeking alternative solutions to scupper her progress. Granted, the Romanian secret police was always ready to believe that spies from all over the world were being sent to infiltrate the sports centre in Oneşti – they had suspected Géza Pozsár's French fiancée, for example – which made them take such alarmist rumours seriously. All the more so since such rumours were confirmed by agents far more competent than Bibire, such as Mili Simionescu, who, on her return from the European Championships in Skien, informed the Securitate that Soviet coach Larisa Latynina had made efforts to limit Nadia Comăneci's success, declaring her to be too young and with plenty of time ahead for her to be able to wait her turn.

In September 1975, at a meeting of the F.I.G.'s Women's Technical Committee held in France, Simionescu once more found herself in the situation of having to stand up to the Soviets and their supporters within Eastern Europe. Ellen Berger and Taissia Demidenko, both deputy chairwomen of the committee, supported a revision of the age requirement: gymnasts would have to reach the age of fourteen in the year of the competition. 'These little girls will never be able to achieve the beauty and interpretative movement of an older gymnast like Turishcheva, and very good gymnasts, such as Hellman Angelika, D.D.R., want to give up gymnastics, because these younger gymnasts receive very high scores,' said Berger, backed up by Demidenko: 'We have forced through the very young and lost gymnasts like Lyukhina, Kuchinskaya. I don't like the mechanical movements of the little girls compared with the artistic movements of gymnasts like Korbut, Kim, Saadi etc.'[3] These discussions took place in a context in which Nadia Comăneci had won the competitions in London and Skien aged just thirteen, and the Soviet gymnasts she defeated included Olympic and World champion Ludmila Turishcheva, aged twenty-two.

In the spring of 1976, after the pre-Olympics tour of Canada and the United States, Corneliu Bogdan, the Romanian ambassador to Washington, sent a telegram to Vasile Gliga, the deputy foreign minister, in which he described the Canadians and Americans' great interest in the Romanian women's gymnastics team. The North American press was full of admiring comment, and the most popular sports programme of the time, *Wide World of Sports*, broadcast on ABC every Saturday afternoon, included in its opening credit a clip of Nadia Comăneci on the uneven parallel bars:

> Given the supremacy of Soviet gymnasts heretofore, the somewhat unexpected success of Nadia Comăneci and the developing Soviet-Romanian rivalry on the eve of the Montréal Olympics have regularly been discussed in almost all commentary. To our knowledge there have not been interpretations and speculations that have gone beyond the sporting nature of this rivalry. Rick Appleman,[4] the director of public relations for the American gymnastics federation, told comrade Ovidiu Ploscaru,[5] second secretary, that during the Toronto tournament in February this year, when everybody stood up to applaud Nadia Comăneci, the head of the Soviet delegation told him: 'probably now you'll start bringing Romanians over to tour the United States.'[6]

The Soviets were correct in predicting that their team would be eclipsed by Romanian gymnasts' victories. Soon, Rick Appleman became a familiar face in Bucharest, developing various Romanian–American partnerships.

With Nadia as the spearhead, with the other gymnasts bringing up her rear, and combined with the efforts of the R.G.F. leadership to combat Soviet score-fixing – unfortunately sometimes using the same methods – Romania began to crave more and more. And the higher the Romanians aimed, the more victories they won. It was a David and Goliath struggle, given the Soviets' resources and their long gymnastics tradition: in the U.S.S.R. gymnastics was organised on scientific principles, they had the largest pool of gymnasts and trainers in the world from which to select, and they could boast a first-class school of sports medicine.

In order to shock their adversaries, Romanian trainers started elaborating increasingly dangerous exercises, more often than not inspired by Soviet exercises. They poached the competition's moves, as they used to say in competitions. Géza Pozsár recalls that Béla Károlyi used to analyse every element executed by the Soviet and East German gymnasts, which he would then copy, while trying to add his own improvements. The Soviet coaches, however, viewed Károlyi as a limited technician, claiming that he achieved results only through excessive work, not through technical brilliance.[7] When it came to choreography, an important part of women's gymnastics, the Romanians stood no chance against the Soviet school of ballet, but Géza Pozsár was inspired enough to invent modern dances moves set to jazz or folk melodic lines, which were to the taste of the public.

After the Montréal Olympics, the Soviet knew that their sole adversary was Nadia Comăneci, and the former collaboration with the Romanians could now exist only at the level of words, spoken because both countries were part of the

Communist bloc. In the spring of 1978, on his return from the Moscow-Riga tournament,[8] Bibire informed the Soviets that the Russians had been very cold towards the Romanians, and they had even avoided spending time with them after the competition, alongside the other delegations from the Communist countries.[9] In Bucharest, when sports lovers talked about Nadia Comăneci, they would opine that the Russians wanted to get rid of her at all costs, even by physically eliminating her. For example, in July 1980, a few days before travelling to Moscow for the Olympics, Nadia was taken to Elias Hospital in Bucharest complaining of pains in her left leg. Rumours immediately spread, to the effect that she had been admitted to hospital suffering from a serious infection of unknown origin. It was claimed that she had been infected after she was pricked by a thorn from a poisoned rose given to her by the Soviet gymnastics delegation.[10] The Securitate found itself having to file a report stating that the rumour bore no relation to reality.

The rivalry with Soviet gymnastics placed huge pressure on coaches and those in charge of the sport in Romania, particularly since it was the Party itself that dictated they be the best in the world and win ever more medals. The Central Committee established in advance of tournaments the number of medals that had to be won and the objective was transmitted from the C.C. Secretariat to the head of the N.C.P.E.S. In the eighth-floor meeting room of the Central Committee, a meeting to lay out the objectives would be held with representatives of the federation, Party secretaries from each institution, and coaches. More often than not, the targets to be met were subjective and perceived as a real burden, but each meeting would unfold in exactly the same way: the head coaches and chairman of the federation would each stand up and praise the Party's care and efforts in the sporting domain, and they would undertake to do everything possible not only to meet the objective but to exceed it.

The reality was obviously known all too well, but nobody dared to object during those comical, absurd meetings, especially since Nicolae Ceauşescu was known to follow women's gymnastics and handball closely, sports at which Romania excelled at the time. 'In the past we would go there, we would compete, and goodbye. On my word, do you remember, at the European Championships,[11] everybody knew that Nadia was European champion but she and I didn't know,'[12] said Károlyi in November 1978, acknowledging that the romantic period of the mid-1970s was over for good.

Elena Ceauşescu personally told Emil Drăgănescu that Nadia had to win three gold medals at the 1980 Moscow Olympics,[13] and the Executive Bureau of the N.C.P.E.S. passed on the directive. The Olympic Games to be held in Moscow had been politicised. The United States and sixty-five other states were boycotting the event.[14] But eighty-one countries were still due to compete, and in the summer of 1980, the U.S.S.R. played host to 130,000 tourists and 5,000 journalists from all over the world. With the United States, West Germany, France,

Italy and other Western countries absent, the Moscow Olympics were seen as a competition between the countries of the Communist bloc, but for gymnastics this was no loss, since the top countries in the sport were all from Eastern Europe.

Nicolae Ceauşescu was eager for Romania to take part in the Olympics because he was determined to show that the Soviets could be beaten on their home turf, and also because he sensed Soviet hostility towards Romania in various gestures. For example, in an issue of *Sputnik* magazine, published by the Novosti press agency and printed in Finland, there appeared a map of the route taken by the Olympic torch, in which the whole of Romania's territory of Dobrudja was shown as lying within the borders of the Soviet Union.[15] After Romania voiced irritation at meetings in both Bucharest and Moscow, the Soviets apologised and ordered that the entire print run be withdrawn[16]

The Romanian national gymnastics squad, headed by Béla and Marta Károlyi, included Emilia Eberle, Dumitriţa Turner, Cristina Grigoraş, Melita Rühn, Rodica Dunca, Marilena Vlădărău and Nadia Comăneci, who was the only gymnast in the team to have taken part in the previous Olympics in Montréal. Nadia was also the oldest member of the squad. The 1976 squad no longer existed, even though at Montréal it had had the youngest average age of any of the top six squads and at the time it had been thought that the Romanians would make few changes between then and the Moscow games.

Gheorghe Gorgoi, Nadia Comăneci's new trainer after she left Deva, did not travel to Moscow. 'Nicolae Vieru asked me nicely not to go, because all the international press would have reported that Béla Károlyi was no longer her trainer and that Romania had made a mockery of itself when Nadia turned up with two coaches in tow,'[17] Gorgoi recalled. In February 1982, journalist Horia Alexandrescu wrote a report for the Bucharest Securitate in which he castigated Nicolae Vieru for the injustice he had been done to Gorgoi in 'sending Nadia Comăneci to the 1980 Moscow Olympics without the coach who actually trained her (Gheorghe Gorgoi), thereby enabling Béla Károlyi to win absolutely undeserved laurels, when the whole gymnastics world thought at the time that the Olympic titles Nadia won in Moscow were also thanks to Béla Károlyi.'[18]

This time, the Securitate embedded just one undercover officer within the Romanian delegation, Captain Traian Oancea of Independent Service D, acting in the official capacity of a N.C.P.E.S. expert. However, he was backed up by fifty-four informers, sportspeople, journalists and official within the four-hundred-strong Romanian delegation.[19]

The tournament was to be among the hardest in which the Romanian gymnasts had ever competed. Not only because they were up against formidable opponents from the Soviet Union and East Germany, such as Nellie Kim, Elena Davydova, Natalia Shaposhnikova, Maxi Gnauck and Steffi Kräker, but above all because they would be on genuinely hostile ground. Many of the fifteen thousand spectators in the Luzhniki Arena whistled Nadia Comăneci when she entered the stadium, a warning of what was to come in the following days of the competition. Yuri Titov upbraided Marin Dragnea, the chairman of the Romanian Olympic Committee and head of the Romanian delegation, for Romanian tourists supposedly behaving 'like hooligans',[20] trying to lay the blame on them for the noisy and often aggressive atmosphere in the stadium, even though it was Russians who booed Nadia and shouted, in Romanian, 'Cazi!' [Fall!] when Nadia was performing on the beam and uneven parallel bars.

The Romanian team made a promising start. On Monday, 21 July, during the compulsory exercises, Nadia Comăneci got her first 10 of the tournament, awarded for her routine on the balance beam, with her performing a confident handspring, backflip and cartwheel. After the compulsories, Nadia was neck and neck with Natalia Shaposhnikova. But on Wednesday, 23 July, during the optionals, which would establish the ranking and the team medals, Nadia made a mistake. In the middle of the arena, another gymnast was performing her floor exercise, accompanied by a *kazachok*, much to the delight of the crowd, who were clapping their hands and whooping, while Nadia was on the parallel bars, in the corner. No sooner had she mounted than she fell. 'It happened so fast that there was nothing I could do to save my performance. One minute I was up there, the next I was on the mat,'[21] recalls Nadia. Her mistake meant she was marked down to 9.50 and the whole team went down in the ranking. In the end, thanks to Eberle and Rühn, who both obtained a 10 on the parallel bars and the vault respectively, Romania managed to overtake East Germany and Czechoslovakia and occupy second place.

The most serious incident came on 24 July, during the individual all-round competition, however. Nadia, who was in fourth place because of her fall on the parallel bars, still had chances of winning gold if she put in almost perfect performances on every apparatus and her opponents made errors. The tension in the arena was so great that even television audiences could feel it, for Nadia had easily closed the gap and was now in second place, behind Elena Davydova. Her next event was the beam, where a score of 9.95 would earn her gold and the title of Olympic champion.

The beam was my final event at the 1980 Games. Yelena Davydova was set to finish on the bars, and if she made no mistakes, she would take the all-around gold. In the competition order, I was to perform second on the beam, and Yelena would be the sixth and final gymnast on the bars. Simple, right? Wrong. After the first competitor finished her beam routine, I prepared for the judges to signal my turn. But they didn't. Instead, they huddled together, and I thought that they were conferring about a score. Meanwhile, the bar routines continued. First, second, third . . . I still waited for my turn on the beam.

Béla instructed me to do some more warm-ups on the floor. As I said, the waiting was the hardest part. The fourth and fifth girls did their bar routines. Impatient, Béla tried to ask the judges what the holdup was, but they had no answer. Yelena did her bar routine—and there were no major mistakes. She received a 9.95. I was finally motioned to the beam. Apart from a slight bobble, I turned in a very solid routine and was scored a 9.85. That was a good number in Moscow; if we'd been in Romania, I probably would have got a higher score.[22]

Romania's gymnasts had to face not only a hostile crowd, but also judging that was grossly manipulated by the Soviets and representatives of other East-European countries, with Yuri Titov and Ellen Berger once more doing what they knew best. 'The judges were lying in wait for the Romanians like brigands in the forest,'[23] as L'Équipe aptly put it, since the international press could not help but notice the judges' brigandry. What also played a part was the outrageous and unjustified prevention of Nadia Comăneci from performing on the beam in her allotted time slot. The panel of judges wanted to make sure she would go on after the Soviet gymnasts so that they could be sure her mark was lower. Likewise, it gave Davydova a chance to perform without being under the pressure that Nadia obtaining a good score would have created. It also meant that Nadia was kept waiting, heightening the psychological tension, which would therefore affect her performance. But even if she showed a hesitation during her performance, the score Nadia received on the beam was unfair.

After she dismounted from the apparatus, all hell broke loose when the Soviet ploy was exposed for all to see. The score of 9.95 should have been out of the question, and the panel of judges deliberated for more than forty minutes, during which time the competition was interrupted. At the time it was alleged that Titov and Berger both played a part, making the other judges award Nadia just 9.85, while Maria Simionescu, the head of the panel, refused to press the button that would display it on the scoreboard. In the end, Soviet representative Kolog Nomus abusively took it upon himself to press the button in Maria Simionescu's stead.

Nadia Comăneci was prevented from winning the title of Olympic champion. Yuri Titov tried to calm down the Romanians by promising them that they would not leave empty-handed. According to Pozsár, who was at the games, Titov dished out the medals as if he were working a market stall, asking the choreographer to reassure Béla Károlyi that on the finals for the individual apparatuses he would give him 'dva zoloty' [two golds].[24]

All this took place not only beneath the eyes of the crowd, but also in front of millions of television viewers, as many channels were broadcasting the event live. Even though the United States and other Western countries were not competing, their press was there to cover the competition, and images of the scandal travelled all around the world. In the West, the conduct of Titov and Berger was widely condemned in the press, but some of the most damning coverage appeared in *Kronen Zeitung*, one of Austria's largest dailies, which on 26 July published a photograph of Nadia Comăneci receiving a kiss from Ellen Berger, with the caption 'The kiss of Judas'.[25] As for the Romanian press, there were biting remarks about the judging not only in the newspapers, but also in radio and television news bulletins. *Scînteia* [The Spark], *România Liberă* [Free Romania] and *Sportul* [The Sport] all praised 'our valiant gymnasts' and noted the existence of unfair scoring at the Moscow Olympics, but carefully avoided drawing any political conclusions. In the Soviet press, monitored by the Romanian embassy in Moscow, there was no mention of the unfair judging. The only Soviet media outlet to respond to criticism in the Romanian press was the Romanian section of Radio Moscow, which said the Romanian gymnasts 'got what they deserved.'[26]

On 25 July, in the finals on the apparatuses – where the rules stated that the only best gymnasts in the team competition were allowed to take part, with no more than two from each country – Nadia Comăneci had her revenge when she won gold on the beam and in the floor exercise, even though she had been up all night, having been summoned to an anti-doping check at two o'clock that morning. But her victories were only secured after furious contestation of her original scores. Romanian diplomats in Moscow described the scene in telegrams to Bucharest. Ştefan Andrei, the Romanian foreign minister, redirected all the telegrams to Nicolae Ceauşescu, to keep informed of the Soviet position in the greatest detail. The following is a telegram sent on 25, describing the events of the previous day:

On the evening of 24 July, the gymnastics competition ended—girls, individual all-round exercise. Demonstrating real patriotic spirit, self-sacrifice, the highest sporting skill and will to win, Nadia Comăneci and the other girls competing (Emilia Eberle and Rodica Dunca) dominated the events, which polarised the attention and esteem of public and specialists and naturally after Nadia Comăneci's performance it ought to have put her in first place and made her overall champion. Unfortunately, as happened on the previous two days, Nadia Comăneci was again marked down by the judges, in circumstances in which her opponents Shaposhnikova and Davydova were awarded by the same judges scores higher than objectively would have been deserved. On the final apparatus, the beam, where Nadia Comăneci performed the exercise almost to perfection, she received only 9.85 points, i.e. exactly as much as 'needed' for her not to come first, but second (the U.S.S.R. and D.D.R. judges awarded Nadia Comăneci scores of 9.80). Normally, the exercise performed would have deserved 9.95, which would have made Nadia Comăneci receive the fully deserved supreme title of overall Olympic champion.

It is to be observed that before awarded the score on the final apparatus, i.e. the beam, the judges deliberated for almost 45 minutes, something unheard of in any other competition, during which time the events were held up, and the stadium, packed to capacity, engaged in an unbelievable uproar and general state of agitation and chaos.

The Romanian judge Maria Simionescu, who was head of the panel of judges for the beam, held a firm position, she did not sign the competition slips, with the announcement of the score awarded to Nadia Comăneci being made by the organisers, the possibility of a subsequent contestation thereby being maintained.[27]

Obviously, over the course of the five tense days the women's gymnastics competition lasted, the Romanian diplomats had discussions not only with the Soviets, who offered them rather sarcastic congratulations and tried to console them by saying 'that's the way the judges are', but also other foreign diplomats in the Luzhniki Arena. According to the Romanians, the foreign diplomats showed 'visible annoyance and surprise', wondering, 'what have they got against Nadia?' The Chinese ambassador told his Romanian counterpart that the Moscow Olympics was 'saturated with a powerful spirit of chauvinism.' At the same time, he remarked that medals were unashamedly awarded to Soviet gymnasts: 'some comments by foreign observers, as well as the observations of Romanian jury members, demonstrate that in the activity of the juries there was co-ordinated action on the part of the representatives of the Comecon countries (particular the U.S.S.R., D.D.R., Bulgarian P.R., H.P.R.) so that medals were allocated before the events to the representatives of those countries.'[28]

On 4 August, at the end of the competition, the official organising committee did not conduct the Romanian delegation to the airport, as would have been usual, even though the delegation also included the chairman of the Romanian Olympic Committee. Károlyi's gymnasts had left for Bucharest on 27 July, taking seven medals with them: two gold (Nadia Comăneci, beam and floor exercise), three silver (team events, Nadia Comăneci, individual all-round event, and Emilia Eberle, uneven parallel bars) and two bronze (Melita Rühn, vault and uneven parallel bars).

As for Captain Traian Oancea, the Securitate's undercover man in Moscow, in his report he described 'the abusive subjective performance of the judges', Yuri Titov's 'hostile' and 'intimidating' attitude, and the presence of the Soviet secret services in the Olympic Village: 'The vice chairman of the U.S.S.R. Council for Physical Education and Sport, Sergey Sychi, in a seemingly friendly conversation with a person from our delegation, which took place in a changing room over vodka, claimed in an domineering voice that they were up to date on everything that went on in the Olympic Village, where everything was monitored.'[29]

At the Moscow Olympics the whole world watched on television as Béla Károlyi protested the judges' decisions, clutching his head in his hands and gesticulating angrily. He also gave brief interviews to the international press, stating that he had never witnessed such unfairness and corruption. Because similar articles were published by the press in Romania, Károlyi thought that once he arrived home, he would be given a hero's welcome, especially since he wouldn't be coming back empty-handed, but with a significant number of medals that had been won with difficulty, in an unfair fight.

In his autobiography he recounts that when he landed in Bucharest, nobody was there to greet him, however, and a few days later he was summoned to the Central Committee, where a number of officials, including Nicu Ceauşescu, the dictator's son, upbraided him for his conduct in Moscow and the fact that he had criticised the organisation of the competition in the international press. Károlyi even feared he might be arrested and took a roundabout route on his way back to Deva, to see whether he was being followed. A few weeks later, the effects of his dressing-down at the Central Committee began to make themselves felt. The funding of the Deva sports centre was drastically cut, a part of the staff left, and nobody phoned from Bucharest.

Károlyi was very despondent in his description of his return from Moscow, as if he had been cast into the wilderness in Deva. In 1982, he told an informer that after the Olympics, 'they were criticised quite harshly even though they had worked in difficult conditions there and still come back with six or seven medals.'[30] His situation did indeed worsen when he lost political support, but he didn't suffer anywhere near as badly as he himself suggests in his autobiography. On his return from Moscow, the airport wasn't deserted, since the entire delegation was greeted by reporters, as photographs in the newspapers of the time bear witness. His name was mentioned in the papers, but this time there weren't any interviews, which was a clear signal that the order had been given not to give him any more publicity. He continued to train gymnasts in Deva and to take them to international competitions, and he was called back to the Central Committee on a number of other occasions, since the Securitate archives reveal 'he was given an audience with the higher leadership of the Party and State'[31] in October 1980 and January 1981.

But it is strange to say the least that Party high-ups in Deva ordered the town's head of the Securitate to cease surveillance of Béla Károlyi. The decision was taken before the Olympics, on 8 July 1980,[32] and the cover of the 'Gymnast' dossier shows that surveillance did indeed cease on 21 August 1980. The last covert recordings made in the Károlyi home date from mid-June, but the reason for this was that he was carrying out renovations and the Securitate officers removed the bugs early lest they be discovered by the workmen. They left a single bug in the dining-room telephone, but this too was removed in August. Normally, surveillance ought to have been stepped up.[33] We believe that the order that came at the beginning of July was not local, but from Bucharest.

Meanwhile, in June 1980, agent 'Nelu's' dossier as a collaborator was also closed, when Pozsár became a member of the Romanian Communist Party, although 'he remained in contact with the organs of the Securitate with the approval of the Party organ as of 25.06.1980'.[34] Both the Deva Securitate and Department One in Bucharest continued to make use of Pozsár to provide them with information about the Károlyi, even though he was no longer officially under surveillance. Pozsár and his wife were very dissatisfied working with the Károlyis at the time. 'Who's stupid enough to work for them [the Károlyis]? Géza does the exercises and Marta takes the credit,'[35] Maria Pozsár complained to Mili Simionescu, claiming that they were struggling financially, whereas Béla and Marta Károlyi scooped up every benefit on offer, from substantial bonuses and free construction materials provided by the school for their villa to small gifts brought by parents wanting them to take their children at the sports centre.

In November 1978, listening in on a conversation between the Károlyis, the Securitate concluded that the two coaches were planning for a normal future. 'We have another five years of our careers left at the most,' Béla told his wife. 'The Los Angeles Olympics. After that we'll stay here. You'll be head of the school and I'll teach the little ones,'[36] replied Marta. To the Securitate, this was evidence that the Károlyis were happy in Deva and weren't planning to defect. In interviews, Pozsár has said that after his return from Moscow, Károlyi quickly realised that any political support he may have had was now gone,[37] and with it also vanished his influence within the R.G.F. and N.C.P.E.S., whereas Nicolae Vieru was waxing ever more powerful. For this reason, Károlyi began to think more and more frequently about leaving Romania. Pozsár confirmed this in a report dated from the end of 1980, in which he states that on 22 October Károlyi told him, 'it's our turn now,' with reference to fleeing the country. But Pozsár also added, 'Béla Károlyi's statement was spontaneous and uncontrolled, for which reason it seems the man in question did not expand on the topic on any other occasion.'[38] A few months later, at the end of March 1981, it nonetheless happened, although the Károlyi's defection was not painstakingly planned, but sooner an impetuous gesture.

In December 1980, Károlyi recounts, he was contacted by a representative of the N.C.P.E.S. for the first time since his return from Moscow. He was told to prepare his gymnasts for a tour of the United States and Venezuela the following year, a major hard-currency money-spinner for the Romanian State. Károlyi was overjoyed at the news, since it meant not an official event, but essentially a private tour of a series of cities, without the pressure of competition. The tour was to be named after Nadia—Nadia '81—and she was to draw crowds eager to see her to venues including Madison Square Garden in New York.

The Romanian delegation left on 4 March 1981 and in addition to the gymnasts it included Béla and Marta Károlyi, Géza Pozsár, Nicolae Vieru and Aurică Stoian from the mass sport and economic section of the N.C.P.E.S. They were due to fly back to Romania on 31 March, which was what happened, albeit less three members of the delegation: the Károlyis and Géza Pozsár. They had chosen freedom, as the saying went at the time, and the act sent a shockwave through Romanian sport and enraged the Communist régime.

The delegation had also included Viorel Trifan, a captain from Department One of the Securitate. His main mission was to keep a watch on Nadia Comăneci, but according to Nicolae Vieru, he made 'nothing but blunders'. For his part, Trifan claimed to have successfully completed his mission, since he never let Nadia out of his sight, shadowing her wherever she went – shopping, disco dancing, hobnobbing with Diana Ross at the singer's home. Because of the incident involving the three defectors, Trifan drew up a detailed report, describing day by day significant events, the tensions between Károlyi and Vieru, his efforts to constrain Nadia's freedom of movement so that she wouldn't be tempted to follow the defectors' example, and the manner in which the Károlyis and Géza Pozsár had vanished from their hotel:

Ministry of the Interior   Top Secret
Department of State Security   Copy. . . .
Department One
No. 161/TV/001604 __ April 1981

REPORT
re. problems resulting from the occasion
of the trip to the U.S.A. and Venezuela
by the women's national gymnastics team

In the period 4-30 March 1981, the women's national gymnastics team effectuated a show tour of the U.S.A. and Venezuela.

The tour of the U.S.A. was organised by the Apel [sic] Sport Corporation in partnership with ABC. Immediately after the plane took off I observed that the Károlyi couple, Stoian Aurică, the head of the delegation, and Vieru Nicolae, the secretary general of the Romanian Gymnastics Federation were carrying significant sums of money in hard currency, as proven by the purchases – liquor and foreign cigarettes – that they effectuated. They did the same thing on the occasion of the stop that the aeroplane made at Vienna airport.

At Kennedy Airport in New York the Romanian delegation was met by Rick Appleman [sic], the organiser of the tour of the U.S.A., and by representatives of the Permanent Mission of the Romanian S.R. to the U.N. After effectuation of immigration formalities in the U.S.A., we made our way to the Summit hotel, situated on Lexington street. Immediately after checking in the first discussion with the organiser of the tour took place regarding the conditions and modalities for implementation of the gymnastics demonstrations. At the insistence of coach Béla Károlyi it was decided that the American side should not provide meals for the delegation, but rather to pay over the equivalent sum in dollars. The next morning Vieru Nicolae and Stoian Aurică had a further discussion with Rick Appleman regarding the material conditions of the tour, on which occasion the person in question handed them a cheque to the value of $25,000 to be transferred to the homeland (in accordance with the contract), as well as the sum of $500 for each member of the delegation (in payment of the cost of meals for the entire duration of their stay in the U.S.A.). Stoian Aurică handed coach Károlyi Béla the total sum due to the gymnasts so that he could distribute it to each gymnast. Subsequently, I ascertained that coach Károlyi Béla had not distributed the sums of money, and on my informing the head of the delegation he asked him why he had not distributed the money. He replied that he would give them the money depending on the results that they obtained in training and the demonstrations. By the end of the tour the sums distributed to the gymnasts varied between $50 and $100 dollars per person.

On the afternoon of 15 March 1981 Cosma Silvia, a former gymnast, a legal emigrant from the homeland, turned up at the hotel where we were staying, with her husband (an engineer) and daughter, a student at the University of Boston, an acquaintance of Vieru Nicolae and Stoian Aurică, who offered to translate conversations with the American side during our stay in New York. In the discussions I had with the person in question, as well as from discussions with the other members of the delegation, I ascertained that she holds a favourable position towards our country, she intends to come to Timişoara this summer to visit relatives and friends.

On the morning of 6 March 1981 the entire delegation made its way to training in 'Madison Square Garden', where the first press conference was held at which representatives of the ABC channel (who filmed training) and reporters from the New York press took part. On this occasion Nadia Comăneci, Béla Károlyi and Nicolae Vieru gave short interviews regarding the manner in which our country's women's national gymnastics team is trained, the training conditions in our country, their future plans and in particular what Nadia Comăneci intends to do in future. After training, a viewing of the film *Caligula* was scheduled. Since Nadia Comăneci did not wish to see the film, I remained with her and Vieru Nicolae at the hotel. At around 17.00 hours, Nadia Comăneci informed me that she had received a telephone call from Oprea Mircea, the American impresario of Ilie Năstase, who conveyed a request on the part of Ilie Năstase to meet at the domicile of American coloured singer Diana Ross. At the request of Nadia Comăneci, I settled with Vieru Nicolae that we should agree to this visit. At 18.00 hours Oprea Mircea[39] came to the lobby of the hotel and conducted us to the International hotel in New York, where Diana Ross has an apartment. Ilie Năstase and Diana Ross were at the dwelling. During the whole 2 hours we were in this apartment the talk was only of the singer's and Nadia Comăneci's work.[40] On this occasion I ascertained that Oprea Mircea was trying to insinuate that in Romania training conditions were poorer than in the U.S.A. He told us that he was originally from the Serbian Banat and that there Romanians had a better life.[41] Since the main topic of discussion was connected with Diana Ross and Nadia Comăneci, I made no comment on Oprea Mircea's asseverations, but finally I told him that he would to better to visit our country, to see for himself the conditions we have. From Diana Ross's home we all went to a nearby discotheque, where we stayed for around an hour, after which we made our way to the hotel.

On 7 March 1918 there was another training session and a meeting with the U.S.A. men's national gymnastics team, with which the tour of the U.S.A. is to be effectuated. On this occasion the manner in which the demonstrations are to be held was established. At the request of the executive director of ABC, Nadia Comăneci and Vieru Nicolae gave interviews to the television channel in question. On returning to the hotel, Pozsár Géza informed me that coach Károlyi Béla was very upset with Vieru Nicolae, who, in his opinion, was using the name of Nadia Comăneci to obtain additional sums of money from the interviews that she gives to American television. I communicated this to the head of the delegation, Stoian Aurică, in order to prevent any incidents among the members of the delegation, all the more so given that coach Károlyi Béla had communicated to me that in the event that Vieru Nicolae did not cease 'to do business', he would cause a scandal in the hotel in front of the American delegation. In this situation, I asked the head of the delegation to lay down the material conditions for these interviews. It was therefore laid down that the incomes resulting from these interviews were payable to the American organiser of the tour, and this was communicated to all the members of the delegation, including coach Béla Károlyi.[42]

On 7 March year in progress another training session was held, after which the whole delegation went on a bus sightseeing tour of the city of New York, and at the insistence of coach Károlyi Béla we stopped at Alexander's shop situated near the hotel, where the man in question, his wife, and Nadia Comăneci effectuated purchases. On this occasion I ascertained that the Károlyi couple had a very long list of purchases that they had to effectuate. Marta Károlyi told me that for the head of the Deva school and his mistress alone they had to buy 4 pairs of jeans, 2 fur coats and footwear, items that they did indeed purchase that day. On the premises of the shop Béla Károlyi made injurious remarks about the deputy chairman of the Hunedoara County People's Council, who on his departure from the country is supposed to have solicited the kind of items that he should bring back for his family. On returning to the hotel, I ascertained that a letter from an American citizen by the name of Charles Andelman had arrived addressed to the delegation, asking about the situation of coach Gorgoi Gheorghe—Nadia Comăneci's official coach.

On discovering this, coach Károlyi Béla uttered swearwords aimed at Vieru Nicolae (who was not present), claiming that he intended to compromise him, that he was supposed to have made known in the U.S.A. the fact that the coach of the national coach is Gorgoi, and not Károlyi Béla.

On 8 March 1981 the official demonstration took place attended as invited guests by members of the Permanent Mission of the Romanian S.R. to the U.N., of the Commercial Agency, and of the Tourism Office. Despite the fact that prior to commencement of the programme the head of our delegation, in my presence, handed to the director of the show a tape and a cassette of our country's anthem, at the official opening the old anthem was intoned. Verifying this issue it resulted that the arena had a tape of the old anthem and that this tape was mistakenly played.

During the break in the show Sasu Ştefan, a former forestry technician in Oneşti, who left the country illegally around 10 years ago, approached the delegation wishing to talk to Nadia Comăneci, whose parents he knew. Since the person in question began to speak hostilely about our country, I moved him away.

On the morning of 9 March 1981 the delegation went to Hartford by bus, where that evening there took place a further demonstration. Over the course of the journey, between Nadia Comăneci and American gymnast Kurt Thomas closer relations of friendship were created, with her being in his company most of the time, and he described to her the material advantages he enjoys (he is a millionaire), as well as his social standing.

On 10 March 1981 we went to Cincinnati by aeroplane and we stayed at the Souffer Inn hotel. Immediately after checking in the Károlyi couple requested that they leave to effectuate some purchases. Together with gymnast Nadia Comăneci and Vieru Nicolae I went into town, visiting nearby shops. On this occasion I ascertained that the Károlyi couple were in possession of large sums of money (Marta Károlyi bought a large gold brooch). I report that during the trip into town, the Károlyi couple kept trying to avoid us when they made purchases. This occurred throughout the tour.

On the morning of 11 March 1981 a training session took place, and in the evening a demonstration took place. After the demonstration Károlyi Béla asked me to communicate to Vieru Nicolae not to keep following him around the shops, otherwise he would molest him. I communicated this to the head of the delegation Stoian Aurică, who convened the whole delegation and made clear that according to his mandate he was drawing attention to the fact that trips were to be effectuated only in groups in order to avoid any persons going missing, particularly the gymnasts, who are very young.

On 12 March 1981 we travelled by bus to Indianapolis, staying at the Hilton hotel. That evening the demonstration took place. During the journey to Indianapolis relations of friendship between Nadia Comăneci and American gymnast Kurt Thomas were accentuated.

On the morning of 13 March 1981 we travelled by aeroplane to Detroit, staying at the Plaza hotel. We were met by priest Iancu Mihai, a very good friend of the leader of the delegation Stoian Aurică, with whom in fact he went into town immediately after the delegation checked in, although both I myself and Vieru Nicolae drew his attention to the fact that it was stipulated that all trips were to be effectuated only in groups. The person in question returned to the hotel at around 24.00 hours, carrying numerous presents received—according to his statement—from priest Iancu and his family. Since Nadia Comăneci had been invited by Kurt Thomas to the hotel discotheque on the evening in question, I accompanied her together with Vieru Nicolae. On this occasion Kurt Thomas gave her the gift of a gold necklace.[43]

On 14 March year in progress Stoian Aurică communicated to us that we had been invited by the Romanian Community in Detroit to the special meeting hall within the precincts of Detroit University. Nadia Comăneci communicated to me that she would not take part in this meeting unless Kurt Thomas was also invited, in which situation I invited him along with another two American gymnasts. The meeting took place at around 14.00 hours, with around 40 persons present and the whole Romanian delegation. In fact, the meeting in question had been arranged to enhance the prestige of priest Iancu Mihai.

On our return to the hotel, choreographer Pozsár Géza communicated to me that in the hotel lobby he had seen Gheorghiu Ştefan, who had left the country many years ago, a friend of Vieru Nicolae. That evening, while with Nadia Comăneci and Kurt Thomas in the hotel park, I saw Vieru Nicolae with Gheorghiu Ştefan and his wife entering the hotel restaurant. Immediately behind them Károlyi Béla also entered the restaurant and positioned himself in such a manner as not to be seen by Vieru Nicolae.

After around 15 minutes Károlyi Béla came up to me and Nadia Comăneci and informed us that Vieru Nicolae was doing business with Gheorghiu Ştefan, to whom he gave money for the next trip to the U.S.A. He also stated that Vieru Nicolae is 'the biggest businessman' in Romanian sport and that on returning to the country he intended to give a detailed report on everything he knew about Vieru Nicolae. I report that on the evening in question the leader of the delegation Stoian Aurică went out with priest Iancu Mihai and his family. Meanwhile Bădulescu Mircea, the former trainer of the men's gymnastics team, a defector to the U.S.A., showed up at the hotel and made contact with Károlyi Béla and Pozsár Géza. Pozsár Géza informed me that Bădulescu Mircea complained about his present circumstances in the U.S.A., that he had not managed to find permanent employment. [. . .]

On 15 March 1981 the demonstration in Detroit took place and immediately after that the journey by aeroplane to Philadelphia. [. . .] In Philadelphia we stayed at the Hilton hotel. On the afternoon of 16 March year in progress the demonstration took place. On this occasion Rujanu Ion, who illegally left the country many years ago, turned up at the table of the Romanian delegation. Since he was making denigrating statements about our country, I moved him away, also with the support of Stoian Aurică.

On 17 March year in progress we travelled by bus to New York together with the American team. Immediately after our arrival in New York, coach Károlyi Béla proposed that the whole delegation make its way to a shop selling electronic items. Together with a representative of the Commercial Agency of the Romanian S.R. we made our way to Street 14, where purchases were effectuated. Coach Károlyi Béla bought 3 music stations, a number of cassette players, including auto radio-cassette players, 2 hunting rifles and other items. Choreographer Pozsár Géza bought 2 music stations, 4 radio-cassette players, as well as other items.

All the items purchases, including the personal luggage of the entire delegation, were stored in a room at the offices of the Romanian Commercial Agency, since we were due to travel to Venezuela the next day.

On the evening of 17 March year in progress, Stoian Aurică, in joint agreement with Vieru Nicolae, Károlyi Béla and the American organiser of the tour, established that after returning from Venezuela the Romanian and the American team would give another demonstration in Washington. The explanation given by telephone to our country was that there would not be a Tarom flight until 30 March year in progress. In actual fact, the demonstration in Washington was effectuated with the aim of obtaining additional sums of money for those in question, which was in fact what was done.

On 19 March year in progress we travelled by Pan Am aeroplane bound for Caracas. At the airport in Caracas we were met by personnel of the Romanian embassy, as well as by Ilou Raia, the organiser of the Venezuela tour.

That evening the first discussions with the Venezuelan side took place regarding the manner in which the tour should proceed. I report that at all the discussions with the discussions with the Venezuelan impresario the consul of the Romanian S.R. in Caracas, Ion Turturică, was present, providing translation and accompanying us everywhere.

On 20 March 1981 we travelled via Maracay to Valencia, the town where the first demonstration was due to be held, after which we returned to Maracay. In Maracay we were invited to the 'Italian House', where a performance was held in honour of Nadia Comăneci. On this occasion, a citizen (he did not give his name) approached the Romanian delegation and told us that he was a member of the Communist Party and asked us not to speak to the chairman of the 'Italian House', since he is of a neo-fascist orientation and carries on activities against the communists in the town in question (the chairman is called Filippo Sindoni). Together with Nadia Comăneci we returned to the hotel earlier, at her request, with the rest of the delegation arriving at around 24.00 hours. In the hotel I stayed in the same apartment as Károlyi Béla and Pozsár Géza. During the night (they were unable to sleep) they cursed Vieru Nicolae, accusing him of thwarting their financial entitlements and of doing 'business' together with Nadia Comăneci. I drew their attention to the fact that in all our talks the consul of our country was present and therefore there could not have been any irregularities. At one point they voiced their intention to search Nicolae Vieru's luggage when he was out of the hotel in order to see what he had bought and how much money he had.

On 21 March year in progress a demonstration took place in Maracay in the company of the Venezuelan men's gymnastics team. After the demonstration, the delegation went by bus to Caracas. On 22 March year in progress the consul of the Romanian S.R. in Caracas Turturică Ion communicated to us that the whole delegation, and Nadia Comăneci in particular, was invited to be the guests of Duzoglou Constantinos, a Greek citizen of Romanian origin, at the 'Platana' club, situated near the city of Caracas. We travelled there by bus. At the club we were met by personnel of the Embassy of the Romanian S.R. in Caracas and by Duzoglou Constantinos. I report that Duzoglou Constantinos is one of the richest men in Venezuela. During our visit to the club (approx. 4 hours) I ascertained that Duzoglou Constantinos was in good relations with the personnel of the embassy of the Romanian S.R. and took a stance favourable to our country.

On 23 March year in progress a training session took place in the arena of the Italian-Venezuelan club in Caracas, and in the evening the demonstration, attended by representatives of the local authorities and the accredited diplomatic corps in Caracas. After the demonstration, coach Károlyi Béla made contact with a citizen with whom he talked for approximately 20 minutes. Via comrade Turturică Ion, the consul of the Romanian S.R. in Caracas, I discovered that the person in question was engineer Zisu Sorin, living for many years in Venezuela. Via this person, Károlyi Béla purchases a safety device for his motorcar.

On 24 March year in progress the final demonstration in Venezuela took place, after which the whole delegation was invited to the domicile of a Jewish citizen of Romanian origin, Jaimei Meier, the chairman of a electro-technical products corporation. At the domicile of this person were present members of the embassy of the Romanian S.R., reporters and businessmen. On this occasion, Pozsár Géza communicated to me that he had talked to Iosifescu Mişu—living in Venezuela since 1973—who made denigrating statements about the living conditions of people in our country compared with those in Venezuela.

On 25 March 1981, the delegation visited the city of Caracas. On the morning of 26 March year in progress the entire delegation went to the 'Simon

Bolivar' international airport in Caracas. In attendance at the airport were representatives of the embassy, of the press and radio-television organs from Caracas. The same day we arrived in New York checking in to the Summit hotel, and the next day were due to travel to Washington, in accordance with the arrangement previously made. I asked the head of the delegation whether in the meantime he had received approval from the home country to put on the demonstration and he communicated to me that it had not arrived, but as things were at a very advanced stage, we could not pull out. The same evening, Pozsár Géza asked me to arrange for him to make telephonic contact with his wife in Deva (he does not speak English), which I did. In my presence he spoke to his wife and communicated to her that he had purchased all the things and items requested and asked her whether there was anything else she wanted, at the same time he communicated to her that he would be returning to the country on 30 March year in progress on a Tarom flight and asked her to wait for him at the airport, since he had a large amount of luggage. I asked him to ask his wife to inform my family that we would arriving in the country on 30 March year in progress. Immediately after the conversation Pozsár Géza began to complain about how much luggage he had, particularly the technical equipment, and did not know how he would cope at Romanian customs.

On the morning of 27 March 1981 we travelled by bus to Washington, where we arrived at around 15.00 hours, checking in to the 'Stadium' hotel, situated on the outskirts of the capital. Immediately after checking in we went to a gymnasium, after which we made a brief visit to the embassy of the Romanian S.R. In the bus there was a violent argument between coach Károlyi Béla, who intended to make purchases, and the head of the delegation, Stoian Aurică, who wanted the whole delegation to visit the environs of the White House. Under these circumstances, we all went to the hotel, where we met the American team. Kurt Thomas invited Nadia Comăneci into town, but I asked him not to do this, since we were tired, an explanation he accepted. Under these circumstances, together with Vieru Nicolae we invited Kurt Thomas to Nicolae Vieru's room, where we offered him Romanian brandy. Nadia Comăneci was also present during the discussion. The discussion dealt in particular with the subject of Nadia Comăneci's return to the U.S.A., to the celebration of the ABC television channel, and in particular to do with the financial resources available to Kurt Thomas.

On the morning of 28 March year in progress the Károlyi couple, Pozsár Géza, Vieru Nicolae and Stoian Aurică went to a nearby shop to effectuate a number of purchases. I remained at the hotel with Nadia Comăneci and Kurt Thomas. They returned to the hotel at 12.00 hours, but without Marta Károlyi, who was late in coming. I ascertained that Károlyi Béla had purchases numerous items of clothing and in particular hunting and fishing implements.

[. . .] From the hotel we went to the hall for the performance, and after the demonstration we travelled directly to New York, where we arrived at around 20.00 hours, checking into the Summit hotel again. After arriving at the hotel, choreographer Pozsár Géza stated in the presence of myself and Vieru Nicolae that it was necessary that that night we take very great precautions with Nadia Comăneci, since it was possible that she might leave with the American gymnast. Together with Vieru Nicolae I took measures that she be given a different room, closer to our rooms (the hotel was very crowded). Under these circumstances, I sat in an armchair at the door to the lift. At 21.30 hours Nadia Comăneci came out fully dressed and on seeing me she communicated to me that Kurt Thomas had invited her to a discotheque. We went down to the hotel lobby where Kurt Thomas and the coach of the American team were waiting. I communicated to Kurt Thomas that Nadia Comăneci could not go on her own with them at night and that it was better that she be escorted. Kurt Thomas made no objection. I telephone Vieru Nicolae in his room and told him to get dressed so that we could go with Nadia Comăneci and the American gymnast. We went to a discotheque nearby, where Nadia Comăneci and Kurt Thomas danced till 24.00 hours, after which we returned to the hotel. On our return to the hotel, choreographer Pozsár Géza communicated to me his dissatisfaction and that of the Károlyi coaches, caused by the fact that the head of the delegation had not given them the money after the demonstration in Washington. The next day, I communicated this to the head of the delegation, who summoned them and gave them the money. He communicated to me that he had given them $100 each, as agreed, although according to information subsequently obtained it transpires that the three received $650 each.

That morning we went to the Romanian Commercial Agency in New York to collect the personal luggage and previously effectuated purchases, which we brought back to the hotel. Throughout this interval the Károlyi couple complained of the fact that they did not have enough suitcases for the purchases they had made, deciding to buy another 2 suitcases, which is what they did. The afternoon of that day we were invited to be the guests of the 'Atalanta' company (which imports meat products from our country), where a meal was served and we stayed for approximately 3 hours. Members of the Romanian Commercial Agency and the Tourism Office were present.

I report that on the afternoon of 29 March year in progress the head of the delegation Stoian Aurică went to the German F.R., where he had established telephonically a meeting with representatives of sports materials companies.

That evening at the hotel I helped Nadia Comăneci to pack her bags, but I had in view the prevention of any unconsidered action on her part. I escorted her to a shop near the hotel to buy foodstuffs. Throughout this interval, Vieru Nicolae was in the hotel bar with the American impresario. When we returned to the hotel choreographer Pozsár Géza communicated to me that he was going to the Károlyi couple's room in order to help them pack their bags. At around 22.30 hours I was called on the telephone by Béla Károlyi who asked me whether I knew where Vieru Nicolae was, since he wanted to communicate to him that he was going into town, having been invited by a family who lived nearby. I communicated to him the place where Vieru Nicolae could be found, insisting that he communicate without delay the fact that he was leaving the hotel. When Vieru Nicolae returned, I asked him whether he had seen the Károlyi family and Pozsár Géza and he communicated to me that they had not met. The Károlyi couple and choreographer Pozsár Géza returned to the hotel at around 01.00 hours in the morning. Pozsár Géza communicated to me that they had been to meet some Hungarians, originally from Cluj-Napoca, an old acquaintance of the Károlyi couple.[44] Since the American team was in the hotel I spent most of the time in the corridor upstairs, since music could be heard coming from Kurt Thomas's room. I report that Nadia Comăneci entered Kurt Thomas's room (where there were also two American gymnasts) and the music was heard until 02.00 hours in the morning.

When Pozsár Géza returned to his room he told me that he had to buy another suitcase, since the two he had already bought previously were insufficient.

According to the prior arrangement, on 30 March year in progress, at 09.30 hours, the entire delegation met in the hotel lobby to make its way to the Alexander's shop. By common consent the entire delegation decided that at 12.00 hours we should all meet at the entrance to the shop, with those who still had purchases to effectuate staying for a maximum of 2 hours in order to have enough time to reach the Kennedy airport. We arrived at Alexander's immediately after it opened and I saw Bella [sic] Károly and his wife at the jewellery counter. Thence they went to the basement of the shop. Pozsár Géza went to purchase a suitcase. Together with Nadia Comăneci and other gymnasts I stayed on the ground floor of the shop. The Károlyi couple and choreographer Pozsár Géza did not arrive at the appointed rendezvous. After waiting for approximately 15 minutes, Vieru Nicolae decided that those who still had purchases to effectuate would remain until 14.30 hours and that we would all meet at the hotel. Since Nadia Comăneci did not wish to remain, I escorted her to the hotel. At the entrance to the hotel we met the representative of the AMF (sports materials) company with whom we had toured the United States, who communicated to me that the bus to take us to the airport had arrived, but apart from Nadia Comăneci and myself no other member of the delegation had arrived. Under these circumstances we decided to wait for them in the hotel lobby. Approximately 30 minutes later, on seeing that nobody had arrived, I went up to the room where I ascertained that the personal belongings and purchases objects were no longer to be found. Under these circumstances I immediately talked to Nadia Comăneci and we decided to go together up to the Károlyi couple's room. I report that in the meantime Vieru Nicolae also arrived at the hotel, whom I immediately informed of the situation that had arisen.[45]

Together with Nadia Comăneci I requested from the hotel staff duplicates of the keys to the Károlyi couple's room, ascertaining that the luggage was gone with the exception of the radio speakers they had purchased. I asked the hotel staff whether they had any knowledge of the situation regarding the Károlyi couple and they told me that they knew nothing. I received the same answer from the representative of the sports materials company (AMF) who was taken by surprise at the act of the persons in question. Under these circumstances I asked Nicolae Vieru to inform the Permanent Mission of the Romanian S.R. to the U.N. Comrade Ion Goritza, adviser, was informed, who instructed us to proceed to the airport and told us that he would communicate the emergency situation to our country. At this point Nadia Comăneci informed me that immediately after she returned to the hotel she was telephoned by a person by the name of Magda, who asked her how she was and whether she had decided to remain in the U.S.A. (the person in question is Magdalena Fintes, originally from Cluj-Napoca, resident in the U.S.A.).

At the Kennedy airport we were met by representatives of the Romanian S.R. Permanent Mission to the U.N., the Commercial Agency and the Tourism Office. At 20.00 hours the aeroplane took off for Amsterdam. Throughout the flight, among the members of the delegation there were discussions connected with the motives that led those in question not to return to our country. The initial reaction of the gymnasts was one of fear for their future (Ecaterina Szabo, Emilia Eberle, Lavinia Agache), after which they voiced their joy at having escaped from the 'terror'.

On arrival, at Otopeni airport we were greeted by the leadership of the National Council for Physical Education and Sport and some representatives of the Romanian sporting press.

Captain Trifan Viorel.[46]

Béla and Marta Károlyi and Géza Pozsár were placed under criminal investigation on 1 April 1981 in absentia for refusing to return to Romania, a crime under the then Penal Code. The Militia conducted searches at the school, where they compiled a long list of 'debits' (sports equipment and materials that had not been surrendered, unpaid bills, and debts incurred as a result of repairs to the villa where they lived). The N.C.P.E.S. filed a civil suit against Béla Károlyi for 'losses to our unit to the sum of 56,246.75 lei, representing the equivalent value of various sports goods.'[47] On 2 April, officers from the Securitate's Department of Criminal Investigation carried out a search of the Károlyi's home, leaving with a long list of goods to be confiscated to recoup the losses or which were deemed to be owned illegally: 4,300 dollars, 1,500 Deutschmarks, and other small sums in various currencies (zloty, pesos, bolivars, roubles etc.), jewellery, five hunting rifles and hundreds of cartridges, medals, stamps, and savings books worth more than 260,000 lei.[48] From Géza Pozsár's home they removed only personal documents, as his financial position did not even begin to compare with that of the Károlyis.

During the criminal investigation, further charges were brought against the three: abuse of trust to the detriment of public property and failure to abide by foreign payments regulations. By 1 July 1981, the case had been tried and sentence passed: seven years imprisonment for Béla Károlyi and six years imprisonment for Marta Károlyi and Géza Pozsár.

Many people wondered why the Károlyis had resorted to such an act when 'not even a minister lived as well as him.'[49] Everybody was surprised, including the Securitate, which had not been able to detect any clue to be able to prevent it. Károlyi had bought his villa in Deva and engaged in costly work to extend it, an investment he would not have made if he had had plans to defect. In discussions in the privacy of their own home – on 13 February 1981 the Securitate had planted bugs once more to find out whether the Károlyis were planning to profiteer during the trip abroad[50] – they were never caught making even the slightest allusion to leaving the country illegally. Not least, the fact that they had left behind significant sums, and the fact that they had made numerous purchases during the tour were further evidence in support of their not having planned to do so.

The Securitate received confirmation that they made their decision only the night before, when they were visited by Ion and Ghizela Olteanu, resident in New York, first from Nicolae Vieru – 'they made the decision during the visit to Ghizela Olteanu'[51] – and then from various agents in the months and even years to come.[52]

The case of Géza Pozsár was different, given he had worked as a Securitate informer for more than six years. He enjoyed great trust. He had met intelligence officers from Bacău, Hunedoara and Bucharest, whose identity he would be able to reveal to the U.S. authorities, as well as the nature of the missions they had given him.[53] The secret police tried to influence Maria Pozsár, who had been left behind in Deva, to persuade her husband to return to the country. There were plenty of reasons for him to come back: his wife and child were waiting for him, and the authorities promised that there would be no repercussions of any kind and he would be able to carry on working at the sports centre.[54] Whereas on learning the news Pozsár's wife had been outraged at her husband's act and blamed Béla and Marta Karoli, a few weeks later she changed her tune and started hoping that Géza Pozsár would manage to bring her and their child to the United States.

This was what happened, thanks largely to the assistance of American sportspeople and managers, including Bart Conner and Paul Ziert, as well as a number of congressmen, headed by Bill Archer.[55] They were joined by the State Department and American press, which exerted pressure on the Romanian Communist régime to agree to reunite the families. Béla and Marta Károlyi managed to be reunited with their daughter six months later,[56] while Géza Pozsár waited for more than a year before his wife and daughter received permission from the Romanian authorities to leave the country.

Károlyi had hoped that his act would garner wide press coverage, but the U.S. media's attention was focused elsewhere, given that on 30 March, the day when he defected, an attempt to assassinate Ronald Reagan was made, an event that dominated the public attention for many days to come. The three Romanians' situation was brought up in the newspapers and on television only a week later, thanks to congressman Bill Archer. The *Washington Post* set the tone, publishing on 8 April a first-page article by Charles Fenyvesi, along with a photograph captioned 'Trainers of Romanian stars, including Comăneci, defect'. Subsequent articles in the U.S. press referred to the Károlyis as 'Nadia's trainer' or 'Comăneci's trainer'.

Although they did not voice any harsh criticism of the Communist régime, they claimed that they had made the decision to defect because they were dissatisfied with the way in which the Romanian authorities were treating them. Fenyvesi, a Hungarian who had escaped to the West in late 1956, mentioned the Hungarian ethnicity of the Károlyis and Pozsár, and a few days later he published a follow-up on their situation entitled 'Comaneci's Trainer'. Other media outlets took up the story after the *Washington Post*, all of them being reported in encrypted diplomatic telegrams sent from the Romanian embassy in Washington:

On 8 April, at 17.15 and 19.15 hours on the state and then federal (the whole U.S.A.) networks, the NBC tv company broadcast two special programmes *Nadia's Trainers*, in the first presented by Barbara Allen footage of Nadia Comăneci on the beam was shown, the news about the Károlyis and Pozsár, who have requested political asylum, their family members left behind in Romania. Then they showed footage from the State Department, where the Department's spokesman informed reporters that the Károlyis and Pozsár had requested political asylum in the U.S.A., that the American authorities were in the process of completing the formalities.

At 19.15 hours, news anchor Roger Mudd revealed that in recent years many escapes to the West from the socialist countries had taken place, but none at this level. The Károlyis' escape is 'a great joy for the whole western world.' After they showed images of Nadia and Károlyi at the Moscow Olympics, it was revealed that the reason for requesting political asylum was dissatisfaction at treatment at the hands of the Romanian Gymnastics Federation. It was recounted that the three fugitives have addressed the U.S.A. Congress in order to be assisted to reunite their families. Likewise, they made the same request to the Romanian government. In the meantime, the U.S.A. government has granted the three leave to work in the United States. Against a backdrop of a photograph of B. Archer, the congressman, it was revealed that he has informed the Romanian ambassador that if the Romanians want the clause (most favoured nation), they should give the three their families as quickly as possible.

In our opinion, the series of publicity actions, the press conference at the State Department, the letter from the American congressmen, the rapid granting of leave to work, reveal that they were planned long in advance and implemented with the co-operation of official American departments. Likewise apparent is the very high-level treatment of the issue on the American side.[57]

Obviously the Romanian Communist régime didn't want to perpetuate the scandal, quickly realising it would be politically damaging. The subject easily veered towards far more sensitive issues, which the Romanian authorities were not prepared to see on the agenda of bilateral talks. For example, based on the Károlyi-Pozsár case, congressmen Schulze and Ritter raised the issue of the rights of Romania's Hungarian minority and their constant infringement, as well as the situation of the 'minority churches', claiming that there was persecution and intimidation. The matter might have escalated into a full-blown debate about the Romanian State's humanitarian record when it came to the reuniting of families, and hundreds or thousands of unsolved applications would have come to light. In this context, the withholding of the most favoured nation clause on the part of the U.S.A. was more and more frequently invoked as a consequence of such a policy, albeit not by the White House or State Department, but for the time being only by members of Congress. For this reason, the Károlyi's daughter arrived in the United States in record time, likewise the rest of Pozsár's family, although the three were officially 'traitors' and had already been given prison sentences.

The Securitate thought about measures to compromise them – which we shall describe below – but these were abandoned as the years passed, particularly given the fact that both the Károlyis and Géza Pozsár continued to have successful careers in the United States, and also the fact that they did not make hostile gestures towards the Communist régime in Bucharest. Károlyi made threatening noises mostly in the letters he sent to Bucharest, in which he suggested that he might make public certain pieces of information.

From time to time, the secret service tried to take advantage of meetings between Károlyi and Romanian informers visiting the United States or when they met him at international gymnastics competitions. In 1982, one such agent reported that Béla Károlyi 'is regretful and cries when he remembers acquaintances he left behind in Romania, claiming that he wasn't ready to stay in the U.S.A., but because of an argument and altercation with the leader of the group, he decided to remain permanently. (. . .) He was also upset at the fact that the group's leader took away the passports that he had on him for the whole squad. When he drinks a lot he remembers the home country and cries. He claimed: "When will those 7 years be over to come back home?"'[58]

A few years later, Károlyi explained his defection from Romania differently. In 1984, during the America Cup, he told Octavian Belu, the trainer of the Romanian national team, 'he regrets the fact that he has remained in the U.S.A. illegally, but he did it at the insistence of his wife Marta.'[59] He also told other members of the Romanian delegation, 'he would not have agreed to remain abroad if his wife had not categorically insisted that they accept the financial offer made by representatives of the Hungarian community in the U.S.A.'[60]

'If you'd stayed too, our princess, I wouldn't have gone back either,' Nicolae Vieru is supposed to have told Nadia Comăneci in the airport. The scene was described to the Securitate by journalist Horia Alexandrescu, who spent many years in Nadia's close circle. 'Neiru didn't deny he said it, but specified that he would have remained . . . out of fear,'[61] added Alexandrescu.

After the return to Romania, the secretary general of the R.G.F. had a lot of explaining to do, particularly since he was also obliged to combat accusations to the effect that he had organised 'a looting and business tour', and that Károlyi 'remained there because of you.' Vieru, covertly recorded by the Securitate talking with Federation colleagues and Nadia Comăneci in a hotel room, had this to say in his own defence: 'He remained there because of him not because of me. The only business I did in America was bringing Nadia back home.'[62]

The Securitate did not forgive Vieru, even if thitherto he had been on friendly terms with them, and by the end of May 1981 they had opened a surveillance dossier on him. The reason for the measure was that in the West 'he influences Romanian specialists and sportspeople with the aim of drawing them into actions that could cause damage to our country's interests'[63] – a reference to the Károlyi–Pozsár case – and Vieru was one of those who had the most significant connections abroad.[64] At the time a certain senior official of the R.G.F. was suspected of habitually profiting from his personal relations and even of knowing in advance that certain sportspeople and trainers intended to flee the country but without informing the authorities. Among the agents who were assigned to monitor Vieru were Maria Simionescu, Atanasia Albu and Aurel Stoian. In addition, as was usual in such situations, bugs were planted in his home and his telephone and letters were intercepted.

'Monica' and 'Lia Muri' confirmed the Securitate's suspicions in their reports. Consequently, after further evidence was gathered and the case was examined by the chairman of the N.C.P.E.S., in the spring of 1982 Vieru was demoted to the position of instructor at the Centre for the Further Training of Cadres in the Sporting Movement. Surveillance was curtailed in April 1986, by which time the

Securitate deemed Nicolae Vieru to have expiated his sins, which is to say, he had ceased to have unofficial relations with foreigners and become more careful in regard to 'his attitude and behaviour'. But in spring 1986, it was also proposed that 'the approval of the Party organs with a view to his use in the gathering of information from the sporting sector,'[65] and 'Vlad' thenceforth ceased to be an official connection of the Securitate and instead became an informer.

As for Nadia Comăneci, she experienced repercussions, but not straight away. In the first phase, the Securitate wished to discover when exactly she discovered the trio's intentions and whether or not she was tempted to join them. Vieru declared that during the tour, 'despite the differences, already well known in Romania, that existed between trainer Béla Károlyi and gymnast "Corina", the former constantly tried to enter the gymnast's graces,' that the night before he fled, he was 'upset, angry and pensive', and Nadia is supposed to have said that he asked her 'whether she was determined to remain or not',[66] but only his vigilant intervention put a stop to Károlyi's plan.

Maria Simionescu recounted to the Securitate what she found out from Vieru during meetings at the federation or in private. For example, the general secretary of the R.G.F. is supposed to have confessed, 'Béla also repeatedly proposed to Nadia that she should remain outside the country,' and at the airport, also according to Vieru's account, she was very depressed, weeping and saying, 'it's all over now, I'll never be able to leave now.'[67]

Béla Károlyi put her in a very unpleasant situation a few months later. On 20 September 1981, he wrote a letter to Ion Păun, the head of the international relations service of the National Council for Physical Education and Sport, in which he described the episode, and Nadia, according to Károlyi, was in on the whole plot:

Recently, in the English press, there was published a declaration attributed to Nadia about the fact that I suggested that she remain in America. Yes, I knew her intention not to return to the country, Appleman, Vieru's 'friend', told me about the arrangement between Kurt Thomas and Nadia, the contract that was due to be signed with a view to a joint tour. Appleman didn't like the idea of Nadia staying behind because of the scandal that would have erupted, and because he would be losing the client with whom he had plans as a foreign gymnast, not as business partner of Kurt Thomas. Vieru knew this just as well, not only did he tell Appleman, but also I personally drew his attention to the fact that it would be well that besides the arrangements with Appleman and the television that he should also see to Nadia's life, which might take 'flight' . . . Anyway, I had a talk with Thomas on the final evening before leaving Washington, on which occasion the lad said that Nadia constantly being there would complicate his situation too much, and dividing the earnings down the middle didn't thrill him as much as in the first flush of enthusiasm. So, in the final 24 hours, the lad didn't go back to New York with the Century Fox representative who was to bring the contracts with a view to the tour and the film, which was to have been shot with the two of them, Nadia and Kurt. Nadia sat with her bags packed waiting for the people to arrive as agreed, but being an 'artist' by nature, she concealed her agitation, and later her fury.[68]

Károlyi's letters could not but fall into the hands of waiting Securitate officers, especially since many of the addressees were informers, as was the case with Ion Păun, alias agent 'Popescu'. Given Károlyi's well-known penchant for distorting reality – 'he cultivates the lie', as agent 'Nelu' was wont to say of him – it was hard even for the Securitate to establish whether he was distorting the facts deliberately or employing a tactic to counter secret service measures to compromise him.

In reality, the letter was sent as a reaction to such measures. Between 9 and 12 September 1981, Nadia Comăneci was in London for the launch of Graham Buxton Smither's *Behind the Scene of Gymnastics*. Her attendance at the event was officially approved because Nadia was accompanied only by Securitate officers and informers: federation trainer Maria Simionescu, journalist Aurel Neagu, and Captain Viorel Trifan of Department One, who posed as a representative of the National Council of Physical Education and Sport. In his post-mission report, Trifan said that everything went well during Nadia's encounters with the British press. When she arrived at the airport, reported Trifan, 'the BBC correspondent asked her whether Béla Károlyi remaining abroad affected Romanian gymnastics negatively. In accordance with instructions received in the home country, Nadia Comăneci answered that this was not the case, as proven by the exceptional results subsequently obtained by our gymnasts.'

It was not this remark that offended Károlyi, but one made later, during a press conference the following day, when the reporters were asked for their question 'before the interviews began so that Nadia Comăneci would have an opportunity to prepare her answers, since it was in English,' a trick that delegations from Communist countries visiting the West employed so that they wouldn't be caught out by inconvenient questions. Asked by the *Daily Express* reporter the opinion of Károlyi's refusal to return to Romania, 'Nadia Comăneci answered that she detested the gesture of him in question and did not believe that in a foreign country he would have the same conditions as he had in the home country.'[69]

Obviously, as Trifan said in his report, Nadia reacted to the reporters' questions 'according to instruction from the home country', which means she had been briefed on what she should say if she ever wanted to travel abroad again. Károlyi must have been well aware of this modus operandi on the Communists' part, given that he himself had frequently been placed in similar situations, when he heaped praises on the régime and Nicolae Ceauşescu in interviews to the foreign press over the course of his career. But Károlyi preferred to write to Ion Păun, and his claims fed later Securitate suspicions that Nadia had been tempted to defect, but had come up against the coach's refusal.[70]

The secret service took note of the few interviews that Károlyi gave to Radio Free Europe during his first months in the United States and concluded that he had 'intensified his obsessions with denigrating the achievements of Romanian gymnastics and damaging the interests of our state.'[71] The Securitate also took into consideration the fact that Károlyi had quickly forgotten the gesture of goodwill made by the régime when it reunited him with his daughter, while Károlyi was irritated by Nadia Comăneci's statements in London, sensing that others would follow.

As a result, the Securitate drew up the 'Katona plan of action', which was approved on 18 December 1981, although the archives give no indication that it was ever implemented. The plan would have had two phases, with the first entailing measures to influence him, the second measures to compromise him. Maria Simionescu, Atanasia Albu, Ion Păun, and others would have sent letters to Károlyi in which they rejected his claims. Likewise, they would 'disinterestedly' communicate with representatives of the United States Gymnastics Federation and 'talk to them about "Katona", describing the exceptional conditions he enjoyed in the Romanian S.R., the support and understanding shown by the Romanian authorities when reuniting him with his family, and that it ought to be the case that they refrain from inappropriate actions.'

In the second phase, 'Lia Muri' would write to Károlyi in a more threatening way, 'making references to his "pedagogical" methods of training the gymnasts', suggesting they could be made public. Such accusations would have been hard to rebut on the Károlyis' part, given that they would be backed up by the most prestigious federation coach in Romania and would probably be confirmed by the gymnasts themselves. There would likely also have been disclosures about 'his mercantile, profiteering spirit'[72] and references to the private lives of the three defectors. Finally, Károlyi was to be revealed as a Securitate agent, not in public, but through a so-called slip-up for the benefit of the U.S. authorities: 'A letter will be drafted in which it will be understood that "Katona" is in contact with the organs of the Romanian Securitate. This will be handed to one of our organs' sources who is travelling abroad in order to be posted to "Katona's" address. We are counting on the fact that the U.S.A. police will intercept this letter and it will create suspicion around him.'[73]

Blithely unaware of what was in store for him, Károlyi continued to send letters to Romania, albeit suspecting they would be intercepted. The letters conveyed messages or warnings to both the N.C.P.E.S. and the Securitate. For example, on 25 October 1981, he wrote to Maria Simionescu, 'it would be in the interest of all of us (. . .) not to dig up the dead.' He of course also mentioned Nadia's statements to the press in London, which had aggrieved him so badly:

the statements I have made to date about the past and present of our girls and team are favourable or at the least reserved. But I'm not convinced that I'll not change my stance in the event that no intervention is made to halt the calumnious statements made by Nadia in England, which the American newspapers have also reported on. Maybe even you yourself could do so especially since you were there with her. I think it's sufficient that you remind Miss Comăneci that I'm the only man who can describe her in her real 'splendour', starting with her 'family', her 'diet', her 'jokes' during training sessions in Bucharest, 1977–78, in Deva, 1978–79, and in particular during the final tour, about which Kurt Thomas would also have a lot of things to say. I hope you have enough arguments to bring her back to the real world, maybe you can also remember a few things about incidents from the period in which you were with her, which likewise it's not desirable (at least I think so?) to have printed in the newspapers. I think you realise how eager the sensational story-hunters are to have me start reacting to an eventual open attack.

Personally, I've not injured her up to now in any way, on the contrary, I want her to remain a symbol of high-quality gymnastics, an idol for children all over the world, even if she is a rotten corpse, as only we, a few people, fortunately know.[74]

In his letter, Károlyi threatened other revelations he might make in future, if the war of statements grew worse, and the Securitate understood, 'he is referring to conflicts that might be made public,'[75] a situation undesirable to the régime in Bucharest. Ultimately, Károlyi and the Securitate both had a similar aim, which was to cast a shroud of silence as quickly as possible, but it took months before each party fully realised that revelations from both sides would have caused damage far too great.

Not everybody was negatively affected by the Károlyis' defection or felt it to be a loss. In Deva, the gymnasts hoped that the departures of the two coaches would bring their dark days to an end, that they would no longer be beaten or have to come up with ingenious methods of hiding food, such as inside the hem of the curtains. In other words, they would no longer be living in a 'concentration camp', as gymnast Rodica Dunca was to describe it decades later. When asked by a reporter whether Béla Károlyi's methods were harsh, she replied, 'harsh is putting it mildly, under conditions in which we were happy if we got away with just a beating. And there were days when we were hit so hard that the blood streamed from our noses. The hunger was our constant enemy.' But so was thirst, since the gymnast also recalled that there were times when 'we had to urinate with the door open. (. . .) They were afraid we might drink water. But we would go inside the cubicle, we would do our business and not flush the water. We would climb up on the toilet and with a glass hidden there, we would scoop water from the cistern up above. We would drink our fill. (. . .) When we took a shower, the same thing would happen. We were guarded and we weren't allowed to tilt our heads back lest we swallowed some water.'[76]

Securitate officer Trifan reported that even in Kennedy Airport, 'the gymnasts' initial reaction had been one of fear for their future (Ecaterina Szabo, Emilia Eberle, Lavinia Agache), after which they expressed their joy at having escaped the 'terror'. In a report written on 21 April 1981, after the Securitate asked her to gauge the mood in Deva, Maria Simionescu also remarked on the gymnasts' elation:

With regard to the mood of the women's squad in Deva after the defection of the Károlyis and Pozsár Géza, the source relates: the great majority of the gymnasts expressed their satisfaction at having escaped from a tyranny, beatings, very nasty words etc., in particular Emilia Eberle, who claimed that at last she would be able to do the vault, since when Béla entered the gym she would be inhibited and unable to coordinate her movements. Likewise, Vlădărău Marilena, Grigoraş Cristina, Szabo Ecaterina, Rühn Melita, and Dunca Rodica were overjoyed. Dunca writes from Oradea: 'we work twice as much now even without the beating.' The gymnasts do not like Agache Lavinia, since, talking among themselves, they said that during the U.S.A. tour she had four falls from the apparatuses, but Béla Károlyi fined her just 50 dollars a fall, while Szabo Ecaterina, who also had 4 falls, was fined 100 dollars for every mistake.[77] Agache, having been Béla's favourite, is more reserved, even upset.[78]

On 14 April 1981, a few days after his return from the tour that created so many problems for him, Nicolae Vieru told a friend over the phone that in the end, 'some good will come from the bad': 'The girls are working, they're progressing and if that lot aren't here any more maybe others will take flight to achieve good things, because now there's nobody to break their wings. Maybe they'll do better than they did.'[79] In the months that followed, he looked for solutions to build a new team of trainers, recruiting Maria Cosma, Adrian Stan, Octavian Belu and others. Adrian Goreac was appointed manager of the squad.

The secret service sought to plant as many informers as possible among the trainers at Deva and promptly to penalise any action regarded as a deviation on the part of those who did not collaborate. For example, Goreac was kept under surveillance because of suspicious relations with foreign citizens, because he had made political comments deemed hostile, and because he was suspected of wishing to defect. For years at a time, he was also at loggerheads with Maria Cosma, another trainer, who had a tendency to 'monopolise' the team and push Goreac to one side,[80] as one agent put it. Unlike Goreac, Cosma had the support of the Securitate, since she was an informer. In Bucharest, a new team was formed along the same lines, with informers given the top positions, since Maria Login, another Securitate agent, had taken over the position of secretary general of the R.G.F. after the removal of Nicolae Vieru. Login enjoyed the respect of other Securitate agents such as Maria Simionescu and Atanasia Albu, who praised her in their reports, while others thought that during her time as secretary general 'she created serious conflicts and misunderstandings among the trainers.'[81]

In the confusion left in the wake of the three defectors, Nadia Comăneci returned to Deva for a few weeks, before going back to Bucharest. According to Atanasia Albu, Nicolae Vieru 'is desperate to try (for the umpteenth time) to avoid responsibility, taking Nadia back to Deva. (. . .) I personally am instigating her to come and train here, arguing that trainer Gorgoi and A. Grigoraş aren't up to scratch, and the Bucharest setting isn't wholesome for her.'[82] But Nadia preferred to remain in Bucharest and train with Gheorghe Gorgoi and Anca Grigoraş, whose goal was now to have her compete in the World University Games to be held in Romania. 'Nadia is a friend of Anca Grigoraş, who has a positive influence on her,' said Maria Simionescu, nonetheless drawing attention to the fact that the training sessions were of 'low intensity': 'There are dissensions between Vieru and Gorgoi as to who trains Nadia, which are voiced even in front of other people.'[83] After the Moscow Olympics, Nadia had expressed a wish to retire. She would soon reach the age of twenty, having spent almost fifteen years of her life in the gym. The World University Games, held in Bucharest in the summer of 1981, were to be the last official tournament in which she competed and at which she won her final medals, all of them gold.

She officially withdrew from competitive gymnastics on 6 May 1984, at a celebratory event organised by the Romanian Olympic Committee and the International Gymnastics Federation. At the Palace of Sports and Culture in Bucharest a tournament was also held, in which a number of top Romanian and foreign gymnasts took part, with Nadia giving a number of demonstrations. Juan Antonio Samaranch, the chairman of the International Olympic Committee, presented her with the silver girdle of the Olympic Order, and the event was extensively covered in the Romanian and international press. ABC obtained the rights for extended coverage, requesting that the Romanians allow the channel to interview Nadia Comăneci and film her in various everyday settings.

Since the team of American presenters that arrived in Bucharest included Chris Schenkel and former gymnast Kurt Thomas, the Securitate took care to monitor Thomas in particular, suspecting him of having tried to persuade Nadia not to leave the United States in March 1981,[84] and of now planning an act of 'kidnapping-treason'. A number of departments of the Securitate (Department One, Department Three, Bucharest Municipality Securitate, and the Foreign Intelligence Centre) were involved 'with the aim of preventing any eventual action of a nature to damage the interests of our country and to ensure conditions for the normal unfolding of this sporting event.'[85] For the whole time he was in Romania, Thomas was followed by surveillance teams wherever he went, which reported on his movements and interactions with Nadia Comăneci minute by minute.

At the ceremony, none of Nadia's trainers were mentioned by name, since the régime viewed most of them dimly. Marcel Duncan and Valeriu Munteanu seemed to have been consigned to oblivion. Béla and Marta Károlyi were traitors, and Gheorghe Gorgoi had in the meantime been reduced to working as an unqualified labourer at the Sport Base Administrations Factory, in punishment for his obvious desire to emigrate.

After her retirement, Nadia's life lost its former glitter, it became increasingly drab, as was inevitable in a communist régime where she was now a state functionary. She completed the higher education she had begun in 1981, and was assisted by Nicu Ceauşescu to get a job as a ballet instructor at the Artistic Ensemble of the Union of Communist Youth. In 1980, she had a salary of 1,920 lei without ever having to show up at work. After the Executive Bureau of the N.C.P.E.S. promoted her to gymnastics trainer, category one, on 1 February 1984 she was also promoted within the Artistic Ensemble of the Union of Communist Youth (U.C.Y.) to ballet maestro, category one, with a salary of 3,350 lei.[86] From 1984 to 1986, she worked in the Sports Commission of the Central Committee of the U.C.Y., and in 1986 she was made a trainer at the Republic Training Centre of the National Squads, where she worked with coach Cornel Bălan.

In 1987, she was transferred to the technical team of the Romanian Gymnastics Federation, having been withdrawn from the squad at her own request, and managed the Oneşti Juniors Centre, which is to say, she performed clerical tasks. In July 1989, she was elected a member of the N.C.P.E.S. and a member of the Executive Office of the R.G.F. After the retirement of Lia Manoliu and Maria Simionescu, she was promised the position of vice-chairwoman of the Romanian Olympic Committee and Romania's candidacy for the Technical Commission of the International Gymnastics Federation.

Nadia got the house she wanted in Bucharest, but had to pay for it, buying it at a reasonable price from the Topalescu family. The owners were waiting for permission to leave the country permanently and approval to sell the property before emigrating.[87] The approvals were granted thanks to the intervention of Nicu Ceauşescu, who speeded up the completion of the paperwork.[88] After Nadia Comăneci purchased the house on Strada Rozmarin in December 1980, the Carpathians Trust renovated the property, but not for free, as they had originally promised, since Nadia had to pay monthly instalments of around 1,000 lei for a long while afterward.

It was in this villa on a quiet street near the House of the People, built in the French style and painted a cream colour, that Nadia Comăneci lived until she left

Romania. It was her refuge. In one room she kept her trophies, and in another the dolls and porcelain she collected. But not even here could she escape the Securitate, since they entered her house, trampling the yellow parquet that contrasted so starkly with the black furniture, to plant bugs at various times.

In the 1980s, Nadia continued to be monitored, but the reasons for this surveillance had changed. Béla Károlyi was no longer in Romania, and the main reason for secret surveillance up to March 1981 had been the conflict between him and Nadia. A few weeks later, in April, the dossier was transferred from Deva to the Bucharest Municipality Securitate,[89] and in the ensuing period the information that was gathered was mainly to do with her progress in training for the University Games. After her official retirement in 1984, 'Department One, as part of a protection plan, measures were taken to discover and prevent any eventual attempt to lure Nadia Comăneci into activities of a nature that might affect the interests of our state through their being exploited for anti-Romanian propaganda purposes,'[90] but such a broad remit could have meant almost anything.

Nadia never expressed political opinions at odds with the Communist régime. She joined the Romanian Communist Party – from which she was expelled on 7 December 1989, after fleeing the country – but she was not attracted to a political career. As the years passed, she appeared in the press more and more seldom, and even then, it was unpolitical. She was not recorded expressing any regret at having remained in Romania or any intention to leave the country illegally. On the contrary, all the information collected via Securitate agents pointed to the absence of any premeditated plan. Any relations she still had with foreign citizens were limited and tightly controlled by the authorities, and her trips outside the country grew fewer and fewer.

One seemingly unanswered question remains: why did her surveillance not come to an end in the later 1980s? The reason seems to have been her social life, albeit not so much the accusation of 'libertinism' to be found in accusatory Securitate reports dated after her defection, which was exaggeratedly said to be capable of affecting her reputation. For the Securitate kept a close watch on Nadia's love life, reporting every relationship she had in the 1980s. Every relationship, that is, except one: the too close relationship she had with Nicu Ceaușescu.

As far as we are concerned, we have not set out in this book to examine Nadia's personal life, since it has nothing to do with her career. We consider such matters to be private and they are of nobody's concern but hers. But the presence of Nicu Ceaușescu in her life cannot be overlooked, given that at the time Romanians regarded him as his father's successor, he held positions in the Party, the highest having been that of general secretary of the Central Committee of the Union of Communist Youth (1983–87), and from 1987 to the fall of the Communist régime, he was first secretary of Sibiu County.

In the archives there is no information about the relationship between Nadia Comăneci and Nicu Ceauşescu for the simple reason that the Securitate was not allowed to gather information about members of the family that ruled Romania. For Nadia's part, when asked to comment on the subject, she has refused to admit that she had any personal relationship with the youngest son of Nicolae and Elena Ceauşescu. She has confirmed that she met him and knew him, given that she once worked for the U.C.Y., but that their relationship was strictly professional. But there are a number of accounts of a personal friendship between them that have become public. These accounts have been given by people who were close to Nadia at the time, including members of her family, and we do not doubt their veracity, even if she herself has denied them and regards them as 'clumsy tales'.[91]

Because of the presence of Nicu Ceauşescu in her life, the Securitate found itself in the situation of having to find unusual solutions when conducting surveillance on her, since there is no trace of the dictator's son in the archive materials. On the one hand, the officers of Service Six of Department One, who were responsible for the areas of education, the legal system, health, and sport, were given the mission of drawing up a protection plan for Nadia. In May 1989, Lieutenant Colonel Marian Ureche, the head of the structure, confirmed that Nadia was kept under surveillance because 'the counter-intelligence protection of her is what is pursued,'[92] and the last officer to carry out this mission was Major Nicolae Roşu, who reported, 'in September 1988 I personally took over the contact.'[93] The analyses written by this structure went to Iulian Vlad, the head of the Securitate, and Tudor Postelnicu, the interior minister, who then presented them to the top of the hierarchy, Nicolae and Elena Ceauşescu. Most of the documents are still preserved in the archives.

On the other hand, we believe that surveillance of Nadia Comăneci was carried out by an ad hoc parallel structure, consisting of a few heads of units and departments, but secret even within the Securitate. The information collected was not collected in any dossier, but went straight to Tudor Postelnicu, who presented it solely to Elena Ceauşescu.

Since the December 1989 Revolution, few politicians of the time have publicly talked about how the Ceauşescus viewed the Olympic gymnastics champion. Significant among those who have is Ştefan Andrei, foreign minister from 1978 to 1985, who claimed that while Nicolae Ceauşescu liked Nadia, Elena Ceauşescu did not.[94] It is known that Elena Ceauşescu meddled in her children's lives, that she interfered in their love lives, and she does not seem to have looked kindly on the relationship between Nicu and Nadia.

In New York in December 1989, when Nadia told the international press that in illegally crossing the border she had risked her life because she wanted to be free and that for years she had not been allowed to travel, she had no way of knowing that it was Elena Ceauşescu who had personally imposed measures to limit her freedom, the most significant of which was a ban on her travelling to the West. Securitate general Aurel Rogojan, the head of Iulian Vlad's cabinet from 1987 to 1989, believes that she was refused a passport because she was in the entourage of the Ceauşescu family: 'As such she became a target for all the espionage services, and this was also known by the Romanian services. This infiltration was attempted via a symbol of Romania. Precisely for this reason she was not allowed to leave the country very often.'[95] The Securitate's fear, probably fuelled by the aberrant demands of Elena Ceauşescu, was that during her trips abroad Nadia Comăneci might make negative comments regarding what she knew about the Ceauşescu family, and that agents of Western secret services would easily have been able to obtain compromising information from her.

Rogojan's wording obviously requires correction: 'not very often' in fact meant 'never', because Nadia's last trip to the West was in 1985. By the end of the 1980s, a world-class gymnast who had travelled all over the world since the age of ten was a prisoner in her own country. Her isolation was all the more absurd given that by the nature of her past career she was invited to take part in the judging of international competitions such as the Olympic Games, the World and European Championships, as well as other international tournaments in which Romania's gymnastics teams competed. As a member of the Sportspersons' Commission of the International Olympics Committee, she was required to take part in the body's meetings and symposiums, which was now impossible. Given that the last time she was able to take part in such a meeting was in 1985, at a congress in Seoul in 1988, it was decided that Nadia Comăneci should no longer be part of the commission.

Not least, she was frequently invited to give interviews, but in the late 1980s the authorities refused to grant her permission to do so. One of the last such refusals came in April 1989, when sports reporter Christophe Roux, from France's Canal Plus, tried to interview her for a programme he was presenting on the world's great gymnasts. The firm hand of Emil Bobu, a member of the Romanian Communist Party's Executive Political Committee and the man in charge of Romanian sport, repeatedly underlined the word 'no' in the N.C.P.E.S. report, even though it suggested that the interview would provide 'good propaganda to presented the wonderful working and living conditions our state provides to sportspeople.'[96]

In March 1988, Major Roşu referred to Nadia's disgruntlement in a summary: 'She is at the same time dissatisfied that the heads of the N.C.P.E.S. have not reacted favourably to any of the invitations that have been made to her to take part in certain ceremonies (Canada), to receive a scholarship (Mexico, England), to give performances with a circus in France etc. and nor has she been allowed fully to exercise the obligations of a member of the F.I.G. Technical Commission, inasmuch as she has been authorised only to travel to socialist countries (in 1987 she made trips to the S.F.R.Y., P.R.B., U.S.S.R. – twice, H.P.R., D.D.R.) which her last trip to a Western country having been effectuated in 1985, to Switzerland.'[97]

In 1989 Nadia received at least twelve invitations to take part in various international championships and meetings with representatives of other gymnastics federations in the West. She was denied permission to go to any of them, and the only foreign trip she was able to make was to Cuba, but only after the Cubans exerted high-level political pressure, as they were very keen for her to attend the Moncada Tournament. The Securitate called upon a number of its informers to make sure that she would 'adopt an appropriate conduct', and Nadia received the news with great satisfaction, telling one of the said informers, 'the ice has been broken at last.' During the trip she was kept under constant surveillance, 'particularly during layovers', to prevent her from being 'separated from the other coaches.' Roşu noted in his report before leaving, 'on the morning of 31.05.1989 I carried out Nadia Comăneci's counterintelligence training, and she undertook to adopt an irreproachable conduct and to abide by the delegation's programme.'

The same day, Nadia, who was delighted, telephoned Major Roşu, and since the call was intercepted, we know today how the brief conversation unfolded:

At 18.55 hours 'Corina' telephoned Roşu, to whom she recounted how she travelled to Sibiu and with whom she arranged to meet tomorrow morning, at 7.40 hours, at the federation, in order to talk.

C. — Todea told me something too. We'll also talk tomorrow morning.

R. — He told you?

C. — He told me that comrade Bobu and comrade Mihalache will be there and that . . .

R. — That's what I wanted us to talk about. The thing is that now you have to act . . . The way you act now will depend . . . you know what I mean.

C. — I know. That's the amazing thing.

R. — That is, a lot of effort has been made for this, but you deserve it.[98]

Her hopes of travelling were once more quickly crushed when in the autumn of 1989 she wasn't even able to take up an invitation to the U.S.S.R. Her frustration was known to the Securitate, specifically Major Roşu, who also knew that Nadia suspected high officials of the Romanian Communist Party of being the ones who put up opposition, but she believed that the Ceauşescus' envy of her huge fame might ultimately be to blame. For this reason, after she fled Romania, Major Roşu believed that her frustration was in part justified.

Her dissatisfaction was caused both by the fact that the <u>trips represented a significant source of income</u> (more than 500,000 lei in the period 1988–89), which would have helped her to pay off debts, but also by <u>the consequences</u>

of her loss of status in the international sporting movement in relation to sportspeople from other countries who are of the same generation, but below her level (Tourishcheva, Kim etc.).

The procedure and the level at which the approvals for her were discussed and given were known, for this reason she does not openly voice her dissatisfaction except in her close circle, also presupposing the motives behind the decisions in question. This situation was known to the leadership of the N.C.P.E.S., which often, in discussions with the objective's officer, presented it as being 'insoluble', although the presence of Nadia Comăneci at these events could have brought many benefits, both at the hard currency level and at the level of promoting our sporting interests along the lines of judging and in other areas.

The situation in question was reported many times, verbally, to the heads of the department. (. . .)

The fact that her trip to Cuba was approved (at the last moment, as a result of intervention by Cuban officials) has been exploited, with it being explained to her that from that moment her conducts and the way in which she undertakes to carry out work assignments will play a decisive rôle in the taking of decisions for subsequent trips.

I report that after this trip Nadia Comăneci seemed more optimistic and was better implicated in realising the tasks assigned by the federation, becoming more co-operative.

In August 1989, the U.S. Gymnastics Federation invited the women's gymnastics squad to effectuate, after the World Championships in Stuttgart, West Germany, a demonstration tour in the U.S.A., in which Nadia Comăneci would also participate, offering the sum of 30,000 dollars. In a discussion with her in question regarding the tour opportunity, she confided that under the conditions in question it was not opportune, since she could obtain a larger sum of money, and from the point of view of the gymnasts it is very tiring, requiring a long period of recuperation. On it being pointed out to her that our squad would be accompanied by Béla Károlyi, Nadia Comăneci gave her usual reaction to hearing that name, stating that she would refuse to go with the squad.[99]

Nadia Comăneci's attendance of the Los Angeles Olympics in 1984, not as a competitor but as a special guest, was painstakingly negotiated by the Romanian authorities with their U.S. counterparts. Peter Ueberroth, the head of the organising committee, negotiated patiently, but accepted most of the Romanians' demands in order to persuade them to take part, given that it was boycotted by the Communist countries, headed by the U.S.S.R. It was said that one of the conditions was that any sportspeople who attempted to defect would not be allowed to stay on U.S. soil but sent back to Romania. The Securitate was satisfied to note that Ueberroth showed a 'receptive and favourable attitude' and 'in press conferences, official contacts with the Romanian delegation and in other circumstances, Peter Ueberroth expressed positive opinions of the Romanian S.R. During the press conference held for Nadia Comăneci, Peter Ueberroth interrupted to put Nicolae Munteanu, an editor for Radio Free Europe, in his place when he asked tendentious questions about the political conditions for our country's presence at the Olympics. At the same time, through his intervention, hostile declarations made by Béla Károlyi about the social-political situation in the Romanian S.R. were prevented from being published in the *Los Angeles Times* daily.'[100]

Nadia Comăneci remembers that she was shocked when she found out that she would be able to travel to the U.S.A.:

> I did not think that the 1984 Olympics would involve me. There was no way I would be allowed to travel to the United States when I wasn't even allowed to go to Europe. But I received a phone call from a government official saying that I would be part of the Romanian delegation. I remember staring at the phone I held in shock because I couldn't believe the government was actually going to let me get on a plane! I was assigned a 'chaperone' for the trip, but I really didn't care that I was going to be watched. I was travelling to America, and I planned to eat, shop, and meet as many fun people as possible. For a brief moment, I felt almost free.[101]

In the Romanian delegation to the Los Angeles Olympics, among the sportspeople, trainers, judges, medical personnel and reporters, the Securitate had a network of ninety-eight agents: forty-six informers, forty-five officers with operational missions, and seven officers tasked with maintaining official relations. They were co-ordinated by three officers, under the usual cover of being advisers or sports instructors.[102] Some had the mission of keeping Nadia under constant watch. The 'chaperone' referred to by Nadia must have been judge and teacher Elena Firea, who had been recruited as an informer as long ago as 1966,[103] and who accompanied her everywhere. The only room into which she did not manage to follow her was the one where Ronald Reagan received her, welcoming her to Los Angeles.[104]

For years later at the 1988 Seoul Olympics, Nadia Comăneci was not part of the delegation. The decision was so aberrant that even the Securitate's informers were surprised by it. On finding out, 'Monica' and 'Cristian' made inquiries at the N.C.P.E.S., where they were given the disarming answer that it was 'an order from above', while Nadia Comăneci herself said, 'she was expecting it, she would have liked to have gone to Seoul, but "that's the situation"'.[105] The Communist régime was not prepared to risk her defection, and from 1985 she was not allowed to travel abroad except to Communist countries.

7
A MOVIE ENDING

Nadia Comăneci never showed any intention to take advantage of a trip abroad in order to defect. It would have been too hard for her to be so far away from family and friends. Sometimes, when she returned from a trip, when her brother Adrian would half-jokingly ask why she hadn't stayed abroad, she would answer that she felt happier at home, in the kitchen, with her pots and pans, at which everybody would laugh. Although she sometimes fell prey to emotion, she was otherwise highly practical. She refused to believe in foreigners, to allow them to inveigle her into projects that seemed unachievable at first sight. She was optimistic by nature, and only acted after making a thorough examination of the situation in which she found herself. In other words, Nadia was not one to daydream.

Consequently, it is all the more obvious that it was the absurd restrictions imposed on her after 1985 that caused her to accept the proposal to flee the country, when the opportunity arose, even if it meant placing her life in danger. All the restrictions in her life convinced her that she should abandon caution and do something that was not in her nature, especially since she knew that if she left Romania, she would never see her family again.

The episode of her escape was rightly regarded as spectacular and captured the imagination of the West, as Le Figaro declared on 1 December 1989: 'Dramas now come to us from Eastern Europe, rather than from Hollywood. In Romania the plots of films are happening in real life. The former champion escaped the country on Wednesday, after she had once been a heroine of the communist system. Real life beats fiction. Many episodes in Nadia's life surpass the fictional.'[1]

In the days after her escape, as the Western media debated all kinds of outlandish theories, there was uproar in Bucharest, too, not in the press, but in government cabinets, and the fury was the greatest at the headquarters of the secret police. As is often the case of intelligence services, the Department of State Security's reputation was often exaggerated. The Nadia Comăneci Case is a good example, revealing as it does Securitate incompetence. Incapable of preventing Nadia's escape and finding out about it only once it had actually happened, the Securitate was caught by surprise, an embarrassing and blameworthy situation for an intelligence service. Nadia Comăneci's escape even created a genuine crisis within the Securitate, which was exacerbated from outside the country by massive international coverage of the event and inside the country by the fury of Nicolae Ceauşescu, in despair at having lost the gymnast who had been the country's 'best advertisement', as *The Independent* aptly put it at the time.

But if the Securitate was incapable of preventing it, when and how did the authorities in Bucharest learn the news that Nadia Comăneci had defected? The information came in the next day, 28 November, at four o'clock in the afternoon. It was received by military counterintelligence officers from Department Four of the Securitate. It was not thanks to their own operational capacities, but sooner an accident – or maybe a deliberate act of defiance on the part of the Hungarians – since they obtained the information from other fugitives who had illegally crossed the frontier the day before and been sent back to the Romanian side surprisingly quickly. Alexandru Cinca, Maria Balea and Maria Ezias,[2] the two women being accompanied by their sons, both minors, had escaped across the border on 27 November and at the Kiszombor border post they had met Nadia Comăneci and the other six members of her group the next morning. Maria Ezias, a Romanian citizen of Hungarian ethnicity, was asked by the Hungarian border guards to translate a part of their discussions with Nadia. Then, at around four o'clock in the afternoon, Alexandru Cinca and Maria Balea and her son had been surrendered to the Romanian authorities, while Maria Ezias and her son had been allowed to remain in Hungary.

The first interrogation of Cinca and Balea took place in the afternoon of 28 November at the base of the Sînnicolau Mare border guard's battalion. They were then taken to a Securitate base and interrogated until midnight. The two were not able to provide very much information, but the mere fact that Nadia Comăneci was out of the country amazed the officers of Department Four, and Colonel Traian Sima himself, the head of Timiş County Securitate, arrived to take part in the interrogation. Alexandru Cinca said, 'Nadia Comăneci was wearing a denim suit and boots, the leather of the heels was scuffed off, she talked to us for a few minutes, saying she crossed a ploughed field, that it had been a bigger balancing act than she'd ever done on the beam and parallel bars, she was in a state of grogginess, she spoke in a breezy sort of way, without any kind of remorse,'[3] and Maria Balea made a similar statement:

I was in the other room when the door opened and I saw the 7 persons who arrived, including Nadia Comăneci. Shortly after that a Hungarian soldier came and took Ezias away to translate to the 7 the questions he asked. (. . .) In the meantime, Nadia Comăneci arrived (. . .), at which point I was left surprised at meeting her in such conditions, telling her I was surprised at meeting her there in such conditions, to which she replied, 'it's a big world.' (. . .)

Nadia Comăneci, who looked tired, argued with a Hungarian soldier because he asked her whether she was really Nadia Comăneci, she was very breezy about it, she wasn't worried at all, she was wearing a denim suit.[4]

On 28 November, at around five o'clock in the afternoon, the entire leadership of the Securitate was informed and the first verifications were made to establish whether the information was true. Confirmation, if it were needed, came the next morning, when Radio Kossuth broadcast the news for all the world to hear. Special Unit R of the Securitate, which intercepted radio broadcasts, in particular radio stations deemed hostile to the Communist régime, made a transcript and immediately sent it to the heads of the Interior Ministry.

On 29 November 1989, Romanian diplomats in Budapest sent their first encrypted telegram on the subject, signed by Traian Pop, the Romanian ambassador to Hungary. The message was brief, merely repeated what was already known from the Hungarian press at that moment. It cited not Radio Kossuth, but the *Magyar Nemzet* national newspaper, which had a reputation for obtaining the best political information and which Romanian diplomatic staff pored over since it was in the habit of publishing anti-Romanian propaganda. The very fact that the news of Nadia's escape was published in *Magyar Nemzet* is a significant detail in itself, since it meant that the authorities had provided reporters with the information during the night in order to meet the morning edition:

To comrade Ion Stoian, minister of foreign affairs,

Allow me to report:
The *Magyar Nemzet* newspaper of 29 November publishes, in the 'Day's events' column, a news item according to which former Olympic and world champion Nadia Comăneci crossed the previous day the frontier into Hungary illegally and asked for asylum. According to the newspaper and radio stations that broadcast the news a number of times, Nadia Comăneci decided to cross the frontier illegally because she was not allowed to operate as a gymnastics trainer abroad.
With respect,
Traian Pop[5]

Ambassador Pop's telegram reached Bucharest at 12.40 hours, more than four hours after the news became public. The delay was not because Romanian diplomats liked to sleep in, but because of the logistics of the time. The embassy staff began work at eight in the morning, and at around nine they reviewed the day's papers and presented to Traian Pop any items that referred to Romania. The diplomats would then hold a meeting and draft telegrams to send to Bucharest after they had been approved and signed for by the ambassador. But even if they were urgent, the telegrams could be transmitted only within certain intervals established for each diplomatic mission.

Telephone calls were avoided for fear of interception. The 'short' telephone, for example, which could be used to call anybody in Bucharest, including the head of state, was seldom employed. According to the rules of the time, it was Moscow that provided channels of communication for the Warsaw Pact countries, which meant that calls to Bucharest were placed via a Soviet operator. The 'short' telephone could hardly provide any secrecy whatever. In the Romanian embassy in Budapest, the telephone set in question was shut inside a cupboard in a disused toilet on the ground floor for fear that it contained microphones. Whenever it happened to ring, a secretary would rush to open the cupboard and bring it to the ambassador's officer, trailing a long wire behind her.[6] As for the ordinary telephone, this was not used for important messages either, as it was presumed that calls were intercepted by the Hungarian authorities.

Given the gravity of the situation, Pop's telegram was presented not only to Ion Stoian, the foreign minister, but also to Nicolae and Elena Ceauşescu. Just three hours later – a very rapid reaction time – Stoian replied to the ambassador indicating two directions for action: 'Comrade Ambassador, (. . .) 1. Carefully monitor whatever Nadia Comăneci does in Hungary: if she makes declarations, their content, meetings with various officials etc. 2. We ask that you inform me via telegrams address only to me about the aforementioned issues.'[7]

Ambassador Pop did not manage to send to Bucharest much information of genuine interest, and the only significant encrypted telegram was sent on 1 December, during the hours when nobody knew where Nadia had gone. The following is an excerpt:

In the given circumstances, we do not have any other information. From the way in which the press and other media have reacted and continue to report, we are entitled to believe that Nadia Comăneci is still in Hungary, where her presence can be exploited by institutions with a stake in it.

We would have to be naïve to believe that the organs with a stake in this will not make use of such an opportunity to obtain various information and data about various circumstances and persons with which she came into contact in the home country.

This belief on our part is also strengthened by a piece of information that came out immediately after her arrival in Hungary, on the part of the Hungarian Olympic Committee, about making contact with and trying to persuade the fugitive to remain in Hungary.

Moreover, if the person in question had left Hungarian soil, it is impossible to rule out that a foreign press agency would not have managed to obtain information that it would have immediately made known to international public opinion.

Ed.: Ovidiu Miron

Traian Pop[8]

Pop was engaging in a certain amount of disinformation here, giving currency to rumours circulating at the time, according to which, 'Nadia Comăneci knows a lot of important secrets'[9] about the Ceauşescu family, and that once she fell into the hands of the Hungarian secret services, they would know how to 'exploit' her. But on closer inspection, it can be seen that this was the opinion of Ovidiu Miron, the diplomat who drew up the telegram, rather than the ambassador himself, and it is known that Miron was an undercover Securitate officer.

The news of the defection both outraged and depressed Nicolae Ceauşescu. According to General Iulian Vlad, the head of the Securitate at the time, 'the departure under such circumstances of Nadia Comăneci provoked not only anger, indignation, but also alarm, in the sense that the frontier was porous, at least in the area in question.' The subject was discussed at a high-level meeting, but unfortunately, all we know about it is to be found in Vlad's memoirs. The head of state probably convened the meeting on the morning of 29 November, and it was attended only by Tudor Postelnicu, the interior minister, Vasile Milea, the minister of defence, Iulian Vlad, the head of the Securitate, and Nicolae Popovici, the prosecutor general. 'All four of us had been summoned after a local shepherd with hundreds of sheep and all the necessary vehicles crossed the border into Hungary, he quite simply crossed the border, as if it hadn't even existed. This occurred not long after Nadia Comăneci had fraudulently left the country, by illegally crossing the frontier.' It is true that not just one but four shepherds had crossed the frontier with their sheep, more than a thousand of them, along with vehicles and machinery, which caused a huge scandal, as well as countless jokes about the alertness of Romania's border guards, who, after an investigation, proved to have been in cahoots with the shepherds.

But in his memoirs Vlad is mistaken as to the timeline of events. In actual fact, Nadia escaped not before but a month after the incident in question, as emerges from documents in the archive of the Ministry of Foreign Affairs, which was monitoring the process to extradite the shepherds. The four had crossed the border illegally on the morning of 1 November, and the next day the Romanian government demanded their extradition and recovery of the vehicles, machinery and livestock. On 27 November 1989, a few hours before Nadia fled the country, the Romanian ambassador to Budapest informed Central Office of the Ministry of Foreign Affairs, 'in the next few days extradition measures are to be taken and a press communiqué connected to this will be given. From the investigations carried out by the Hungarian organs, they have signalled that one of the four Romanian citizens is no longer to be found on Hungarian soil and it is supposed that he has returned to Romania taking with his two horses.'[10]

Two weeks after the shepherds' escape, there was another unpleasant incident on the border between Hungary and Romania. On the morning of 15 November, two Hungarian officers and five soldiers armed with machine-guns climbed out of an all-terrain vehicle and five of them crossed the frontier on foot, with the aim of observing Romanian territory. When challenged by a Romanian border patrol, the five ran back over the border, and over the days that followed, there was an angry reaction on Romania's part: explanations were demanded from the Hungarian side and the Hungarian ambassador to Bucharest was summoned to the Ministry of Foreign Affairs in Bucharest to be informed that his government had made an illegal incursion.

'The head of state was utterly outraged, and rightly so,' recalls Iulian Vlad. This was hardly surprising when the shepherds had blithely crossed the border with their flocks – one of them had even come back again, also clandestinely, bringing two horses with him – when armed Hungarian border guards had insolently strolled across the line of demarcation, and when, to top it all, Nadia Comăneci had escaped over the border just a few days later. Ceauşescu therefore had every reason to be furious and to react harshly. As was his wont in such situations, he will have cast the blame on all and sundry, his voice trembling and unsteady, accusing them of 'treason' and 'consorting with the enemy'. Vlad describes the reaction in his own style: 'The analysis of the head of state, since, as I said, we had been convened, was very harsh and stern, particularly towards the Minister of Defence. Some very stern criticisms were aimed at Minister Milea, but obviously nor did the others, including the Securitate, escape criticism. And rightly so, since inside the country, or as far as the ploughed frontier strip, there were a host of other organs that ought to have known what was happening within the zone in question and to have taken the necessary preventative measures.'

During that tense meeting the issue of border security was discussed, the question being how it was possible for the Romanian military to have been humiliated by a series of such serious incident within the course of just one month. After the meeting Milea, Postelnicu, Vlad and Popovici went by helicopter straight to the border, having been ordered by Ceauşescu personally to supervise an investigation. Two weeks later, the investigation was completed and measures were implemented, the most significant being that the border guard would no longer answer to the Ministry of National Defence but directly to the Ministry of the Interior, as laid out in Decree No. 313 of 11 December 1989.

We do not know what Ceauşescu had to say about the Nadia Comăneci case at the meeting. We do not know whether he ordered the Securitate to kidnap her and bring her back, an order that only the head of state could give. Ceauşescu, who was impulsive and brooked no opposition, would have been capable of giving such an order, particularly if he was egged on by his capricious and aggressive wife, who was known not to be able to stand Nadia Comăneci. If such an order was indeed given, it would have been verbal, leaving no trace in the archives. But would the Securitate have been capable of carrying it out?

Probably not, since there would have been only a very narrow window of opportunity, during the seventeen hours Nadia was in Szeged, which would have been the most convenient place to capture her. But since the Securitate discovered her escape after four o'clock in the afternoon on 28 November, that window of opportunity became even narrower. Nor should it be forgotten that a kidnap operation would have had to be carried out in foreign, even hostile, territory, where General Department Three of the Hungarian Interior Ministry was already alert to such a possibility and had assigned Nadia discreet protection at the Hotel Royal. The Romanian agents themselves would have been in danger and their mission would have been greatly complicated. But by the morning of 2 December, Romanian time, Nadia was already on U.S. soil, which meant that such a plan was rendered moot, as such a mission would have been all but impossible, as well as politically catastrophic.

Whether or not such a plan existed will never be known, as the late head of the Securitate remained silent on the question in his memoirs, where the only mention of Nadia's escape that he makes in his account of the meeting with Ceauşescu is that her action was inexplicable. Ultimately, Nadia Comăneci was a privileged person, Iulian Vlad was to admit almost three decades later, and 'thanks to her great talent and achievements, she received from the Romanian State support that it is hard to appreciate today, great support from every point of view. This was also because she had become a certain symbol.'[11] Securitate General Aurel Rogojan was of the same opinion, saying, 'she was privileged by the régime. Particularly her mother. At the time you need all kinds of permits, you had to queue up. She didn't have to do that.' Ceauşescu wanted not regrets, but a detailed explanation, backed up with evidence, and only the régime's secret service could provide it. Why had such a privileged person wanted to escape? Who helped her? And above all, which of the country's enemies was behind this disgraceful incident?

A present-day observation on the part of Rogojan might serve to elucidate the opinion that the Securitate formed at the time and how it ought to be presented to Ceauşescu, at least in the form of a hypothesis: 'But if we don't have documents, I don't know how important our words are. And there aren't any documents, because things like that aren't put down on paper. What can I tell you? That the American president [George H. W. Bush] gave the nod that he wanted the girl? That stuff isn't written down anywhere, there's nowhere to come up with any documents. It was all well planned by the C.I.A. and other agencies. Little does it matter which. But it was aimed at denigrating Ceauşescu.'[12] In a subsequent interview, Rogojan declared just as categorically that in his opinion, 'the C.I.A. organised Nadia Comăneci's extraction . . . it was a provocation.'[13] Therefore, the Securitate believed that it was a C.I.A. operation, with Nadia's escape being one phase in a complicated joint U.S.–Soviet plot to oust Nicolae Ceauşescu from power.

Another theory that circulates today, concocted by reporters who interviewed locals in Cenad, suggests that Nadia illegally crossed the border with the assistance of the Securitate or at least a faction thereof. Asked to comment on this theory, Aurel Rogojan has said: 'I don't think any part of the Securitate helped Nadia, but I'm not excluding the possibility that at the individual level there might have been Securitate traitors. At the frontier, too, it's possible she may have been helped by Romanians, but you should know that the Rahova Penitentiary was full of border officers that had been arrested. They made a lot of money.'[14]

The 'mysteries' of a so-called operation 'Nadia's Defection', orchestrated by the C.I.A. or a part of the Securitate will continue to exist and circulate for as long as the facts and the archive documents are interpreted erroneously or maliciously, and for long as Nadia Comăneci keeps her own counsel, as she has hitherto. As we have seen, even the heads of the Securitate lent credence to the possibility of C.I.A. involvement, based on real information obtained during the investigation. But in reality, Nadia's plan to escape was simple, and she put it into effect without the help of any intelligence service, be it Romanian or foreign.

Besides Nadia, the other main character in this spectacular story is Constantin Panait, whom she introduced as 'my friend' and whom she insisted on thanking for his help in front of the crowd of reporters that met her at Kennedy Airport when she landed on U.S. soil. A driver by profession, Panait had become a U.S. citizen after swimming across the Danube to Yugoslavia in June 1981 and making his way to America, where he became a construction worker. From the summer of 1987 he started visiting his relatives in Romania every year, whom he told about the free and prosperous life he was now leading, earning seventy to eighty thousand dollars a year. On 4 November he visited Romania once again, this time with Aurel Talpoş, another brother of Nadia Comăneci's guide, who had also escaped Romania in September 1981. Panait and Talpoş, who had met in exile, entered the country by the Stamora Moraviţa border crossing, each driving a car rented in Vienna.

The inquiry conducted after Nadia's escape reconstructed Constantin Panait and Aurel Talpoş's route, the towns through which they passed and the people with whom they came into contact. Witnesses declared that Panait met Nadia in the evening of 14 November at a party held at the Sima family home. Costel, as his friends called him, had been brought to the party by singer Ion Dolănescu, a close friend of Nadia's, who introduced him to the others as 'my godson from Florida',[15] not a status to be envied especially, since Dolănescu had around two hundred godsons at the time. 'After the two were introduced at the Simas' house, Nadia and Costel were inseparable',[16] recalled Adrian Comăneci, Nadia's brother, a few days later, under interrogation.

They visited Poiana Braşov, where Nadia met Aurel Talpoş, and then Sinaia, and they were together all the time they were in Bucharest. On 18 November, to travel with Panait around the country, Nadia took time off work, and a few days later she put in for sick leave via her sister-in-law Liliana Comăneci, announcing that she would return to work on 29 November.

On 19 November, at the suggestion of Panait and together with a number of other people, Nadia made her first visit to the area of the border, for the declared purpose of visiting Aurel Talpoş's relatives. Although the journey was long and tiring, she begged her mother to go with her, which she agreed to do. On 25 November, when she made a second trip, she did likewise, this time insisting that Adrian and Liliana Comăneci come with her. Her presence in the two border towns was noticed by all the locals, as well as by the Militia and Securitate officers who monitored the area, registering all incoming visitors, since Nadia attended a number of parties and meals for large numbers of guests in Cenad and Sînnicolau Mare. As was to be expected, the locals were enthused to see the famous gymnast among them, especially since she didn't make a big thing of her stardom and was willing to sign autographs and chat to people, and spent the night wherever she could find a spare bed.

In actual fact, as Nadia was later to recount, her openness about being there was a tactic to lull the suspicions of the authorities. It was Panait's idea, as Nadia has admitted: 'Constantin (. . .) knew of a way for me to get out of Romania. He had a friend with some family close to the border with Hungary. He suggested we visit that family for a party and get the government used to my socialising with people who lived by the border. If I just went one time, it would cause suspicion. But if I went and returned several times, it might result in a laxer attitude on the part of the police and give both me and the handful of other Romanians who planned to defect with Constantin enough time to cross the border before an alarm was sounded.'[17]

On the evening of 27 November, Adrian and Liliana returned to Bucharest by train, after Nadia and Constantin Panait dropped them off at Timişoara Station. Having plenty of time at their disposal, they spent a few hours in the Continental Restaurant, then said goodbye to each other. Nadia told Adrian, 'we'll talk on the phone', and said to Liliana, 'take care of yourselves.'[18] Nadia and Constantin Panait returned to Cenad, where another party was being held, this time in the house of Gheorghe Talpoş, to bid Constantin Panait and Aurel Talpoş goodbye, as they were flying back to America the next day. At the party, Nadia Comăneci said she would be going back to Bucharest. After midnight, the group of nine left the guide's house while the others continued to party and drove a few kilometres down the road to Sînnicolau Mare before dropping off the defectors in a field on the right. Constantin Panait and Aurel Talpoş then drove the two cars to the Nadlac border post, which they crossed legally, and then continued to Szeged, where they would meet the others the next morning.

The Securitate investigation determined that Panait was the ringleader, that he had persuaded Nadia to take that bold and risky step, after confessing to her that he was already helping his relatives and Talpoş's friends to flee the country, and assuring her that the plan was feasible because he had paid a trustworthy guide who knew the area like the back of his hand. As the Securitate put it, 'he exploited the unstable and impressionable nature of Nadia Comăneci.'[19] But in Nadia's eyes, 'Meeting Constantin made me feel as if a window had been cracked open, and suddenly, a fresh breeze carried the promise of a different future than the one to which I'd resigned myself.'[20]

Had the C.I.A. organised the whole operation, it would not have been out of the question that Nadia would have been provided with support when she arrived in Hungary, a communist country which, unlike Romania, was starting to demolish the Iron Curtain that divided it from the West. But on the morning of 29 November, when Radio Kossuth first broadcast the news of her defection, she had already set off on a second adventure. She and the other members of the group, whom Panait and Talpoş had picked up in Szeged, were heading by car for the border with Austria, with the aim of making a second illegal border crossing and reaching Vienna.

It was a six-hour car journey to the Austrian border. A few months previously, Hungary and Austria had relaxed the strict border régime, with foreign ministers, Gyula Horn and Alois Mock, symbolically cutting the barbed wire that divided their two countries. The act was taken in support of East Germans who, pretending to holiday in Hungary, were trying to cross over into Austria and thence reach the German Federal Republic. Nadia and some of her companions no longer had identity papers, as they had left them in the Royal Hotel in Szeged, and they did not have passports. As a result, wary of Austrian border guards, who made random checks of travel documents at the customs post, they stopped a few kilometres from Sopron, the Hungarian border town. 'Constantin decided to leave us at a café while he drove through to see whether he would be stopped,' Nadia recalls. 'When he returned, he told us that he had, in fact, been stopped and that it was too dangerous to try to drive across the border with us. We would have to cross at another spot . . . at night.'[21] For this reason, a few hours later they repeated what they had done at the border between Romania and Hungary. Once again, Panait and Talpoş waited on the other side with the cars until the rest of the group could clandestinely cross the border and reach Austrian soil.

This time, the crossing was shorter, but there were still plenty of obstacles. They walked alongside a barbed wire fence, hoping to find a breach. Before long they found it and crossed over into no-man's-land. On the other side was another fence, which they also passed through a breach. Then they walked through a forest clearing, crossed a disused railway line, skirted another fence, reached a vineyard, crawled under barbed wire. Soon they came to a path that led to the road where Panait and Talpoş were waiting for them.[22]

In Vienna, they checked into the Ibis Hotel, and the next day the members of the group went their separate ways. The others went to the Traiskirchen refugee camp, twenty-six kilometres from Vienna, while Nadia and Panait went to the United States embassy, but found it closed, meaning they had to return the next morning, on 1 December:

> Constantin took me to the American embassy in Austria because I wanted to ask for political asylum. I remember walking through the doors and telling the first person I met that I was Nadia Comaneci and I wanted asylum. It created quite a spectacle and a flurry of activity. I felt like every paper had been dropped at the mention of my name. People in the embassy stared at me as if I were a ghost. An official told me that the people in the embassy had heard I'd defected but that no one knew where to find me. If I'd had the ability to communicate better, I would have told him that over the last few days, I didn't even know where I was myself.
>
> 'What do you want to do?' the official asked me.
>
> 'I want to go to America,' I replied.
>
> 'When?'
>
> 'As soon as possible.'
>
> 'There's a Pan Am flight leaving in two hours, you're on it,' he said with a smile.[23]

Once she arrived in New York, the whole world, which had been following the story with interest and jubilation, knew Nadia was safe. A new chapter opened in Nadia's life, perhaps not so spectacular as thitherto, but just as important and, at least at first, just as arduous, as her fame as a gymnast put her in the glare of the spotlight of the world's media.

In the opposite hemisphere, however, an unnatural, embarrassed silence had descended on Bucharest. U.S. diplomats, knowing that the Romanian authorities might cause them more unpleasantness than they had to cope with already, urged the few officials that still visited the country at the time to cancel all but essential trips. For example, Harry G. Barnes Jr., the U.S. ambassador to Romania from 1974 to 1977, had been due to take part in a seminar of the International Research and Exchange Board (IREX) in Bucharest that December. On 30 November the U.S. embassy sent a telegram to the State Department in Washington, saying: 'Bearing in mind that the IREX seminar has been cancelled, please inform us whether former ambassador Barnes is still thinking of coming to Romania on 9 December. We assume that he will cancel the trip. If he is still thinking of coming, please remind him that we are obliged to discourage him from doing so, not only because of Romania's surprising decision to cancel the IREX seminar, but also because of a probable reaction to Nadia's defection.'[24]

Ordinary Romanians had also found out the news by now, secretly commenting on it in satisfaction, but there was no official reaction on the part of the régime and information about the defection was forbidden. The Department of State Security launched a vast inquiry that marshalled all the resources at its disposal.

Department One Domestic Intelligence (Military Unit 0610) was tasked with investigating Nadia Comăneci, her relatives, and everybody of her acquaintance. Colonel Gheorghe Raţiu, the head of the department, was in charge of the 'Corina' case, centralising information from intelligence structures in Bucharest and around the country, including the Bacău, Bihor, Hunedoara and Timiş county inspectorates of the Securitate. The county inspectorates monitored and interrogated all those persons who had ever been in contact with Nadia within their jurisdictions. Timiş County Securitate also carried out a detailed investigation of the manner in which the group of seven had managed to cross the border. Bucharest Municipality Securitate called on the assistance of the Militia to round up those suspected of involvement in the defection and interrogate them.

Department Three Counterespionage (Military Unit 0625) was tasked with identifying Romanians and foreigners of Nadia's acquaintance who had contacts with enemy intelligence services, and with the assistance of the Foreign Intelligence Centre, the Securitate's foreign espionage wing, information relative to the inquiry was gathered from abroad.

Special Units T, F, and S and Independent Service D were other structures that played a direct part in the investigation and in implementation of the counteraction plan. Special Unit T (Military Unit 0639) planted bugs and intercepted telephone calls, Special Unit F (M.U. 0672) kept suspects under surveillance, Special Unit S (M.U. 0647) intercepted letters, and Service D (M.U. 0682) drew up a plan to disinform not only Romanian and international public opinion, but also enemy secret services, to counteract and diminish the devastating effect on the communist régime from the propaganda standpoint. Hundreds of officers and informers, some of them working under their own identities, others posing as diplomats, journalists, sportspeople and coaches, were involved in a vast operation both within Romania and internationally.

All Nadia's close relatives, friends, ex-boyfriends, and mere acquaintances were targeted by the Securitate, and the same went for each member of the seven-strong group of defectors of which she had been part. Those suspected of having been accomplices or being in possession of information were subjected to various forms of investigation, from intercepted telephones and correspondence to interrogation and searches of their homes. In the first few days of the inquiry, at least nineteen of Nadia's relatives and acquaintances found themselves in this situation.[25] Given the proportions of the investigation, by the beginning of December the Securitate had already managed to gather all the essential information, to bring to light the entire sequence of events and the persons involved in them.

Ştefania Comăneci and Adrian Comăneci, Nadia's brother, and his wife Liliana were justifiably regarded as the most important sources of information to the investigation. They lived in Bucharest, but at different addresses. Adrian and Liliana lived in Nadia's house on Strada Rozmarin, while Ştefania lived alone in a three-room flat in a building of Strada Polonă, having divorced Gheorghe Comăneci in 1980. All of them had low-level jobs. Ştefania, who had just seven years of schooling, was a cashier at the Progress Sports Club. Adrian was employed as an unqualified worker in the Bucharest Metro, while studying for an electronics degree at night school, and Liliana was a cashier and ticket collector at the Aviatorilor metro station.

With the exception of her father, who lived in Oneşti and whom she met only rarely, all the other members of Nadia's immediate family were suspected of having been party to her crime of leaving the country. The Securitate was unable to countenance that she would not have told them of her intentions or asked for their support. Consequently, they were monitored and investigated. Special Unit T planted bugs in Ştefania Comăneci's and Adrian's homes, which relayed continually until 20 December 1989, the date on which the final transcripts were made. Their telephone calls were also intercepted, as both Nadia's mother and her brother suspected from the very start. The telephone intercepts and recordings made using hidden microphones were sent to Department One on a daily basis, where they were studied by Gheorghe Raţiu, who thereby tried to determine how deeply they had been involved in the defection.

Nadia's family first became aware that something was seriously wrong on the evening of 28 November, when two high officials from the Romanian Gymnastics Federation, Nicolae Vieru and Vasile Chiorean, came to Ştefania's home, where Adrian and Liliana were also present at the time. The federation had never sent anybody to look for Nadia when she was missing, but always phoned to check up on her. Obviously, Vieru and Chioreanu were acting at the behest of the Securitate, who wanted them to confirm the alarming news they had received a few hours after the Hungarian authorities returned fugitives Alexandru Cinca and Maria Balea. Adrian Comăneci remembered that at around eight that evening, 'comrades Vieru and Chiorean from the federation came to the house and informed us that the general (Marin Dragnea) had sent them to look for Nadia because she hadn't turned up to work for 2 weeks. I told that that we knew she was ill, but we didn't know where she was right then. The comrades in question chided us for not knowing, why hadn't we checked up on her etc., to which we replied it wasn't the only time she'd disappeared and not got in touch, giving the example of when she'd been admitted to hospital and the family hadn't been aware of it, because usually she didn't inform us.'[26]

While Adrian and Liliana knew Nadia's intentions and were complicit, encouraging her to flee the country, her mother knew nothing. In a short interview she gave in December 2019, she herself said, 'I think it was on 30 November, my son Adrian came to see me. He brought it up in a roundabout way, told me to sit down and said that Nadia had defected and that he didn't say anything to me so as to protect me.'[27] But in one of the statements she made during the investigation, on 9 December 1989, she admitted, 'on 29 Nov. 1989 at around 17.00 hours the children came to see me at work (Adrian and his wife), they informed me that they'd been to Timişoara and that Nadia had stayed there and probably she'd fled on the night of 28 Nov. or that she'd cross on the evening of 29 Nov. together with a number of other people.'[28] The thread of the story was further tangled by Liliana, who on 2 December stated under interrogation, 'Nadia's mother, in my opinion, did not know her daughter's intentions until the evening of 28.xi. year in progress, which was confirmed to me at her house. On receiving the news, her reaction was as if she hadn't known anything about it. She started to cry, she was worried about the life her daughter would now lead. To her surprise, Nadia had done the opposite of what she had once confessed to her "that she will never leave the country illegally".'[29]

Whatever the truth may have been, among the Securitate documents have been preserved transcripts of the telephone calls that Ştefania Comăneci made on the evening of 29 November after she came home from work, from which it is apparent that she discovered Nadia's adventure at the same time as other ordinary Romanians, listening to Free Europe after six o'clock, and the news took her by surprise. She was telephoned by an unknown woman who urged her to listen to Free Europe before hanging up. She was shocked, wept, and continued to talk on the telephone out of a need for reassurance and in an attempt to find out more. That evening, Ştefania Comăneci probably received more calls than she had since Nadia became Olympic champion at Montréal in 1976:

'Corina II'[30]

At 18.25 hours, Ştefania, 'Corina's' mother, was phoned by a friend, Sima, who tried to find out about 'Corina', but the former, apparently very cheerful, answered, 'my daughter is in the mountains, at Poiana Braşov.'

At 18.35 hours, Ştefania was phoned by a woman who told her to listen to the radio news about 'Corina', after which she hung up.

At 18.50 hours, Ştefania telephoned Sima (84.06.59, Sima Victor — Bulevardul Metalurgiei — 22, Block B, floor 3, flat 59) telling him, 'a woman phoned, I don't know who, and she told me about "Corina" leaving.' Sima Victor seemed just as surprised as Ştefania, neither of them being able to believe it (note—although they had listened to the radio).

At 19.00 hours, Ştefania phoned back and reproached Marcela Sima, in tears, for not having told her soon about 'Corina' leaving. Marcela tried to calm her down, offering to help her . . . moral support, inviting her to her house, but Ştefania was too 'devastated' to go.

At 19.54 hours, Ştefania was phoned by Ileana, who asked her whether the news about 'Corina' was true. Ştefania, cheerful, asked her not to talk about such matters over the phone.

At 20.10 hours, Ştefania was . . . consoled by Dida, to whom she declared that she did not know anything, the news . . . 'paralysed her', she was thinking 'about what was in store for her'. Ştefania's wish is for her daughter to return, since not even she understands her action under the circumstances . . . 'When she could have done it whenever she was away.' Dida confirmed that on Saturday 'Corina' was at the Cişmigiu restaurant, where she works, with Adrian, Liliana and 'with another lad'. Ştefania supposes that 'now her house will be confiscated and they'll be left homeless.'

At 20.20 hours, Ştefania was called by Ileana, whom she told about 'Corina's' departure. Ştefana, feigning desperation (. . .), repeated to her what she had heard on Free Europe about 'Corina'. Advised to go to 'Corina's' house to remove valuables, to prevent their confiscation, Ştefania replied that 'there's nothing I can do, I've got nowhere to take the things.' Ştefania does not know where 'Corina's' car is, she thinks 'she left with it'. Ileana told her that she should avoid talking on the telephone 'because it's intercepted'.

At 20.40 hours, Ileana Popescu telephoned back and gave Ştefania details about 'Corina', details she had found out 'just now' from 'a television engineer'. Ileana is sure that '"Corina's" destination is the U.S.A.' and that 'good will come of the bad'.

At 20.50 hours, a certain Rodica, 'Gregor's sister', congratulated Ştefania for 'Corina's' deed. Ştefania, admitting that 'I'm drugged up', claimed that she placed her hope only in . . . God. Rodica assured her that 'it'll be alright', which Ştefania does not believe, but hopes.

At 21.15 hours, Dan Sima, the son of Marcela and Victor, voiced his 'indignation' at the act of 'Corina' who . . . 'could have taken me with her, instead of going alone . . .' Dan Sima congratulated Ştefania and said 'a million kisses to you.'[31]

For her part, Ştefania Comăneci telephoned her son at around twenty to eight, who 'didn't even know, he found out from the neighbours and promised his mother that they – he and Liliana – would come to her house, to have something to eat and drink a beer.'[32] Adrian was lying of course, as a means of protecting her, as well as himself, realising that the telephone call might be intercepted. But from the partial recording made on 1 December it is apparent that in the days that followed the three did not have a respite to meet due to the investigation that had begun in the meantime. Ştefania complained to acquaintances over the telephone 'about the fact that she is being investigated, that they made an inventory of her possessions. She does not know what is happening with her son since she hasn't spoken to him for two days.'[33]

From 29 November, she made a habit of recording on cassette tapes the morning and evening news bulletins broadcast by Free Europe. The same as every other Romanian, she did not have access to the international press, but only to Western radio stations with Romanian-language services. Funded by the U.S. Congress, Free Europe was the radio station most widely listened to in Romania, as it was very balanced and avoided broadcasting any alarmist. Nadia's mother always had a cassette tape at the ready to record the latest news and commentaries about her daughter, which she would then listen to over and over again, along with the unseen agents of Unit T, who logged her listening habits.

On 2 December, when her son and daughter-in-law visited her, they talked for around an hour, and Ştefania probably found out more information about Nadia's adventure than she had been able to glean from her cassettes. They also talked about the interrogations they had been put through so far, in order to get their stories straight in future. The Securitate was unable to obtain a usable recording of their discussion however:

> At around 21.18 hours Adrian arrived at the house with Lili. He asked Ştefania to play him the cassette with the recording of news about 'Corina' (from F.E.). After it finished, she put on a cassette of folk music, at loud volume, and the three talked in a whisper (unintelligible).
>
> At 22.00 hours they listened to the news bulletin (and obviously this broadcast was recorded too!). When the broadcast on 'Corina' finished the mother and son whispered together, and Lili put on another cassette of folk music (at loud volume). It seems that the two were telling each other about the questions the interrogators had put to them. After the cassette finished, those in the house don't come back on because now they are in the kitchen, from where they can be heard only faintly.
>
> At 22.30 hours they turn the volume of the music up again, so it cannot be established when the young couple left.
>
> At 23.00 hours she listens once more to the radio Free Europe broadcast — which she had recorded when the young ones were at her house. Ştefania goes back over some passages which she doesn't understand very well.
>
> After 23.30 hours the house is silent.[34]

From the way in which discussions developed from 29 November to 19 December 1989,[35] both at 'Corina I', Nadia's house, where Adrian lived, and 'Corina II', Ştefania's flat, we are able to come to a number of conclusions, which the Securitate will also have drawn as they examined the surveillance materials. Ştefania Comăneci was torn in two opposing directions, unable to conceal her contradictory feelings from friends and acquaintances. Her initial reaction turned to despair and defiance, against the backdrop of the interrogations to which she was subjected and which heaped pressure on her – some of them lasted for hours at a time – and finally, after 10 December, she seems to have resigned herself to the situation. It was, of course, quite easy for the Securitate to manipulate her, as shown by the covert recordings, as well as the procès-verbaux of the interrogations, which provide clues as to the plan to influence her.

Some of those who contacted her were informers who had been instructed to do so, either to update her on the news with the purpose of gauging her reaction – such as the unknown woman who phoned her on 29 November, telling her to listen to Free Europe before hanging up – or to glean information from her. But above all, their mission was to convey messages to her as a means of influencing her behaviour.

As a rule, such persons remain nameless in the documents, instead being referred to as 'citizens'. One such incident took place on 1 December, at a time when Ştefania Comăneci had not yet got over the initial shock and avoided talking on the phone, telling acquaintances to call her later or the next day. At 15.40 hours she was phoned by a woman, a 'citizen', who, although asked to call back, insisted on continuing the conversation. At one point, Ştefania tells her, 'now she has this misfortune', at which the 'citizen' wonders what "Corina" lacked here, but she was thinking only of herself. Ştefania, almost in tears, tells her that that is right, she thought only of herself, she did not realise that she had brought misfortune down on her head and everybody else's.'[36]

Emil Cerbu, a close friend of Ştefania's, warned her on the evening of 8 December that her defector daughter shouldn't 'denigrate the country, it would be a shame, because these folk have toiled and they toil, in the cold, without food, but they toil, and it would be a shame for her to denigrate them.'[37] Obviously, Nadia's mother could not foresee that in the very near future the Communist régime would collapse, that Romania would become a democracy, and that she would be reunited with her daughter in a matter of months. The immediate threats were far more real and frightening. 'Misfortune' meant not only losing her privileges, having gone overnight from the mother of a champion to the mother of a traitor, but also the danger of losing her job, maybe even her home, and above all, the fact that now she had to endure a torturous investigation that might have gone on for years. The Securitate had already ascertained that family members were afraid of this outcome, since at the end of November they were heard 'expressing the fear that their house and valuables might be confiscated.'[38] Under the circumstances, it is no wonder that in early December Ştefania Comăneci was often recorded saying that her daughter's adventure had 'destroyed' her in her old age, that if she had known what she intended, she would have tried to stop her, while also expressing her conviction that Nadia hadn't done it 'on her own, she was forced to by somebody.'[39]

But even so, she received encouragement from plenty of people who admired her daughter's act, and who recommended that she resist the interrogations and pressure. Ştefania Comăneci spent time with these people, listening to the cassette recordings of Free Europe broadcasts and reminiscing about Nadia, as happened on 10 December: 'Ştefania puts on a cassette recording of F.E. news broadcasts about "Corina's" defection, she shows the visitors mementos of her (a dedication written in a Bible by the priest who baptised "Corina"?)'[40] and the next day, when she told a friend that Nadia 'is a grown-up, she does what she wants, there's nothing I can do to change her.'[41]

Depending on how the investigation and information collected from agents and covert recordings evolved, the Securitate constantly altered its tactics as a way of increasing the pressure on family members and obtaining as much intelligence as possible. There were daily interrogations at the Militia headquarters. Ştefania, Adrian and Liliana often at their meals at friends' homes, since they didn't have time to do housework or even to report to work. Whereas during the first days of the investigation, they requested unpaid leave from work, around a week later they found themselves in the situation of being refused the time off. The Militia told them that they would receive exemptions, but this did not happen and they were therefore in danger of losing the jobs due to absenteeism. On 3 December, Ştefania told her neighbour, 'the lady from downstairs', that Adrian and his wife 'have been stopped from coming to her house, so that they would not try to get their stories straight together.'[42] Outgoing calls from both her telephone and her son's were blocked, allowing the Securitate to control the flow of information to the benefit of the investigation.

Adrian and Liliana Comăneci were undergoing an even worse ordeal, since they were suspected of having been Nadia's accomplices. In an interview he gave in 2009, Nadia's brother briefly recounts the hardships he endured:

On the first evening after the defection I was with my wife and another couple at a restaurant and we came back at eleven p.m. In front of my gate were two Militia cars, and the officers bundled us inside. Then the interrogations began. They held us there the whole night. I kept telling them 'no', I told them that I didn't know anything about her wanting to leave. Simultaneously, they began an investigation. In the morning they made me sign to say I agreed to them searching the house. I didn't have any choice. But later I found out from the neighbours that the whole night, while we were at the station, they saw lights burning in the house. So, I think they'd already entered without my permission.

They entered the next day, too, in my presence. They kept asking me where the money was, where the gold was, whether we had drugs. They placed a seal on the trophy room, where Nadia had all her cups, all her medals. They did an inventory of all the goods, we couldn't use the telephone for outgoing calls any more, only incoming ones. Then we were handed over to another team, from the Capital Militia. More interrogations. Then they told us: 'Don't keep telling us you don't know, we have proof that you went to Sînnicolau Mare.' They'd checked and found out that we'd been recorded entering the town, and they even discovered my wife's file at the dentist's. They kept trying to get out of me who the guide was and who organised it all. They made us draw diagrams of who was sitting where at the table during the night of the party in Sînnicolau.

They took Mama away too. They took her to the station, after which they brought her home and for a few days they stayed with her in the house. They didn't sleep there, they came in the morning and left in the evening. Things were becoming harder and harder, they stayed like that until two days before the events in Timişoara. It was then that they more or less left us in peace. They had information that things would be happening there and they weren't interested in us any more.[43]

The conduct of the three during the investigation seems to have followed a pattern that would suggest an initial intention to coordinate with each other. Obviously, it wasn't hard for the Securitate to detect this pattern, which led them to discourage meetings between Ştefania and Adrian and Liliana. It also wasn't hard for the interrogators to catch them out, since their first statements were full of untruths: 'One day, they held me eight hours and kept trying to get something out of me, but they could not find anything. I maintained the same position from start to finish,' Ştefania Comăneci said in the same interview, but her handwritten statements suggest the opposite. On 20 November, at five p.m., when her interrogation began, she described how she found out that her daughter had crossed the border illegally, but she lied when she was asked whether she had met Constantin Panait at the Simas' home on 14 November. Likewise, she claimed that in November she had not left Bucharest, even though Nadia had taken her to Timişoara and Sînnicolau Mare, where she had been seen by numerous witnesses.

Mrs Comăneci then altered her statement, admitting that she had met Panait in mid-November, and on 3 December she signed a statement that she had found out about her daughter's defection on 29 November, at around seven p.m., from Adrian and Liliana Comăneci: 'I said it couldn't be true, who could she have left with, and they told me that she arranged to leave with Panait C-tin. I asked how could she leave and where to, my son answered that there was a shepherd who took Nadia and another 6 persons across in exchange for 10 thousand lei per person.'[44]

Mrs Comăneci's son and daughter-in-law were placed in the same situation. Under interrogation on 30 November, Adrian declared that the news had shocked him, having learned of it from a neighbour on 29 November at around midday. 'Our reaction was one of complete bewilderment, and it was hard to calm Mama

Figure 7.1 Photo taken by the Securitate on 8 December 1989, during a surveillance of Adrian Comăneci, Nadia Comăneci's brother, and his wife in Bucharest. (Archive of the National Council for Study of the Securitate Archives [A.C.N.S.A.S], Documents Archive, dossier 13346, vol. 24, leaf 115.)

Figure 7.2 Photo taken by the Securitate on 8 December 1989, during a surveillance of Adrian Comăneci, Nadia Comăneci's brother, and his wife in Bucharest. (Archive of the National Council for Study of the Securitate Archives [A.C.N.S.A.S], Documents Archive, dossier 13346, vol. 24, leaf 115.)

down,'[45] he declared, and to justify his ignorance, he added that lately Nadia had been increasingly irascible and hadn't allowed any questions about her personal life. However, he made the mistake of declaring that in November he had not taken any trip outside Bucharest, despite witnesses from Sînnicolau Mare and Cenad confirming that he and his wife had visited the area. The interrogators therefore knew he was lying. On 2 December he admitted that Nadia had told him of her plan, asking him to sell her house and car without going to a notary public to draw up the contracts so that the authorities would not find out. Adrian went to a friend from lycée, Mihai Ioan, to draw up the contracts of sale, and he told him of Nadia's intentions. As he mentions in the interview, a few days later he was made to identify the persons who had been at the parties in Sînnicolau and Cenad, and also the place where they had the meals, with the interrogators showing him photographs of his sister and Constantin Panait at the airport in New York. Unlike Adrian, Liliana admitted as early as 1 December that she had visited Cenad, and the next day she confessed to having known about Nadia's plan. Nadia had told her, 'very adamantly, "I'm sick of everything and I can't take any more," without giving me any explanation.'[46]

During the interrogation, Adrian was forced to confess to all kinds of minor but untrue details that would bear out the theory that his sister had planned her defection painstakingly. For this reason, there were moments when he tried to refuse to make any further statement. On the other hand, both he and his wife did everything possible to coach each other on what to say and to make sure they got their stories straight. For example, they both confessed on the same day that they had known of Nadia's plan, and they described how she made her intentions known to them in an identical fashion. Playing their rôles, Adrian Comăneci said he was 'bewildered' at it, Liliana that she was 'completely taken aback'.

On Wednesday, 22.11 year in progress, I arrived home at 4 in the morning, I went to sleep in Nadia's small bedroom and woke up at around 9–9.30 since there was noise coming from the kitchen. Having quickly put a few clothes on I went to the kitchen, where Nadia and Costel Panait were drinking coffee. Nadia introduced me to Costel, after which she took me into her big bedroom and said: 'Adi, we have to transfer ownership of the house and car to you because I'm leaving with Costel.' Demanding an explanation, she replied: 'I'm crossing the border and Costel has arranged everything.' As I showed my bewilderment at what she told me, she answered: 'Costel will explain it to you better.' We both went to the kitchen, where Nadia told Costel to go with me and explain. We both went into the big bedroom, where, after I asked him, hey brothers, what are you thinking of doing, he answered that he was taking Nadia across the border, everything was arranged, and when I interrupted saying the risk is great and don't get her involved in such a situation, he answered that it's no problem and that <u>if it's not going to be possible he won't expose her to any risk</u>, that Nadia is going to sign the house and car over to me. I <u>proposed to go with Nadia to draw up the contracts legally with a notary public, to which one of them said: 'that's not possible because it will be glaring' why Nadia is giving away her house and car</u> just like that, all of a sudden. In the end, we decided to write out the contracts by hand (in the presence of witnesses), and that we'd draw them up after we got back from Sinaia.[47] (. . .)

Adrian Comăneci

On 22.xi year in progress in the morning when we woke up (that night my husband had been at work, he came back in the morning and didn't come upstairs to my room), after I got dressed I went down to the kitchen where first of all Adrian and Costică Panait came in, I'd met him at Mr Sima's name-day party, where he was introduced by Ion Dolănescu as his 'godson from Florida', and after 15 mins. Nadia came in.

In the kitchen they ate something, had coffee, around 30 mins. (because he had to be at work at one), after which Adrian (when Costel and Nadia were out of the room) informed me that Nadia was leaving, but for me that was enough and I asked him where she was going, he said she was leaving the country. He didn't specify whether legally or illegally or the date or the circumstances in which she was going to do it.

This news obviously didn't come as any joy to me and, as is natural, I asked Nadia whether it was true. She told me 'YES', and getting this definite answer I wanted to know what had led her to do it, to which she said: 'I'm sick of everything, I can't stand it any more.' With tears in my eyes I tried to persuade her not to leave us and especially (after I realised she wanted to cross the border illegally) that the risk was very great. She didn't want to have any kind of discussion about this action, which is why I was completely taken aback and I was left in tears probably because of the fact that I wasn't in her situation, I was much more aware than she was and I could discern that even so it wasn't a good thing what she wanted to do.[48] (. . .)

Liliana Comăneci (indecipherable signature)

In addition to relatives, nobody deemed significant to the success of the investigation escaped surveillance, and in the initial phase, telephone calls were intercepted and the Militia took people in for questioning. If grounds for suspicion were established, extended surveillance and interrogation were employed. Nadia's friends, past and present, and her ex-boyfriends were also targeted, no matter how famous they might be; celebrity was no protection against the Securitate. The reports of Department One Domestic Intelligence show that 'O.T.

measures of the T.C.I. type'[49] were applied for in the case of singers Ion Dolănescu (code name I.D.) and Benone Sinulescu (code name 'Sandu'), and actor Ştefan Bănică Jr. (code name 'Banu') immediately after Nadia's defection, that is, 'from 29.xi.1989 until clarification of the case', with the aim of obtaining 'information regarding Nadia Comăneci's defection to a foreign country (connections, preparations, enabling circumstances etc.)'[50]

The information gathered did not reveal any involvement on the part of the celebrities, quite the opposite. Folk singer Ion Dolănescu, who introduced Panait to Nadia's circle, found out about her defection on 29 November from friends he talked to on the phone between two concerts, since he had just got back from Tîrgovişte and was about to go to Piteşti. In a conversation with a relative on 1 December, actor Ştefan Bănică Jr. said, 'I wasn't any more,' with reference to the fact that their relationship had been over for some time, 'but even so, it's a shock!'[51] A few days later, when asked about it by somebody else during a telephone conversation, he mentioned that he had been summoned to the Interior Ministry. Attempting to confirm American involvement, the Securitate was also interested in obtaining information about Béla Károlyi, who for a short space of time was suspected of having helped Nadia to defect, but nothing could be proven.

In the meantime, Nadia tried to sow confusion among the Romanian investigators by giving false information to the international press about how she had planned to flee the country. For example, she stated that she had met Constantin Panait two years previously and that her parents, brother and sister-in-law hadn't known anything about her intentions. But it was not difficult for the Securitate investigators to disprove what she said when they had witnesses who were there when Nadia met Panait for the first time, at the Simas' party, and when Adrian and Liliana had confessed their complicity at the beginning of December.

A major investigation was also underway at the border, including the particular stretch of no-man's-land the seven fugitives were thought to have crossed. 'Along the frontier strip no traces of their crossing into Hungary were found,'[52] states a report dated 29 November, as if there were any chance of the frozen ground preserving their footprints. But the investigation that counted the most was the one carried out in the towns that Nadia and her family visited. It was discovered that Lieutenant Nina Stanciu and Major Eugen Dinescu of Timiş County Securitate – Dinescu was in charge of five frontier towns, including Cenad – knew in advance that Nadia Comăneci and U.S. citizens Panait and Talpoş were in the area, but failed to grasp their intentions and, even more seriously, to report them to their superiors in Timişoara and Bucharest. The two acknowledge their failure, but justified it by arguing that Nadia had been monitored by the head of the Cenad station, Sergeant Pintea Grigore, and by a Securitate informer in Sînnicolau Mare, codenamed 'Aurora', who had been at some of the parties that were held.

On 19 November, Stanciu declared, 'source "Aurora" informed me that gymnast Nadia Comăneci was in the company of two foreign citizens and other persons from the town of Sînnicolau Mare, holding parties with relatives of fugitive Talpoş Aurel, in the village of Cenad,'[53] immediately reporting it to Major Dinescu, in charge of Cenad village and contacted Border Guard Battalion 68 Sînnicolau Mare. For his part, Dinescu made the following statement:

> I was aware of the fact that on 19.xi.1989 he (Aurel Talpoş) held a party in Sînnicolau Mare to which Nadia Comăneci and Paraschiv Gheorghe from Bucharest came, as well as another American citizen originally from our country with his mother. On 20.xi.1989, via source 'Aurora' who was at this party, I established that there was no evidence of aspects that might be of interest in the line of security work, for which reason I did not report to the professional leadership.
>
> Likewise, I was also aware of the fact that on 25.xi.1989 at the home of the aforementioned Talpoş Gheorghe in Cenad a further party was held to which Nadia Comăneci once more came. I did not have information from which it was apparent that any person taking part intended to leave the country illegally, but I did bear in mind that the town was near the frontier with Hungary (. . .). For these reasons, with the commandant of the militia of the Sînnicolau Mare and those manning the Cenad militia station, I took measures to reinforce the border post at the entrance to the town and to organise ambushes from the said building. To this end, via Lieutenant Stanciu Nina the organs of the Border Guard Battalion were informed and took measures to reinforce the guard at the frontier.
>
> On the morning of 26.xi.1989, all those at the party were taken from the area, and Talpoş Gheorghe was given a written warning by the officer in charge of the militia post.
>
> Source 'Aurora' who was also at this party informed me that no security problem was posed. For all these reasons I did not report to the professional leadership.[54]

Source 'Aurora' confessed that when she put discreet questions to Constantin Panait, Aurel Talpoş and Nadia Comăneci, 'they made no reference to frontier issues or other issues connected to Romanian state policy. Referring to her personal situation, Nadia Comăneci said that in Romania she was materially very well off, and professionally she didn't think she could possibly have achieved more.'[55] But 'Aurora' had not been vigilant enough, she had not constantly monitored what the people at the party said and did. But what measures could the Securitate take against one of its own informers for such a failure?

Sergeant Pintea of the Militia, in charge of the Cenad post, is not recorded as saying he suspected Nadia of embarking on such a perilous enterprise. Unlike the Securitate officers, he did take a number of measures to cover himself, however, since on 25 November he reported to the militia in Sînnicolau Mare the list of those who had entered and left the Cenad area, which included Nadia's name, but he also reported that the persons 'did not pose problems connected to the BORDER POST.'[56] On the other hand, even though on 26 November he notified Gheorghe and Aurel Talpoş in writing that they should stop coming to parties in Cenad, he himself was at one of the last parties. As Liliana Comăneci stated under interrogation, at the party Pintea had said something that ought to have aroused the Securitate's suspicions. According to Liliana, Pintea said that he was there 'because such parties are usually held in advance of every frontier crossing.'[57]

Today, Grigore Pintea claims that Nadia herself confessed to him her intention to defect, and during the final party, when they went outside into the yard, she asked him to join the group, but the then militia sergeant declined, for fear that his family would suffer at the hands of the Securitate. But he didn't report her since he thought that important people in Bucharest supported her act. 'Nicu Ceauşescu wanted to meet me, to shake my hand, and he thanked me for the way I'd acted,' recalls Pintea, who believes the dictator's son was congratulating him because 'I knew how to file the paperwork properly.' Accompanied by Traian Sima, the head of Timiş Securitate, Ion Deheleanu, the head of Timişoara Militia, and 'seven or eight' other people, Nicu Ceauşescu arrived in the area a few days after the event, according to Pintea, who has not forgotten the brief talk he had with him: 'We went inside, he congratulated me, he asked me whether she had said anything bad about him, about his dad . . . What was I supposed to tell him? Because I knew everything she said. I said no, she spoke very nicely, they didn't have anything against you.'[58]

Traian Sima stated, 'full responsibility devolves upon me as head of security, I have to take responsibility for the shortcomings that appear in the activity of the apparatus that I command,'[59] but he did not neglect to cast the blame on Stanciu and Dinescu, who had not reported to the Timişoara Securitate Nadia's presence in the area.

The declarations of all the Timiş Securitate officers regarding Nadia Comăneci's 'escape' all end on the same penitent note, suggestive of their fear for their future careers. They confess to a 'lack of professional judgement' and the lightness with which they carried out their orders, while undertaking not to allow such mistakes to happen again. The declarations made by officers from the Bucharest Securitate are no different, although the wording is slightly different: 'lack of professional orientation and foresight' and 'lack of professional maturity'. While some of them accepted personal responsibility, they also had the courage to point to a collective failure on the part of the Securitate.

For example, Major Nicolae Roşu of Department One, the officer in charge of the 'Sport' objective, tasked with liaising with Nadia Comăneci, stated that he was unable to prevent her defection because there were gaps in the surveillance and protection measures, that there were not enough undercover agents in her entourage, but also because 'the decision to go abroad was taken at the last moment,'[60] which is to say, unexpectedly.

> The reconnaissance and preventative measures in the case of Nadia Comăneci did not rise to an appropriate level, which prevented apprehension of the moment in which she in question took the decision to go abroad illegally. This was due both to the lack of sources capable of penetrating the entourage and the private conceptions of her in question, and to the sporadic employment of special working methods (the small number of means relative to the problem assigned to the jurisdiction of the department and the recent changes arising in the operational situation).
>
> The decision to go abroad was taken recently, under advantageous circumstances, to which in large part contributed the non-approval of any trip abroad. The cancellation of the trip to the U.S.S.R., about which she probably found out, and the fact that it had not been officially communicated to her whether she was allowed to go to Spain, likewise played an important part.
>
> I reported verbally to the leadership of the department (the locum tenens who directed the department) the new issues arising in the case after September 1989.
>
> Many of the shortcomings that exist in this case are also due to the fact that since July 1989 a series of negative events (defections) arose in the 'Sport' matter, which required much time to examine and clarify in the circumstances in which I did not have available to me any officer to deal with the reconnaissance work. Both officers assigned to the matter—Captain Gherghe Florea and Captain Niculescu Lucian—had other missions, and I myself, in September and October, was taking a refresher course at the Grădiştea school.[61]

Because of the direct professional relationship that he had with Nadia Comăneci, Major Roşu had to account above all for the fact that he had not even suspected that Nadia wished to defect. In a number of reports, he explained that he did not have the manpower to monitor Nadia's trips around the country, that 'all the persons consulted subsequent to the commission of the act of fraudulently crossing the frontier' had given assurances that 'Nadia Comăneci is not capable of such an action', while other Securitate officers around the country did not provide him with any 'information via which I might have been alerted to the presence of Nadia Comăneci in Poiana Braşov or in the counties adjoining the state frontier in the company of foreign citizens.'[62]

Although the heads of the Securitate suspected C.I.A. involvement in the whole affair, the evidence gathered by the investigators themselves put paid to the theory. The simple fact that the two men who organised the illegal border crossing were Romanians who had acquired U.S. citizenship was not proof in itself. Besides, during investigations, it had been established that neither Panait nor Talpoş had any special training, but were ordinary people without any higher education. The investigation files also prove beyond all doubt that Nadia Comăneci and Constantin Panait met completely by chance, rather than as a result of any conspiracy. Not least, it is worth emphasising that the Securitate officers recognised that Nadia 'had certain dissatisfactions connected to her earnings and the fact that she was not given permission to travel abroad when invited by various international sports organisations and national federations.'[63] Nor do any of the documents in the archives make any mention of Nadia having been ensnared in a plot by any foreign political power.

Further proof that the C.I.A. was not involved was Nadia's conduct in early December, when she mostly declined interviews with the press. If her defection had been part of such an operation, American intelligence would have sought to make use of her to disseminate criticism of Nicolae Ceauşescu and the Romanian Communist régime, as she would have provided the perfect mouthpiece. But Nadia herself made use of the powerful weapon of the international press only in very few situations and with serious reservations when it came to any political statements.

Maybe Sergeant Pintea of the Militia, regarded by locals as an 'exceptionally good and decent man', really was Nadia's accomplice in a way. He didn't help her, but he did keep quiet about it when he discovered her intentions. As for the support that 'a part of the Securitate' might have provided Nadia in crossing the frontier clandestinely, we believe this was in fact the case, albeit in the form of incompetence on the part of officers including Major Dinescu and Lieutenant Stanciu, as well as their network of informers in the Cenad-Sînnicolau area. They made the fugitives' escape easier by thinking they were in control of events and didn't have to inform their superiors, who would have demanded additional measures.

In November 1989, the fraught political context within Romania – the Fourteenth Congress of the Romanian Communist Party – obliged the Securitate to demonstrate heightened vigilance, tightening the screws on a population already under draconian surveillance. For example, under operation 'Forum 89'[64] all foreign citizens visiting Romania during the Party Congress were placed under counterintelligence surveillance. But Constantin Panait, who was a U.S. citizen, passed under the radar. Had Department 320 of the Bucharest Securitate, in charge of 'American counterespionage' within the city, picked up on his presence in the city, they would have found plenty to arouse their suspicions. In 1987, when Panait had first returned to Romania, he had been summoned to the headquarters of Bucharest Securitate to answer questions, but in 1988 and 1989 he was left alone, having been deemed not to meet 'the criteria that would indicate him as a foreigner who needs to be kept under watch as a priority.'[65] The criteria in question were listed as follows: 'Inasmuch as Panait Constantin did not have a higher education, did not work in a setting where secrets were gathered, had not been detected as having connections with persons party to secrets and did not visit the country often, he was not designated a counterespionage person of interest and no verification measures were implemented regarding him.'[66] But the Securitate did not realise its mistake until Panait was already out of the country.

Major Eugen Dinescu's lack of experience – he had been working in the Securitate for around two years – and the youth and inexperience of Lieutenant Stanciu provided an unhoped-for advantage for the fugitives. So too did the indifference of the heads of the Romanian Gymnastics Federation, who were not alerted by the fact that Nadia was constantly absent from her desk, requesting days off and medical leave. Had it been anybody else, they would probably have taken a dimmer view, but they had become accustomed to the former Olympic champion's little whims and absences from work.

All these circumstances considerably improved the fugitives' chances of success. Sometimes a plan will succeed not because it has been painstakingly put together, but simply because a favourable conjunction of circumstances happens to arise. And this was why Nadia was able to win her victory over the Securitate.

In its first report on the crisis situation, drawn up at the beginning of December 1989, Department One stated, 'after she reached the outside, Nadia Comăneci, in numerous interviews, has declared that she left the country illegally, "choosing freedom", inasmuch as she was not allowed to take part in sports competitions abroad, to which she had been invited. To date the person in question has not engaged in virulent hostile actions.'[67]

Encouraged by this, the Securitate thought up a number of measures to discourage the foreign 'reactionary' persons or groups that aimed to exploit the defection, thereby damaging the security and interests of the Communist régime. By placing under surveillance Nadia's family and friends, the Securitate were able to identify and block any channels by which information on the subject could be sent from Romania to foreign countries. They verified whether there were friends or relatives who might be thinking of fleeing the country in the immediate future or who might contact foreign journalists, and Nadia's personal documents, video recordings, medals and trophies were confiscated to prevent them from being smuggled out of the country.

The Securitate took a firm approach to the people they interrogated during the investigation, but the pressure applied was psychological rather than physically violent. The main aim was to persuade Nadia not to engage in hostile political actions. As a consequence, they pressured family members, both directly and via informers, with a view to influencing them 'so that in the event that she in question contacts them they will determine her to adopt the correct attitude and not to be caught up in anti-Romanian activities.' When they were finally allowed to contact her, the Securitate wanted Nadia's relatives to tell her that 'measures have not been taken against them by the authorities, and they have remained in the same jobs.'[68] In a subsequent phase, they were to select agents to convey messages aimed at influencing or, if necessary, discouraging her.

Because they had to travel abroad as part of their jobs, the officials of the National Council of Physical Education and Sport and the Romanian Gymnastics Federation were given instructions as to what to say on the subject during meetings with foreign partners in general and journalists in particular. The following is a summary of the plan drawn up on 11 December, which laid down the line from which nobody was allowed to deviate: Nadia Comăneci was valued in Romania for her talent and achievements; she was provided with support to complete her education at the Institute of Physical Education and Sport and to attend course to obtain her international judge's certificate; she had considerable incomes, had bought a large house, custom-made furniture, a car, and other valuables; she was employed as a trainer of the women's gymnastics team, made frequent trips abroad, most recently to Cuba, and had been due to travel to Spain and the U.S.S.R.; she enjoyed freedom, comfort, admirers, but had a chaotic personal life and an entourage who were a negative influence on her; her relationship with Béla Károlyi had been cold, dominated by a strong personal dislike; the Romanian Gymnastics Federation had taken the decision to appoint her in the near future to the Women's Coaching Committee of the International Gymnastics Federation, replacing Maria Simionescu, and the Romanian Olympic Committee was to offer the post of vice-chairwoman after Lia Manoliu retired; which is why her departure surprised everybody and is an incomprehensible act, condemned by all those in sport and her family members, who believe 'she was corrupted, lured by promises and lies by foreigners, gold-diggers, who aim to profit from her fame, and to denigrate and compromise the good results of Romanian sport'; but at the same time, 'it is believed that Nadia Comăneci cannot adapt to the western lifestyle, she will not succeed (due to mental instability) in achieving results as a gymnastics trainer and given her feelings towards Béla Károlyi (which can't change overnight), there cannot be any prospect of a collaboration between the two.'[69]

At the same time, agents of the espionage department, primarily those who worked in the foreign press, were also to be instructed to 'discredit and compromise her.'[70] It was believed that there was sufficient factual information that could be used to this end, one example being the complicated nature of the relationship she had with Béla Károlyi over the course of time. This line of attack was to be finalised by the Securitate by 25 December.

After Nadia Comăneci's defection, Romanian sportspeople attending international tournaments and competitions were subject to even more stringent conditions. Selection was more rigorous, background checks more thorough[71] and Securitate officers and informers were more numerous among the members of delegations.[72] Constantin Oprița, the chairman of the N.C.P.E.S. in 1989, decided that no gymnasts were to take part in competitions from November to December 1989, although the Central Committee had given its approval, which led to the loss of hundreds of thousands of dollars and further tarnished the prestige of Romanian sport.

'Now, God knows what would have happened later if the Revolution hadn't come,' said Nadia's mother in 2019. It was true: when the political upheavals of late December 1989 placed the Ceaușescu's in the situation of fighting an ultimately hopeless battle to remain in power, the Nadia case abruptly lost all importance. The whole world watched with bated breath as events unfolded in Romania and the Communist régime crumbled like a sandcastle, with the loss of more than a thousand lives over the course of just a few days, and ending with Nicolae and Elena Ceaușescu being hauled before a firing squad on 25 December 1989.

The Securitate investigation into the Nadia case ended on 19 or 20 December 1989. By now the secret police were faced with far more pressing problems, given the uprising that had started in Timișoara on 16 December and spread to the rest of the country. Only the first phase of the investigation had been completed, which minutely examined the defection itself, the persons involved, and those persons' degrees of culpability. The next phase was to have implemented measures to deal with the international fallout and to influence Nadia Comăneci positively, on the one hand, while also compromising her, on the other. But there was no more time for that. The Securitate had not even had time to collect from the house on Strada Rozmarin the items they had confiscated during the search and stored in sealed sacks. Among various documents deemed to be of interest, the sacks were also stuffed with the medals and trophies that Nadia had won during her career as a gymnast.

In lieu of an epilogue

In the 1980s, Romania continued its series of successes at major international women's gymnastics competitions, most notably winning the Olympic title at Los Angeles in 1984, at which Ecaterina Szabo also won three gold and one silver medal, Simona Păucă one gold, and Lavinia Agache one bronze. Of course, the other Communist countries that usually dominated the sport were boycotting the Los Angeles Olympics, but even so. Romania's gymnasts delighted the American crowds, but one of the most moving moments of the competition was when all the spotlights in the stadium were turned on Nadia Comăneci and she was given a standing ovation.[73]

At the time, the more than eighty thousand spectators in the Memorial Coliseum who saluted Nadia, as well as her millions of admirers worldwide, did not know that she was living a life of restrictions, earning a wage equivalent to about one hundred and fifty dollars a month. They did not know that Securitate officers and informers shadowed her, watching her every step, both in Romania and abroad, or that her private life was invaded in the crassest possible way.

Did Nadia Comăneci enjoy a life of privilege during the Communist régime, as Iulian Vlad, the head of the Securitate, later claimed? In reports compiled by the secret police after her defection, there are paragraphs pointing out that she had led a pleasant, comfortable life, that she owned a villa with seven rooms and annexes at no. 23, Strada Rozmarin and her own Dacia 1300 motorcar.

General Aurel Rogojan made a point of saying that Nadia did not have to queue outside food shops. Given the serious food shortages at the time, only the genuinely privileged were able to avoid queuing. But Nadia Comăneci was more famous worldwide than Nicolae Ceauşescu himself, so even if she had been obliged to join a long queue outside a food shop, she would have been recognised immediately and probably been invited to go straight to the front, in token of admiration for her sporting achievements for the nation. Thanks to her fame and the widespread admiration she enjoyed, Nadia was able to befriend petrol station and food shop managers, who made her life easier by procuring rationed goods for her. In the secret service reports filed in December 1989, we discover: 'Nadia Comăneci had a wide circle of contacts, consisting of persons in positions of responsibility, particularly in retail, via whom she solves problems of supplies and problems of a monetary nature.'[74]

The truth was that Nadia was not financially well off. Every month she had to pay instalments on repairs carried out on the house in Strada Rozmarin, and often she found herself in the situation of having to sell personal items in order to make ends meet. In winter, she slept in the kitchen because the house was poorly heated. Whenever she was able, she was generous towards her friends, and she was courteous to strangers. The Communist régime had exploited her both financially and politically, subjecting her to a complicated life full of restrictions in return. What privileges and honours she did receive were deserved, although they fell far short of her genius as a gymnast and the sacrifices she had made.

Under Communism, Nadia Comăneci's life could be likened to the uneven parallel bars: a straight line of conformity, predictability, and the strict control to which she always had to submit, and running alongside it, fixed there permanently, inescapably, the Securitate, keeping her under surveillance, influencing her, sometimes unobtrusively, sometimes overtly.

In the early 1990s, living in the United States and for a time Canada, Nadia faced hardships and she made plenty of awkward decisions that might have tarnished her reputation. Had the Romanian Communist régime survived, the Securitate would not doubt have exploited such missteps. But within a short time, supported by former gymnastics champion Bart Conner and manager Paul Ziert, she found her path once more and the world continued to hold her in high esteem. Although now far away from Romania, she never stopped honouring the place where she was born and from where she rose to become a champion. In 1994, from the first money she earned in the United State, Nadia Comăneci donated one hundred thousand dollars to the Romanian Gymnastics Federation, and over the years she has continued to support Romanian gymnastics both financially and morally.

Today, her name can be found in the International Gymnastics Hall of Fame. She was named Sportsperson of the Twentieth Century alongside figures such as Pelé, Muhammad Ali and Mark Spitz. She has been voted one of the most influential one hundred women of the last century. These are among many gestures of appreciation that remind us of the exceptional part that Nadia Comăneci, the gymnast whose name is synonymous with perfection, has played in the history of sport.

NOTES

Chapter 1

1 The 'triple border' (Latin). Romania's most westerly point, next to the town of Beba Veche, Timiş County, where the borders of Romania, Hungary and Serbia meet. In 1920, a three-sided boundary stone was erected here, emblazoned with the arms of the three neighbouring states.

2 Cristian Timofte, 'Dosare cenzurate. Operaţiunea Nadia. Fuga Nadiei Comăneci din România (II)' [Censored Files. The Nadia Operation. Nadia Comăneci's Escape from Romania], *Monitorul de Neamţ*. http://monitorulneamt.ro/dosare-cenzurate-operatiunea-nadia-fuga-nadiei-comaneci-din-romania-ii/ (retrieved 3 February 2020).

3 George Paraschiv, *Primăvară în decembrie* [Spring in December], Editura Ad Literam, Bucharest, 2010, p. 31.

4 Nadia Comăneci, *Letters to a Young Gymnast*, Basic Books, New York, 2004, p. 140.

5 Comăneci, *Letters* . . ., pp. 140–1.

6 Marius Tucă, Irina Cristea, 'Paşaport spre o viaţă liberă' [Passport to a Free Life], *Jurnalul*, https://jurnalul.antena3ro/scinteia/special/pasaport-spre-o-viata-libera-528703.html (retrieved 3 February 2020).

7 George Paraschiv, *Primăvară* . . ., pp. 33–4.

8 Cristian Timofte, 'Dosare cenzurate'.

9 The Department of State Security, known in Romanian as Securitatea [The Security] for short, was the principal and most powerful secret service of the Romanian communist régime from 1948 to 1989.

10 Comăneci, *Letters* . . ., p. 142.

11 Comăneci, *Letters* . . ., p. 142.

12 George Paraschiv, *Primăvară* . . ., pp. 39–44.

13 According to Nadia Comăneci, Pál Schmitt, the chairman of the Hungarian Olympic Committee at the time, later told her that he was the one who sent a representative to the frontier to welcome her and provide her with assistance.

14 George Paraschiv, *Primăvară* . . ., pp. 39–44.

15 Unfortunately, at present there are no final statistics, accepted by all researchers in the field, with regard to the phenomenon of the 'frontierists'. The official figures obtained from archive documents are not thought to be reliable given that the reports filed by the guards at the border posts are incomplete and because many frontier

incidents were not reported for fear of restrictive measures. In addition, persons who disappeared after illegally crossing the frontier were not recorded in the statistics. It is known, however, that at the end of the 1980s the number of illegal border crossings from Romania to Hungary increased dramatically. Whereas in 1987 there were fewer than 1,000 cases, by 1988 there were 7,182 and by 1989, 19,006 (see Nagy József, *Dezvoltarea locaţiei teritoriale, a activităţilor, a organizării şi a numărului de poliţişti de frontieră din 1958 pînă în 1998* [The Development of the Territorial Deployment, Activities, Organisation and Number of Frontier Police Officers from 1958 to 1998], PhD dissertation, Budapest, 2000, p. 211, cited by Paul Horváth and Dr Sallai János in 'Evaporarea cetăţenilor români spre Europa de Vest, cu ajutorul Ungariei, între 1985-1989' [The Drain of Romanian Citizens to Western Europe with the Assistance of Hungary between 1985 and 1989], http://horvathpal.com/wp-content/uploads/2020/02/evaporare.pdf (retrieved 15 February 2020); Marina Constantinoiu, Istvan Deak, 'Frontieriştii. Cum fugeau românii de communism şi cine le-a frînt aripile' [The Frontierists. How Romanians fled communism and who broke their wings], 12 March 2016, http://miscareaderezistenta.ro/frontieristii/frontieristii-comunism-romania-26432.html (retrieved 15 February 2020).

16 See Alexandru Ghişa, 'România şi Ungaria în ultimii ani ai Războiului Rece (1987-1989)' [Romania and Hungary in the Final Years of the Cold War], Editura Curtea Veche, Bucharest, 2011.

17 Paul Horváth, Dr Sallai János, 'Evaporarea cetăţenilor români . . .'

18 See Alexandru Ghişa, 'România şi Ungaria în ultimii ani ai Războiului Rece (1987-1989)', in Laurenţiu Constantiniu (ed.), *In memoriam acad. Florin Constantiniu. Smerenie. Pasiune. Credinţă* [In Memoriam Academician Florin Constantiniu. Humility. Passion. Faith], Editura Enciclopedică, Bucharest, 2013.

19 Researcher Roland Olah, who has made a painstaking examination of the archives in Romania and abroad, has to date identified 614 persons whom the Hungarian authorities handed back to Romania's border guards in 1989.

20 See Roland Olah's account of the phenomenon: 'Aspecte socio-demografice privind transfugii români arestaţi de grănicerii maghiari în anul 1987' [Socio-demographic aspects of Romanian frontier crossers arrested by Hungarian border guards in 1987], *Crisia*, No. 47, 2017, pp. 189–97, https://crisia.mtariicrisurilor/ro/pdf/2017/R%20Olah.pdf (retrieved 20 February 2020).

21 Immediately after the Montreal Olympic Games of 1976, when Nadia Comăneci enjoyed a spectacular rise to fame, a number of rumours about her ethnicity appeared in the international press, which claimed that her family were Transylvanian Hungarians and her real name was Anna Kemenes. According to the stories, 'the gymnast's change of name and place of birth are supposed to have been premeditated by the Romanian authorities, the same as in other cases, with the aim of denationalising the Hungarian element in Romania.' The Securitate monitored and analysed the information in various secret reports, drawing the conclusion that it was part of a campaign conducted by Hungary for the purpose of 'unmasking the systematic practice of denationalisation pursued by the Romanian organs in Transylvania.' Even though the stories were pure fictions that could easily have been discredited, there was no official protest on Romania's part (A.C.N.S.A.S., S.I.E. archive, dossier 31452, vol. 2, p. 234).

22 The information was provided by witnesses Maria Balea and Alexandru Ciucă, both of whom were present when the team that made the video recording arrived.

According to Maria Balea, 'during the period of time we were at the Hungarian border post on 28 November 1989, at ten a.m. they came to interview and film Nadia', while Alexandru Ciucă states, 'around 20–30 minutes later a group of six people arrived with a television equipment, a camera, microphones and cables, to interview Nadia Comăneci, which lasted around 30–40 minutes, translating into Hungarian the answers and the questions they put to Nadia Comăneci.' Maria Balea also stated that she didn't know what Nadia Comăneci said during the interview because it was in English (A.C.N.S.A.S., Documents archive, dossier 13346, vol. 25, pp. 139, 156, 158 verso).

23 In 1989, General Department III was the shorter name for the Hungarian intelligence service. The Minister of the Interior's General Department of State Secret Services (III. Állambiztonsági Csoportfőnökség) oversaw Department III/I Espionage, Department III/II Counterespionage, Department III/III Counterespionage Internal Dissent (Belső reakció elhárítása), Department III/IV Military Counterespionage, and Department III/V Technical Operations.

24 Reference to Ion Mihai Pacepa's *Red Horizons. Chronicles of a Communist Spy Chief*, Washington D.C., Regnery Gateway, 1987), which struck a heavy propaganda blow against the Ceauşescu régime. In the summer of 1978, General-Lieutenant of the Securitate Ion Mihai Pacepa (1928–2021), Nicolae Ceauşescu's personal adviser and second-in-command of the Securitate's Foreign Information Department, defected to the United States and was granted political asylum.

25 A.C.N.S.A.S., Documents archive, dossier 13346, vol. 25, p. 5.

26 *The Daily Egyptian*, 1 December 1989, Vol. 75, No. 252, https://opensiuc.lib.siu.edu/cgi/viewcontent.cgi?article=1000&context=de_December1989 (retrieved 20 February 2020).

27 In a conversation with the author of this book, Nadia Comăneci stated that no such telephone call between Teodora Ungureanu and herself took place, as she did not have the opportunity to make telephone calls during that interval.

28 Statement made by the MTI agency on the afternoon of 30 November, https://rendszervaltas.mti.hu/Pages/Newsaspx?se=1&wo=nadia&sd=19890101&ed=19901231&sp=0&ni=230053&ty=1 (retrieved on 20 February 2020).

29 Statement made by the MTI agency on the morning of 1 December 1989, https://rendszervaltas.mti.hu/%20Pages/News.aspx?se=1&wo=nadia&sd=19890101&ed=19901231&sp=0&ni%20=222571&ty=1 (retrieved 20 February 2020).

30 A.C.N.S.A.S., Documents archive, dossier 13346, vol. 24, p. 71. Although the Documents archive attributed these headlines to the 'Evening Star' newspaper, it is unclear which Evening Star newspaper the headlines come from.

31 Comăneci, *Letters . . .*, p. 148. See also: https://www.nytimes.com/1989/12/13/us/scorn-gives-comaneci-a-lesson-in-image.html

32 Comăneci, *Letters . . .*, p. 148.

33 See the detailed monitoring of the foreign press carried out by the Securitate, in A.C.N.S.A.S., Documents archive, dossier 13346, Vol. 24, pp. 25–106. The subject is also explored by Florian Banu, 'Noiembrie 1989—plecarea din România a Nadiei Comăneci: ultima lovitură de imagine data regimului Ceauşescu' [November 1989—Nadia Comăneci's departure from Romania: the final blow to the image of the Ceauşescu regime], in Cosmin Budeancă, Florentin Olteanu (eds.), *Sfîrşitul* *regimurilor comuniste. Cauze, desfăşurare şi consecinţe* [The End of the Communist Regimes. Causes, Evolution and Consequences], Institute for Investigation of the Crimes of Communism and Memory of Romanian Exile, Făgăraş Country Memorial to the Anti-Communist Resistance, Editura Argonaut, Cluj, 2011, pp. 80–99.

Chapter 2

1   Ioan Chirilă, *Nadia*, Editura Sport-Turism, Bucharest, 1977, p. 9.

2   *Letters to a Young Gymnast*, pp. 12–13.

3   A.C.N.S.A.S., Documentary archive, dossier 13346, vol. 26, p. 311 verso.

4   Ioan Chirilă, p. 35.

5   *Letters to a Young Gymnast*, p. 16.

6   Ioana Adobricăi, Maria Pop, Istoria unui Liceu, Liceul unei Istorii [The History of a Lycée, the Lycée of a History], Editura
Magic Print, Oneşti, 2006, p. 12.

7   After Gheorghiu-Dej's death in March 1965, the State Council of Ministers decided to rename Oneşti after him. Although the town was named Gheorghe Gheorghiu-Dej up to 1990, when it reverted to Oneşti, I have used the original (and current) name in this book.

8   At the time, Oneşti had a population growth of 216.9 per cent, the highest in Romania (Rozalia Verde, Teodor Verde, *Monografia municipiului Oneşti în date şi evenimente (1458-2003)*, Editura Magic Print, Oneşti, 2003, p. 114.

9   Emanuel Fântâneanu, *Inscripţii pe columna gimnasticii româneşti*, Editura Tracus Arte, Bucharest, 2017, p. 69.

10 In the Union of Physical Education and Sport's report on the Romanian Gymnastics Federation, we find: 'for years there has been an attitude of tolerating the shortcomings in the training of the gymnasts at the former Constructorul association. Instead of being interested in fostering young elements, coaches Duncan Marcel and Ruja Felicia have limited themselves to a small number of gymnasts, Instead of finding in sporting activity a means to strengthen morals and raise a healthy younger generation, they have preached and supported the infiltration of concepts of stardom, of skiving off work, of bunking off training sessions without any managerial measures even being taken against them.' It was also emphasised that the old bourgeois ideology was still influential among gymnasts, given that during training 'they use the expressions "mister" and "missus", which are elevated to the rank of "civilised salon relations", and they consider themselves to be part of a category for which the dear word of the working class, the word "comrade" is not meaningful enough,' as well as the fact that 'the coaches still tolerate it when they permit themselves to call their trainer by his first name,' for example, 'Marcel' rather than 'comrade Duncan' (Central National Historical Archives, National Council for Physical Education and Sport archive, dossier 497/1958, p. 88 and dossier 553/1958, pp. 110–19.

11 Maria Simionescu (1927–2012) graduated from the Physical Education Institute in 1953. She was appointed a federal trainer in 1956. She was deputy chairwoman of

the Romanian Gymnastics Federation from 1990 to 2005. In 1972 she became a member of the Technical Committee of the International Gymnastics Federation (F.I.G.). She was a member of the F.I.G. judges' commission, taking part in every major competition (the Olympics and World Championships) from 1972 to 1996. She was awarded the title of Emeritus Trainer and in 2000 the National Cross for Loyal Service, First Class.

12 Nicolae Vieru, *Călătorie în lumea gimnasticii*, Fundaţia Nadia Comăneci and Editura Evenimentul şi Capital, Bucharest, 2015, p. 114. Vieru mentions that Maria Simionescu was assigned to Oneşti in 1964, but the Securitate archives would indicate that it was 1965 or 1966. For example, in a discussion with Lieutenant Colonel Vasile Miriţă that took place in September 1976, Gheorghe Braşoveanu, said: 'the first gymnastics group was founded in Gh. Gheorghiu-Dej in 1964–65 by Duncan Marcel, a trainer send by the Romanian Gymnastics Federation, and in 1965 he was joined by Simionescu Mili, a federation trainer, and teachers Ipate, Miclăuş, and Braşoveanu Gheorghe. Likewise, in September 1976, informer 'Măgureanu' states in a report, 'teacher Simionescu and his wife arrived in Oneşti at the end of 1966 and worked in parallel with coach Duncan until he left' (A.C.N.S.A.S., Informers archive, dossier 5189, vol. 1, pp. 75, 81.

13 Interview with Gheorghe Condovici, 12 June 2020.

14 Justin Gafiuc, 'Duncan a descoperit-o pe Nadia, Károlyi a dus-o la perfecţiune' (Duncan discovered Nadia, Károlyi brought her to perfection', *Gazeta Sporturilor*, https://www.gsp.ro/gsp-special/ superreportaje/oamenii-care-l-au-cunoscut-pe-marcel-duncan-il-descriu-ca-pe-un-antrenor-foarte-pasionat-si-un-mare-iubitor-de-copii-duncan-a-descoperit-o-pe-nadia-Károly-a-dus-o-la-perfectiune-282811.html (retrieved 4 July 2020).

15 Interview with Anca Grigoraş, 11 June 2020.

16 In 1969, 180 pupils were enrolled at the lycée. Lessons were taught in makeshift classrooms housed in dormitory blocks for unmarried factory workers until the decision was made to move Lycée No. 2 to a new building, which allowed the lycée to move into the vacated building. When it opened, it was officially named the General Educational Lycée with a Physical Education Programme for Training in the Branch of Girls' Sporting Gymnastics and soon thereafter became a centre for training female Olympic gymnasts. In 1976, it became Gymnastics Real-Humanist Lycée No. 2, in 1977 the History-Philology Lycée, in 1993 the Nadia Comăneci Sports Lycée, and in 2003 the Nadia Comăneci Sporting College. Although it is no longer producing champion gymnasts, the lycée can boast that it gave Romania eight Olympic titles, ten world titles, eight European titles, and more than 270 national titles in women's gymnastics.

17 In Romania, after the installation of the Communist régime, the old sports organisations were disbanded on the grounds that they were 'reactionary'. They were replaced with various centralised structures in charge of sport, such as the Union of Romanian Sports Federations and the People's Sports Organisation. From 1949, copying the Soviet model of organisation, national sport was run by the following governmental organisations: the Committee for Physical Culture and Sport from 1949 to 1957, the Union of Physical Culture and Sport from 1957 to 1967, and the National Council for Physical Education and Sport from 1967 to 1989. The National Council was in effect a ministry of sport, subordinate to the Sports Section of the Central Committee of the Romanian Communist Party. The heads of the structure were influential at the highest political level as long as they did not display any opposition to Party decisions regulating sport.

18 For an analysis of the Communist régime's propaganda apparatus in the world of sport, See Valentin Vasile, 'Aproape o jumătate de veac de sport şi propaganda în România (1945-1989)' (Almost half a century of sport and propaganda in Romania), *Caietele CNSAS, Reeducare şi propagandă*, Year 8, No. 2 (16), 2015, pp. 259–317. Edelman, Robert, and Christopher Young, eds. *The Whole World Was Watching: Sport in the Cold War*. Palo Alto: Stanford University Press, 2019.

19 Maria Simionescu and Marcel Duncan were joined in 1968 by 'Mihai Ipate and Gheorghe Braşoveanu from Oneşti, Tatiana and Titus Livius Isar from Lugoj, Maria and Mircea Bibire from Bacău, Maria Raicu and Kuhn Norbert from Timişoara, Valeriu Munteanu and Natalia and Petre Miclăuş from Bucharest, Florica and Florin Dobre from Craiova, and Gheorghe Gorgoi from Cluj. All of them arrived with their own gymnasts' (Ioana Adobricăi, Maria Pop, *Istoria unui Liceu, Liceul unei Istorii*, Editura Magic Print, Oneşti, 2006, p. 11).

20 A.C.N.S.A.S., Informers archive, dossier 5189, vol. 1, p. 161.

21 Béla Károlyi and Nancy Ann Richardson, *Feel No Fear. The Power, Passion, and Politics of a Life in Gymnastics*, Hyperion: New York, 1994, p. 32.

22 Nicolae Vieru (1932–2016) became a federal trainer in 1965, and from 1967 to 1983 he was secretary general of the Romanian Gymnastics Federation, serving as chairman between 1990 and 1999 and between 2000 and 2004, before being named honorary chairman in 2006. He was an international referee, an expert at the Higher Training Centre of the National Council of Physical Education and Sport (1983–90), a member of the Executive Committee of the International Gymnastics Federation, to which he was appointed at the 1976 Montreal Congress, prior to the Olympic Games. He was also deputy chairman of the International Gymnastics Federation. In 2002 he was named Emeritus Trainer. His other medals and awards include: Order of Sporting Merit, 2nd Class (1976), Order of Sporting Merit, 1st Class (1981 and 2004), National Loyal Service Medal, 1st Class (2000), National Loyal Service Medal, rank of Chevalier (2002) (see the biography in Emanuel Fântâneanu, p. 195, and Nicolae Vieru, *Călătorie în lumea gimnasticii*),

23 Nicolae Vieru, p. 115.

24 Justin Gafiuc, 'Duncan a descoperit-o pe Nadia . . .'.

25 A.C.N.S.A.S., Documents archive, dossier 13346, vol. 5, p. 384 verso.

26 Ioan Chirilă, pp. 14–15. According to Gheorghe Grunzu, chairman of Oneşti Municipal Council for Physical Education and Sport, the hall was officially opened on 5 August 1968 (Ioana Adobricăi, Maria Pop, p. 104).

27 A.C.N.S.A.S., Documents archive, dossier 13346, vol. 5, p. 369.

28 Justin Gafiuc, 'Duncan a descoperit-o pe Nadia . . .'.

29 Nicolae Vieru, p. 116; Ioana Adobricăi, Maria Pop, p. 96.

30 A.C.N.S.A.S., Documents archive, dossier 13346, vol. 5, p. 369.

31 *Feel No Fear*, p. 43.

32 *Sportul*, 22 April 1973, Year 29, No. 7391.

33 *Sportul*, 10 May 1975, Year 21, No. 8016.

34 D. Dimitriu, *Nadia Comăneci şi echipa de aur* (Nadia Comăneci and the Golden Team), Editura Sport-Turism, Bucharest, 1976, p. 54.

35 At the time, Dumitru Dimitriu was deputy chairman of the Bacău County Council for Physical Education and Sport. His book, published in October 1976, includes countless paeans to Nicolae Ceauşescu, whose involvement in the development of sport the author regards as essential and inspiring. A close friend of Béla Károlyi, Dimitriu also include biased information in his book, praising Béla and Marta Károlyi to the skies.

36 Ioan Chirilă, pp. 18–19.

37 A.C.N.S.A.S., Informers archive, dossier 5189, vol. 1, p. 159.

38 A.C.N.S.A.S., Documents archive, dossier 13346, vol. 5, p. 107.

39 A.C.N.S.A.S., Documents archive, dossier 13346, vol. 26, p. 175.

40 A.C.N.S.A.S., Informers archive, dossier 5189, vol. 1, p. 137 verso.

41 A.C.N.S.A.S., Informers archive, dossier 5189, vol. 1, p. 75.

42 A.C.N.S.A.S., Informers archive, dossier 5189, vol. 1, p. 76.

43 A.C.N.S.A.S., Informers archive, dossier 5189, vol. 1, p. 78.

44 A.C.N.S.A.S., Informers archive, dossier 5189, vol. 1, p. 81.

45 A.C.N.S.A.S., Informers archive, dossier 5189, vol. 1, p. 83.

46 Gheorghe Simionescu actually arrived in Oneşti in September 1969, when he was appointed head of the lycée.

47 A.C.N.S.A.S., Informers archive, dossier 5189, vol. 1, p. 136–136 v.

48 *Sportul*, 6 May 1975, Year 31, No. 8013.

49 Nadia Comăneci, interviewed by Andreea Esca, 2017 for the *La radio cu Andreea Esca* programme on Radio Europa FM, https://www. youtube.com/watch?v=p5jweed_bg4 (retrieved 12 June 2020).

50 Nadia Comăneci, pp. 16–17. In *My Own Story*, Nadia says, 'We were taught an elementary form of gymnastics by Mr Duncan who "coached" me for the first two years of my involvement in this exciting new activity,' and that later 'I was training under a Mr Munteanu, who was an excellent coach. Technically brilliant with a perfect understanding of the movements of the sport, he laid the foundations upon which Béla and Marta were then able to build' (Nadia Comăneci, *Nadia. My Own Story. The Autobiography of Nadia Comăneci*, Proteus Books: London, New York, 1981, pp. 29, 32.

51 Justin Gafiuc, 'Duncan a descoperit-o pe Nadia . . .'.

52 Justin Gafiuc, 'Béla Károlyi primeşte cu ironie idea că Marcel Duncan a fost primul antrenor al Nadiei' (Béla Károlyi reacts with irony to the idea that Marcel Duncan was Nadia's first trainer), *Gazeta Sporturilor*, https://www.gsp.ro/sporturi/gimnastica/Béla-Károlyi-primeste-cu-ironie-ideea-ca-marcel-duncan-a-fost-primul-antrenor-al-nadiei-stiu-pe-multi-care-au-descoperit-o-283086.html (retrieved 14 June 2020).

53 Ioan Chirilă, p. 25.

54 *Letters to a Young Gymnast*, pp. 25, 27.

55 A.C.N.S.A.S., Informers archive, dossier 5189, vol. 1, p. 149.

56 Although the archive sources point to different years for when Valeriu Munteanu resigned as a trainer in Oneşti and returned to Bucharest, with some saying 1971, others, 1972, we believe it was in the summer of 1971. He continued to teach physical education at the Dumitru Petrescu Lycée in Bucharest, and from October 1975 to August 1979 he taught in Casablanca, Morocco. From 1981 to 1983 he was under Securitate surveillance, suspected of wanting to leave the country illegally.

57 *Sportul*, 1 April 1970, Year 26, No. 860 (6294).

58 *Sportul*, 25 November 1970, Year 26, No. 1094 (6528).

59 Interview with Mariana Cojanu David, 9 July 2020.

60 A.C.N.S.A.S., Informers archive, dossier 5189, vol. 1, p. 75.

61 Ioana Adobricăi, Maria Pop, p. 106.

62 A.C.N.S.A.S., Informers archive, dossier 5189, vol. 1, p. 155.

63 A.C.N.S.A.S., Informers archive, dossier 464970, p.23.

64 In other books on the subject, Nadia Comăneci is said to have been given a 6.20, but we believe this is mistaken.

65 *Sportul*, 26 April 1972, Year 28, No. 7038.

66 *Sportul*, 3 July 1972, Year 28, No. 7014.

67 *Sportul*, 26 April 1972, Year 28, No. 7038.

68 *Sportul*, 15 June 1972, Year 28, No. 7086.

69 *Feel No Fear*, p. 45.

70 *Sportul*, 24 July 1972, Year 28, No. 7125.

71 *Sportul*, 14 November 1972, Year 28, No. 7236.

72 Pete Shilston, 'Champions All. Empire Pool, Wembley, London. April 12, 1975', *Gymnast*, Vol. 17, No. 6, June 1975, p. 25.

73 Carol Garabet Stabişevschi, pianist, teacher at the Institute of Physical Education and Sport in Bucharest. Béla Károlyi regarded him as one of the best pianists in the country and in 1974 asked him to join his team. Stabişevschi composed music for Romania's gymnasts at three Olympics, and in October 1977, while on tour in the United States, decided not to return to the country. Informer 'Nelu', a friend of Stabişevschi, described him as an 'indolent sort, who didn't do much work, vindictive by nature, quite thrifty, most of the time he came back to the country with all the money he earned, in a word, nothing gave anybody to suspect that he might do such a thing.' In March 1980, he managed to reunite with his family, after the authorities allowed his wife and daughter to leave Romania (A.C.N.S.A.S., Documents archive, dossier 13346, vol. 26, p. 167, and Network archive, file 118837, p. 18 verso).

74 Ioana Adobricăi, Maria Pop, p. 28.

75 For a description of the competitions in which the Oneşti gymnastics team trained by Béla and Marta Károlyi took part, see Emanuel Fântâneanu, and D. Dimitriu, *Nadia Comăneci*.

76 *Letters to a Young Gymnast*, p. 32.

77 A reference to the three original moves, with an exceptional degree of difficulty, that Nadia Comăneci performed on the parallel bars.

78 *Sportul*, 8 May 1975, Year 31, No. 8014.

79 *Sportul*, 10 May 1975, Year 31, No. 8016.

80 D. Dimitriu, p. 125.

81 *Sportul*, 18 November 1975, Year 31, No. 8152.

82 *Letters to a Young Gymnast*, p. 36, and *Feel No Fear*, pp. 54–6.

83 https://stirea.wordpress.com/2011 /11/12/nadia- comaneci-a-amenintat-ca-se-va-omori/ (retrieved 4 July 2020).

84 A.C.N.S.A.S., Documents archive, dossier 13346, vol. 26, p. 187 verso.

85 Iosif Sîrbu met a tragic end in September 1964, committing suicide because of the incurable illness from which he suffered. The Olympic champion had been kept under surveillance by the Securitate after criticising the régime. In his Securitate file, he is said to have been in the habit of telling 'various jokes critical of our régime' and of being given to 'outbursts hostile to the régime and the Party leaders, outbursts that have a negative influence and create an inappropriate attitude among the collective of which he is part', of 'slandering Party leaders' and 'lauding the quality of the armaments and technology in the capitalist countries', and praising the standard of living in the West. In 1958 he was censured by the Party, as the Securitate suspected 'he intends to betray the homeland,' after informers reported that during an upcoming trip to the West, Iosif Sîrbu planned not to return to Romania. On 23 September 1964, a day before he committed suicide, he wrote a farewell note, titled 'Confession', but in which he did not mention any political reason. The Communist press in Romania brought him back to public attention whenever the Romanian team was getting ready to travel to the Olympics, but merely mentioned that Sîrbu 'is no longer among us' (A.C.N.S.A.S., Informers archive, file 397453, pp. 20, 34, 220–1, 265.).

86 The Committee for Physical Education and Sport's report on the performance of gymnast Elena Leuşteanu at the Melbourne Olympics states: 'Individually, the best performance was by Elena Leuşteanu, who came fourth place overall, third in the floor exercise, sixth on the beam and vault. After six events she came first overall, but botched the dismount on the beam and uneven bars. The potential of this gymnast is much greater, but she does not put serious work into her training' (A.N.I.C., National Council for Physical Education and Sport archive, dossier 345/1956, p. 23).

87 *Feel No Fear*, p. 57.

88 Ioan Chirilă, p. 117.

89 Mircea Cărbunaru, 'Am fost o sportivă de echipă' (I was a team sportswoman), interview with Georgeta Antohi (Gabor), *Sportul Brăilean*, December 2018, Year 10, No. 10, p. 4.

90 Ioan Chirilă, p. 118.

91 A.C.N.S.A.S., Informers archive, dossier 133808, p. 5.

92 Ioan Chirilă, p. 122.

93 Nicolae Vieru, pp. 22–3.

94 *Sportul*, 23 July 1976, Year 32, No. 8326.

95 See *Les Grands Duels du Sport*, a documentary film by Jean-Christophe Klotz for Arte: https:// www.youtube.com/watch?v=84e_dCONe8s (retrieved 23 June 2020).

96 *Letters to a Young Gymnast*, p. 1.

97 *Letters to a Young Gymnast*, p. 15.

98 Sandra Sobieraj Westfall, 'Michelle Obama: "Gloves Are Off" to Bring Olympics to Chicago', *People*, 29 September 2009. https://people.com/celebrity/michelle-obama-gloves-are-off-to-bring-olympics-to-chicago/ (retrieved 4 July 2020).

99 *Letters to a Young Gymnast*, p. 45.

100 *Letters to a Young Gymnast*, p. 48. Archive footage from Romanian Television can be seen at https:// www.youtube.com/watch?v=PbDhWZlvEgU (retrieved 4 July 2020).

101 A.C.N.S.A.S., Documents archive, dossier 13346, vol. 26, p. 320.

102 *Sportul*, 29 July 1976, Year 32, No. 830.

103 Mihaela Andra Wood, *Superpower: Romanian Women's Gymnastics during the Cold War*, PhD thesis, University of Illinois, Urbana-Champaign, 2010, p. 17. https:// www.ideals.illinois.edu/handle/2142/16106 (retrieved 28 June 2020).

104 Gheorghe (Gogu) Rădulescu (1914–91), member of the Central Committee and Executive Political Committee of the Romanian Communist Party, minister, deputy prime minister.

105 Over the years a number of stamps were issued celebrating both Nadia Comăneci's performance at Montréal and her stature as a gymnast, not only in Romania, but also in countries including North Korea, Equatorial Guinea, Mongolia, Azerbaijan, the Gambia, Guyana, Mozambique and the Netherlands. In Romania, the first stamp was issued in 1976 and very quickly sold out, after which it could only be found on the black market for a price equivalent to an average month's salary at the time.

106 Ilie Verdeţ (1925–2001), member of the Central Committee Secretariat, member of the Permanent Praesidium of the Executive Committee, prime minister (1979–93).

107 Leontu Răutu (Lev Oigenstein) (1910–93), member of the Central Committee and Executive Political Committee, in charge of propaganda, the main Communist ideologue during the period when the Party leader was Gheorghe Gheorghiu-Dej.

108 János Fazekas (1926–2004), member of the Central Committee and the Executive Political Committee of the Romanian Communist Party, minister and deputy prime minister.

109 Vasile Dîba (1954-), canoeist. At the Montréal Games he won Romania's first canoeing medal in the K1 – 500 metres event.

110 Iosif Banc (1921–2007), member of the Central Committee and the Executive Political Committee of the Romanian Communist Party, minister, deputy prime minister.

111 Ion Ioniţă (1924–87), member of the Central Committee and substitute member of the Executive Political Committee of the Romanian Communist Party, minister, prime minister.

112 Richard Winter (1934–94), member of the Central Committee and substitute member of the Executive Political Committee of the Romanian Communist Party, minister.

113 Petre Lupu (Pressman) (1920–89), member of the Central Committee of the Executive Political Committee of the Romanian Communist Party, minister, ambassador.

114 A.N.I.C., C.C. of the R.C.P. archive, Chancellery Section, dossier 72/1976, pp. 56–8, Stenogram of the meeting of the Executive Political Committee of the

R.C.P. on 18 August 1976; Report on the participation of the delegation of Romanian sportspeople at the Olympic Games and proposals regarding the decoration and financial recompense of medal-winning sportspeople (with thanks to historian Armand Goşu for bringing this document to our attention).

115 *Sportul*, 29 July 1976, Year 32, No. 8330.

Chapter 3

1 By Presidential Decree No. 2050 of 18 August 1976, the Socialist Republic of Romania awarded honours not only to the sportspeople and trainers, but also to a number of activists in the National Council for Physical Education and Sport and to a number of sports journalists.

2 A.C.N.S.A.S., Informers archive, dossier 5189, vol.1, p. 83.

3 According to Nadia Comăneci, the car the authorities promised was not given to her, but bought by her family from the cash prize she was given.

4 This is untrue, since Nadia Comăneci received the highest honour.

5 *Feel No Fear*, pp. 62–3.

6 A.C.N.S.A.S., Informers archive, dossier 5189, vol.1, p. 83.

7 A.C.N.S.A.S., Documents archive, dossier 13346, vol. 26, p. 303 verso.

8 A.C.N.S.A.S., Informers archive, dossier 5189, vol. 1, p. 69.

9 A.C.N.S.A.S., Informers archive, dossier 5189, vol. 1, p. 9.

10 A.C.N.S.A.S., Informers archive, dossier 5189, vol. 1, p. 123.

11 *Feel No Fear*, p. 62.

12 A.C.N.S.A.S., Documents archive, dossier 13346, vol. 22, pp. 246–7, 248–9. In Securitate jargon, 'source' denoted a person within an intelligence network or provider of information. A 'source' who was also a Party member had the special task of informing the Securitate about activity within particular field, with the permission of Party organs, but his or her status was equivalent to that of an ordinary informer. The code '161' denotes Department One, Service 6, Bureau 1, while 'NI' are the initials of the officer with whom the 'source' liaised at the time, namely Nicolae Ilie.

13 'Trustworthy person' (or 'official person') meant an informer who had not been officially recruited but assisted the Securitate to carry out various operations. Usually, trustworthy persons were employed because they held particular responsibilities or positions in a given professional setting, allowing them to take part in operations to influence or disinform others.

14 A.C.N.S.A.S., Documents archive, dossier 13346, vol. 22, p. 383 verso.

15 A.C.N.S.A.S., Documents archive, dossier 13346, vol. 22, p. 379 verso.

16 A.C.N.S.A.S., Documents archive, dossier 13346, vol. 22, p. 384 verso. A person under scrutiny and selected with a view to recruitment. The Securitate would carry out a study of the person in view in order to establish whether he or she met their criteria, which assessed the candidate's ability to provide information, his or her willingness to collaborate, his or her risk of revealing the collaboration, and identified means of constraint or blackmail that might be employed in the event of a refusal to collaborate, and so on.

17 A.C.N.S.A.S., Informers archive, dossier 1589, vol. 1, p. 166.

18 A.C.N.S.A.S., Documents archive, dossier 13346, vol. 26, p. 132.

19 A.C.N.S.A.S., Network archive, dossier 118837, p. 65.

20 A.C.N.S.A.S., Informers archive, dossier 5189, vol. 1, p. 111.

21 The Varna World Gymnastics Championships were held in October 1974.

22 Roxana Maha, 'Fuga soţilor Károlyi în SUA sub umbrela securistului' (The Károlyis' defection to the U.S.A. under the umbrella of the Securitate officer), *Cotidianul*, 17 August 2007, https://www.hotnews.ro/stiri-arhiva-1039663-fuga-sotilor-Károly-sua-sub-umbrela-securistului.htm (retrieved 5 July 2020).

23 A.C.N.S.A.S., Informers archive, dossier 133808, p. 2.

24 A.C.N.S.A.S., Documents archive, dossier 13346, vol. 26, pp. 49 verso, 135.

25 Justin Gafiuc, 'Aflaţi cine este omul care i-a turnat la Securitate pe Károlyi şi Nadia' (Find out who was the man who informed on Károlyi and Nadia to the Securitate', *Gazeta Sporturilor*, 25 June 2009, https://www.gsp.ro/gsp-special/anchetele-gazetei/aflati-cine-este-omul-care-i-a-turnat-la-securitate-pe-Károly-si-nadia-144304.html (retrieved on 27 July 2020).

26 David Lease, TSL Interview, https://www. youtube.com/watch?v=BHmbPjuVEvk& feature=youtu.be&fbclid=IwAR2394NoteTh_HPSrvvHANGwX0kmeh0Su89cwvU2 yK0e22pcjs rlolUA 6Kfvfscn8Y (retrieved 27 July 2020).

27 Regarding Évelyne Nelet, the young Frenchwoman, the Oneşti Securitate reported: 'there are materials from which it results that she is interested in discovering highly detailed information about Romanian gymnastics and our gymnasts, particularly Nadia Comăneci. The informer met her at the World Champ. in Varna and over the course of 2 months she came to our country twice. (. . .) She is suspected and it may be believed that she has connections or relations with an espionage service' (A.C.N.S.A.S., Network Archive, dossier 118837, p. 110).

28 A.C.N.S.A.S., Network archive, dossier 118837, p. 79 verso.

29 A.C.N.S.A.S., Informers archive, dossier 133808, p. 3.

30 A.C.N.S.A.S., Network archive, dossier 19620.

31 A.C.N.S.A.S., Network archive, dossier 118837, p. 138 verso.

32 A.C.N.S.A.S., Network archive, dossier 13346, vol. 26, p. 472.

33 A.C.N.S.A.S., Network archive, dossier 13346, vol. 24, p. 139, vol. 26, p. 467.

34 A.C.N.S.A.S., Network archive, dossier 13346, vol. 34, p. 130.

35 A.C.N.S.A.S., Network archive, dossier 13346, vol. 26, p. 8–9.

36 A.C.N.S.A.S., Network archive, dossier 13346, vol. 26, p. 327.

37 A.C.N.S.A.S., Network archive, dossier 13346, vol. 26, pp. 317–18.

38 A.C.N.S.A.S., Network archive, dossier 118837, p. 74.

39 A.C.N.S.A.S., Informers archive, dossier 5189, vol. 1, pp. 165 and verso.

40 A.C.N.S.A.S., Documents archive, dossier 13346, vol. 5, p. 384.

41 A.C.N.S.A.S., Network archive, dossier 13346, vol. 10, p. 185.

42 A.C.N.S.A.S., Network archive, dossier 13346, vol. 5, p. 381 and verso.

43 A.C.N.S.A.S., Informers archive, dossier 5189, vol. 1, p. 163.

44 A.C.N.S.A.S., Informers archive, dossier 5189, vol. 1, p. 163.

45 A.C.N.S.A.S., Informers archive, dossier 5189, vol. 1, p. 164.

46 A.C.N.S.A.S., Documents archive, dossier 13346, vol. 26, p. 49 verso.

47 A.C.N.S.A.S., Documents archive, dossier 13346, vol. 26, p. 302.

48 A.C.N.S.A.S., Documents archive, dossier 13346, vol. 26, p. 170 verso.

49 A.C.N.S.A.S., Documents archive, dossier 13346, vol. 26, p. 565.

50 A.C.N.S.A.S., Documents archive, dossier 13346, vol. 26, p. 304.

51 See *Athlete A*, a Netflix documentary, produced by Bonni Cohen and Jon Shenk in 2020, and the podcast *Heavy Medals*.

52 The file number and date were added to the letter by the Securitate officer who processed the anonymous letter.

53 A.C.N.S.A.S., Documents archive, dossier 13346, vol. 26, pp. 333–4.

54 A.C.N.S.A.S., Documents archive, dossier 13346, vol. 26, pp. 331–2.

55 A.C.N.S.A.S., Documents archive, dossier 13346, vol. 26, p. 135.

56 A.C.N.S.A.S., Documents archive, dossier 13346, vol. 26, p. 133.

57 A.C.N.S.A.S., Documents archive, dossier 13346, vol. 26, p. 170.

58 A.C.N.S.A.S., Documents archive, dossier 13346, vol. 26, p. 231 verso.

59 Ioan Chirilă, p. 17.

60 See *The Annual of the Oneşti Physical Education Lycée*, 1969–970, Classes 1–11, in Ioana Adobricăi, Maria Pop, pp. 77–9.

61 A.C.N.S.A.S., Informers archive, dossier 5189, vol. 1, p. 81.

62 Interview with George Condovici, 12 June 2020.

63 Ioan Chirilă, p. 27.

64 https://themedalcount.com/2020/01/18/a-history-of-the-average-age-in-womens-gymnastics/ (retrieved 7 July 2020).

65 *Feel No Fear*, p. 39.

66 D. Dimitriu, p. 55.

67 NBC interview with Nadia Comăneci. https://www.youtube.com/watch?v=W5267w6VRPk (retrieved 7 July 2020).

68 Ioan Chirilă, p. 95.

69 See Ioan Drăgan's informer file, A.C.N.S.A.S., SIE archive, dossier 1387.

70 Ioan Drăgan, *Martor la 8 Olimpiade* (Witness to Eight Olympics), Bucharest: Editura Porus, 1992, p. 33.

71 Nicolae Vieru, p. 117.

72 A.C.N.S.A.S., Documents archive, dossier 13346, vol. 26, p. 178 verso.

73 Ioan Chirilă, p. 100.

74 Ioan Drăgan, p. 34.

75 Marin Dragnea (1923–2020), army general (reserves). Graduate of the School for Infantry Offices (1943–44), Special Infantry School (1947–48) and the K. E. Voroshilov Higher Academy of the Major General Staff (1952–54). From 1948 onward he was appointed to a number of political functions within the army: political locum tenens of the commander of the Third Battalion of the Third Battle Regiment (1947–48), political locum tenens of the Third Tank Brigade (1948) and the Ninth Tank Brigade (1949), political locum tenens of the Second Alpine Troops Division (1949–51), Commander of the First Alpine Troops Division (1951–52), Commander of the Fifth Infantry Division (1952), commander of the Fortieth Army Corps (1954–56), commander of the Thirty-Eighth Army Corps (1956–58), locum tenens of the commandant of the Third Military Region (1958–60) and of the Third Army (1960–69), commander of the Cluj Territorial Military Command (1969–73). From 1973 he was active in sport as deputy chairman (1973–74 and 1977–81) and chairman (1974–77 and 1981–84) of the N.C.P.E.S., chairman of the Romanian Olympic Committee (1973–82) and deputy minister of tourism and sport (1982–84).

76 Interview with Anca Grigoraş, 11 June 2020.

77 A.C.N.S.A.S., Documents archive, dossier 13346, vol. 26, p. 360.

78 A.C.N.S.A.S., Documents archive, dossier 13346, vol. 26, p. 353.

79 Mircea Cărbunaru, p. 5.

80 Michael Atkinson (ed.), *Battleground Sports*, vol. 1 (A-O), Westport: Greenwood Press, 2009, p. 116. Also see the Romanian Television documentary *Adevăruri despre trecut: Fabrica de 10 – Bătaia e ruptă din aur* [Truths about the Past: The Top Marks Factory – Corporal Punishment is Golden], minute 12.30 https://youtube.com/watch?v=FWtv-Skt718

81 A.C.N.S.A.S., Documents archive, dossier 13346, vol. 25, p. 274.

82 A.C.N.S.A.S., Informers archive, dossier 5189, vol. 1, p. 107.

83 Ioan Chirilă, p. 29.

84 A.C.N.S.A.S., Informers archive, dossier 5189, vol. 1, p. 178 verso.

85 Géza Pozsár provided details about such incidents in a report dated 5 October 1976, after the Olympic squad returned from Montréal. According to 'Nelu', 'before leaving for Montréal, there were violent arguments between Maria Simionescu and the Károlyis about training. A girl, Milea Luminiţa, ran away from training because of the harsh discipline imposed by Béla Károlyi. This discipline consisted in restricting the amount of food to a minimum and painstaking control of the schedule, plus a very high volume of work' (A.C.N.S.A.S., Network archive, dossier 118837, p. 59).

86 A.C.N.S.A.S., Documents archive, dossier 13346, vol. 5, p. 363–4.

87 A.C.N.S.A.S., Informers archive, dossier 5189, vol. 1, p. 77. Luminiţa Milea informed the author of this book that Béla Károlyi forced her to take off her plaster cast, which she did, 'but the next day Dr Bora came and when he saw me without the cast, he protested and sent me to the Sports Medicine Centre to have it put back on. I wore the plaster cast on my leg for another two weeks. When you were in plaster, it didn't mean you sat on the bench looking at the other girls, but you did whatever was possible . . . and it was possible. So, I would say that I didn't practice without a cast, but with a cast' (correspondence with Luminiţa Milea-Răileanu, 4 April 2022).

88 A.C.N.S.A.S., Informers archive, dossier 5189, vol. 1, p. 78.

89 A.C.N.S.A.S., Informers archive, dossier 5189, vol. 1, p. 78 verso.

90 A.C.N.S.A.S., Documents archive, dossier 13346, vol. 26, p. 285.

91 A.C.N.S.A.S., Documents archive, dossier 13346, vol. 26, p. 303 verso.

92 A.C.N.S.A.S., Network archive, dossier 431466, p. 7.

93 Ioan Chirilă, p. 64.

94 A.C.N.S.A.S., Documents archive, vol. 26, pp. 276, 285 verso.

95 A.C.N.S.A.S., Informers archive, dossier 264686, vol. 1, p. 2.

96 A.C.N.S.A.S., Network archive, dossier 431466.

97 A.C.N.S.A.S., Informers archive, dossier 134909.

98 A.C.N.S.A.S., Documents archive, dossier 13346, vol. 26, p. 171.

99 A.C.N.S.A.S., Network archive, dossier 120782, vol. 1, p. 10.

100 A.C.N.S.A.S., Network archive, dossier 120782, vol. 2., pp. 38–38v.

101 A.C.N.S.A.S., Network archive, dossier 118837, p. 69.

102 A.C.N.S.A.S., Network archive, dossier 431466, p. 8.

103 A.C.N.S.A.S., Documents archive, dossier 13346, vol. 26, p. 285 verso.

104 Carmen Dumitru, paediatrician, doctor of medical sciences, doctor of physical education medicine. From 1960 she was head of the laboratory and then director at the Sports Medicine Centre, Bucharest. She also taught in the Physical Education Medicine Department of the Medical Faculty of Bucharest University, the Medical Inspection Department of the Physical Education Institute, Bucharest, and the Pharmaceutical Medicine Institute.

105 A.C.N.S.A.S., Documents archive, dossier 13346, vol. 26, p. 524–525.

106 Sophia Jowett, Svenja Wachsmuth, 'Power in coach-athlete relationships. The case of women's artistic gymnastics', Roslyn Kerr, Natalie Barker-Ruchti, Carly Stewart and Gretchen Kerr (eds.), *Women's Artistic Gymnastics. Socio-cultural perspectives*, New York: Routledge, 2020.

107 Interview with Mariana Cojanu David, 9 July 2020.

108 A.C.N.S.A.S., Documents archive, dossier 13346, vol. 5, p. 404.

109 *Feel No Fear*, p. 9.

110 Interview with Mariana Cojanu David, 9 July 2020.

111 *Letters to a Young Gymnast*, p. 51.

112 Denis Grigorescu, interview with Géza Pozsár published in *Adevărul*, 'Nadia Comăneci a fost singura gimnastă care a scăpat nebătută de Béla Károlyi' (Nadia Comăneci was the only gymnast who escaped being beaten by Béla Károlyi'. https://adevarul.ro/international/statele-unite/ exclusiv-coregraful-Géza-poszarnadiacomaneci-fost-singura-gimnasta-scapat-nebatuta-Béla-Károlyi-1_5f1ae40a5163ec4271514ebd/index.html (retrieved 2 August 2020).

Chapter 4

1 A.C.N.S.A.S., Documents archive, dossier 13346, vol. 26, p. 420.

2 Nicolae Vieru, p. 117.

3 A.C.N.S.A.S., Documents archive, dossier 13346, vol. 24, pp. 281–2.

4 A.C.N.S.A.S., Documents archive, dossier 13346, vol. 26, pp. 551–60.

5   A.C.N.S.A.S., Documents archive, dossier 13346, vol. 26, pp. 561–5.

6   A.C.N.S.A.S., Documents archive, dossier 13346, vol. 26, p. 420.

7   A.C.N.S.A.S., Documents archive, dossier 13346, vol. 26, p. 419.

8   *Feel No Fear*, pp. 71, 73.

9   *Letters to a Young Gymnast*, p. 57.

10 *Letters to a Young Gymnast*, p. 65.

11 A.C.N.S.A.S., Documents archive, dossier 13346, vol. 26, p. 3.

12 A.C.N.S.A.S., Informers archive, dossier 5189, vol. 1, p. 78.

13 A.C.N.S.A.S., Documents archive, dossier 13346, vol. 5, p. 370.

14 A.C.N.S.A.S., Informers archive, dossier 5189, vol. 1, p. 137.

15 A.C.N.S.A.S., Documents archive, dossier 13346, vol. 26, pp. 301–2.

16 Mircea Cărbunaru, p. 5.

17 A.C.N.S.A.S., Documents archive, dossier 13346, vol. 26, p. 42.

18 A.C.N.S.A.S., Documents archive, dossier 13346, vol. 26, pp. 572–4.

19 A.C.N.S.A.S., Network archive, dossier 118837, p. 59.

20 A.C.N.S.A.S., Informers archive, dossier 5189, vol. 1, pp. 150–3.

21 A.C.N.S.A.S., Documents archive, dossier 13346, vol. 26, p. 303 and vol. 5. p. 371.

22 According to a report filed by Department One at the beginning of October 1976, 'the father of gymnast Gabor Georgeta, removed from the squad by coach Károlyi Béla, signalled that he does not understand why the organs of the Militia talked to his daughter and examined the notebook in which she writes down her personal problems. Furthermore, they asked whether his daughter intends to remain abroad illegally' (A.C.N.S.A.S., Documents archive, dossier 13346, vol. 5, p. 381).

23 A.C.N.S.A.S., Documents archive, dossier 13346, vol. 26, p. 303.

24 A.C.N.S.A.S., Informers archive, dossier 5189, vol. 1, p. 46.

25 A.C.N.S.A.S., Informers archive, dossier 5189, vol. 2, pp. 386–386v.

26 A.C.N.S.A.S., Informers archive, dossier 5189, vol. 2, p. 385–385v.

27 A.C.N.S.A.S., Documents archive, dossier 13346, vol. 26, p. 319.

28 A.C.N.S.A.S., Documents archive, dossier 13346, vol. 5, p. 381.

29 A.C.N.S.A.S., Documents archive, dossier 13346, vol. 26, p. 303.

30 A.C.N.S.A.S., Documents archive, dossier 13346, vol. 26, p. 304.

31 *Sportul*, 28 October 1976, Year 332, No. 8394.

32 *Sportul*, 9 November 1976, Year 32, No. 8403.

33 *Sportul*, 2 October 1976, Year 32, No. 8376; *Sportul*, 6 November 1976, Year 32, No. 8401.

34 Virgiliu Radulian, deputy minister of education (1968–71), chairman of the national Pioneers Organisation (1968–75) and director of the Institute of Pedagogical and Psychological Research (1975–82).

35 On 14–15 December, Nadia Comăneci was invited to London by the BBC to be awarded the trophy for best sportsperson of the year. Given her tense relationship with Béla Károlyis, she was accompanied by Nicolae Vieru rather than her coach.

36 The finals of the National Championship and the Romania Cup, held in Cluj on 17–19 December 1976.

37 A.C.N.S.A.S., Documents archive, dossier 13346 vol. 26, pp. 283–284v.

38 A.C.N.S.A.S., Documents archive, dossier 13346 vol. 26, pp. 267–270.

39 A.C.N.S.A.S., Documents archive, dossier 13346 vol. 26, p. 265 verso.

40 A.C.N.S.A.S., Documents archive, dossier 13346 vol. 26, pp. 259–259v.

41 A.C.N.S.A.S., Informers archive, dossier 5189 vol. 2, p. 371.

42 A.C.N.S.A.S., Documents archive, dossier 13346 vol. 26, pp. 241–6.

43 A.C.N.S.A.S., Documents archive, dossier 13346, vol. 5, pp. 340–340 v.

44 Part of the Mercury Foreign Trade Enterprise, subordinate to the Ministry of Foreign Trade. During the Communist period, Mercury shops sold various imported consumer products, from food to shoes, clothes and hunting rifles.

45 A Securitate officer noted in the margin next to Károlyi's claim about the search of his apartment, 'None of it is true' (A.C.N.S.A.S., Informers archive, dossier 5189, vol. 1, p. 58).

46 A.C.N.S.A.S., Documents archive, dossier 13346 vol. 5, pp. 340–340v.

47 A.C.N.S.A.S., Documents archive, dossier 13346 vol. 26, pp. 234–234v; A.C.N.S.A.S., Network archive, dossier 118837, p. 44.

48 A.C.N.S.A.S., Documents archive, dossier 13346 vol. 26, p. 207.

49 Physical education teacher Ilie Istrate was recruited as an agent in November 1951 and given the code name 'Carter', but because of poor health he was dropped in 1954. In the mid-1960s he was under surveillance because of his connection with foreign citizens suspected of carrying out espionage for Holland (A.C.N.S.A.S., Network archive, dossier 101518 and Informers archive, dossier 433646).

50 A.C.N.S.A.S., Documents archive, dossier 13346 vol. 265 p. 353.

51 A.C.N.S.A.S., Documents archive, dossier 13346 vol. 26, p. 211.

52 A.C.N.S.A.S., Documents archive, dossier 13346 vol. 26, p. 27.

53 A.C.N.S.A.S., Documents archive, dossier 13346 vol. 26, p. 360.

54 A.C.N.S.A.S., Documents archive, dossier 13346 vol. 26, pp. 371, 428.

55 A.C.N.S.A.S., Documents archive, dossier 13346 vol. 26, p. 166.

56 A.C.N.S.A.S., Documents archive, dossier 13346 vol. 26, p. 505.

57 Ioan Drăgan.

58 A.C.N.S.A.S., Documents archive, dossier 13346 vol. 26, p. 28.

59 A.C.N.S.A.S., Documents archive, dossier 13346 vol. 26, p. 429.

60 A.C.N.S.A.S., Documents archive, dossier 13346 vol. 26, p. 43.

61 *Feel No Fear*, p. 73.

62 A.C.N.S.A.S., Informers archive, dossier 5189 vol. 1, p. 40. See also the interview with David Lease.

63 In the report, Nadia Comăneci is referred to as 'the objective' or 'Ob.' and Teodora Ungureanu as 'T'.

64 CBS, which in association with Romanian Television produced the documentary *Nadia — With Love From Romania*, directed by Dick Foster and Sterling Johnson.

65 Flip Wilson, a famous American comedian, the host of the *Flip Wilson Show*.

66 In a report dated 22 December 1976, Securitate Captain Niolae Ilie states, 'one of the members of the American film crew that filmed the Olympic team of the Romanian S.R., during filming gave as a present a gold bracelet to gymnast Nadia Comăneci. A scene that that they recorded on film, at the intervention of the Romanian side it was destroyed. When coach Béla Károlyi heard that Nadia had received this bracelet he intervened in a completely unacceptable way, forcing Nadia to give back the bracelet, claiming that she wasn't allowed to receive such gifts. These aspects unpleasantly surprised the American delegation, all the more so when subsequently they offered Béla Károlyi a Polaroid camera which he accepted without comment. In the final part of the American team's stay in Oneşti the coach did not allow them to say goodbye to Nadia, claiming that she had her leg in plaster, which wasn't true, since during a school break they had seen Nadia running in the school yard' (A.C.N.S.A.S., Documents archive, dossier 13346, vol. 26, p. 277).

67 Ştefania Comăneci unsuccessfully laid claim to the sum of ten thousand dollars. In his memoirs, Nicolae Vieru gives the following account: 'After the tournament in America at a celebratory meal in New York, I received from the American federation a cheque for ten thousand dollars for Nadia. According to the rules of amateur sport, she wasn't allowed to receive the money, so the cheque was made out to the federation. I surrendered it in Romania, but it didn't go to Nadia, despite her mother's insistence, which resulted in a scandal and the cancellation of the U.S.A. tournament in 1979' (Nicolae Vieru, p. 137).

68 Source 'Lily' told Nicolae Ilie: 'Throughout the trip to Spain, coach Károlyi Béla was harsh in his behaviour to the gymnasts and to Nadia Comăneci and Teodora Ungureanu in particular. In this respect he hit Nadia while she was having her body weight checked and seeing she was 42.5 kg he told her she had to lose 1 kg. In the opinion of the source 42.5 kg was the optimum weight. He hit Teodora Ungureanu during training, when she performed a figure incorrectly, which caused her to cry for 3 hours. This situation caused the 2 gymnasts to declare to the source that after the European Championships [of May 1977] that they wouldn't work with coach Károlyi Béla any more' (A.C.N.S.A.S., Documents archive, dossier 13346, vol. 5 p. 339.

69 At the time it had been decided that Nadia Comăneci should train in Bucharest with Iosif Hidi, Gheorghe Condovici and Atanasia Albu.

70 A.C.N.S.A.S., Documents archive, dossier 13346, vol. 26, pp. 417–21.

71 A.C.N.S.A.S., Informers archive, dossier 5189, vol. 1, p. 50.

72 A.C.N.S.A.S., Documents archive, dossier 13346, vol. 26, p. 206 verso.

73 A.C.N.S.A.S., Documents archive, dossier 13346, vol. 26, p. 207.

74 A.C.N.S.A.S., Informers archive, dossier 5189, vol. 1, p. 45

75 Nicolae Vieru, p. 105.

76 Nadia Comăneci was to open the competition on the beam and was the last in the floor exercise, although each gymnast's place in the rankings was perfectly well known. This might suggest a fix on the part of the judges, in order to make their calculations the easier in the event that they decided to mark down Nadia in favour of other gymnasts.

77 A.C.N.S.A.S., Documents archive, dossier 13346, vol. 26, p. 354.

78 *Letters to a Young Gymnast*, p. 61.

79 Nicolae Vieru, p. 106.

80 Nicolae Vieru, pp. 106–7.

81 *Feel No Fear*, p. 69.

82 A.C.N.S.A.S., Documents archive, dossier 13346, vol. 26, p. 207.

83 A.C.N.S.A.S., Documents archive, dossier 13346, vol. 26, p. 212–212v.

84 *Letters to a Young Gymnast*, p. 62.

85 A.C.N.S.A.S., Documents archive, dossier 13346, vol. 26, p. 504.

86 The Romanian delegation brought a number of objections to the knowledge of the organisers of the European Championships in Prague. These were to do with not only with the way in which the scores were altered in the vault contest. For example, they objected to Ellen Berger's decision to withdraw Maria Simionescu from the judging panels of major international competitions on the grounds that the first deputy chairwoman of the Women's Technical Commission could not also be a judge. Likewise, she neglected to include her in the jury of the Prague European Championships, and she was reinstated only after the R.G.F. protested to the F.I.G. They criticised the manner in which lots were drawn, as well as the decision to remove from the judging panels representatives from Spain, Belgium, the United Kingdom and Portugal, who were known not to be influenced by the Soviet Union or the Communist bloc countries. At the same time, the panel for the uneven parallel bars was made up of judges from the German Democratic Republic (Sylvia Hlavacek), Czechoslovakia (Alena Prorocova), Holland (Leni Lens) and Austria (Grete Doeber), who were deemed hostile to Romania's gymnasts and were biased towards those of the U.S.S.R. and other Communist bloc countries. Not least, they condemned a number of judging guidelines to the effect that new elements presented at the Montréal Games were no longer to be considered new at the Prague European Championships.

87 Nicolae Vieru, p. 108.

88 *Sportul*, 16 May 1977, Year 33, No. 8553.

89 A.C.N.S.A.S., Documents archive, dossier 13346, vol. 26, pp. 215–21.

90 See the telegram from the U.S. embassy in Bucharest sent to Washington, Moscow, Berlin, Belgrade, Budapest, Prague, Sofia, Warsaw and Munich. https://aad.archives.gov/aad/createpdf?rid=1119 00&dt=2532&dl=1629 (retrieved 8 September 2020).

91 A.C.N.S.A.S., Documents archive, dossier 13346, vol. 26, p. 213.

92 A.N.I.C., National Council for Physical Education and Sport archive, dossier 345/1956, p. 30.

93 A.N.I.C., National Council for Physical Education and Sport archive, dossier 345/1956, p. 23.

94 Georgia Cervin, 'Gymnasts are Not Merely Circus Phenomena; Influences on the Development of Women's Artistic Gymnastics During the 1970s', *International Journal of the History of Sport*, 2016, p. 10.

95 Associate Press, 'U.S. Gymnastics Officials Level Charges', *St Petersburg Times* (Florida), 24 July 1976, quoted in Georgia Cervin, p. 10.

96 A.C.N.S.A.S., Informers archive, dossier 18002, vol. 1, p. 88.

97 A.C.N.S.A.S., Documents archive, dossier 13346, vol. 5, pp. 372–3.

98 A.C.N.S.A.S., Documents archive, dossier 13346, vol. 26, p. 376.

99 A.C.N.S.A.S., Documents archive, dossier 13346, vol. 26, p. 375.

100 A.C.N.S.A.S., Network archive, dossier 118837, p. 99.

101 A.C.N.S.A.S., Documents archive, dossier 13346, vol. 5, pp. 377, 385 verso.

102 A.C.N.S.A.S., Documents archive 13346, vol. 34, pp. 111–12 and vol. 10, p. 187.

103 *Feel No Fear*, p. 60.

104 David Lease interview.

105 A.C.N.S.A.S., Documents archive, dossier 13346, vol. 26, p. 265.

106 Georgia Cervin, p. 11.

107 *Sportul*, 16 May 1977, Year 33, No. 8553.

108 A.C.N.S.A.S., Documents archive, dossier 13346, vol. 5, p. 385.

109 A.C.N.S.A.S., Documents archive, dossier 13346, vol. 5, p. 447.

110 A.C.N.S.A.S., Informers archive, dossier 18002, vol. 1, p. 15.

111 According to the coaches of the Romanian squad at that time, the Securitate suspected Yuri Titov of being an undercover K.G.B. agent, holding the rank of colonel, but was unable to obtain evidence to support this.

112 A.C.N.S.A.S., Documents archive, dossier 13346, vol. 5, pp. 402–3.

113 A.C.N.S.A.S., Documents archive, dossier 13346, vol. 26, p. 496.

114 A.C.N.S.A.S., Documents archive, dossier 13346, vol. 26, p. 207 verso.

115 A.C.N.S.A.S., Informers archive, dossier 1035, vol. 1, p. 17 verso.

116 A.C.N.S.A.S., Informers archive, dossier 1035, vol. 1, p. 17–17 verso.

117 A.C.N.S.A.S., Documents archive, dossier 13346, vol. 26, p. 212 verso.

118 Nicolae Vieru, pp. 108–9.

119 A.C.N.S.A.S., Documents archive, dossier 13346, vol. 5, p. 313.

120 A.C.N.S.A.S., Documents archive, dossier 13346, vol. 5, pp. 327–9 verso.

121 A.C.N.S.A.S., Documents archive, dossier 13346, vol. 5, pp. 311–13.

Chapter 5

1 In 1987, Gheorghe Condovici, gymnastics trainer at the Ministry of National Defence's Steaua Club, holding the rank of major, defected from Romania. On the morning of 25 October, while taking part as a judge at the World Championships in Rotterdam, he vanished from the hotel where the Romanian delegation was staying. He subsequently settled in West Germany. He was placed under criminal investigation in Romania, but given the events of December 1989, he was not brought to trial or convicted (A.C.N.S.A.S., Penal archive, dossier 59503).

2 A.C.N.S.A.S., Documents archive, dossier 13346, vol. 26, p. 32.

3 A.N.I.C., National Council for Physical Education and Sport archive, dossier 553/1958, p. 90.

4 A.C.N.S.A.S., Documents archive, dossier 13346, vol. 26, p. 5 verso.

5 A.C.N.S.A.S., Documents archive, dossier 13346, vol. 26, pp. 25–25v.

6 A.C.N.S.A.S., Documents archive, dossier 13346, vol. 26, p. 405.

7 A.C.N.S.A.S., Network archive, dossier 46446.

8 For further details on the professional career of Dr Carmen Dumitru, see the collection of interviews published by Maria Oprea, *Culoarul campionilor* (The Hall of Champions), Bucharest: Editura Amaltea, 2003.

9 This seems to have been an exaggeration on the part of witnesses from the time. But the Securitate did have a plan that sprang into action whenever Nadia Comăneci ran away from the sport complex: 'In the event that she leaves the training centre without permission, she will try to reach acquaintances in Bucharest, Focşani, Oneşti, Oradea, Piteşti, or Deva. To go elsewhere in the country, she might take the train or hitch a ride in a car from the Colentina Avenue.' The document gives the names of all the persons with whom she might hide and their addresses, including Benone Sinulescu and Irina Loghin (A.C.N.S.A.S., Documents archive, dossier 13346, vol. 26, pp. 18–19).

10 Interview with Gheorghe Condovici, 12 June 2020.

11 A.C.N.S.A.S., Documents archive, dossier 13346, vol. 26, p. 378.

12 Interview with Carmen Dumitru, 20 October 2020.

13 A.C.N.S.A.S., Documents archive, dossier 13346, vol. 5, pp. 314–15.

14 A.C.N.S.A.S., Documents archive, dossier 13346, vol. 26, p. 478.

15 Kurt-Walter Szilier, member of the Dinamo Bucharest club, rank of lieutenant, member of the men's Olympic squad. On 15 October 1982 he was sent with gymnast Dimitrie Valentin Sîrbu to West Germany to take part in an international competition, but they both failed to return when they were due to on 25 October 1982. On 9 November, they were placed under criminal investigation, accused of desertion among other things. In March 1983, Szilier was sentenced in absentia to five years and ten months imprisonment (A.C.N.S.A.S., Penal archive, dossier 115234).

16 A.C.N.S.A.S., Documents archive, dossier 13346, vol. 26, p. 460.

17 A.C.N.S.A.S., Documents archive, dossier 13346, vol. 26, p. 6.

18 A.C.N.S.A.S., Documents archive, dossier 13346, vol. 26, p. 478.

19 The international gymnastics contest held in Shanghai on 17–18 June 1978, at which Romania was represented by Nadia Comăneci, Marilena Neacşu, Angela Bratu, Carmen Savu, Dumitriţa Turner, Rodica Dunca, Mirela Oancea, Anca Grigoraş and Dan Grecu, Ion Checicheş, Nicolae Operescu, Kurt Szilier, Radu Branea, Romulus Bucuroiu, Gabriel Popescu. Although Atanasia Albu suggests in her report that Nadia Comăneci and the Romanian team were victorious at the contest, in reality the Chinese team was the winner, with Nadia taking part only in the team events (9.95 on the beam, 9.90 on the vault, uneven parallel bars and floor exercise). In the apparatus events, Chinese gymnasts Liu Ya-chun and Chu-Cheng won gold and silver, while Anca Grigoraş won bronze.

20 A.C.N.S.A.S., Informers archive, dossier 18002, vol. 1, p. 54.

21 A.C.N.S.A.S., Documents archive, dossier 13346, vol. 26, p. 386.

22 A.C.N.S.A.S., Documents archive, dossier 13346, vol. 26, pp. 440–440v.

23 *Letters to a Young Gymnast*, pp. 66–7.

24 Although presented as an autobiography, *My Own Story* was written by Graham Buxton Smither after obtaining permission in 1978 to interview Nadia Comăneci. Since he had promoted Romanian gymnastics throughout the world, Buxton Smither was well liked by Maria Simionescu and Nicolae Vieru, and the Romanian Gymnastics Federation agreed to his proposal to write the book. Nadia Comăneci did not know about the details of his plan. As a photo-reporter, Buxton Smither had also worked with the Romanian press, but he was monitored by the Securitate whenever he visited the country. The international press said of the book that it was 'written with bitterness, if not even spite' (*Le Figaro*): 'This book in any event fits in with a Romanian Gymnastics Federation campaign to blacken the names of the Károlyis, who defected to the United States last year' (A.C.N.S.A.S., Documents archive, dossier 13346, vol. 34, p. 143).

25 *Nadia. My Own Story*, pp. 47–8.

26 *Scînteia Tineretului*, 21 November 1981, Year 36, Series 2, No. 10105.

27 A.C.N.S.A.S., Documents archive, dossier 13346, vol. 24, pp. 260–260v and vol. 1, p. 331.

28 A.C.N.S.A.S., Documents archive, dossier 13346, vol. 24, pp. 253–253v.

29 A.C.N.S.A.S., Documents archive, dossier 13346, vol. 24, p. 261 verso.

30 Correspondence with Graham Buxton Smither (1 August 2022).

31 Interview with David Lease.

32 Nicolae Vieru, p. 30.

33 Ministry of Foreign Affairs Central to Paris Embassy, telegram no. 2/03454/8 May 1984 (Diplomatic Archive of the Ministry of Foreign Affairs, France 1984 archive, dossier 639, p. 2.

34 Quoted in https://www.latimes.com/archives/la-xpm-1990-02-19-sp-869-story.html (retrieved 28 September 2020).

35 *The Magic and Mystery of Nadia* was a gymnastics demonstration broadcast on ABC in 1990. The show was choreographed by Paul Ziert and it marked Nadia Comăneci's first appearance in the U.S. media since her escape from Romania, as well as her first reunion with Béla Károlyi on American soil.

36 Bart Conner interview with Nadia Comăneci for *The Magic and Mystery of Nadia*, ABC Sports, www.youtube.com/watch?v=IV-fiGyub XM (retrieved 28 September 2020).

37 See the reports written by Dr Valeriu Cazan, Captain Nicolae Ilie, and informer Maria Simionescu, A.C.N.S.A.S., Documents archive, dossier 13346, vol. 26, pp. 375–377v, 389–90.

38 A.C.N.S.A.S., Documents archive, dossier 13346, vol. 26, pp. 17–19, 21–2.

39 A.C.N.S.A.S., Documents archive, dossier 13346, vol. 5, p. 281 verso.

40 A.C.N.S.A.S., Documents archive, dossier 13346, vol. 26, p. 394.

41 A.C.N.S.A.S., Documents archive, dossier 13346, vol. 26, p. 387.

42 A.C.N.S.A.S., Documents archive, dossier 13346, vol. 26, pp. 389–90.

43 A.C.N.S.A.S., Documents archive, dossier 13346, vol. 26, pp. 384–5.

44 A.C.N.S.A.S., Documents archive, dossier 13346, vol. 26, p. 395.

45 A.C.N.S.A.S., Documents archive, dossier 13346, vol. 26, p. 21 verso.

46 A.C.N.S.A.S., Network archive, dossier 118837, p. 5.

47 A.C.N.S.A.S., Documents archive, dossier 13346, vol. 26, p. 150.

48 *Feel No Fear*, p. 75.

49 *Feel No Fear*, p. 76.

50 Not long thereafter, the Romanian Gymnastics Federation decided to train the women's gymnastics squad in Deva. From 1973 to 1982, the head of the school was Mihai Bănulescu, regarded as the Securitate as a member of the Károlyis' circle: 'From the existing information it transpires that Béla Károlyi used him for personal ends in solving domestic and recreational problems. Despite this he did not regard him as close' (A.C.N.S.A.S., Documents archive, dossier 13346, vol. 5, p. 52).

51 *Sportul*, 4 February 1978, Year 34, No. 8776.

52 A.C.N.S.A.S., Informers archive, dossier 5189, vol. 2, p. 349.

53 John Barr and Dan Murphy, *Start by Believing. Larry Nassar's Crimes, the Institutions that Enabled Him, and the Brave Women Who Stopped a Monster*, New York: Hachette Books, 2020, p. 26.

54 Information about the Károlyis' abuses was made public by Emilia Eberle (Trudi Kollar) in 2008 in an interview with KCRA, a Sacramento television channel. See also Episode One of the Heavy Medals podcast: https://30for30podcasts.com/heavy-medals/

55 A.C.N.S.A.S., Documents archive, dossier 13346, vol. 24, pp. 47–8.

56 A.C.N.S.A.S., Documents archive, dossier 13346, vol. 26, pp. 146–7.

57 A.C.N.S.A.S., Documents archive, dossier 13346, vol. 26, pp. 380–2.

58 *Sportul*, 16 September 1978, Year 34, No. 8965.

59 *Sportul*, 7 September 1978, Year 34, No. 8957.

60 *Feel No Fear*, p. 83.

61 *Letters to a Young Gymnast*, p. 68.

62 A.C.N.S.A.S., Documents archive, dossier 13346, vol. 26, p. 379.

63 A.C.N.S.A.S., Informers archive, dossier 18002, vol. 1, p. 56–7.

64 A.C.N.S.A.S., Documents archive, dossier 13346, vol. 26, p. 514.

65 A.C.N.S.A.S., Documents archive, dossier 13346, vol. 26, p. 379.

66 A.C.N.S.A.S., Informers archive, dossier 5189, vol. 1, p. 27.

67 A.C.N.S.A.S., Informers archive, dossier 5189, vol. 2, p. 229.

68 A.C.N.S.A.S., Informers archive, dossier 5189, vol. 2, p. 224–8.

69 A.C.N.S.A.S., Documents archive, dossier 13346, vol. 26, p. 145.

70 A.C.N.S.A.S., Informers archive, dossier 5189, vol. 2, p. 224–228v.

71 See the commentaries of Jim McKay and David Hartman for ABC Sports: https://www.youtube.com/watch?v =PRLe EU5Ix9c (retrieved 15 October 2020). During a commentary for ABC Sports in 1978 Cathy Rigby also mentioned rumours that Teodora Ungureanu and Nadia Comăneci had not trained with Béla Károlyi for a time due to 'misunderstandings': https://www.youtube.com/watch?v=CcZD8y6c-tw (retrieved 15 October 2020).

72 The author refers to the order in which the gymnasts entered during the compulsory and the optional exercises, which was established by the trainer. It is known that due to subjectivity, the judges awarded the first gymnasts to enter lower scores, while the final contestant were marked less severely. In this particular case, according to Nicolae Vieru, Nadia Comăneci was initially placed by Béla Károlyi among the first gymnasts from the Romanian team to enter. In the finals on the apparatuses, the order is picked by lot. Nicolae Vieru's claim is backed up by Captain Nicolae Ilie, part of the Romanian delegation to Strasbourg, under the cover of being a sports trainer from the Romanian Olympic Committee. In the report he wrote on returning to Romania, Ilie claimed: 'Within the women's gymnastics squad there was a mood favourable to a world-class competition, with the exception of the participation in this contest of gymnast Nadia Comăneci, who because of her body weight did not succeed in realising complete training at the level of the team. There were discussions regarding the order of the gymnasts in the team, with Béla Károlyi favouring Emilia Eberle over gymnast Nadia Comăneci (A.C.N.S.A.S., Documents archive, dossier 13346, vol. 5, pp. 465–6).

73 Nicolae Vieru, p. 64.

74 *Sportul*, 25 October 1978, Year 34, No. 8998.

75 A.C.N.S.A.S., Documents archive, dossier 13346, vol. 5, p. 425.

76 A.C.N.S.A.S., Documents archive, dossier 13346, vol. 5, pp. 424–5.

77 *Sportul*, 30 October 1978, Year 34, No. 9002, and 1 November 1978, Year 34, No. 9004.

78 *Letters to a Young Gymnast*, p. 74.

79 A.C.N.S.A.S., Informers archive, dossier 5189, vol. 2, pp. 212–13.

80 See Bob Ottum, 'The Search for Nadia', *Vault. Sports Illustrated*, 19 November 1979, https://vault. si.com/vault/1979/11/19/the-search-for-nadia-the-author-plunges-into-the-mists-of-transylvania-in-quest-of-the-worlds-favorite-gymnast-nadia-comaneci-she-had-been-perfect-then-she-had-faded-from-view-now-it-develops-there-is-a-new-nadia (retrieved 18 October 2020).

81 *Sportul*, 2 December 1978, Year 34, No. 9031.

82 Béla Károlyi liked to call Nadia Comaneci 'Grigore' (a boy's name) when he was pleased with her.

83 A.C.N.S.A.S., Informers archive, dossier 5189, vol. 2, pp. 217–18.

84 A.C.N.S.A.S., Informers archive, dossier 5189, vol. 2, p. 211.

85 Nicolae Vieru, p. 119.

86 A.C.N.S.A.S., Documents archive, dossier 13346, vol. 26, pp. 116–17.

87 A.C.N.S.A.S., Documents archive, dossier 13346, vol. 26, pp. 437–8.

88 A.C.N.S.A.S., Informers archive, dossier 5189, vol. 2, p. 204.

89 A.C.N.S.A.S., Informers archive, dossier 5189, vol. 2, p. 172 verso.

90 A.C.N.S.A.S., Informers archive, dossier 5189, vol. 2, p. 292–3 verso.

91 Major Dumitru Iovan of Deva Securitate.

92 A.C.N.S.A.S., Informers archive, dossier 5189, vol. 2, p. 99.

93 A.C.N.S.A.S., Documents archive, dossier 13346, vol. 26, p. 6 bis verso.

94 Interview with Gheorghe Condovici, 12 June 2020.

95 A.C.N.S.A.S., Informers archive, dossier 5189, vol. 2, p. 212 verso.

96 *Sportul*, 19 January 1979, Year 35, No. 9070.

97 A.C.N.S.A.S., Documents archive, dossier 13346, vol. 26, p. 379 verso.

98 A.C.N.S.A.S., Documents archive, dossier 13346, vol. 26, p. 484.

99 Since then, only Russian gymnast Svetlana Khorkina has repeated this performance.

100 A.C.N.S.A.S., Informers archive, dossier 5189, vol. 2, p. 153–153v.

101 *Sportul*, 15 May 1979, Year 35, No. 9167.

102 A.C.N.S.A.S., Documents archive, dossier 13346, vol. 26, p. 10–11.

103 Nicolae Vieru, p. 65.

104 *Feel No Fear*, p. 88.

105 *Feel No Fear*, p. 90.

106 Nicolae Vieru, p. 66.

107 *Letters to a Young Gymnast*, p. 87.

108 A.C.N.S.A.S., Informers archive, dossier 5189, vol. 2, p. 93 verso.

109 A.C.N.S.A.S., Informers archive, dossier 5189, vol. 2, p. 89 verso.

110 A.C.N.S.A.S., Informers archive, dossier 5189, vol. 2, p. 87.

111 *Letters to a Young Gymnast*, p. 86.

112 A.C.N.S.A.S., Informers archive, dossier 5189, vol. 1, pp. 19–20.

113 A.C.N.S.A.S., Documents archive, dossier 13346, vol. 29, p. 151 verso.

114 A.C.N.S.A.S., Documents archive, dossier 13346, vol. 26, p. 128.

115 A.C.N.S.A.S., Documents archive, dossier 13346, vol. 26, pp. 123–30.

116 The code name for Béla Károly in Securitate surveillance files.

117 A.C.N.S.A.S., Informers archive, dossier 5189, vol. 2, pp. 253–8.

118 A.C.N.S.A.S., Informers archive, dossier 5189, vol. 2, pp. 87, 91, 93v.

119 A.C.N.S.A.S., Documents archive, dossier 13346, vol. 26, p. 130.

120 A.C.N.S.A.S., Documents archive, dossier 13346, vol. 5, p. 392.

121 A.C.N.S.A.S., Informers archive, dossier 163281, vol. 1, pp. 8–9.

122 The code name for Géza Pozsár in Securitate covert surveillance documents.

123 A.C.N.S.A.S., dossier 5189, vol. 2, pp. 75–75v.

124 A.C.N.S.A.S., dossier 5189, vol. 2, pp. 60–3.

125 A.C.N.S.A.S., dossier 18002, vol. 1, pp. 57–8.

126 A.C.N.S.A.S., dossier 18002, vol. 1, p. 64 verso.

Chapter 6

1 Mircea Bibire, gymnastics coach, former political prisoner. While a pupil in lycée, he was caught up 'in a group of pupils reading books of a subversive nature' and 'sentenced to three years of correctional imprisonment.' He was recruited by Bacău County Securitate after his release in September 1950, subsequently dropped, and recruited once more in 1979. His reports, signed 'Liceanu' and 'Stanciu Mircea', focused on the group of trainers in Oneşti, particularly Gheorghe Gorgoi, who used to make what were considered 'hostile' political remarks (A.C.N.S.A.S., Network archive, dossier 428414).

2   A.C.N.S.A.S., Network archive, dossier 428414, vol. 2, p. 22.

3   A.C.N.S.A.S., Documents archive, dossier 13346, vol. 5, pp. 375–6.

4   Richard E. Appleman, businessman, sports promoter, founder of Applesports, Inc., a sports marketing company. With the support of the United States Gymnastics Federation, Appleman's company organised numerous demonstration tours of the United States by international Olympics squads, including those from the U.S.S.R. and Romania.

5   Ovidiu Ploscaru, Romanian diplomat in Washington from 1970 to 1978. The Securitate suspected him of having a close relationship with F.B.I. agents. He settled in the United States in the 1990s.

6   Telegram from Washington No. 083 816, 28 March 1976, 01.00 hours (AMAE, encrypted Telegrams archive, entries, Washington, 1976, vol. 2, pp. 42–3). My thanks to Ciprian Niţulescu for pointing out this document.

7   David Lease interview.

8   Tournament for senior gymnasts from the Communist bloc, whereas the Friendship Cup was for juniors.

9   A.C.N.S.A.S., Network archive, dossier 428414, vol. 3, p. 17.

10 A.C.N.S.A.S., Documents archive, dossier 13346, vol. 5, p 451.

11 I.e. the Skien European Championships of 1975.

12 A.C.N.S.A.S., Informers archive, dossier 5189, vol. 2, p. 217.

13 Ioan Drăgan, p. 44.

14 In December 1979, after the invasion of Afghanistan, Jimmy Carter declared that Soviet military action was a grave breach of international rules and demanded an immediate withdrawal, otherwise there would be serious consequences to the relationship between the two superpowers. A few months later, Carter made the decision to boycott the Olympics, taking a more aggressive stance towards the Soviet Union and making a clear statement that Soviet foreign policy, particularly the invasion of Afghanistan, could not be tolerated by the international community. The U.S. President also demanded that the games be moved to Greece, a proposal rejected by the International Olympic Committee.

15 Sputnik, No. 7, 1980. Route of the torch passed through Greece, Bulgaria, Romania and the U.S.S.R.

16 See telegram from Bucharest no. 1/06350, 22 July 1980 (AMAE, Encrypted telegrams archive, outgoing, Bucharest, January-October 1980, vol. 1, p. 357) and telegram from Moscow no. 051 347, 25 July 1980 (AMAE, Encrypted telegrams archive, incoming, Moscow, July-September 1980, vol. 6, p. 79).

17 Interview with Gheorghe Gorgoi, 27 October 2020.

18 A.C.N.S.A.S., Informers archive, dossier 18002, vol. 1, p. 98 verso.

19 A.C.N.S.A.S., Documents archive, dossier 13346, vol. 1, pp. 260–3, 282, and vol. 22, pp. 149–50.

20 Telegram from Moscow no. 051 311, 21 July 1980, 23.30 hours (AMAE, Encrypted telegrams archive, incoming, Moscow, July-September 1980, vol. 6, p. 23).

21 *Letters to a Young Gymnast*, pp. 99–100.

22 *Letters to a Young Gymnast*, p. 102.

23 *Sportul*, 26 July 1980, Year 35, No. 9536.

24 David Lease interview.

25 Barush Hazan, *Olympic Sports and Propaganda Games. Moscow 1980*, New Brunswick, N.J.: Transaction Books, 1982, p. 194.

26 Telegram from Moscow no. 051 398, 3 August 1980, 14.00 hours (AMAE, Encrypted telegrams archive, incoming, Moscow, July-September 1980, vol. 6, p. 158).

27 Telegram from Moscow no. 051 339, 25 July 1980 (ibid., p. 65).

28 Telegram from Moscow no. 051 398, 3 August 1980, 14.00 hours (ibid., p. 159).

29 A.C.N.S.A.S., Documents archive, dossier 13346, vol. 1, pp. 359–61.

30 A.C.N.S.A.S., Documents archive, dossier 13346, vol. 5, p. 256.

31 A.C.N.S.A.S., Informers archive, dossier 18002, vol. 1, p. 64.

32 A.C.N.S.A.S., Documents archive, vol. 26, p. 49.

33 Surveillance was broken off when it was deemed to have achieved its aim, when the target no longer engaged in hostile actions, when he was sent to prison or died, when he was recruited as an informer and genuinely collaborated with the Securitate. None of these was the case with Béla Károlyi in July 1980.

34 A.C.N.S.A.S., Informers archive, dossier 184960, p. 16.

35 A.C.N.S.A.S., Documents archive, vol. 5, pp. 429–30.

36 A.C.N.S.A.S., Informers archive, dossier 5189, vol. 2, p. 204.

37 In some interviews, Pozsár has said that while they were still in Moscow, Béla Károlyi read in a newspaper that the then prime minister Ilie Verdeţ had been sacked. The news depressed Károlyi, who is supposed to have told Pozsár, 'this is the end.' But we think Géza Pozsár must have been mistaken, since Ilie Verdeţ continued as prime minster till 1982.

38 A.C.N.S.A.S., Documents archive, dossier 13346, vol. 5, pp. 304–5.

39 Next to Mircea Oprea's name, the words 'F.B.I. agent' have been pencilled in.

40 In his autobiography, Nicolae Vieru recounts the episode as follows: 'In the evening I went with Nadia to a restaurant at the invitation of Ilie Năstase, then we visited Diana Ross at her home. She had three little daughters who were all over Nadia. We watched Diana's latest big concert in Los Angeles, then together we went to the largest discotheque in New York, where we sat at the same table as actor and director Robert Duvall. Evidently, all the while we were accompanied by Securitate officer Trifan, who had the mission to protect Nadia but instead made nothing but blunders' (Nicolae Vieru, p. 139).

41 Pencilled note: 'possibly former Iron Guard'.

42 Pencilled note: 'inaccurate'.

43 The gymnasts were not allowed to go to the disco, but in this case Nadia Comăneci was allowed to do so since the entire gymnastics tour was named after her. In another Securitate report on the tour, it is stated that necessary measures were taken to prevent Nadia going to private meetings or the disco unaccompanied: 'During the U.S.A. tour, Comăneci Nadia befriended U.S.A. gymnastics champion Kurt Thomas, a member of the U.S.A. men's gymnastics team, which gave the scheduled demonstrations jointly with our country's team. The aforementioned placed constant pressure on Romanian gymnast Nadia Comăneci to lure her to day and night shows in bars, discotheques etc. At the intervention of Vieru Nicolae and the attendant of gymnast Comăneci Nadia she was prevented from going without a chaperone' (A.C.N.S.A.S., Documents archive, dossier 13346, vol. 26, p. 61).

44 Ion and Ghizela Olteanu, who had been P.E. teachers in Cluj and moved to the United States in 1976.

45 In the event of a sportsperson or member of the delegation disappearing, the Securitate officer was required to inform the head of the delegation, to gather detailed information from the others about the circumstances of the disappearance, to undertake measures to look for them, to inform the organiser demanding that a search be made for the person and that he or she be brought back to the delegation, and to inform the Romanian diplomatic mission in the country in question (A.C.N.S.A.S., Documents archive, dossier 13346, vol. 1, pp. 1–2).

46 A.C.N.S.A.S., Informers archive, dossier 18002, vol. 1, pp. 38–44.

47 A.C.N.S.A.S., Penal archive, dossier 13179, vol. 1, p. 7.

48 For a statement of the goods confiscated, see A.C.N.S.A.S., Documents archive, dossier 5143, vol. 11, pp. 21–4 and A.C.N.S.A.S., Penal archive, dossier 13179, vol. 1.

49 A.C.N.S.A.S., Documents archive, dossier 5143, vol. 11, p. 41.

50 A.C.N.S.A.S., Documents archive, dossier 5143, vol. 11, p. 29.

51 A.C.N.S.A.S., Penal archive, dossier 13179, vol. 1, p. 67.

52 A.C.N.S.A.S., Documents archive, dossier 13346, vol. 1, p. 292 and vol. 26, p. 53.

53 A.C.N.S.A.S., Informers archive, dossier 184960, p. 17.

54 A.C.N.S.A.S., Documents archive, dossier 5143, vol. 11, pp. 316–17.

55 In April 1981, thirteen members of the Chamber of Representatives signed a letter in which they demanded the proceedings be speeded up. The signatories were B. Archer, R. Schulze, G. Vander Jagt, F. Guarini, B. Frenzel, D. Pease, K. Hance, J. Jones, D. Rostenkowski, T. Downey, L.A.S. Bafalis, J. Shannon, and E. Jenkins. Romanian diplomats in Washington informed Bucharest of the congressmen's move a few days later: 'At 17.00 hours, on 8 April, we received, by courier of the U.S.A. Congress, a letter sent by congressman Bill Archer. In the envelope was a letter signed by 13 members of the Chamber of Representatives. They addressed the embassy on behalf of the Károlyis and Pozsa who "requested political asylum last week", asking that they be granted assistance to hasten the necessary arrangements to reunite their families, i.e. for the Károlyis' daughter and Pozsár's wife and daughter to come to the U.S.A. The letter shows that all the signatories are members of the Subcommittee for Trade of the Chamber's Ways and Means Committee, which will re-examine this year the clause and it is shown that the granting of this special status will be based on the understanding that the Romanian government intends to make efforts to ameliorate outcomes in the area of emigration and reunification of families. In this context direct allusion is made to the analysis of the clause and permission for these three persons to emigrate as soon as possible — the family rights of the fugitives in question' (Telegram from Washington no. 073 402, 14 April 1981, 21.00 hours, AMAE, encrypted telegrams archive, incoming, Washington, March-June 1981, vol. 2, p. 79).

56 See also Mike Davis, 'How Béla and Marta Károlyi Got Their Daughter out of Romania', https://themedalcount.com/2020/03/21/how-Béla-and-marta-Károlyi-got-their-daughter-out-of-romania/ (retrieved 11 November 2020).

57 Telegram from Washington no. 073 389, 10 April 1981, 2.00 hours (AMAE, Encrypted telegrams archive, incoming, Washington, March-June 1981, vol. 2, p. 61).

58 A.C.N.S.A.S., Documents archive, dossier 5143, vol. 11, p. 10.

59 A.C.N.S.A.S., Documents archive, dossier 13346, vol. 23, p. 13.

60 A.C.N.S.A.S., Documents archive, dossier 13346, vol. 23, p. 24.

61 A.C.N.S.A.S., Informers archive, dossier 18002, vol. 1, p. 99.

62 A.C.N.S.A.S., Informers archive, dossier 18002, vol. 2, p. 9.

63 A.C.N.S.A.S., Informers archive, dossier 18002, vol. 1, p. 1.

64 According to the legislation in force (Decision No. 18 of the Council of Ministers, 1972, which was never made public), relations with foreigners was allowed only via the country's ministries, people's councils, and the organisations and enterprises subordinate to the said ministries. The Securitate saw to the manner in which this law was obeyed and to combating 'unofficial relations with foreigners'.

65 A.C.N.S.A.S., Informers archive, dossier 18002, vol. 1, p. 140–1.

66 A.C.N.S.A.S., Documents archive, dossier 13346, vol. 26, p. 53.

67 A.C.N.S.A.S., Informers archive, dossier 18002, vol. 1, p. 48.

68 A.C.N.S.A.S., Documents archive, dossier 13346, vol. 31, pp. 16–17.

69 A.C.N.S.A.S., Documents archive, dossier 13346, vol. 24, pp. 251–2.

70 To date, Nadia Comăneci and Béla Károlyi have made conflicting statements about this episode in the books they have published. Károlyi has said that he told Nadia even before he went shopping that he was not going back to Romania, and that she started to cry and beg him not to abandon her ('let me stay with you'): 'Nadia I cannot take that responsibility. I am here in the middle of nowhere, surrounded by strange people who speak a language I do not know. I don't know where I am going to eat or sleep tomorrow. I don't even know what I am going to do tomorrow, but I'm a grown person and I have to take whatever comes. I can't guarantee you a decent life or a safe environment here.' Likewise, he told her that she had to finish college in Romania and 'If you stay here everyone in the world will think that I kidnapped you, that I made you stay and go through the nightmare that we are most likely going to face' (*Feel No Fear*, p. 111). 'I don't recall that morning,' says Nadia Comăneci, describing the incident as follows: 'All I remember is that the night before Béla defected, I ran into him in the hallway of our hotel. It was late, and I was going to my room to pack. We were alone, and Béla said softly that he was thinking of not going back. I thought he was joking or that he might be checking to see if I was thinking of defection so that he could stop me. "Whatever," I said with a smile and went to my room. I had been trained for so many years not to react to anything that what Béla said didn't register as being even possibly for real. The next morning was our last

opportunity to shop in New York before returning home, and all of the gymnasts were excited. I ran into Béla before I set off, and he mentioned again that he was thinking of not going back. Once more, I ignored the idea, and its implications. When I returned from the stores, I went to my room to finish packing. We had a team meeting at noon, and Béla, Marta, and Géza weren't there. I assumed they were still shopping. I went to my room, and the telephone rang. It was a woman who said, "Béla asked me to call and see if you want to stay in the United States or return to Romania." "I am going home," I replied and hung up the phone' (*Letters to a Young Gymnast*, pp. 117–18).

71 A.C.N.S.A.S., Documents archive, dossier 13346, vol. 31, p. 9.

72 At the time, it was claimed that Béla Károlyi attempted to profit financially from the connections he made in foreign countries. For example, besides the various sums of money that he was supposed not to have declared to the head of the delegation, it was alleged that during tours Károlyi was in the habit of requesting hunting rifles and dogs from representatives of gymnastics federations, receiving them as gifts. 'How is it possible for measures not to be taken against him when he is capable of selling out the country for a rifle?' Géza Pozsár asked the Securitate officer to whom he reported such information. It was Pozsár who most frequently made such allegations in his secret reports, and another informer reported that he accused Béla Károlyi of being 'the biggest crook in the world' (A.C.N.S.A.S., Informers archive, dossier 5189, vol. 1, p. 38, Documents archive, dossier 13346, vol. 26, pp. 7, 206 verso, 513).

73 A.C.N.S.A.S., Documents archive, dossier 13346, vol. 31, pp. 9–10.

74 A.C.N.S.A.S., Documents archive, dossier 13346, vol. 24, pp. 306–9.

75 A.C.N.S.A.S., Documents archive, dossier 13346, vol. 31, p. 285.

76 Decebal Rădulescu, interview with Rodica Dunca, *Pro Sport*, reproduced at https://atelier.liternet.ro/articol/28/Cosmin-Staniloiu/Crime-cu-premeditare-in-gimnastica.html

77 Although the gymnasts received a daily stipend during foreign trips, the reports of Securitate informers show that Béla Károlyi kept the money and didn't give the gymnasts the full sums, but kept a large part for himself. To justify this theft, he invented a system of fines for the gymnasts' mistakes.

78 A.C.N.S.A.S., Informers archive, dossier 18002, vol. 1, pp. 47–8.

79 A.C.N.S.A.S., Informers archive, dossier 18002, vol. 2, p. 18.

80 A.C.N.S.A.S., Documents archive, dossier 13346, vol. 5, p. 155.

81 A.C.N.S.A.S., Documents archive, dossier 13346, vol. 5, p. 126.

82 A.C.N.S.A.S., Informers archive, dossier 18002, vol. 1, p. 59–60.

83 A.C.N.S.A.S., Informers archive, dossier 18002, vol. 1, p. 51.

84 A.C.N.S.A.S., Documents archive, dossier 13346, vol. 33, p. 290.

85 A.C.N.S.A.S., Documents archive, dossier 13346, vol. 33, p. 290.

86 A.N.I.C, C.C. of U.C.Y., Cadres archive, dossier C/1117 and dossier C/893. My thanks to historian Mihai Burcea for pointing out these documents.

87 A.C.N.S.A.S., Documents archive, dossier 13346, vol. 24, p. 232.

88 Interview with Gheorghe Gorgoi, 10 November 2020.

89 A.C.N.S.A.S., Documents archive, dossier 13346, vol. 34, p. 137.

90 A.C.N.S.A.S., Documents archive, dossier 13346, vol. 25, pp. 6, 34.

91 In addition to articles that have appeared in the press, we also came across such accounts in the interviews we conducted when researching this book, but we have decided not to publish them, deeming them to be an intrusion into Nadia Comăneci's personal life.

92 A.C.N.S.A.S., Documents archive, dossier 13346, vol. 25, p. 33.

93 A.C.N.S.A.S., Documents archive, dossier 13346, vol. 25, p. 34 verso.

94 *Stăpînul secretelor lui Ceaușescu. I se spunea Machiavelli. Ștefan Andrei în dialog cu Lavinia Betea* (The Master of Ceaușescu's Secrets. They Called Him Machiavelli. Ștefan Andrei in Conversation with Lavinia Betea), ed. Cristina Deac, Florin-Răzvan Mihai, Ilarion Țiu, Bucharest: Editura Adevărul, 2011, p. 335.

95 Ștefan Both, 'Misterele operațiunii *Fuga Nadiei*' (The Mysteries of the Nadia Defection), interview with Aurel Rogojan, *Adevărul*, 25 July, https://adevarul. ro/locale/timisoara/misterele-operatiunii-fuga-nadi ei-a-facut-parte planul-americano-sovietic-indepartare-ceausescu-traseul-parcurs-gimnasta- noiembrie-1989-1_55b 23cc6f5eaafab2ce5 cb9b/index.html (retrieved 4 May 2020).

96 A.C.N.S.A.S., Documents archive, dossier 13346, vol. 24, pp. 161–2.

97 A.C.N.S.A.S., Documents archive, dossier 13346, vol. 24, p. 145.

98 A.C.N.S.A.S., Documents archive, dossier 13346, vol. 24, pp. 164–5.

99 A.C.N.S.A.S., Documents archive, dossier 13346, vol. 25, pp. 35–6.

100 A.C.N.S.A.S., Documents archive, dossier 13346, vol. 1, p. 289. See also Peter Ueberroth, *Made in America*, New York: William Morrow, 1985; Harold E. Wilson Jr., 'The Golden Opportunity: Romania's Political Manipulation of the 1984 Los Angeles Olympic Games', https://www.academia.edu/27607071/THE_GOLDEN_ OPPORTUNITY_ROMANIAS_POLITICAL_MANIPULATION_OF_THE_1984_ LOS_ANGELES_OLYMPIC_GAMES (retrieved 8 December 2020).

101 *Letters to a Young Gymnast*, p. 126.

102 A.C.N.S.A.S., Documents archive, dossier 13346, vol. 1, pp. 147–62.

103 A.C.N.S.A.S., MFR Bucharest archive, dossier 100063.

104 Images of Nadia Comăneci waiting to be received by Ronald Reagan in Los Angeles can be viewed at minute 9.53 in the footage available at https://www.youtube.com/watch?v=hvhSGFc+Vek (retrieved 28 November 2020).

105 A.C.N.S.A.S., Documents archive, dossier 13346, vol. 24, p. 147.

Chapter 7

1 A.C.N.S.A.S., Documents archive, dossier 13346, vol. 24, p. 66.

2 Or Ezicas in some Securitate documents.

3 A.C.N.S.A.S., Documents archive, dossier 13346, vol. 25, p. 118–19.

4 A.C.N.S.A.S., Documents archive, dossier 13346, vol. 24, pp. 155–6.

5 Telegram from Budapest no. 021 853, 29 November 1989, 12.40 hours (AMAE, Encrypted telegrams archive, incoming, Budapest 1989, vol. 7, p. 4).

6   George Albuţ, 'Din memoriile unui diplomat roman la Budapesta, 1981-1990' (From the memoirs of a Romanian diplomat in Budapest, *Oraşul*, Year 7, Nos. 31–2 (2014), pp. 17–20.

7   Telegram from Ministry of Foreign Affairs Central no. 20/015 837, 29 November 1989, 16.30 hours (A.M.A.E., Encrypted telegrams archive, outgoing, Budapest 1989, vol. 1, p. 465).

8   Telegram from Budapest no. 021 867, 1 December 1989, 15.00 hours (A.M.A.E., Encrypted telegrams archive, incoming, Budapest 1989, vol. 7, pp. 28–9).

9   Állambiztonsági Szolgálatok Történeti Levéltára (Historical Archives of the Secret Services, Á.B.T.L.) 2.7.1. NOIJ III/A 221-64-213-89. A BRFK Állambiztonsági szervének III/A alosztályának 1989. December 01. 213-számú jelentéséboől (My thanks to historian Bandi István for pointing out this document and providing it).

10 Telegram from Budapest no. 021 841, 27 November 1989, 15.00 hours (A.M.A.E., Encrypted telegrams archive, incoming, Budapest 1989, vol. 6, p. 429). The persons who illegally crossed the frontier with their livestock were Ioan Bratu, Naomi Ileana Roman, Viorel Moţ, and Cătălin Tilică. The Romanian State began extradition procedures to try them for banditry, theft, fraudulent crossing of the frontier, and other infractions of Hungarian and Romanian law.

11 Aurel I. Rogojan, *Iulian N. Vlad—confesiuni pentru istorie*, Baia Mare: Editura Proema, pp. 441–4.

12 Ştefan Both, previously cited article.

13 *Puterea umbrei. Istorii din lumea informaţiilor secrete. De la Ceauşescu la Băsescu, General brg. (r.) Aurel I. faţă în faţă cu Dan Andronic*, Baia Mare: Editura Proema, 2019, p. 508.

14 *Puterea umbrei*, p. 508.

15 A.C.N.S.A.S., Documents archive, dossier 13346, vol. 25, p. 219.

16 A.C.N.S.A.S., Documents archive, dossier 13346, vol. 25, p. 195.

17 *Letters to a Young Gymnast*, p. 132.

18 A.C.N.S.A.S., Documents archive, dossier 13346, vol. 25, p. 224, 326.

19 A.C.N.S.A.S., Documents archive, dossier 13346, vol. 25, p. 7.

20 *Letters to a Young Gymnast*, p. 132.

21 *Letters to a Young Gymnast*, p. 143.

22 George Paraschiv, *Primăvară . . .*, 49–54.

23 *Letters to a Young Gymnast*, pp. 145–6.

24 Telegram from the U.S. Embassy in Bucharest, 30 November 1989, https://foia.state. gov/Search/Results.aspx?searchText=nadia&beginDate=&endDate=&spublished BeginDate=&publishedEndDate=&caseNumber= (retrieved 10 June 2020).

25 A.C.N.S.A.S., Documents archive, dossier 13346, vol. 25, p. 2.

26 A.C.N.S.A.S., Documents archive, dossier 13346, vol. 25, p. 192.

27 Octavian Pescaru, 'Fuga Nadiei Comăneci în SUA', *Gazeta Sporturilor*, https://www. gsp.ro/sporturi/gimnastica/fuga-nadiei-comaneci-in-sua-si-o-teorie-halucinanta-care-a-aparut-dupa-dezmintita-vehement-de-fosta-gimnasta-si-de-familie-pe-nadia-o-chema-anna-kemenec-si-este-unguroaica-584 432.html (retrieved 10 June 2020).

28 A.C.N.S.A.S., Documents archive, dossier 13346, vol. 25, p. 294.

29 A.C.N.S.A.S., Documents archive, dossier 13346, vol. 25, pp 326–7.

30 'Corina II' was the code name for Ştefania Comăneci's house, while 'Corina I' was the code name for Nadia's house, where Adrian and Liliana also lived.

31 A.C.N.S.A.S., Documents archive, dossier 13346, vol. 27, p. 86–9.

32 A.C.N.S.A.S., Documents archive, dossier 13346, vol. 27, p. 103 verso.

33 A.C.N.S.A.S., Documents archive, dossier 13346, vol. 27, p. pp. 71–5.

34 A.C.N.S.A.S., Documents archive, dossier 13346, vol. 27, pp. 71–5.

35 Although the final transcript is dated 20 December 1989, we believe it was made by Special Unit T the day before and sent to Department One (Domestic Informers) the next morning.

36 A.C.N.S.A.S., Documents archive, dossier 13346, vol. 27, p. 79–80.

37 A.C.N.S.A.S., Documents archive, dossier 13346, vol. 27, pp. 22–3.

38 A.C.N.S.A.S., Documents archive, dossier 13346, vol. 25, p. 15.

39 A.C.N.S.A.S., Documents archive, dossier 13346, vol. 27, p. 22.

40 A.C.N.S.A.S., Documents archive, dossier 13346, vol. 27, pp. 16–17.

41 A.C.N.S.A.S., Documents archive, dossier 13346, vol. 27, p. 13–15.

42 A.C.N.S.A.S., Documents archive, dossier 13346, vol. 27, p. 66–8.

43 Marius Tucă and Irina Cristea, interview with Adrian Comăneci for *Jurnalul* newspaper, https://jurnalul.antena3.ro/scinteia/special/adrian-comaneci-politia-a-facut-inventar-la-tot-ce-era-in-casa-528707.html (retrieved 10 June 2020).

44 A.C.N.S.A.S., Documents archive, dossier 13346, vol. 25. pp. 290–1.

45 A.C.N.S.A.S., Documents archive, dossier 13346, vol. 25. p. 193.

46 A.C.N.S.A.S., Documents archive, dossier 13346, vol. 25. p. 323.

47 A.C.N.S.A.S., Documents archive, dossier 13346, vol. 25. pp. 230–1.

48 A.C.N.S.A.S., Documents archive, dossier 13346, vol. 25. pp. 328–9.

49 Operational Techniques of the Telephone Conversation Interception type.

50 A.C.N.S.A.S., Documents archive, dossier 13346, vol. 25. pp. 135–6.

51 A.C.N.S.A.S., Documents archive, dossier 13346, vol. 25. pp. 123–4, 128.

52 A.C.N.S.A.S., Documents archive, dossier 13346, vol. 25. p. 17 verso.

53 A.C.N.S.A.S., Documents archive, dossier 13346, vol. 25. p. 58.

54 A.C.N.S.A.S., Documents archive, dossier 13346, vol. 25. pp. 59–60.

55 A.C.N.S.A.S., Documents archive, dossier 13346, vol. 25. p. 136.

56 A.C.N.S.A.S., Documents archive, dossier 13346, vol. 25. p. 41.

57 A.C.N.S.A.S., Documents archive, dossier 13346, vol. 25. p. 222.

58 Interview with Grigore Pintea, 23 April 2020.

59 A.C.N.S.A.S., Documents archive, dossier 13346, vol. 25. p. 52.

60 A.C.N.S.A.S., Documents archive, dossier 13346, vol. 25. p. 37 verso.

61 A.C.N.S.A.S., Documents archive, dossier 13346, vol. 25. p. 37 verso.

62 A.C.N.S.A.S., Documents archive, dossier 13346, vol. 24. pp. 140--142.

63 A.C.N.S.A.S., Documents archive, dossier 13346, vol. 25. p. 6 verso.

64 The Securitate operation to protect the Fourteenth Party Congress.

65 A.C.N.S.A.S., Documents archive, dossier 13346, vol. 25. p. 44.

66 A.C.N.S.A.S., Documents archive, dossier 13346, vol. 25. p. 45.

67 A.C.N.S.A.S., Documents archive, dossier 13346, vol. 25. p. 7 verso.

68 A.C.N.S.A.S., Documents archive, dossier 13346, vol. 25. p. 10 verso.

69 A.C.N.S.A.S., Documents archive, dossier 13346, vol. 25. pp. 13–14.

70 A.C.N.S.A.S., Documents archive, dossier 13346, vol. 25. p. 11 verso.

71 Those travelling to foreign countries as part of their jobs were verified by the Securitate over a number of months. The operation, codenamed 'The Traveller', entailed checks into the subject's behaviour socially and within the family, his circle of friends, any relatives living abroad, interaction with foreigners, political views, vices, hobbies etc. The primary aim of 'The Traveller' was to establish whether the person under investigation intended to remain abroad. Usually, investigations were carried out by Special Unit F at the request of other department of the Securitate (Department One, in the case of sportspeople), with the assistance of the Militia. Permission to travel was granted only after the special unit concluded from its investigations that the subject did not show any 'unusual aspects'. After the defection of Securitate general Ion Mihai Pacepa in 1978, the Securitate had harshened the rules for foreign trips, introducing operation 'Alpha', aimed at trips of less than three months, and 'Atlas', for longer stays. More often than not, people travelling abroad were recruited as informers (Stejărel Olaru, Georg Hebrstritt, *Stasi şi Securitatea*, Humanitas, Bucharest, 2005, pp. 174–7.

72 The list of measures taken after Nadia Comăneci's defection can be found in A.C.N.S.A.S., Documents archive, dossier 13346, vol. 10. p. 252 and vol. 24, p. 14.

73 Nicolae Vieru, p. 30.

74 A.C.N.S.A.S., Documents archive, dossier 13346, vol. 25. p. 1 verso.

INDEX